Your Child's Emotional Health

Philadelphia Child Guidance Center

Your Child's Emotional Health

PHILADELPHIA
CHILD GUIDANCE CENTER
WITH JACK MAGUIRE

Produced by The Philip Lief Group, Inc.

Macmillan Publishing Company
New York

Maxwell Macmillan Canada
Toronto

Maxwell Macmillan International
New York   Oxford   Singapore   Sydney

This book is not intended as a substitute for the professional advice of a doctor or mental health professional. The reader should regularly consult a physician or appropriate health care practitioner in matters relating to health, particularly with respect to any symptoms that may require diagnosis or medical attention.

Macmillan Publishing Company   Maxwell Macmillan Canada, Inc.
866 Third Avenue   1200 Eglinton Avenue East, Suite 200
New York, NY 10022   Don Mills, Ontario M3C 3N1

Macmillan Publishing Company is part of the Maxwell Communication Group of Companies.

Library of Congress Cataloging-in-Publication Data
Your child's emotional health / the Philadelphia Child Guidance Center,
    with Jack Maguire.
        p.   cm.
    Includes index.
    ISBN 0-02-577371-2
    1. Emotions in children.   2. Emotional problems of children.
I. Maguire, Jack.   II. Philadelphia Child Guidance Center
BF723.E6Y67   1993
649'.1—dc20   92-25481

Published by arrangement with The Philip Lief Group, Inc.
6 West 20th Street
New York, NY 10011

Macmillan books are available at special discounts for bulk purchases for sales promotions, premiums, fund-raising, or educational use. For details, contact:

Special Sales Director
Macmillan Publishing Company
866 Third Avenue
New York, NY 10022

10   9   8   7   6   5   4   3   2   1

Printed in the United States of America

This book is dedicated to Margie Ouellette
and to her children,
Amanda, Carly, and Brittany.
I am proud to be a part of their family.

Contents

Part Three
ADOLESCENCE:
AGE THIRTEEN TO AGE TWENTY

Preface

C hildren seldom say that they need help. More often their behaviors tell us that they do. They may suffer vague, slowly evolving difficulties at home, at school, or with their peers. Or they may exhibit sudden, marked changes in their conduct and mood that pervade every aspect of their lives.

Each year, thousands of children, adolescents, and their families get help from Philadelphia Child Guidance Center (PCGC). As one of the foremost centers in the country for child and adolescent psychiatric care, PCGC offers services that are specialized and individually designed to meet the needs of each child and family. Often working in closely cooperative teams, staff members help families recognize, expand, and mobilize their strengths to make life more fulfilling for the affected child as well as for the family as a whole.

Since PCGC's origin in 1925 as one of the first centers in the world devoted to child psychiatry, it has enjoyed an international reputation for its excellent treatment and innovative research. The founding director, Frederick H. Allen, M.D., was the first board-certified child psychiatrist in the United States as well as one of the first psychiatrists to address the problems of the child in the context of the family. Within his historic thirty-year tenure, PCGC achieved a leadership position in the study and treatment of emotional problems affecting children from birth through adolescence.

Later, under the auspices of Director Salvador Minuchin, M.D., PCGC pioneered the development of structural family therapy, a systems-oriented approach that views diagnosis and treatment of a child in the context of the family and social relationships in which she or he lives. Included in that context are the child's extended family, friends, caretakers, school, and all agencies in the culture at large—social, legal, religious, recreational, and health oriented—that influence the child's life.

Today, under the clinical direction of Alberto C. Serrano, M.D., PCGC's staff of 230 professionals provides a broad range of diagnostic and therapeutic programs that directly benefit the mid-Atlantic region of the United States and serve as models for other diagnostic and therapeutic programs throughout the nation and abroad. Thanks to its strong affiliation with the University of Pennsylvania Medical School, The Children's Hospital of Philadelphia, and Children's Seashore House, PCGC is a major component of one of the most advanced health-care and health-care research centers in the country.

This books draws upon the unique experience and expertise of PCGC to offer you, as parents, practical guidelines for raising your child to be emotionally healthy. Specifically, it helps you perform the following, especially challenging activities:

■ identify and assess your child's emotional states, problems, capabilities, and needs;

■ develop an effective parenting style that best suits you and your child as individuals;

■ address the most common and most troublesome emotional difficulties that can arise in the course of your child's life;

■ ensure the emotional well-being of all family members during any emotional crisis experienced by your family as a whole or by your child individually;

■ determine if and when you, your family, and your child need professional help in managing emotional difficulties;

■ secure the professional help that is most appropriate for you, your family, and your child, according to the situation at hand.

Love for a child comes naturally to a parent and can go far toward giving a child emotional security. Parenting skills, however, are also required to meet a child's emotional needs, and they do *not* come naturally. Instead, parents must learn them.

This book is specially designed to help parents help themselves so that they in turn can help their children. Underlying everything that PCGC does—and represents—is the belief that family members have the ability to work together to solve their problems and that each family member can achieve a new and more rewarding life in the process.

Acknowledgments

Among the many people outside Philadelphia Child Guidance Center who were helpful in putting this book together, I'd like to give special thanks to Eva Weiss, to The Philip Lief Group as a whole, and to Natalie Chapman, my editor at Macmillan. Their "writer guidance" was invaluable.

Part One: The Early Years

BIRTH TO AGE SIX

Introduction

The human memory relies on words and language skills to identify, record, and preserve all that an individual may encounter in life. It is small wonder, therefore, that most adults have very sketchy memories of their childhood before they began school and almost no vivid memories of it before they began to speak.

The early years of life have a mysterious and elemental quality that an adult can only recapture by caring for children who are going through them. Within this special caretaking relationship, adults learn again to see the world in nonverbal ways, and they confront anew the tremendous turmoil of an existence governed so much more by raw feelings than by processed thought. It's a learning and confrontational process for adults that is not only inspiring to their lives as individuals but also vital to their effectiveness as parents.

In emotional terms, the years between birth and age six for a child are the best of times and the worst of times. Periods of paradisal bliss and security, seldom to be realized in later years, alternate wildly and unpredictably with times of unspeakable torment and despair, the likes of which are rarely, if ever, experienced by adults.

A parent is never more important to a child's physical and emotional well-being than during this time span. Therefore, it is critical that parents enter into their very young child's world single-mindedly and wholeheartedly, progressing with her or him through that world as safely and delightfully as possible.

Fortunately, the most effective aid a parent can offer a very young child is also the easiest to offer: love. In the absence of any other surety, love alone can guide both parent and child through the darkest emotional crisis. To ensure that it stands the best chance of doing so, here are three other general truths to keep in mind about the overall emotional life of children under six:

1. Every human being is born into life with a unique temperament and begins exhibiting a distinct personality right away.
The mind of a baby is not a blank slate, awaiting the impress of time and experience to produce a characteristic "self." At birth, an infant

already possesses a personal temperament, which can be defined as an innate set of tendencies to act and react in certain ways. Throughout life, this "core" temperament will determine whether she or he is basically easygoing or high-strung, tough or vulnerable, meek or bold, playful or serious, sociable or individualistic, and many other qualities that words are hopelessly clumsy in defining.

From a parent's point of view, this means remaining ever aware of the fact that a child under six is a person in her or his own right. Therefore, much of your relationship with your very young child, from the moment of birth, has to be worked out like any other that exists between two human beings: by identifying, accepting, and appreciating the similarities and differences in your respective personalities.

Your child is not mature enough—or independent enough—to meet you halfway in this process, so you'll have to be especially understanding to make up the difference. But throughout this process, you shouldn't expect your child to be just like you, nor should you feel that you are necessarily the "prime mover" of your child's behavior.

---

2. It's far more important simply to pay ongoing attention to children under six than it is to act or react in specific ways.

Parents of very young children are overinclined to be "doers." So much sheer physical work is required to attend to the basic needs of the child—food, sleep, clothing, shelter, cleanliness, and safety—that parents assume that a similar expenditure of effort is needed to "do something" about a child's emotional well-being.

In fact, there is much that you as a parent can do to promote and safeguard your child's emotional health, but overdoing can easily lead to emotional exhaustion for every member of the family. Your first and foremost responsibility is simply to watch over your child. This involves keeping calmly and persistently attuned to her or his moods and behaviors so that you know your child well and, consequently, when it's appropriate to be concerned.

---

3. Always remember that a child under six is paying especially close attention to you.

Because they are so dependent on their parents, children this young can be incredibly sensitive to how their parents feel, act, and react. Again, they mentally and emotionally process what they witness in "noncommunicable" ways that are difficult for adults to detect or appreciate.

Although your child under six may not be capable of grasping the "adult" meaning of your moods and behaviors, don't ever assume that she or he is not "old enough" to be influenced by your moods or behaviors. Be particularly mindful of how you interact with others, cope with stressful situations, or express your feelings in the presence of your very young child. The more constructively you manage your own life, the better example you will set.

Also, it's important to be honest about your moods and behaviors. Any falseness is immediately apparent and inevitably distressing to a very young child's "unsophisticated" mind. Don't lie about your feelings or actions. And don't deny—either to your child or to others in her or his presence—what your child knows to be true. Always be truthful, and it will serve both you and your child well throughout your lives together.

The information offered in this section of the book is designed to help you develop and enjoy a relationship with your very young child that nourishes her or his emotional health. Specific guidelines are organized according to the following topics:

1. SLEEPING *(Page 17)*

■ common sleeping patterns and emotional problems associated with sleeping

■ how to manage bedtime resistance, nightmares, and night terrors

■ what to do about problems associated with early rising and late sleeping

2. EATING *(Page 30)*

■ common eating patterns and emotional problems associated with eating

■ how to manage eating resistance, food fussiness, and disruptive table manners

3. SEXUALITY *(Page 33)*

■ milestones in sexual development, curiosity, and activity, and emotional issues associated with those milestones

■ how to prevent, or cope with, the sexual abuse of your very young child

■ how to minimize, or deal with, awkward sexual behavior

■ how to avoid harmful gender stereotypes in raising your child

4. SHYNESS AND AGGRESSION *(Page 45)*

■ why your child may be basically shy or aggressive and emotional problems associated with these traits

■ how to help your child cope with, and overcome, problems relating to shyness or aggression

5. FEAR *(Page 53)*

■ how fears develop in very young children; how to recognize them and how to manage them

■ a timetable of common fears at different ages

■ how to prevent, and deal with, fear associated with a hospital stay

■ at PCGC: pain management for very young children

6. DEPRESSION AND STRESS *(Page 64)*

■ causes and effects of depression and stress in very young children

■ how to prevent, manage, and overcome common problems associated with depression and stress

■ how to help your very young child remain emotionally stable through a divorce, a remarriage, a traumatic event, or a death of a loved one

7. SEPARATION ANXIETY *(Page 77)*

■ what "separation anxiety" is and why very young children experience it

■ how to cope with, and overcome, separation anxiety

8. DISCIPLINE *(Page 81)*

■ common disciplinary challenges and emotional issues associated with them; general guidelines for handling them successfully

■ how to issue commands effectively

■ how to handle the "gimmes" and the grabs when shopping with your very young child

■ how to manage whining and tantrums

■ how to evaluate and enhance your child's ability to self-discipline

9. TOILET TRAINING *(Page 98)*

■ myths versus facts regarding toilet training

■ guidelines for managing toilet training with a minimum of emotional stress both for you and for your very young child

10. SIBLINGS *(Page 102)*

■ common types of sibling conflict and how to deal with them

■ how to prepare your very young child emotionally for the birth of a new baby

11. PLAY *(Page 108)*

■ how play contributes to the emotional well-being of your very young child

■ how to ensure that your child plays well: alone, with you, and with others

■ group games that are appropriate for the early years

■ why children develop imaginary playmates and how to cope with them

12. TRANSITIONAL OBJECTS *(Page 115)*

■ what constitutes a "transitional object" and why it is important to a child's emotional well-being

■ how to help your child benefit from, and outgrow, transitional objects

■ why children suck their thumbs and rock their heads; how to cope with these behaviors

13. STORYTELLING *(Page 120)*

■ how storytelling contributes to the emotional well-being of very young children

■ how to invent, choose, and tell stories effectively

■ "read aloud" book suggestions for various emotionally distressing situations

14. DAY CARE *(Page 128)*

■ how day care affects the emotional health of very young children

■ how to choose and monitor day-care services

■ emotional issues relating to early education

15. PSYCHOTHERAPY *(Page 135)*

■ how to determine if your child might need psychotherapy

■ how to chose an appropriate therapy and an appropriate doctor/therapist

■ the meaning behind special diagnoses: mental retardation, autism, and attention-deficit hyperactivity disorder

■ at PCGC: preschool at-risk program

The Early Years:
An Emotional Time Line

Although it is particularly difficult to define what is "normal" in the emotional life of a child under six, here are some very broad guidelines:

BIRTH TO SIX MONTHS OLD

■ becomes increasingly affectionate and demonstrative toward parents, smiling at them often and frequently responding with eagerness to facial gestures and speech

■ derives repeated joy from specific sights, sounds, and movements

■ develops ability to calm self down on certain occasions

SIX MONTHS TO ONE YEAR OLD

■ responds more and more specifically and appropriately to different types of facial gestures, speech, and interactions

■ tests environment more and more for possibly pleasurable experiences

■ develops multiple ways to initiate "love play" and to seek comfort

ONE YEAR TO EIGHTEEN MONTHS OLD

■ increasingly seeks and derives pleasure out of particular play activities

■ begins responding cooperatively and appropriately to different tones of voice (e.g., for commands)

■ develops more and more ability to control anger and dissatisfaction

■ copies behavior and emotions of others

■ seeks and develops distinct interactions with different people (especially other very young children)

EIGHTEEN MONTHS TO TWO YEARS

■ increasingly practices "pretend" games, including "pretend" emotional reactions

■ builds a repertoire of distinctly different gestures and vocalizations to express different feelings

■ occasionally seeks solitude and quiet when emotionally confused or upset

■ develops more and more ability to "read" emotional states in other people (especially parents)

■ initiates increasingly appropriate and constructive responses to other people's (especially parents') emotional states

■ works with parents to develop "codes" for communicating and managing different feelings

TWO TO THREE YEARS

■ develops ability to throw—and recover from—temper tantrums

■ increasingly initiates behavior or interactions to test emotional state—or emotional responses—of other people

■ troubles or delights self more and more with own imagination and play

■ seeks to communicate more and more feelings with specific words

■ worries more and more about the potential occurrence of distressing events

■ seeks repeated reassurance about well-being of self and family

THREE TO FOUR YEARS

■ develops increasing interest and skill in controlling emotions

■ practices "manipulating" emotions of others (especially peers)

■ starts being concerned about gender identity, modifying her or his emotional expression accordingly

■ focuses affection on parent of opposite sex, resulting in some degree of competitive antagonism toward parent of same sex

■ initiates discussions about emotional issues

■ begins exhibiting strong emotional responses—positive and negative—to dreams

FOUR TO SIX YEARS

■ seeks specific constructive outlets for emotional tension (e.g., drawing or playing particular games) in a calm and deliberate manner

■ begins making and appreciating rational judgments about causes and effects of emotions

■ becomes increasingly self-reliant in terms of pleasing self and resolving emotional disturbances

■ demonstrates more and more empathy for, and curiosity about, other people (especially peers)

■ interacts in more emotionally responsible and resilient ways with others (especially peers)

■ seeks and respects justice in emotional conflicts

At PCGC:
Early Childhood Therapy

By far the most neglected and least-defined area of psychotherapy in general involves the social-emotional problems of early childhood. Very young people are most often troubled by the same basic emotional problems that trouble adults: depression, anxiety, trauma, or grief. The manner in which such difficulties arise—or reveal themselves—in very young children tends to differ according to the following developmental stages:

THE INFANT

During infancy, social-emotional problems are interwoven with the baby's ability to regulate internal sensory processes and to make secure parental attachments. Thus, there may be "unusual" illnesses, motor-development problems, and eating or sleeping difficulties or a lack of appropriate or pleasurable responsiveness to parents.

THE TODDLER

During toddlerhood, social-emotional development is closely linked with the child's growing abilities to explore the environment, communicate, and begin individuation from her or his parents. Thus, the most common cause or effect of social-emotional problems involves some *temperamental* factor, such as an "unusual" inability to manage fear, anger, or self-control.

THE PRESCHOOLER

During the preschool years, social-emotional development is intensely involved with the increasing complexity of thought, reasoning, and communication in the child's life. Thus, the most common cause or effect of social-emotional problems involves some *cognitive* or *interpersonal* factor, such as an "unusual" lack of self-confidence, patience, or curiosity or an "unusual" amount of conflicts with, or withdrawal from, other children.

We have developed an Early Childhood Program to offer information and support to parents who are in any way concerned about their very young child's psychological development and to provide diagnostic, treatment, and outpatient services that are tailored to the needs of the individual child as well as her or his community of family members and caretakers.

With this general picture in mind, a multidisciplinary team

of professionals screens three major areas in each child's life to determine if she or he is, in fact, experiencing "unusual" social-emotional problems:

1. the child's sensory, motor, and cognitive development; temperamental characteristics; and problem-solving style

2. parental child-rearing strategies and family functioning as a whole

3. the child's relationships with other systems, such as day care, health care, and extended family networks

The program team members then use all the information and insights they have gathered to devise a specific treatment plan for the child's individual social-emotional problems. Such a plan always includes family counseling and, depending on the situation, may also feature psychosocial intervention in the child's day-care or preschool environment.

If you think that your child could benefit from this type of intervention, look for similar programs in your area.

At PCGC: Psychological Testing in the Early Years

Mental-health professionals, physicians, day-care workers, preschool personnel, and other specialists frequently make decisions that have a profound influence on very young children's lives. Historically, psychological testing has been a widely used and valued method for providing such professionals with the proper information to make those decisions.

Psychological testing is generally employed to determine individual differences and needs by providing specifics about a very young child's abilities, strengths, personality style, and emotional functioning. Psychological testing is also helpful in evaluating the actual or potential effects on very young children of significant situational events, such as starting kindergarten, moving to a new home, coping with a serious illness, or going through a parental divorce.

For infants and toddlers, psychological testing provides data about levels of acquisition of basic sensation-processing, motor-coordinating, communicating, learning, and adapting skills. In addition to direct observation by one or more professionals, tests that we most frequently recommend or use for these purposes are the Bayley Scales of Infant Development, the Denver Developmental Screening Test, and the Vineland Adaptive Behavioral Scales.

For preschoolers, psychological testing provides screening data about educational and intellectual levels, cognitive strengths and weaknesses, social adaptability, and school readiness. In addition to direct observation by one or more professionals, tests that PCGC most frequently recommends or uses for these purposes are the Wechsler Primary and Preschool Scale of Intelligence, the McCarthy Scales of Children's Abilities, the Stanford-Binet Intelligence Scale, and the Kaufman-ABC.

We believe that the more the family is informed about the testing and the more they are involved in the testing process, the more useful the evaluation is to them. Therefore, we employ and advocate the following testing process:

■ Before the testing begins, the psychologist (or test administrator) meets with the child and parents to identify the reasons why testing is being sought, obtain relevant background history, address any initial questions or concerns the parents have, and explain the testing process.

■ It helps to have between two and four short, separate testing sessions rather than one long one. That way, fatigue factors are minimized, and a fuller range of the child's behavior or capabilities can be observed or tested.

■ When testing is completed, the results are discussed with the family and, if appropriate, the child.

For more information about psychological testing of very young children, consult your physician or a local mental-health agency.

Psychosomatic Illness

By definition, a psychosomatic illness is a genuine physical illness that has psychological as well as biological causes (*psy-*

cho: the Greek root for mind; *soma*: the Greek root for body).
More technically, such an illness is known as a *psychophysiological disorder*. As a rule, when the underlying psychological problem is effectively addressed, the physical symptoms
of the illness are greatly alleviated and may disappear.

The body and the mind are so interconnected that almost
any illness can be said to have a psychosomatic component.
However, certain stress-sensitive illnesses are commonly
thought to be especially psychosomatic in nature, such as ulcers, headaches, stomachaches, asthma, high blood pressure,
and skin rashes or blemishes.

Among children in the early years, it is very difficult to
determine whether a given physical illness is especially psychosomatic in nature. In part, this is due to the relatively
limited manner in which they are able to verbalize their emotions or their physical sensations and needs.

Another factor complicating such a diagnosis is the tendency
among children in this age range to be less inhibited about
expressing their emotional problems behaviorally. Are we to
infer from this proclivity that such children are *less* likely to
suffer from psychosomatic illnesses because they have otherwise discharged their emotional stress? Or are we to assume
that such children are *more* likely to suffer from psychosomatic
illnesses because their other (i.e., behavioral) reactions to emotional stress are so strong? Who can say?

In some cases involving very young children, a particular
illness may appear to be undeniably psychosomatic in nature
because the behavior that it produces is so much like stress-
related behavior. Nevertheless, it can't be labeled psychosomatic because no particular psychological problem can be
established as a common trigger.

For example, consider *colic*, one of the more common illnesses associated with infants. Its main symptom is frequent,
long-lasting crying "jags" that indicate strong physical pain,
but the precise cause of this pain is maddeningly difficult to
pinpoint. It may or may not be related to diet, but it is most
often relieved by sustained parental attention and protection
from all but the most low key and monotonous stimuli. One
widely used treatment for colic is to take the baby on a long
car ride so that she or he can be lulled to sleep by the nearness
of the parent and the humming of the engine.

On the surface, colic appears to be a psychosomatic illness,
but there is no way to tell for sure. The child whose parents
are consistently very loving and attentive is just as likely to

develop it as the one whose parents are consistently abusive or neglectful. And the child whose environment is consistently free of annoying, excessive, or unpredictable stimuli is just as likely to develop it as one whose environment is consistently bombarded by such stimuli.

As the parent of a very young child who suffers an illness, you need to be careful not to assume too much or too little. Whether or not a major source of your child's illness is, in fact, some emotional problem, it is always therapeutic to provide your sick child with emotional comfort and security and seek to alleviate obviously stressful conditions that she or he has recently experienced. At the same time, avoid labeling your child's illness "psychosomatic" without clear and convincing evidence (through professional consultation) that such a diagnosis is warranted. Otherwise, you may wind up subjecting yourself and your child to unwarranted guilt and responsibility.

Cognitive Development

Separate from, but interrelated with, a child's emotional development is her or his cognitive development. The expression "cognitive development" refers to a child's ability to perceive, think, and remember. As such, it is more closely associated with intellectual capabilities than with psychological makeup.

How a child feels is bound to affect how she or he perceives, thinks, and remembers—and vice versa. However, the particular cause-and-effect relationship between a child's cognitive and emotional development is dependent on many biological and social variables and differs greatly from individual to individual. Therefore, any useful picture of such a relationship in the case of a specific child can only be drawn in the context of comprehensive therapeutic treatment.

Among the many theories concerning cognitive development in children, that of the French psychologist Jean Piaget is the most popular. It divides a child's cognitive development during the early years into two distinct, age-related stages that can be described as follows:

1. Sensory-motor thinking
This stage is associated with infancy. The child acquires the ability to identify and remember different facets of the phys-

ical world (e.g., faces, sounds, toys, smells, foods). The child also learns to connect certain perceptions with particular physical actions (e.g., judging distances, moving within a given set of physical parameters, anticipating the course of simple gestures and events).

2. Intuitive and representational thinking

This stage is associated with toddlers and preschoolers. The child acquires language skills, recognizes major differences in individual points of view, formulates simple stories, ideas, or plans, and develops an understanding of basic time-and-space concepts.

During the middle years (ages six to thirteen), a child goes through the *concrete operations* stage of cognitive development, during which she or he develops logic and the ability to perform core intellectual activities, for example, reading, writing, computing, and experimenting. Thereafter—that is, through adolescence and adulthood—an individual is involved in the *formal-operations* stage of cognitive development, during which she or he refines intellectual capabilities and learns to conceptualize more and more philosophically.

1.

Sleeping

Popular wisdom aside, to sleep like a baby is not necessarily to do so peacefully. Natural—and individual—sleeping patterns change dramatically over the course of the first six years of life, and each new one brings with it additional challenges for both the child and the parent.

Bedtime Resistance

In the first place, there is often a big difference between a very young child's physical need to sleep and that of the family as a whole to follow a regular schedule of sleeping and wakeful periods. This difference in itself can generate all sorts of individual and interpersonal emotional crises, especially as a child matures and the *desire* to go to sleep becomes increasingly independent of the physical *need* to do so. Whether they are actually tired or not, two-year-olds who are ushered to bed before they want to be there have difficulty understanding what is happening: Are their parents punishing them? Rejecting them? Or simply incapable of appreciating how they feel?

Nightmares

In the second place, upsetting or puzzling events in a very young child's waking life are highly likely to disturb her or his sleeping life as well. People of all ages have nightmares from time to time, but they are most apparently bothersome to children between the ages of three and five, a time when they are just beginning to develop self-consciousness and vivid, self-centered fantasies. As a result, they are uniquely preoccupied, on an emotional level, with every possible threat to their success and well-being. If their fledgling powers of reason and imagination can't come to terms with a real or perceived threat during the day, then their dreams may well take it on at night.

Night Terrors

A "night terror" is an altogether different form of sleep disturbance that is especially prevalent among very young children. Characterized by eye opening, screaming, and sometimes thrashing around wildly in bed, night terrors are most commonly displayed by kids between the ages of six months to four years, usually in the early part of the night.

To the outside observer, a child experiencing a night terror seems to be reacting to an especially bad nightmare. On the contrary, brain-wave studies have shown that night terrors do not occur during dreaming periods but during the deepest levels of sleep, when mental activity is at a bare minimum. In fact, people manifesting night-terror symptoms usually remain unconscious throughout the experience regardless of whether their eyes open, their bodies move, or they speak.

Experts don't know for sure what causes a night terror, but all the evidence indicates that the source is a sudden and transitory pain or discomfort that "shocks" the child's nervous system. Frightening as it can be to the parent, a night terror is seldom symptomatic of any serious physical or psychological problem, nor does it have any lingering aftereffects. In most cases, sufferers don't even recall the experience when they wake up. However, if night terrors have a pattern of occurring more often than once every four months, it's a good idea to seek professional help.

Here is a timetable detailing the normal evolution of the three disturbances already mentioned—bedtime resistance, nightmares, and night terrors—as well as other sleep-related issues in the emotional life of a child from birth through age five:

BIRTH TO SIX MONTHS

Unless hunger, colic, illness, or pain intervenes, infants this young will typically fall asleep whenever they need to. Parents can assume that any period of wakefulness—however inappropriate it may be to an adult's daily schedule—is natural or "normal" for the child and not a sign of emotional restlessness.

SIX MONTHS TO ONE YEAR

Usually during this time span, children develop the capacity to energize themselves—or to be excited by outside stimuli—to the point where they might not fall asleep naturally. Such excitement might be triggered, or reinforced, by separation anxiety: The child either fears losing her or his parent(s) by lapsing into sleep or doesn't want to face a loss of consciousness all alone. A child may also be excited to wakefulness by a specific emotionally charged situation over which she or he has no control: for example, being put to bed in an unfamiliar room or while an exceptionally lively household occasion is still in progress.

Whatever the case, you can no longer take for granted that your child will succumb automatically to sleep whenever fatigue sets in. This is the time when you need to begin making conscious and consistent efforts to ease the transition between waking and sleeping for your child. Meanwhile, your child will probably rely more and more heavily on her or his own very helpful tension-discharging strategies, such as rocking in bed or thumb-sucking.

During this age span, children may begin experiencing night terrors, another indication that their nervous systems are much more strongly affected by outside stimuli. They may also start having nightmares; but because children this young are unable to communicate verbally, it's difficult to tell. Assuming they are capable of having a nightmare, they do not appear to be as frequently or dramatically upset by nightmares as three- to five-year-old children are.

ONE TO THREE YEARS

During these two years, children are even more susceptible to feelings that will make them want to stay awake. In addition to fearing that their parents just want to get rid of them, children start developing fears that specific things might happen to them once they are all alone in the darkness of their bedroom. Bugs might crawl over their bodies, or a monster might emerge from the closet.

Moreover, children in this age range have more detailed and retentive memories. Thus, while they're lying in bed, they begin to miss specific light-and-sound stimulations they've come to enjoy during the day. Sometimes they feel this loss so acutely, it's as if they thought that going to bed meant saying good-bye forever to their favorite pleasures.

Faced with more reasons not to go to sleep willingly, one-to-three-year-old children develop increasingly devious strategies to put off that final "good night." As communication skills get better, they progress from crying in bed to making a seemingly unending series of complaints and demands: "I don't want to," "I'm not tired," "I want a glass of water," "Give me another kiss." As powers of locomotion improve, they may go beyond merely thrashing in bed or refusing to lie down under the covers to leaving the bed altogether, either to roam around other rooms or to settle in the bed of a parent.

The variety of activities employed by an individual one- to three-year-old child to forestall sleep is usually very wide ranging. Therefore, handling bedtime resistance calls for a multifaceted, experimental response from the parent. Above all, children in this age range need help in learning to relax so that they can be both physically and emotionally ready to sleep when it's appropriate to do so.

THREE TO SIX YEARS

In general, children from three to six years old are more accepting of bedtime. They may not go to sleep right away, but they are willing to get into bed and say good night with much less fuss than when they were one to three years old. Still, occasional problems may occur.

Around the age of four, a child is sufficiently independent in spirit to appreciate having a "big" bed and an emotionally satisfying bedroom environment. Depending on the child, the latter might entail special bedclothes, reassuring pictures on the wall, and/or rearrangement of furniture that creates distinctly different areas for play, dressing, and sleep.

As indicated earlier, children from three to five are especially prone to have upsetting nightmares. It's perfectly normal during these years for them to have a nightmare as often as once or twice a week. Each specific nightmare should be taken seriously, because that approach will help the child resolve any real-life issues that caused the nightmare. However, no severe emotional disturbance is indicated unless the child has the same nightmare a number of times in close succession. In this case, you may want to consult with a professional.

The Importance of Dreaming

In 1953, researchers at the University of Chicago discovered that human beings exhibit rapid eye movement (known as REM) while they are dreaming. In other words, our eyes move around to "watch" our dreams just as they operate to see the sights of our waking life.

Following through on this discovery, sleep scientists have established that all human beings go through several dreaming cycles in the course of each night's sleep. What particularly fascinates child psychiatrists, however, is that very young children dream far more hours per day than adults, beginning with the first sleeping period after birth.

A child under the age of one dreams approximately 40 percent of fourteen sleeping hours a day, for a total daily dreaming time of 5.6 hours. By contrast, a twenty-one-year-old dreams only about 20 percent of eight daily sleeping hours, which amounts to 1.6 hours of dreaming per day.

Since normal, ongoing body functions do not take place without a life-sustaining reason, what purpose do dreams serve? And why is dreaming apparently so much more important to an infant than to an adult?

The prevailing theory is that dreams help the human mind process daily experiences and that infants have an especially strong need for this function. While dreaming, the mind plays with its emotional and conceptual faculties, testing their strengths and weaknesses against life's mysteries and ambiguities. In this manner, it maintains its own psychological health.

Infants are just starting to develop individual psyches; hence, the need for more extensive dream time. To an infant, the mental play of dreaming is especially fresh and compelling, while everything about life is mysterious and ambiguous.

Managing Nightmares

Whether or not the *cause* of a child's nightmare is a troubling issue or event in daily life, the *effect* of the nightmare all by itself can be very emotionally upsetting. When your child complains about a nightmare, here are some steps you can take to alleviate the effects of that nightmare and possibly eliminate its cause:

■ *Allow your child to wake up naturally rather than interrupting her or his sleep.*

To be jolted awake can be just as startling as the nightmare itself, and it may prevent your child's dreaming mind from reaching its own constructive "solution" to the nightmare. A nightmare that is strong enough to cause moaning and thrashing will usually provoke a child to wake up.

■ *Don't insist that the nightmare wasn't real.*

To your child, the nightmare was very real. Instead, assure your child calmly and reasonably that she or he is safe and that anything that happens in a nightmare can never really bring any harm. It may help to compare a nightmare to a television program—something that is "real" to the child but different from the way that her or his life is "real."

■ *Don't play fantasy games to get rid of the nightmare.*

If a child believes that a wicked little man is crouched under the bed, don't pretend to scare him away. As far as the child is concerned, this technique may be reassuring for the moment but not for good: The wicked little man could always return, or another wicked little man could come in his place. Instead, show the child that there *is* no such monster under the bed at that moment without either suggesting or denying that there ever *was* one under the bed.

■ *Encourage your child to describe the nightmare in as much detail as possible.*

Ask step-by-step questions about what happened in the nightmare and what your child felt as it progressed but avoid commenting or passing judgment on what your child tells you. If your child is allowed to "talk it out" without being distracted by your reactions, chances are it will lose its power to terrify. In addition, you'll learn more about how your child's dreaming imagination works, what scares your child, and, possibly, what may have triggered the nightmare in the first place.

■ *Ask your child to draw a picture of what was scary in the nightmare.*

Like "talking out" a nightmare, this activity enables your child to externalize scary images, thereby rendering them less threatening.

■ *Ask your child to describe what she or he could do to make things better if the same experience were to occur again.*

This request induces your child to rehearse coping strategies, both consciously and subconsciously, that will help her or him manage this specific type of nightmare, if it recurs, as well as similarly upsetting nightmares and real-life situations.

■ *Take appropriate measures to make your child feel more emotionally secure at night.*

If your very young child is afraid of falling asleep because of the possibility of a nightmare, the result can be a physically and emotionally harmful pattern of sleeplessness. To prevent this, it makes sense to foster a greater sense of security by leaving the bedroom door ajar or a night-light on or playing a radio softly. If your child wakes up from a nightmare and is especially upset, consider letting her or him sleep the rest of that night with you.

Managing Night Terrors

■ *Don't expect that your child can hear you or even sense your presence.*

A child in the throes of a night terror is still deeply asleep, even if her or his eyes are open and she or he is screaming, talking, and/or moving around. Indeed, the strongest indication that a child is having a night terror instead of an unusually severe nightmare is that she or he doesn't respond appropriately to outside stimuli even though she or he appears awake. Thus, your child may be screaming, "Mommy, Mommy, where are you?" while you are holding her or him in your arms.

■ *Don't wake up your child unless absolutely necessary.*

Typically, an episode of night terror lasts only a few moments, and the child returns to a normal sleeping pattern with no ill effect. Therefore, to avoid escalating the child's panic, it's best to let it run its course rather than waking the child.

If you hold your child, be gentle and don't resist any strong efforts to break free. Remember, your child doesn't realize that you are there. If your child gets out of bed and moves around, follow her or him and do what you can to prevent accidents. Assuming you are physically strong enough and meet with no resistance, pick your child up and carry her or him back to bed.

An exception to the "don't wake up" rule: anytime your child's movements threaten to result in injury. When this happens, you should definitely rouse the child to wakefulness, but do so gently. If possible, try waking your child by wiping her or his face with a washcloth soaked in warm water.

■*Don't expect your child to remember having a night terror after awakening.*

To keep from worrying your child unnecessarily, it's best not to mention the episode at all unless she or he brings it up. The latter sometimes happens when the child awakens during the night terror itself. In any event, your response to the incident should be calm rather than concerned.

Managing Bedtime Resistance

There are two main schools of thought regarding how to handle a toddler (one to three years old) who cries instead of going to sleep:

1. Assuming the toddler isn't genuinely hungry or in pain, let her or him cry. Difficult as it is to ignore a crying child, you should recognize that she or he is simply releasing tension— something that everyone must learn for oneself and that the child will eventually become better at.

2. Go to the toddler and stay in the room, while performing some soothing activity, until she or he has calmed down. Then leave the room. Over time, the toddler's fears regarding bedtime will disappear.

In practice, individual mothers and fathers must experiment with both schools of thought and arrive at a compromise strategy that works not only for their child but also for them.

Generally, toddlers respond best if there is a regular going-to-bed routine that offers a gradual release from you and the day. When you put a one-year-old to bed, try staying in the room for a while, reading or performing some other relatively quiet activity by yourself. Month by month, spend less and less time in the room after you've said good night.

As soon as a child begins to talk, crying as a sleep-resisting activity gradually gives way to calculated defiance and manipulation. To prevent this or to keep it within manageable limits, regular going-to-bed routines assume even more importance.

Having a good routine isn't necessarily a matter of sticking to the same *bedtime* every night. While an overall consistency in bedtime is helpful, a child is not always tired at the same time night after night, nor does the same routine bedtime always suit the family schedule. Instead, having a good routine means preserving the same basic bedtime *ritual* every night, one that creates a peaceful, reassuring transition between waking and sleeping. Here are some suggestions:

■ *Let your child know when it's time to get ready to go to bed.*

Give ten or fifteen minutes' notice *ahead* of the time when your child is expected to be in bed. This will enable your child not only to do something, or finish doing something, before bedtime but also to get into a "bedtime" frame of mine.

■ *Make sure anything your child may need during the night is within reach of her or his bed.*

Children often put off falling asleep by asking for things they "need": a glass of water, a favorite toy, a tissue. Anticipate such needs and keep the area around the bed well stocked.

■ *Help your child follow a definite sequence of activities before retiring.*

In addition to using the bathroom and undressing, these activities might include putting playthings away, saying good night to family members and pets, and arranging stuffed animals on the bed for sleep.

■ *Give going to bed a ceremonial quality.*

For example, while you and your child walk into the bedroom together, sing a certain song together only at that time. Or light a candle after your child gets under the covers and blow it out after you've said your final good night. Such ceremonial touches influence children to take bedtime more seriously.

■ *Do something special with your child after she or he is tucked in for the night.*

Telling or reading stories is the ideal activity because it works the best to pacify your child. But you can also play quiet games or talk about what happened that day. There should be a well-defined pattern to whatever you do together so that the session can begin and end in a predictable, easy manner. If you tell stories, set a limit of no more than two stories. If you play a game, the game should have a built-in ending. If you talk about what happened that day, structure the conversation according to a certain fixed pattern of questions (e.g., ending a talk about the day with the question "What did you do right before you came to bed?" [answer], and "What are you going to do now?").

■ *Follow a definite rule about saying good night.*

When it's time for your child to be left alone to sleep, say good night in a prearranged, "inviolable" way (e.g., "Night, night until tomorrow"). Stick to this final declaration as much as possible, appealing to the fact that you've already said your special "good night" if your child tries to prolong bedtime.

Managing Early and Late Risers

Getting the day off to a good start is just as vital to a very young child's psychological health as ending it well. Many children routinely wake up much earlier—or later—than their parents. In most cases, this is not a symptom that the child is getting more or less sleep than necessary or that she or he is suffering from some sort of sleep-disturbing emotional problem. Nevertheless, it can create havoc within the family, which will inevitably wind up stressing the nervous systems of parent and child alike.

If your very young child is an early or late riser, first find out whether there are grounds for being concerned about her or his physical or emotional well-being. Monitor sleeping and waking patterns closely for a couple of weeks. A child who sleeps about the same number of hours each night, wakes up in a good mood, and doesn't appear to tire easily during the day is probably getting all the sleep necessary and is not suffering from a sleep-disturbing physical or emotional problem.

Next, take whatever action you can to help your child stay in bed longer or rise earlier, depending on which course of action is necessary for the family as a whole to function effectively. Patience and limited expectations are essential: It's very difficult to change a child's natural inclination to get out of bed or stay in it, especially if she or he is between one and a half and two years old.

GUIDELINES FOR EARLY RISERS

■ *Don't try putting your child to bed later in hopes that she or he will sleep longer as a result.*

This technique usually doesn't work; and even if it does, it's not worth the possible ill effects of tampering with your child's normal bedtime.

■ *Talk to your child firmly and responsibly about the issue.*

Tell your child to stay in bed without disturbing you until you come to get her or him. Reassure your child that you will not let her or him sleep "too long." (Children sometimes fear having done so when they first wake up.)

■ *Give your child suggestions and rehearsals for falling back to sleep.*

Make "falling back to sleep" a more fun thing to do for your child. Explain and demonstrate how to lie quietly, how to keep one's eyes closed, and how to think of peaceful things so that falling back to sleep can be more easily accomplished.

■ *Outfit your child's bedside with toys, water, and a little food.*

If given the chance, young children are capable of entertaining themselves and satisfying their simple hunger and thirst needs. Increase the odds that they will do this upon awakening by making it more convenient for them. Place quiet toys, a glass of water, and/or some simple crackers (such as graham crackers) within reach of the bed.

■ *Reinforce positive behavior with praise.*

Congratulate your child whenever she or he stays in bed and doesn't disturb you.

GUIDELINES FOR LATE RISERS

■ *Don't try putting your child to bed earlier in hopes that she or he will rise earlier as a result.*

It's unlikely to work, and interfering with your child's normal bedtime may only create yet another problem.

■ *Talk to your child firmly and responsibly about the issue.*

Tell your child that getting out of bed earlier will allow you to begin the day together in a better way. Ask her or him what each of you could do to help achieve this goal.

■ *Make early morning as pleasant as possible for your child.*

If your child can anticipate a few moments of play with you upon awakening or a special breakfast treat, she or he may eventually take the initiative to get up earlier.

■ *Suggest and rehearse behaviors that will make waking up easier.*

Practice simple stretching exercises with your child and give her or him simple phrases to speak that will make waking up more successful and enjoyable. For example, show your child how to take turns stretching each arm and leg in a particular sequence while saying, "I'm going to have a great day today."

■ *Try waking your child with your voice before rousing her or him physically.*

Children need to become responsible for waking themselves. If you consistently shake your child awake, the process is postponed. If, instead, you awaken your child with a soft voice, she or he must still make an independent effort to come to full consciousness.

One note of caution: Observe your child closely before disturbing her or his sleep. If you notice rapid eye movement under the eyelids, your child is dreaming, and it's less emotionally jarring for the child to remain asleep until dreaming has stopped.

Above all, don't yell. It's far too disruptive to your child, to you, and to anyone else within earshot. If a soft voice won't do the job, it's better to proceed to gentle physical arousal.

■ *Try giving your child an alarm clock.*

If your child persists in sleeping late and nothing works but physical arousal, you might want to try an alarm clock. To underscore the importance of this step to both of you, you can go together to buy the clock and then show your child how to use it. This will make your child much more responsible for her or his awakening, which should help matters considerably.

■ *Reinforce positive behavior with praise.*
Every time your child gets up at an appropriate time for the family, offer your admiration and thanks.

CASE:

Shedding Light

Eight-month-old Kelly cried every night after she was put to bed. Her parents had installed a night-light in her bedroom, but it didn't seem to help much. Kelly still started crying the instant her mother or father switched off the main light.

One night, as Kelly's father was carrying her into the bedroom, Kelly reached out her hand toward the light switch. Her father carried her over to the switch and let her play with it for a while, turning it off and on. That night, for the first time in many nights, Kelly didn't cry when her father switched off the light. Thereafter, it was a rare night when she did cry.

What a very young child doesn't know can hurt him or her emotionally. Even a small piece of knowledge given to a brain starving for knowledge can have a strong and positive impact.

2.
Eating

So much attention today is focused on getting children to eat the right things that much more common and potentially more serious issues are obscured: getting children to eat at all and getting them to eat in a manner that isn't emotionally upsetting to them and the people around them. While children under six years old seldom suffer from major eating disorders with psychological roots—such as self-imposed starvation (anorexia) or deliberate binging (bulimia)—they commonly experience a wide range of problems in coming to terms with the eating schedules, diets, and contexts that are imposed on them by the outside world.

Each child has a unique set of idiosyncratic eating tastes and habits. Consequently, experts have difficulty making general statements about what is normal for very young children, when it is appropriate to expect problems, or how to go about dealing with troublesome situations.

The first year of a child's life tends to go relatively smoothly as far as eating is concerned. The child eats heartily, if messily, and usually doesn't seem upset during feeding times (except sometimes when there is a greater-than-normal amount of distraction in the immediate environment, such as during a large family dinner).

Problems such as consistently being finicky about certain foods, refusing to eat, or misbehaving while eating—all of which are closely related—rarely develop before age two, at which point children have gone through a natural reduction in their appetite. Most often, such problems do not become seriously bothersome until the child is age three or older.

If your child exhibits one of these eating problems, the first and foremost guideline is not to worry unnecessarily about whether she or he is getting the "proper" nutritional input, especially if she or he gives every other indication of being healthy. Keep close track of what your child eats over a week's time, consult with your pediatrician, and accept the latter's judgment. Then experiment with these suggestions, depending on the specific nature of your child's problem:

■ *Be as patient as possible and avoid making a big deal out of your child's poor eating habits.*

Remember that time heals many bad eating habits of children this young and that any extra attention associated with their poor eating habits—even negative attention—can reinforce those habits.

■ *Make mealtimes as calm and as free from competing stimuli as possible.*

Try feeding your child alone, away from others. She or he shouldn't eat with older children and adults until ready to do so. Provide plenty of time and space to eat but don't let mealtime drag on longer than thirty minutes at the most. Your child needs to learn to take advantage of eating times while they last.

■ *Note what times of day and under what circumstances your child eats best and try to arrange mealtimes accordingly.*

You may find out that your child eats best when you're in the proper mood to serve a meal, when no one else is home, or just after you've played with or washed her or him.

■ *If your child must join the rest of the family for a meal, avoid arguments and problematic situations.*

Don't insist that your child eat certain foods, eat in a certain way, or display certain table manners. Also, don't expect to eat your own meal undisturbed by your child!

Follow your child's lead and allow whatever behavior least interferes with the rest of the family. Also, try to prevent or downplay arguments between you and other family members over your child's behavior at the table. They can only lead to a more stressful mealtime for everyone.

■ *Don't offer your child food between meals.*

Get your child to accept the fact that there are certain times when it is more appropriate than others to eat, since doing so requires your cooperation.

■ *Introduce new foods singly and in a pleasant, low-key manner.*

Don't make a big fuss over new foods. In fact, try at first to present them to your child without making any comment whatsoever. Remember that children over two years old appreciate an attractive presentation. Food doesn't have to be offered in a gourmet manner, but nice eating utensils and pleasant-looking portions can make a difference in getting the child to start eating.

■*Don't force your child to eat when she or he won't.*

You can make several calm efforts to try to persuade your child to eat; but don't override a final no by shoving food into your child's mouth. This can only aggravate an eating problem.

■*If your child repeatedly refuses to eat or consumes what you perceive to be too little, serve small portions of what your child likes best.*

First, do whatever you can, following your child's lead, to get your child to eat and enjoy the food in an acceptable manner. Once this goal is accomplished, you can pay more attention to *what* is eaten.

■*Do not offer your child a highly desired item with little nutritional value until she or he eats at least a small amount of a more nutritional food.*

This is a time-honored technique that can be very effective with most children. Just be careful not to abuse it. Save it for especially important times; and while you should always stick to your bargain, you should do so in a calm, matter-of-fact manner, without theatrics.

■*Don't worry very much about table manners until other, more significant problems have been overcome.*

Acquiring good table manners is a fairly sophisticated skill. You can't expect too much until your child is around seven or eight and has learned through increased socialization that manners in general are important. Make your child aware of what good table manners are— and encourage any effort made to develop them—but don't insist that your child display good manners against her or his will.

■*If you can't help being concerned about your child's eating habits, by all means consult your pediatrician.*

It's better to be safe than sorry. Rely on your pediatrician's judgment about whether the problem is emotional in nature and, therefore, whether to consult a child psychologist or psychiatrist.

3.
Sexuality

Few things are more difficult for an adult to appreciate than the sexuality of a very young child. Once the major hormonal changes of puberty have begun, sexual feelings are irrevocably imbued with eroticism—the drive to have physical union with another person. Thus, in the adult world, sexuality turns into a moral issue, with countless individual and social distinctions between what is good and what is bad, what is acceptable and what is not. To a very young child, however, sexual feelings are not erotic; they simply provide sensory pleasure. And rather than compelling a child to mate with another person or reconcile all sorts of complicated emotional reactions, they merely inspire curiosity.

In the evolution of a human being, sexuality first manifests itself as an instinctive response to physical stimulation. The genitalia themselves may not be the initial target of stimulation, but they wind up registering that stimulation; and this response cycle begins much earlier than is commonly realized.

Ultrasound photography has shown that males have erections even before birth; and although ultrasound photography is not yet capable of observing the female fetus's genitalia as closely, there's every reason to infer that females experience prebirth sexual stimulation as well. Shortly after birth, both males and females have shown that they are physiologically capable of achieving orgasm.

Infants can trigger their own sexual feelings by kicking, rocking, or rubbing against their clothes; or sexual feelings can be triggered in infants when their bodies are touched, caressed, and lulled by their parents and caretakers. As infants mature into toddlers, many of their favorite activities can produce sexual pleasure as a side effect: jumping, bouncing, wrestling, sliding, swinging, and seesawing.

Eventually, toddlers start responding to sexually charged images and situations that exist in their environment. Around age two, children begin exhibiting a keen interest in parts of the body—not just their own but that of others as well, especially those that have a different type of genitalia. Children from age two to five also like to mimic the sexual nuances of adult behavior that they see at home, on television, or in printed matter. They playfully undress themselves, assume provocative poses, or make flirtatious body movements.

Aside from the personal embarrassment such activities may cause you, particularly if they occur in public, they are harmless and unlikely to preoccupy a child's attention for more than a moment or two at a time. It may be appropriate in certain situations for you to help your child control or discontinue a specific act of sexual behavior; but if you make too big an issue of such behavior, you may inhibit your child's early sexual learning, which may result in sexual problems later in life.

On a more positive level, there are ways in which you can help a very young child—even as young as two years old—respect and enjoy her or his sexuality. That male genitals are much more visible than female sexual organs can cause very young children of either sex a considerable amount of worry. Girls may need to be convinced that their bodies are just as beautiful and as marvelously equipped as male bodies. Boys may need to be reassured that their penises will not fall off (an anxiety that can lead to frequent masturbatory "double checks"). Both boys and girls need to be told, in a general way, *how* their genitalia will change as they grow older so that they won't jump to distressing conclusions.

By the age of three, a child usually begins forming a romantic attachment to the parent of the opposite sex (or, lacking this person, to some other adult of the opposite sex or to adult members of the opposite sex in general). In doing so, the child is not motivated by erotic feelings but by social and psychological forces.

In their eagerness to express their freshly appreciated gender identity, three-year-olds are compelled to imitate the male and female relationships that they observe in the adult world. Girls will compete with mother for father's attention; boys will compete with father for mother's attention. It's an ebbing-and-flowing process that usually peaks around age six but can continue for another year or two. By age eight, a child typically seeks self-expression through a more direct and mature identification with the parent of the same sex.

During these turbulent years when a child's interest and affections are increasingly focused on the parent of the opposite sex, there is little that parents can do except to be patient and understanding. Girls should be given more time alone with their fathers—and boys, with their mothers—provided it doesn't interfere unduly with the amount of time that mothers and fathers need to be alone together. As children are taught that their own rights will be respected by their parents, they should also be taught to respect their parents' rights.

It's not unusual for children in this age range to strike out at the "competitive" parent. For example, a very young daughter may be quick to scream "I hate you!" at her mother anytime her mother does something disagreeable, especially whenever her mother thwarts her efforts to claim her father's exclusive attention. In such a case, the rejected parent should not take the outburst personally. It is the parent's role, not the parent as an individual, that the child finds so intolerable.

If you are verbally abused in this way, bear in mind that very young children are just learning to master their emotions as well as their language skills. Therefore, what they impulsively blurt out in a moment of strong emotion is very likely to be crude and misleading. Don't reinforce such behavior by saying something like "It hurts me to hear you say that" or "I don't like you very much, either, when you say nasty things." Remain calm and let your child know that you still love her or him.

Another less extreme but no less upsetting form of rejection-behavior is for the frustrated child to avoid contact with the rival parent or to express consistently a preference to be with the parent of the opposite sex. Again, the best strategy is to remain calm and allow the child to do as she or he wishes, assuming it doesn't create any undue complications. Assure the child that it's okay with you if she or he would rather be with the other parent but that you'd like to spend time together later.

It's perfectly normal for a phase of repeated verbal abuse or avoidance to last as long as a month. If the behavior persists at the same level of intensity for more than a month, then there may be an underlying problem—such as a stressful situation within the family (e.g., marital discord, an impending birth, or an exceptional disruption of normal routine)—that is aggravating the child's relationship with the parent she or he is rejecting. If you think that there may be a specific reason that your child is so consistently manipulating one parent against another, then it may be wise to consult with a child psychiatrist or psychologist to find out how best to manage the problem.

As for sex education in general, it is never too early to begin. In fact, the earlier you start, the easier it is. As a child grows older, the significance of sex becomes increasingly more complicated. Therefore, take immediate and appropriate advantage of any opportunity your child gives you to talk about sexual matters, such as a question related to sex or some behavior that manifests her or his sexuality.

In conversations with your very young child about sex, be direct. Talk to your child in the particular manner that you and your child have developed for discussing interesting subjects. And avoid misnaming parts of the body or inventing "short-cut" fantasy explanations for sexual processes. These cover-up strategies can create unnecessary and even harmful confusion and embarrassment later. For example, a child told that a baby grows in the mother's stomach may actually become nervous about what she or he eats.

In any type of educational endeavor, preparation is all-important. The sex-related questions most commonly posed by a child between the ages of two and six are as follows:

Why don't I have a penis? Breasts? Genital hair?

Where do babies come from? Can I have a baby?

What does "[sex-related term or expletive]" mean?

Anticipate such questions and any others that you feel your child may ask. Then prepare ways to answer them truthfully, in the manner that's most comfortable to you, that's most likely to satisfy your child's natural curiosity, and that teaches your child to associate sexuality with personal responsibility.

For example, in answer to your daughter's question about why she doesn't have a penis, you may want to say simply, "Because you're a girl, you have a vagina instead of a penis. Boys don't have a vagina. A vagina is a private part of a girl that is just as special as a penis is for a boy." In answer to your child's question "Can I have a baby?," you may want to say, "No, your body has to grow up more before you can have a baby. And it takes two grown-up people to make a baby— a man and a woman. The best way for them to have a baby is when they are in love and want to stay together to raise their baby in a family."

Sexual Abuse of the Very Young

Tragically, children of *any* age can be victims of sexual abuse. The abuser of a child age six or under is most likely to be someone who is in frequent contact with the child—a family member, a relative, a friend, a neighbor, or a caretaker, who may consider the abuse itself a harmless bit of fun, even an act of love. Nevertheless, it is an outrageous violation of the child's privacy and emotional well-being, and it can easily turn physically dangerous as well.

No matter how young the victim of sexual abuse is, the long-term psychological damage is potentially horrible. Assuming the abuse is not painful, a child-victim under six years old probably won't regard the sexual activity as "wrong" but will certainly be puzzled about how such an experience factors into intimate relationships with others. If the abuse occurs repeatedly (which is more likely than not in cases involving children), a victim this young will be totally unable to deal with the overstimulation and will eventually intuit from the abuser that something strange and bad is going on. If the child tries to end the abusive behavior, the abuser might resort to emotional or even physical retaliation.

To help prevent child abuse, make sure very young children understand that if anyone touches them and makes them feel "funny," they should first tell the person to stop and then come to you and let you know what has happened. Also, you should avoid using exaggerated language when you advise children to respect adults. For example, don't say to a very young child, "Always do what the baby-sitter says."

If you suspect that your very young child has been sexually abused, look for physical evidence in a routine manner that won't scare the child. Although it's difficult to detect behavioral signs of sexual abuse, be alert to the possibility of abuse if your child does any of the following:

■ exhibits an unusual degree of preoccupation with sexual matters or with her or his genital area;

■ communicates aspects of sexual abuse in drawings, games, or fantasies (e.g., pictures of a larger figure molesting a smaller figure or doll play involving sexual seduction);

■ displays a radical change in behavior, especially involving fear, anger, or withdrawal in regard to a specific individual, situation, or place.

If your child offers any hint that sexual abuse has occurred, calmly encourage her or him to talk freely, without making any judgmental comments. Don't refute what your child says or react with astonishment. Take everything your child says seriously and assure her or him that telling you was the right thing to do. (Abusers often swear their victims to secrecy and threaten them with punishment for disclosure.) Finally, tell your child that you will take action to make sure that he or she is safe and that the abuse won't happen again.

If the suspected abuse has occurred *within* the family, immediately contact your local Child Protection Agency. If the suspected abuse has occurred *outside* the family, immediately contact your local police department or district attorney's office. Anyone reporting to these agencies in good faith is immune from prosecution. These agencies will advise you about what steps you should take, given the situation. Among the recommended steps will almost certainly be consulting with a pediatrician and a child psychologist or psychiatrist.

Managing Awkward Sexual Behavior

PUBLIC REMARKS OR DISPLAYS

There will inevitably be times when your very young child will embarrass you with remarks or displays of a sexual nature while the two of you are among other adults inside or outside your home. Perhaps the mere presence of other physically mature sexual beings excites your child to behave in this manner. Maybe your child instinctively knows that the best time to indulge in this kind of behavior is when others are around to temper your reaction. Most likely your child has just unwittingly chosen to do something perfectly natural at the wrong time.

If your child asks you a question about sex where other people can overhear you, don't betray your discomfort or frustrate your child's healthy curiosity by saying that you'll answer the question later. Instead, answer the question briefly in general terms and try to lead the conversation elsewhere.

If your child undresses in public, resist the impulse to scold. Instead, take your child gently aside (if possible), quietly explain that there's a rule people follow about keeping their clothes on in public, and say that you want her or him to remain dressed when other people are around.

If your child calls attention to someone else's sexual characteristics in a voice loud enough to be overheard, the same basic strategy applies, with an added appeal to the child's innate capacity for empathy. Take your child gently aside (if possible), quietly explain that other people feel uncomfortable when they hear someone talking about them, and say that you don't want her or him to behave in such a way.

SEXUAL GAMES

Beginning around age two and a half and continuing until around age seven, most children remain ever eager to explore similarities and differences in physical sexual characteristics with their peers. As with any venture into the unknown, they tend to conduct this activity in the safely structured context of a game—either "show," in which the participants take relatively formal turns exhibiting their genitals in an agreed-upon manner; "house," in which the participants imitate mother and father by getting naked in front of each other; or "doctor," in which the participants "scientifically" investigate each other's genitals.

Children in this age group who engage in sexual games are motivated by intellectual curiosity, not erotic drive, and so their exploration seldom progresses beyond observing each other, nor does it feature any of the emotional give-and-take associated with romantic love. From a psychological point of view, the greatest potential danger of such sexual play to the participating child lies in the way in which an adult witness handles the situation. If an adult's direct intervention or follow-up is too strong, abrupt, or disapproving, the child is bound to experience a mixture of confusion, embarrassment, shame, and guilt that she or he will subconsciously attach to sexual matters in general.

Whenever you interrupt children in the middle of sexual games, do so gently. Explain to the children that a body is something private and that they should keep their clothes on when they play together. Whenever you are compelled, after the fact, to talk to your child about sexual play, first ask your child what she or he did, then offer the "privacy" explanation and the "keep your clothes on" guideline.

MASTURBATION

Masturbation is a natural way for a very young child to explore and enjoy her or his sexuality. At this stage of life, it consists of a wide progression of activities building in intensity, from tentatively crossing the legs or rubbing the genitals while fully clothed to undressing and vigorously fondling the genitals.

Because masturbation represents a healthy activity for the very young child, your goal in managing your child's masturbatory habit should not be to prohibit it but, rather, to get her or him to regard it as a personal activity that should be performed only when alone. Whenever you observe your very young child doing what you suspect is masturbating, first find out in a casual, nonthreatening way if masturbation is, in fact, what is going on. If you haven't already identified it to your child as "the private thing," then ask your child if the activity is making her or his genitals feel good. Once you've established that your child is masturbating, identify and explain it as "the private thing."

INTRUSION ON PARENTAL SEXUAL ACTIVITY

Disconcerting as it can be for your child to appear unexpectedly when you're having sexual relations, try to remain as composed as possible. First tell your child that you are enjoying your "private time" now. ("Enjoy" is an important word, since it may appear to your child that you're being hurt or bothered.) Then ask your child to leave you alone for a while, with the assurance that you will spend time together later. Of course, the most effective strategy is to anticipate such an intrusion and take measures (such as locking the door) so that you won't be interrupted.

QUESTIONS AND ANSWERS

Gender Stereotypes

■ *Are there any innate differences in emotional makeup between males and females?*

It is virtually impossible to prove that a child's gender in itself predetermines anything about her or his emotional makeup. However, recent scientific studies suggest that females do have a stronger inborn tendency toward empathy and altruism than males.

For example, it's been repeatedly demonstrated that newborn females are quicker to cry in response to another infant's cry than are newborn males and that girls under five years old try more often and more earnestly than their male counterparts to come to their mother's aid when she seems troubled. Moreover, females of *all* ages have been shown to be more adept than males at interpreting emotional states in other people. (Most tests of this nature involve responding to photographs of people expressing strong emotions that are already known to the test administrator.)

Perhaps evolution has favored this trait in women as a mothering skill or as a means of surviving among physically stronger men. Whatever the case, there is no other scientific indication of any difference in innate emotional makeup between males and females.

■ *How do parents commonly tend to stereotype emotional differences between very young boys and very young girls?*

In stereotypical terms, very young boys are regarded as being emotionally stronger and less complex than their female counterparts. Therefore, parents in general are likely to treat very young girls far more delicately and sensitively than they do very young boys.

If a girl under the age of six does something naughty, she typically receives a mild rebuke and a careful explanation of what was wrong with her behavior. If a boy under six does the same thing, the punishment is typically harsher and the explanation (if any) more superficial.

In expressing affection to children in this age range, parents are usually more effusive in their language and gestures with girls than they are with boys. Moreover, in giving commands, parents are inclined to be more circumspect with girls than with boys. Assuming, for instance, that a father wants his daughter to join him, he tends to couch the command in relatively polite language: "Sweetheart, would you come over to Daddy, please?" Assuming that the same father wants his son to join him, he tends to be more abrupt: "Son, come over here."

In reality, there is no scientific basis whatsoever for believing that males are inherently stronger and less complex in their *emotional* makeup than females. (That boys seem to be more inclined toward rough *physical* behavior is a different issue.) Nor is there any logic to support a particular mode of parental treatment as intrinsically better for one sex than the other.

■ *How can gender stereotyping harm young children emotionally?*

Anytime you think of, or act toward, someone in a stereotypical manner—or influence another to react similarly—you are denying her or his unique identity as a human being, and any such denial can be emotionally frustrating to the victim.

This is just as important to remember when that "someone" is a very young child as it is when dealing with a fully grown adult.

It's humanly impossible to be 100 percent "correct"—that is, nonstereotypical—in your thinking and behavior. However, as a general rule, you should strive to treat a child according to her or his individual personality and not according to how you think "a little boy" or "a little girl" *should* be treated.

■ How can parents fight against gender stereotyping in the world and raise emotionally well balanced children?

Gender stereotyping usually begins at birth. If the infant is male, the socially approved color for clothes and playthings is a cool blue, and the appropriate decorative motifs include wild animals, sports equipment, and streamlined stripes or checks. If the infant is female, the color is a soft pink, and the motifs include kittens, flowers, and luxuriant frills.

These distinctions imply major differences between very young males and females; but as far as the children themselves are concerned, there are no apparent differences in feeling or behavior for years to come. Until children are around three or four years old, parents can effectively combat gender stereotyping simply by being careful not to treat a little girl as if she were different from a little boy and vice versa. This means not only resisting the tendency to cooperate with artificial gender distinctions in clothing and playthings but also giving a child of either gender the same kind of attention and care.

When children reach the age of four or five, they begin responding on their own to the gender stereotypes they see everywhere in the world around them, and parental efforts to fight against these stereotypes become much more problematic. On the one hand, it is impossible to deny that male and female stereotypes exist and that they have a major influence on human affairs and relationships. On the other hand, children are naturally and irresistibly drawn to enact such stereotypes in order to bolster the newly emerging sense of who they are.

The best that you can do to fight gender stereotypes at this stage in your child's life is to continue setting a good example. As much as possible, try to behave the same way toward male as you do toward female children and guard against stereotypical gender behavior in your own adult life. In two-parent households, the more fathers and mothers share the same child-raising responsibilities, the better. In one-parent households, it helps to make sure that the child has one special adult of the opposite sex with whom she or he can interact on a regular and frequent basis.

Meanwhile, allow your child to experiment with stereotypical gender roles as she or he wishes. It doesn't do much good to give your four-year-old son a doll if he'd rather have a dump truck or to pressure your five-year-old daughter to play baseball with the boys if she'd prefer to bake cookies with the girls. However, it can do a lot of good to expose your daughter or son to a wide range of different toys and activities, regardless of male and female stereotypes, and to avoid encouraging stereotypical gender behavior at the expense of giving your child full freedom of choice.

If your child's stereotypical behavior is injurious to someone else emotionally or physically, you should intervene as constructively as possible to help her or him appreciate the nature of the offense. For example, if you witness your five-year-old daughter striking a male playmate and then taunting him by saying, "Boys can't hit girls," you should immediately tell her that people shouldn't hit each other at all, regardless of whether they are boys or girls.

The Oedipus/Electra Complex

According to Sigmund Freud, a child between the ages of four and six typically experiences an intense romantic attraction to the parent of the opposite sex (or, in the absence of this parent, to some other adult of the opposite sex who plays a major role in her or his life). In response to this powerful attraction, the child also experiences a strong feeling of competitiveness and even anger toward the parent of the same sex (or toward any adult interested in—or involved with—the love object).

In the case of boys, Freud called this phenomenon an Oedipus complex, after the legendary Greek hero and supposed orphan who unknowingly killed his father and married his mother. In the case of girls, he called it an Electra complex, after the daughter of the Greek king Agamemnon, who killed her mother out of obsessive love for her father. These Greek myths are to be taken not as *literal* portrayals of a real child's possible feelings for her or his parents but, rather, as *symbolic* exaggerations of the passionate, mysterious, and troubling forces that can disturb a child's emotional tranquillity during the early years of life.

Essentially, this stage in a child's emotional development is normal and very significant. It marks the passing of "infantile" sexuality (which lacks any specific outside target and is felt throughout the body in general) and the beginning of "mature" sexuality (which focuses on a particular love object and is more restricted in feeling to the genitals).

It is assumed that all children go through this stage. However, some are more conscious of their feelings than others, some experience such feelings earlier or later than others, and many offer no easily observable manifestations of such feelings.

Parents of a child who is undergoing this stage of emotional development need to be especially tolerant of any attempts their child makes to bond more closely with a love object and to withdraw from, or compete with, a rival. As distressing or obnoxious as such behaviors can sometimes be, they are early and vital experiments in dealing with adult feelings.

4.
Shyness and
Aggression

Every child sometimes behaves shyly and sometimes aggressively. It all depends on the particular social circumstance and the overall emotional state in which that situation is entered. But apart from this dynamic, some children are predisposed to be shy consistently; others are inclined to be aggressive. Most often, their behavior appears to be a matter of inborn temperament.

Recent scientific studies suggest that inherently shy people are more easily aroused physiologically. In other words, their nervous system naturally functions in such a way that they become more quickly and profoundly excited by any change in stimuli. Thus, physicians and mental-health professionals have begun to refer to such people as "highly reactive" rather than "shy."

In highly reactive individuals, the shyness itself is an instinctive behavior designed to protect them from a physiological—and, possibly, emotional—overload. As for inherently aggressive people, science hasn't come up with a similar explanation for why some people are demonstrably more bold, assertive, or uninhibited than the norm.

Apart from a child's intrinsic temperament, there are other explanations for an ongoing tendency to behave either shyly or aggressively. Children under six who are unusually big, small, or ill or who are otherwise very different physically from their surrounding peers might develop either a shy personality to avoid attracting attention or an aggressive personality to compensate for what they perceive as a liability. Family relationships can also play a role. A child raised in a very competitive family may choose either to retreat from the competition by being shy or enter into the competition by being bold.

Birth order is yet another possible factor. For example, the "baby" of a family with numerous children is often inclined to be shy, which may be the net effect of so many other people taking care of her or him. If such a child were compelled to be more independent, a more aggressive personality might emerge. Conversely, the oldest child in a family with numerous children is typically inclined to be bold, perhaps because she or he can claim superiority over the other children or feels responsible for protecting the younger children.

Until a child is around two years old, it's very difficult to identify with any certainty a predisposition toward either shyness or aggression. After the age of two, a child begins to function as a distinctly separate individual and to interact more with others, especially peers. It is during these social encounters that the child's behavior is the most illuminating. If the child tends to let others make decisions, lead in games, do most of the talking, or commandeer all the desired toys, then it's possible that she or he is essentially shy. If the child tends to be the decision maker, the leader, the talker, and the toy grabber, then it's possible that she or he is essentially aggressive.

The degree to which a child likes to touch or hug, or to be touched or hugged, is not a reliable indicator of whether she or he is shy or aggressive by nature. The limits a child sets on body contact with someone else can have many contributing factors, not the least of which may be the relative sensitivity of her or his skin.

For similar reasons, whether a child tends to cling, or not to cling, is also not necessarily an indicator of inherent shyness or aggressiveness. Usually a child outgrows an idiosyncratic need to cling or not to cling by age six. Assuming such behavior isn't accompanied by other disturbing symptoms (for example, consistently crying while refusing to let go of a parent or running away in fear when touched), there's no need to be concerned.

Whatever the case, it's important to realize that shyness and aggression in themselves are neutral attributes—each having its own fair share of positive and negative applications. There is no reason to worry about a child's being basically shy or aggressive unless that personality trait is clearly and repeatedly causing emotional turmoil in the child or in others.

Many parents have difficulty accepting this advice, especially in the case of a shy child. Western culture puts such a premium on aggression in human affairs that parents tend to worry inordinately about their shy child's ability to hold her or his own against others later in life. It's vital for these parents to remind themselves that many creative and successful people have been, and are, shy by nature and that this very trait was a major factor in their success.

On the whole, parents are much less apprehensive about raising an aggressive child. Some parents do worry whether their aggressive child will also turn out to be compassionate; but, again, this is not an issue that requires parental intervention unless definite and irrefutable problems have arisen that are directly attributable to the child's lack of compassion.

Even when an aggressive child does tend to act without a proper degree of compassion, the parents can't expect to change the fundamental predisposition to be aggressive. All they can reasonably hope to do is to change the *manner* in which the child exercises that predisposition. Long-term research indicates that only about one-third of the individuals who are basically shy or basically aggressive as children (combined, an estimated 40 percent of the population) ever change much by the time they are adults.

In the life of a child under six years old, it's unlikely that any major or complicated problems will occur having to do with her or his inherent shyness or aggression (although the likelihood is higher for kids under six who are in day care or nursery schools). Most of the problems for kids under six are situational and easy to spot. Some examples follow:

■ a shy child being regularly bossed around by another child (not necessarily an aggressive one);

■ an aggressive child regularly making other children cry (not necessarily shy ones);

■ a shy child refusing to come out of her or his room when company visits and wants to see her or him;

■ an aggressive child disturbing everyone at a family gathering by demanding constant attention.

After a child reaches age six, at which time academic and social pressures increase enormously, her or his natural shyness or aggression can become much more problematic. Therefore, it is wise to be on the lookout for a consistent pattern of shyness or aggression in the behavior of your child *under* six so that you can intervene at critical moments by giving your shy child a gentle push or by gently restraining your aggressive child. Just be sure to proceed with caution. A few incidents do not a shy or a bold child make. And the majority of children do not seem to have a strong predisposition in either direction.

Managing a Child's Shyness

Here are guidelines for helping your child deal with problems she or he may be having, or creating, as a result of being inherently shy:

■ *Focus your attention on each situation as it happens, not on your child's personality or overall behavior.*

Your six-year-old is too young to understand generalities. If you accuse her or him of being too shy or refer to any history of inappropriately shy behavior, you will simply confuse your child, creating even more feelings of helplessness and hopelessness.

Only address the issue of shyness as it relates to an incident that is very fresh in your child's memory. Structure your remarks so that they refer to the problematic nature of the situation itself, not the "wrongness" of the way your child acted. For example, if your child has a miserable time at a party because she or he is too shy to enter into the party games, lead her or him to see how the games—or the people playing them—might appear scary in some way but in fact are nonthreatening and even fun. You might even try playing the very same games with your child at appropriate times so that she or he can come to enjoy them better.

■ *Make sure your child knows that she or he has a right to express feelings and needs.*

After an episode of shyness, elicit from your child what her or his feelings and needs were at the time. Indicate that it is all right not only to have such feelings and needs but also to act on them in relationships with others.

If your child is not forthcoming on these issues, try simply telling your child about her or his rights in such matters either by referring directly to the incident at hand or by sharing a story that refers to the incident indirectly. You might also help your child release repressed emotions by suggesting that she or he draw a picture or play a particular game.

■ *Engage your child in activities that will help bolster self-confidence.*

First, identify those activities that your child seems to enjoy and master. Then praise your child for skill in those activities and encourage more frequent participation in them.

To deal with specific situations in which your child appears to lack self-confidence, some form of role-playing or "rehearsal" might be helpful. Ask your child to join you in creating an imaginary version of the target situation—one in which the child can feel safer and more empowered. Shy children often see their own way out of their shyness once they are asked to put themselves in a bolder child's shoes or pretend that they are doing something they've been too shy to do in real life.

■ When possible, help ease your child into potentially difficult situations.

If you realize ahead of time that your child is likely to be shy about interacting with another person or taking part in a certain event, be sure to do what you can to smooth the path. Don't be obviously directorial; work subtly to do whatever you can to make the difficult situation less threatening.

Before it occurs, let your child know what to expect and encourage a positive attitude. Just take care not to be too dramatic in your description of the event. Otherwise, your child might feel pressured to have a similar response to it.

Arrange your child's actual entrance into the event so that it occurs at a good time for the child and isn't too abrupt or overwhelming. As much as you can without coddling, assist the child in becoming acclimated to the situation before leaving her or him alone.

■ Tactfully intervene in situations where you witness another child taking unfair advantage of your child.

When your shy child is playing with another child or with other children, it's not appropriate for you to watch over them like a hawk. You may only reinforce your child's tendency to lack self-reliance. However, it is appropriate to check into the play situation very discreetly from time to time.

If you happen to see your child being treated unfairly during one of your "check-ins," step into the situation and clarify calmly and simply who has what rights. At any age, but especially when they are under six years old, children need adult help in such matters. They are not always able—or willing—to sort them out on their own.

■ Praise your child's efforts at being more independent and more constructively assertive.

Whenever your child does behave in a manner that is self-confident and appropriately bold, be sure to point out how much you admire that act. Again, the focus should be on what the child *did*, not on the *child*.

■ *Set a good example of self-confidence and self-assertion.*
Children in general notice far more than their parents think they do; this may be especially true in the case of shy children, who tend to be very reflective. Let your child see you standing up for your rights when it's necessary or taking the initiative in a difficult or novel situation.

Managing an Aggressive Child

Here are guidelines for assisting your child in dealing with problems she or he may be having, or creating, as a result of being inherently aggressive:

■ *Make it clear that you disapprove of what happened in a specific situation and not of your child.*
Aggressive children are quick to become angry or resentful, especially if they feel their very identity is being attacked. Accept your child for who she or he is and direct your remarks about aggression toward each negative situation as it comes to your attention.

■ *Teach your child to appreciate that other people have rights and needs that must be respected.*
Referring to a very recent situation in which your child ignored or violated someone else's rights, you should establish what those rights were and why they needed to be respected. Aside from direct discussion, one of the best ways to do this is to role-play, giving your child the other person's part.

In your role-play, re-create the specific situation in which your child behaved with inappropriate aggression and then handle that situation more appropriately. For example, suppose that your child recently caused a problem by grabbing a playmate's toy. In your role-play of this situation, you as your child should politely ask for permission to play with the toy. If that permission is not granted, then you should bargain politely to see if you can work out a compromise (e.g., playing with the toy in a couple of minutes). If that doesn't work, then you should accept the other child's judgment and find something of your own with which to play.

A subtler way to teach appreciation for others' rights is by telling rights-related stories and then engaging your child in a discussion of them. You might also try exposing your child to television programs or movies that you know discuss rights in a manner that is appropriate to your child's age level and rights-related experiences.

■ *Engage your child in activities that will exercise her or his capacities for self-control and compassion.*

Whenever someone close is in need of help or attention, propose to your child something that she or he might do: make a card, a visit, a phone call or do some simple task for the other person's benefit. Some aggressive children are "tamed" by learning to care for a pet.

■ *Anticipate problematic situations and let your child know what you expect.*

Faced with a situation in which you know your child may be inappropriately assertive, take a few moments to discuss how you'd like to see things go. Avoid being accusatory. Simply enlist your child's natural "take-charge" proclivity in making the event a pleasant one for every person involved. Aggressive children have an unfortunate tendency to act before they think, and this kind of preparatory strategy session helps circumvent that tendency.

■ *If you actually see your child abusing another child's rights, don't hesitate to referee.*

Self-management is a very troublesome task for an aggressive child, so your calm intervention in a deteriorating situation can keep matters from getting totally out of hand. Guard against being punitive. Clarify what's fair given the situation at hand, gain everyone's commitment to fair play, and then withdraw.

■ *Always praise appropriate self-control.*

When your normally aggressive child deliberately exercises self-discipline due to a sense of compassion or fairness, let her or him know at the soonest appropriate moment that you're very proud of that behavior.

■ *Set a good example of fairness and self-control.*

The more your child sees you acknowledging the rights of others, the more she or he will be prepared to do the same. What doesn't come naturally to a child needs to be role modeled.

CASE:

Caught in the Act

Taylor and Mike, both age four, had been good playmates for almost a year. One day, when Mike showed Taylor his new toy truck, Taylor yelled, "Give that to me!" and grabbed for it. Mike let him take it out of his hands and immediately started crying.

Taylor's father, who had observed the scene, knelt down next to Taylor and said in a soft voice, "I know how much you'd like to play with that truck, but it's not yours. It's Mike's. And he feels bad now that you've taken it away from him. Please give it back to him now. Later on, you can ask him in a nice way if you could play with it for just a little while. Okay?" Taylor agreed and returned the truck. In a few moments, the friends resumed playing together happily.

Mike's mother had also observed the scene. She did nothing at the time because Taylor's father stepped in to handle matters. Afterward, however, she recalled the scene for Mike and asked him, "Why didn't you say no to Taylor and keep him from grabbing your truck?" Mike, clearly confused by his own behavior, could only answer, "Taylor's my friend."

Wanting to help Mike realize that he would not have lost Taylor's friendship just by refusing to give him the truck, Mike's mother asked her son to pretend that Taylor had a new toy car. "Would you stop being Taylor's friend if he didn't let you play with his car one time?" she asked. "No," Mike answered with conviction. Sometimes children need a little parental coaching to see their way out of misconceptions.

5.
Fear

Children under the age of six live in a world that is far more baffling and emotionally challenging than their parents can comprehend, despite having been children once themselves. In this "under six" world, everything remains relatively new and therefore potentially unsettling.

To complicate matters, it's difficult for the very young inhabitants of this world to distinguish between what is real (like the death of a grandparent) and what is imaginary (like the death of a similar person on television or in a dream). Each passing hour can bring a fresh round of puzzlement, surprise, and shock; and as children under six live through these hours, they are acutely aware of their smallness and powerlessness compared to adults.

Although parents may not be able to reenter the confusing world of the very young, they can certainly appreciate that children living in such a world are bound to experience a wide range of different kinds, as well as many individual incidents, of fear. The true wonder of childhood is that children are usually able to grow through their fears so quickly—a powerful testament to their inner resources of hope, rationality, and self-preservation.

When parents are faced with their children's fears, the biggest single problem besetting them is an agonizing tendency toward over-protectiveness. You can't possibly shield your child from all fears; and even if you could, it wouldn't always be wise to do so. Giving vent to fear can often be an effective and healthy way for a child to deal with a troubling situation. For example, a fear of dogs can inspire a child to develop safer, more respectful, and more rewarding conduct toward animals of all kinds. A fear of separation from a parent teaches a child to appreciate caretaking, manage anger, and feel empathy for people in need of human contact.

What you as a parent can and should do is to monitor your child's fears in a discreet and practical manner so that you can help your child process more significant fears as constructively as possible. If a certain fear is not seriously disabling and doesn't last longer than three or four weeks at a stretch, there's no need to worry about your child's overall emotional health. However, if a certain fear continues to preoccupy your child for more than a month or if it prevents your child from leading a normal life, then therapy should be considered. It's also wise to check with a professional whenever an episode of strong fear triggers physical symptoms in your child, such as a rapid heartbeat, dizziness, headache, nausea, or incontinence.

Timely and intelligent handling of unusually strong childhood fears is essential for both the present and the future emotional health of a child under six. Left to itself, a persistent or especially severe childhood fear can ultimately lead to an adult phobia: an ongoing, intractable, and unreasonable anxiety regarding something in particular. Among the more common phobias of this type are acrophobia (fear of heights), claustrophobia (fear of enclosed spaces), and any one of a number of animal-related phobias (like entomophobia, or fear of insects).

Until your child is able to communicate fears verbally, there is little you can do except to "read" them through your child's nonverbal behavior and then minimize the grounds for them as much as practically possible. Once your child is capable of conversing with you about these fears, there are a number of ways that you can help her or him manage them so that they don't turn into serious problems:

---

1. *Respond to your child's fear with equanimity and compassion.*

Be respectful of your child's feelings but not overly solicitous. A shower of concern and attention not only rewards a child for being afraid but also risks scaring her or him into being even more fearful.

Conversely, don't belittle or dismiss the fear or resort to teasing or anger in an effort to change the fearful attitude. If your child sees these types of responses, she or he may cease to complain of fear, but chances are strong that the fear will still be present, all the more emotionally injurious for being suppressed.

---

2. *Gently encourage your child to discuss the fear.*

Being careful not to express your own opinions prematurely, ask your child to describe her or his fearful experience(s) and feeling(s). The more informed you are about the nature of the fear, the better you can help your child deal with it. At the same time, the more your child talks about the fear, the more likely she or he is to work through it.

Don't press if your child is reluctant to discuss the fear in much detail. Otherwise, you may unwittingly force her or him to become frightened all over again. If your child says that she or he doesn't want to talk about it, comment that you are really interested in knowing more about it, giving her or him a second chance to talk. If your child insists on remaining silent, leave it at that.

Whether or not your child is willing to talk about the fear, you might try inviting her or him to express the fear in a drawing. Children are often much more comfortable creating visual images than they are expressing themselves verbally, and the results can be even more therapeutic.

3. Reassure your child regarding the feared object or situation and her or his own coping skills.

Be honest in your assessments. If possible, speak from your personal experience of encountering similar objects or situations and of observing your child's displays of courage and resourcefulness in analogous circumstances.

4. Engage your child in discussing constructive ways to cope with the fear.

Coax your child to volunteer ideas before offering your personal suggestions. A child will be much more interested in carrying through a plan that she or he has personally generated. At the end of such a discussion, work toward some form of commitment, no matter how tentative, to a particular plan. Be careful not to make the plan too detailed or time-specific so that there's no serious risk of failure.

5. Be especially patient with your child.

As much as possible, allow your child to confront and master the fear at her or his own pace. For a brief time after the fear develops, your child may need to go through a passive period of self-recovery without taking any direct action to overcome the fear. Give your child up to several weeks before expecting to see any improvement.

If necessary, you can gently move things along by engineering situations in which your child can *gradually* come to terms with the fear. This step-by-step acclimatization technique is used to cure adult phobias. Suppose, for example, that your child is afraid of dogs, is apparently unable to overcome this fear on her or his own initiative, and is routinely exposed to dogs at the homes of playmates and relatives. First, you might arrange a special time for you and your child to observe puppies from a safe distance, such as at a pet store. If that experience is pleasurable, you might then set up a secure situation in which your child can pet a puppy for as long a time, or as short a time, as she or he wishes. If all goes well, you might take the next step: giving your child an opportunity to spend some supervised time with a full-grown dog—during which time you can teach your child specific coping skills.

6. Encourage your child to engage in activities that will serve to counterbalance the fear.

Physical play helps many people discharge feelings of hostility, frustration, or depression—all feelings that can underlie, or accompany, a specific case of fearfulness. Drawing and performing small tasks can serve the same purpose, plus these activities enable children to prove to themselves that they *can* exercise self-control and mastery over the outside world.

7. Tactfully watch and support your child's progress in coping with fear.

Without repeatedly compelling your child to report her or his fear-related experiences and feelings to you, keep track of how she or he appears to be managing the fear. If you witness your child confronting a formerly feared object or situation in a competent, self-assured manner or if your child tells you about such a confrontation, be sure to offer your praise.

8. Set a good example.

In developing a fear of something, your child may be taking cues from you. Watch what you say and do to make sure you aren't inadvertently and inappropriately communicating anxiety to your child.

9. Anticipate potentially fearful situations and take reasonable measures to make them less fearful.

You don't want to be overprotective with your child, but this doesn't mean you can't be protective to an appropriate degree. For example, if you know your child has a fear of strangers and you're about to hire a new baby-sitter, make arrangements for your child to spend some time with the sitter in advance, while you are present. If your child fears scary-looking faces, it may be a good idea not to have her or him waiting at the door when Halloween trick-or-treaters come by or to ask the latter to let your child see their real faces underneath their masks.

A Timetable for Fears

Children typically experience different types of fears at different stages in their physical, cognitive, and emotional development. Among the most prevalent age-appropriate fears are the following:

BIRTH TO SIX MONTHS

- any loud and sudden noise
- any quick movement on the part of another person
- falling or being dropped
- loss of support in general

SEVEN MONTHS TO ONE YEAR

- specific loud noises (such as a garbage disposal)
- strangers in general
- being dressed, undressed, or changed
- tub and basin drains (where the child bathes)
- heights
- helplessness when faced with unexpected situations

ONE TO TWO YEARS

- specific loud noises
- separation from a parent
- strangers in general
- tub and basin drains (where the child bathes)
- sleeping in general (loss of consciousness and nightmares)
- personal injury
- loss of control over physical and emotional functions

TWO TO TWO AND A HALF YEARS

- specific loud noises
- separation from, or rejection by, a parent
- strange peers
- toilets (especially flushing)
- nightmares
- changes in the environment (e.g., moved furniture, altered living spaces)
- bad weather (especially thunder and lightning)

TWO AND A HALF TO THREE YEARS

- large, looming objects

- strange peers

- unusual occurrences and changes in routine

- loss or movement of objects

- nightmares

CASE:

Weathering the Storm

When Carly was two and a half years old, she developed a fear of storms. She would get quiet and watchful whenever the sky turned dark. If it began to rain heavily, she would start crying. Thunder and lightning would elicit shrieks of terror.

Carly's parents decided to distract her attention from storms by turning stormy times into party times. When a storm hit, they would announce, "Time for a party!" Then they would lay out a blanket in the family room, play with some of Carly's toys, listen to music, and eat special treats.

The first three times Carly's parents did this, she would forget her fear for short intervals while the party was going on, but a rise in the wind or a sharp peal of thunder frequently prompted another spell of anxious behavior. By the fourth storm party, however, she was no longer surprised by feelings of fear, and she continued to remain composed after the party, even though the storm was still raging.

Eventually, a full-fledged, parent-run storm party was no longer necessary. Carly had learned to seek entertaining distraction on her own.

CASE:

Battle of the Bugs

One afternoon four-year-old Jason was helping his father clean the garage. He balked when it came to removing some empty boxes from a dark corner, telling his father, "I don't want any bugs to get me."

The first thing Jason's father did was to try to put this fear into perspective. "What *kind* of bugs?" he asked. "Flying bugs," Jason answered. Later, they consulted a book of insects, and Jason's father asked him to indicate which "flying bugs" were the worst and which weren't really so bad. This activity made both Jason and his father realize that what scared him the most were flying insects that made noises: droning houseflies and beetles and buzzing bees, hornets, wasps, and mosquitoes.

With the assistance of the insect book and a rented video-tape, Jason's father helped him appreciate the lives that these insects led and the roles that they played in the biological scheme of things: providing food, transferring pollen, decomposing waste matter, and fertilizing the soil. He also managed to trap individual specimens of some of the feared insects under a drinking glass so that Jason could observe them safely at a close distance. Armed with this new understanding of his former enemies, Jason lost his fear within a couple of weeks.

Managing Fear of the Hospital

When your very young child needs to stay in the hospital overnight or longer for medical tests, treatment, or surgery, don't assume that she or he will be afraid of the experience in the same way that an adult would be. Most very young children harbor no preconceptions of what a hospital visit, a serious illness, medical care, or a painful recuperation might entail. If your child does exhibit fear (and some do not), it's almost certainly because of this lack of knowledge as well as the fact that she or he is leaving home, loved ones, and familiar daily routines.

Here are some suggestions for preventing or handling a very young child's fear of the hospital:

■ *Seek advice from your physician.*

Your physician has no doubt dealt with such fear many times and knows techniques and resources that may help you. Furthermore, she or he can alert you to potential fear-provoking aspects related to the specific situation at hand. In any event, your physician will be able to put your child's fear into perspective for everyone's peace of mind.

■ *Fully inform your child, in a manner appropriate to her or his intelligence level, about what is going to happen.*

Don't lie to your child or make promises that may not come true (e.g., "It won't hurt," "You'll enjoy it," or "I'll be with you all the time"). As soon as you're able, go over the realities of the situation without instilling undue anxiety but also without leaving your child unprepared for the possible pain or fear that may be involved.

■ *If practical, let your child visit the hospital in advance and witness you talking with the physician about the visit.*

This will eliminate a great deal of the shock element when it's time for your child's scheduled stay. Your physician, or someone on the hospital staff, can probably help arrange this exploratory visit so that your child has a pleasant time.

■ *Plan something fun for your child to do after the hospital stay.*

Anticipation of this posthospital event will help your child put up with some of the negative things that may occur while in the hospital.

■ *Accompany your child as much as practical or possible during the hospital stay.*

Some hospitals have facilities for a parent to stay overnight or longer with the child. Many allow a parent to accompany the child into operating and treatment rooms. Whatever the situation, let your child know when to expect your presence during the hospital stay and when not to (reassuring your child, in the latter case, that you will be waiting for her or him afterward).

■ *When the hospital experience is over, continue to refer to it casually as long as it still seems to be on the child's mind.*

This strategy invites your child to share—and thereby discharge—any residual fears or confusions about the experience.

At PCGC:
Pain Management for
Very Young Children

Compared to all that we know about the emotional and physiological factors relating to *adult* pain, there is a surprising
lack of information and education about the emotional and
physiological factors relating to *children*'s pain. As a result,
many misconceptions exist, such as the false notions that children, especially infants, do not feel pain as intensely as adults
and that they are essentially incapable of managing the pain
they do feel.

The best way for hospitals and clinics to assist child patients
and their families in coping more intelligently with severe or
chronic pain is to coordinate medical, psychological, nursing,
physical therapy, and technological resources into an integrated treatment plan. Increasingly, hospitals and clinics are
aiming in this direction.

The guiding philosophy of this kind of "pain management"
plan is to minimize the child's pain as much as possible while
at the same time increasing her or his ability to function. For
example, in the Pain Management Program conducted by The
Children's Hospital of Philadelphia and the Philadelphia Child
Guidance Center, a pain management team of professionals is
assigned to each case. To treat the physical aspects of pain,
physicians on these teams rely on new medications, old medications used in new ways, and innovative techniques in administering medications. To address the psychological aspects
of pain, psychiatrists and psychologists on these teams rely on
various nonmedical methods to help the child cope with pain
and to assist the family in managing stress factors associated
with the pain. Among these nonmedical methods are the following:

ACTIVE LISTENING

Children in pain often feel that other people—especially
adults—are incapable of understanding or appreciating what
they are going through. Team members always exercise active
listening skills when they are working with a child, and they

teach family members and caretakers to do the same. Here are the main active listening skills:

■ establishing trust with the child;

■ encouraging the child to talk openly about painful experiences;

■ not interrupting or "speaking for" the child;

■ never questioning what the child says about her or his pain;

■ demonstrating that you understand and respect what the child has said.

BIOFEEDBACK

Using a computer, child patients are able to see or hear their own physiological reaction to pain. This helps them put the pain into a more realistic perspective and inspires them to work effectively toward reducing it.

For example, a girl with chronic leg pain can attach computer-connected electrodes to her leg and then engage in very simple relaxation techniques aimed at easing her leg pain. As these techniques change the level of her skin conductivity, thus indicating a relaxation of her leg pain, she sees the change registered by the computer: A train appears on the screen and runs downhill on a track. Through this kind of activity, she learns to channel her attentive energies more and more toward *controlling* her physiological reaction instead of just *expressing* her discomfort.

SELF-HYPNOSIS AND RELAXATION

Many techniques exist for teaching a child how to relax, including deep muscle relaxation or visual imagery. The techniques chosen for a specific case depend on the age of the patient and the nature of the pain.

Take, for instance, the relatively extreme case of a five-year-old boy with cancer who is frightened of bone-marrow aspirations. His anxiety makes the procedure even more painful than it naturally is. To alleviate this anxiety, the boy can be taught to visualize an imaginary line running from the back of his neck to the place on his body where he feels that pain and then to imagine that he himself is turning the wire on and off. Eventually, he can learn to "let go" of his pain when the wire is "off" and thereby tolerate the temporary procedure with much less discomfort.

PAIN DIARY

A pain diary is a written account—often supplemented with simple drawings, charts, or graphs—of when and where the pain occurs, what seems to precipitate the pain, and how intense the pain is (e.g., on a "pain is . . ." scale of "slight," "bad," "very bad," or "awful"). By assisting a child in keeping such an account, family members can help themselves and their child gain a more tangible understanding of the pain and therefore have more control over pain-related experiences.

FAMILY COUNSELING

Counseling for some or all of the child's family members can help ease ongoing or intermittent tensions that may be contributing to the child's pain. In addition, such counseling can teach family members how to cope with the personal and interpersonal difficulties caused specifically by the child's illness as well as how to assist the child in coping more effectively with her or his pain, given the overall family situation at hand.

Look for hospitals or clinics in your area that provide pain management programs similar to the program described above. If none is available, consult your physician or mental-health professional about creating a similar kind of treatment plan for your child.

6.
Depression and
Stress

A human being is never too young to be depressed or stressed out. However, the nature of potential depression and stress varies according to age. For children under six, such experiences are, thank goodness, relatively overt and fleeting. Annoying as it may be for a parent to endure several hours of intermittent crying and whining, it's better on the whole for both parties than if the child were to respond to the same depressing or stressful stimulus with several uninterrupted days of secret suffering.

This doesn't mean that depression or stress is not as important an issue for a very young child as it is for an older child or adult. If ignored or handled inappropriately, it can create an emotional vulnerability in a very young child that may last throughout life, rendering future episodes of depression or stress all the more difficult to prevent, endure, or combat.

Technically, depression refers to a state of sadness characterized by emotional despair and physical lethargy. In very young children, depression can sometimes manifest itself in a disguised form, for example, as anger, irritability, or hyperactivity; but this kind of "disguised" depression (i.e., depression revealing itself in nonstereotypical ways) is far more common among older children and adults.

Almost always, no matter how old the victim, depression is triggered by a loss or sense of loss. In the case of a person this young, it's usually associated with major changes affecting the family at large, such as those attending severe marital discord or separation, a divorce, a remarriage, a sudden health crisis, a death, or a family move.

In contrast to a depressive episode, a stress reaction is a very generalized "shock" response to any event that is especially unfamiliar and disturbing, such as experiencing a period of unusual activity at home, witnessing a violent crime on television, or hearing about a major car accident that occurred down the street. The stress response typically manifests itself as some combination of two or more of the following emotions: fear, disgust, resentment, hate, anger, panic, or overexcitement.

To a child under six, so much of life is disturbing and/or unfamiliar that one might expect frequent stress reactions of high intensity. In fact, children in this age range are inclined to be so emotionally resilient that stress reactions of any significance—ones that last longer than a couple of hours for two- to three-year-olds and longer than a couple of days for four- to six-year-olds—are fairly few and far between.

Because depression and stress in a very young child are so likely to accompany each other or result in similar emotional manifestations, they can be managed in the same basic manner:

■*Always take seriously any indication that your child is depressed or having a stress reaction.*

Emotionally speaking, a child is weakest at such times. You can easily make matters worse by insisting that her or his feelings are inappropriate, making light of them, or ignoring them altogether.

While you don't want to respond to a depressive episode or a stress reaction with visible anxiety, take care to deal directly and compassionately with *every* such episode that comes to your attention. The potential cost of not doing so to the future emotional health of your child can be great—certainly too great to risk.

■*Work gently to clarify the cause of the depression or stress reaction and why it is manifesting itself the way it is.*

Without pressuring your child to respond, ask questions that will tell you more specifically *what happened* to make her or him depressed or stressed out and *how she or he feels* about that situation or event. Try to avoid such leading questions as "Was it [x] that made you so scared?" You may inadvertently put words in your child's mouth or give your child yet another reason to be upset. Of course, if this strategy doesn't work and the situation is relatively serious, then it may be advisable to ask your child if she or he is concerned about particular things that you feel may be involved.

It's also a good idea to talk with other knowledgeable people inside or outside the family about the possible cause and effect of your child's depression or stress reaction. Just be careful to give your child's testimony the most weight. Also, make sure that your child's self-esteem and relationships with others won't be negatively influenced by your investigation. For example, don't let your child overhear you discussing her or him with someone else; and don't reveal anything to your

other children that might embarrass her or him unless you think it's
absolutely necessary.

■ *Allow your child to express emotions freely, without interruption or censorship.*

At first, be patient with outbursts that are unkind, misinformed, irrational, or otherwise objectionable. Then, after the child has reached
a stopping point, make your own contribution toward putting your
child in a better frame of mind.

This strategy not only provides you with more insight into your
child's problem; it also provides your child with an opportunity to
release negative feelings and, in the process, discover more positive
ones.

■ *Offer consoling information and support.*

Make sure your child is not suffering from gross misconceptions about
what has occurred, what is going to occur, or the extent to which these
occurrences are threatening. Without lying, reassure your child that
she or he is loved and is safe. Offer to do whatever you can to make
her or him feel better.

It's fine to propose remedies or distractions to your child but don't
indicate that she or he is wrong not to accept one of them. A vital
part of the support you need to offer in such a situation is letting your
child know—directly or indirectly—that you are willing to allow her
or him to go through this period at her or his own pace.

■ *Do what you can behind the scenes to alleviate your child's depression or stress reaction.*

Try to maintain a home atmosphere that is peaceful. Minimize the
chances that your child will be exposed to emotionally jarring situations in real life, on television, or in the movies. Give your child the
freedom to do as she or he wishes, within reason; but also be prepared
to give your child a reasonable amount of extra attention if it is sought.

■ *Observe closely how you, your child, and other family members handle your child's depression or stress reaction for as long as it lasts.*

How an incident of depression is handled can reveal a great deal about
each member of the household, and family dynamics in general, that
you might not otherwise notice. Over time, you may discern a pattern
in how you, your child, and other members of the family instigate,
manage, or fail to manage your child's periods of depression or stress
reactions. If you should ever have to seek professional help to cope
with your child's intractable, recurring, or unusually severe depres-

sion or stress reaction, such background information can be extremely valuable.

■*Anticipate the occurrence of similar incidents of depression or stress reaction in the future.*

Armed with the knowledge you've gained from specific incidents of depression or stress reaction in the past, you can take steps to prevent or forestall future incidents of a like nature or prepare your child and other family members to manage them more effectively.

For example, if you know from experience that your child gets upset when not permitted to go on special trips with older siblings, you might do the following:

> ■In a casual, conversational manner, inform your child ahead of time about the special excursion so that she or he doesn't feel left out of a secret.

> ■Make sure that your older children know about this delicate situation and that they take care not to brag about the trip in their younger sibling's presence.

> ■Set up in advance something special that your child can look foward to doing at the same time as the excursion.

> ■Arrange for your child to be away at the precise time that older siblings leave home.

Coping with a Divorce

Very young children can understand two friends or two siblings having a quarrel and separating for a certain amount of time thereafter, but their minds can't process all the ramifications of a divorce. They tend to confuse a divorce with a death: Whatever it may be, it means that someone (in this case, Mommy or Daddy—or both, in cases of split custody) won't be around as much anymore. Mercifully, their short-term emotional reaction to either a death or a divorce is apt to be fairly subdued as long as the event isn't accompanied by violent outbursts or radical changes in the child's day-to-day life.

To date, there is no reliable research establishing whether it is better for children of *any* age if their divorced parents continue to live together, split custodial responsibilities, or assign such responsibilities to only one of the parents. Nor has one particular type of visitation pattern proven to be the most successful (assuming the pattern itself is regular and dependable). Too much depends on the individuals involved: The specific divorce arrangement that works for one family may not work at all for another.

However, if you and your spouse are divorcing, there are some generally effective guidelines you can follow to help your very young child accept and endure the divorce with a minimal amount of emotional turmoil:

■ *As soon as possible, let your child know that you are divorcing but that she or he will continue to receive the love and care of both parents.*

Preferably, you and your spouse will make this announcement together, sending a signal to your child that both you and your spouse are in agreement about the divorce and that all of you will be sharing the experience. Check to make sure that your child realizes not only that you are not going to stay married or live together anymore but also that each of you will continue to be active participants in your child's life.

■ *Assure your child that she or he is not in any way responsible for the divorce.*

Children are very self-centered by nature. Never underestimate their capacity to feel that the divorce is somehow their fault or that their love for both parents should be enough to make their parents abandon the idea of divorcing. Take every appropriate opportunity to remind your child that the divorce is the result of irrevocable differences between mother and father and is not due to anything that concerns her or him.

■ *As the divorce unfolds, keep your child informed.*

Often the most difficult part of a divorce for a very young child is being aware that something "big" is going on but not actually knowing what's happening. Left in complete ignorance, the child is free to imagine that things are worse than they really are or to hope for the best—only to be cruelly disappointed later on.

It isn't appropriate to share with your child *all* the stress-producing details and feelings associated with ironing out your divorce arrangements, but your child should be kept up to date in general terms on such matters as:

■ When is the noncustodial parent leaving?

■ Where will the noncustodial parent be living?

■When can your child next expect to see the noncustodial parent?

■ How frequently—and in what context(s)—will she or he be able to see the noncustodial parent in the future?

■ When can she or he next expect to see both parents at the same time?

■ How frequently—and in what context(s)—will she or he be able to see both parents together in the future?

■ When will the divorce be official?

■ What happens after the divorce is official?

No matter how specific you can or cannot be in answering these questions, the ongoing dialogue concerning these matters will afford your child the opportunity to come to terms with the change that is largely taking place behind her or his back.

■ Try not to disrupt the normal pattern and tenor of your child's day-to-day life.

The more familiar the rest of your child's daily life is, the more secure she or he will be in the face of any changes caused by the divorce. Don't impose "new order" rules and routines at home unless they are absolutely necessary because of the absence of the other parent. You need to allow your child to appreciate that a parental divorce does not mean the end of the world.

■ Guard against taking out your frustrations over the divorce on your child.

Although it may be very difficult, try not to alter your behavior toward your child during the divorce. Don't lean on her or him more heavily for emotional support, don't become more critical of her or his conduct or attributes, and don't demand that she or he be more understanding because of what you are going through.

■Maintain good communication and cooperation between yourself and the other parent regarding matters affecting the child.

Don't allow your child to see or hear the two of you fighting about her or him and don't slip in your responsibility to keep the other parent informed about the child you share. If you and the other parent are able to demonstrate to your child that you are equally well informed about her or his life and that you are acting in concert regarding her or his welfare, your child will adjust to the divorce much more smoothly and readily.

Coping with a Remarriage

Assuming a child under six has gradually become familiar with a parent's spouse-to-be before the actual wedding, the remarriage should be accepted with very few problems, if any. A child this young is not nearly as inclined as an older child to compete with the new stepparent for her or his natural parent's affection or to resent the new stepparent's assumption of a role that once belonged to her or his other natural parent.

To ensure that your remarriage gets off to a good start without serious emotional repercussions to your child under six, follow these steps:

■ Make sure that you and your partner agree on how to raise your child.

This will prevent arguments between the two of you about the child that could wind up making her or him feel insecure. Ideally, your child should continue to be raised in the manner that's familiar, at least for a while. Any changes should be introduced very gradually.

■ Talk privately with your child about your new partner and the marriage.

You and your new partner should make an effort to do many things *together* with your child so that your child will accept the two of you as a parental team. Just remember that it is also important for you to spend some time *alone* with your child during which you can discuss her or his new stepparent and this new phase of family life.

Don't pressure your child to reveal her or his feelings. They may not be very strong or identifiable, given her or his young age and lack of experience with such matters. Instead, reveal your own feelings first and then ask if your child has any questions or thoughts about what's happening.

This is your opportunity to clear up any misconceptions your child may have about your partner as an individual, the role of a stepparent in general (often misconstrued as a threatening one because of fairy tales), the role and feelings of the other natural parent, and/or the remarriage. Even if your child has no questions or misconceptions, she or he will appreciate the fact that you are concerned and that you value her or his opinion.

■ *Frequently reassure your child of your continuing love and devotion.*

As you spend more and more time with your partner, your child needs to hear more and more often that you care just as much about her or him and will always be there to provide comfort and safety.

■ *As much as practical, indulge any tendencies your child may have to cling to you or to your new partner.*

It is normal for children during this period to cling to their natural parent, because they fear losing a love they've had all their life, or to the new partner, because they're afraid she or he will "go away," as the former partner did. In either case, don't be too quick to discourage the clinging as long as it isn't interfering with your plans. Your child can benefit from a heightened sense of security and some extra affection at this time.

■ *Don't be concerned if your child doesn't respond as enthusiastically to the marriage as you had hoped.*

Your child may seem emotionally "flat" during the transition period. If so, she or he is probably just waiting to see what happens. Again, children under six have a very limited concept of what a marriage or a remarriage means, so they can't be expected to rise to the occasion automatically.

■ *Be sure to allow times for you and your partner to enjoy your relationship apart from your child.*

Often new couples make the mistake of catering to their very young child so much that they deny themselves the time alone together that they need to maintain a strong and loving relationship. In the long run, this time alone together is also essential to the child's well-being, since it tends to make the couple more effective in their parenting and to teach the child to be more independent.

Make an effort to spend some time alone with your partner each day. Above all, avoid taking your child on your honeymoon. If it is completely impractical to leave the child with someone else right after the wedding, then postpone the honeymoon until it *is* practical.

Coping with Bad News

Very young children do not react to traumatic and stressful events in the same way that older children or adults do. When they hear about, or witness, something scary happening, they lack the cognitive ability to judge such an event in terms of why it happened, what it means, and whether it threatens them directly. Instead, their reaction is entirely emotional and can easily escalate into full-fledged panic or depression. Here are some tips for preventing such an emotional overreaction.

■ *Control your child's exposure to potentially disturbing images on television, in movies, and in printed materials.*
The line between fantasy and reality is very faint and flexible to a child under six. A make-believe image is just as likely to be frightening as a true-life happening.

As much as practically possible, don't allow your child to see shows or materials that may contain upsetting subject matter. If you're not sure whether a specific program your child wants to watch will be upsetting, watch it with your child so that you can offer reassurance and explanation at appropriate moments (e.g., a comment that the actors are just pretending, a description of how a particularly disturbing special effect might have been achieved, or a guarantee that what is happening on-screen won't happen to your child).

■ *Talk with your child as soon as possible about upsetting incidents in real life that are likely to reach her or his attention.*
This includes family crises (e.g., a serious illness, a marital separation, or a job loss), calamities in the neighborhood (a murder or a building burning down), and major national and international catastrophes (a war or an earthquake). You don't need to say much. Indeed, saying too much may frighten your child. And children at this stage in their development can't fully comprehend such matters as death, the economic problems attending a reversal in family fortune, or the reason why one group of people are fighting with another.

Whatever the crisis, calamity, or catastrophe, the best course of action is simply to inform your child about it in a simple, nondramatic way and to reaffirm your child's personal safety and security. Hearing about the event first from you rather than some other source will make it seem less alarming. In addition, your taking the initiative in this way leaves the door open for the child to communicate to you—then or later—any particular fears he or she may experience related to the event.

■ *Be alert for signs that your child is responding over-anxiously to bad news.*

Common signs that a child is experiencing stress include nightmares, aggressive play, long periods of withdrawal or silence, increased attachment to one or both parents, loss of appetite, or an increase in angry or irritable behavior. You shouldn't worry about these responses unless they become excessive, at which point you should talk with the child about her or his stressful feelings and do what you can to alleviate them by offering reassurance and distraction.

■ *Help your child discharge anxiety in constructive ways.*

Many children respond well to drawing or role-playing about what is bothering them or to hearing stories that offer soothing commentary relative to the disturbing event. Depending on the situation, your child may actually be able to take a positive role in the event: for example, by making a get-well card for a sick person.

Coping with a Death

Until children reach the age of five or six, they can't begin to understand what death really means. The most prevalent misconception is that death, like sleep, is a temporary state of being that can be reversed. Television cartoons, fairy tales, and "play dead" games feed this misconception, as does the inexplicable (to them) appearance and disappearance of people in their day-to-day lives.

Lacking the ability to appreciate the permanence and gravity of death, very young children are not likely to respond to a specific death with strong emotions. An exception may be if a child actually witnesses a sudden and shocking death, such as a parent suffering a massive heart attack or a pet being run over by a car. In such a case, the child will no doubt have a much more severe stress reaction than in cases where the death is not witnessed or is less violent.

Whatever the case, a child this young does not appear to experience the type of immediate, prolonged, and demonstrative grieving period for a dead loved one that an older child or an adult typically does, nor should she or he be influenced to do so. Nevertheless, a very young child does need help to realize what has happened and to make the emotional transition from life with a loved one to life without that person.

When death claims someone near and dear to your child, here are some suggestions for making that realization and transition easier:

■ Tell the truth about the death.

Children under six do not require lengthy medical or theological discussions about what death is like. They do need to be informed that their loved one has died and therefore won't be around anymore.

Saying that the deceased loved one has "gone away" without indicating that it's forever merely postpones the inevitable. Worse, your child will ultimately have a more difficult time accepting the death because of your well-meaning but confusing lie.

Saying that the loved one has "gone to sleep," even if you do indicate that it's forever, is also not advisable. It could make your child more fearful of sleep. This doesn't mean you can't *compare* death to sleep in terms of appearance and peacefulness.

Yet another problematic approach is to say that God took away the loved one. Your child might fear that she or he—or some other loved one—will be next, hopeless against the inscrutable workings of fate.

When you talk about the death, mention the general cause of death: sickness, injury, or old age. Again, details aren't necessary. What matters is that your child is not left completely in the dark. Depending on the maturity of your child—emotionally and intellectually—and on the nature of your relationship with each other, you may or may not choose to discuss details about the dying process or to reveal that a particular death was self-inflicted, murder, or the result of some catastrophe.

■ *Share your feelings about the death in an appropriate manner.*

Any death that has an emotional impact on your child will most likely have a similar impact on you. If the death involves someone very close, such as your spouse, your parent, or another child, it will have an especially strong and lasting effect on your behavior.

Emotionally intuitive as children are, your child will be aware of this impact on you whether you refer to it or not. The best policy, therefore, is to let your child know up front how you feel. It will make each of you feel less alone.

In expressing your emotions, be honest but ever mindful of your child's limited capacity to understand or share your reaction. You shouldn't frighten your child by appearing out of control or by using overly dramatic language (e.g., "I don't know how I'm going to keep on living"). However, you should prepare your child for the fact that you may not be functioning in quite the same way for a while.

■ *Allow your child to live her or his normal life as much as possible immediately after the death.*

Ideally, your child will be able to remain at home and engage in the predictable round of daily activities that provide an ongoing sense of security. This will minimize any fear your child may have that the death is going to alter her or his world in a radical way.

If the ideal is not possible, do whatver you reasonably can to make day-to-day life for your child the same as it was before the death. Mention the death to day-care workers, teachers, and any other adults who regularly interact with your child. Inform them that you want your child's normal routines maintained as much as possible.

■ *Offer your child some formal means of acknowledging the death and saying good-bye to the departed loved one.*

If the person who has died was very close to your child, and if it's at all practical, your child should attend the funeral so that she or he can feel like a part of the community of people who mourn the death. Don't burden your child, however, with a role in the funeral that is overly demanding.

In addition, try to arrange a more personal ceremony for your child to provide an outlet for any privately distressing feelings harbored about the death. Consider having a few minutes of silence together, saying a prayer, planting a tree in honor of the deceased, or visiting the grave. Check your local library and bookstores for material that suggests consoling activities for very young children who have recently lost a loved one.

■ *If possible, allow a reasonable amount of time for the child to get over the death before introducing any major change into her or his life.*

It's best not to take your child on a long trip, enroll your child in a new day-care center, or invite friends or family members to make extensive visits until at least a few weeks have passed and you've been able to determine that your child is accepting the death well. When a pet dies, put off getting a new one for at least a few weeks.

Very young children do tend to recover from a bereavement faster than older children and adults. But you don't want to rush the process or frustrate it by introducing yet another stressful event into their lives before they are emotionally ready for it.

7.

Separation Anxiety

Around six to nine months of age, children begin to recognize, cognitively and emotionally, that their parents are separate beings who may leave their company for extended periods of time. No longer does the absence of a parent simply inspire a fear in a child that her or his needs might not be met. From that point until the child is around two to three years old, it can trigger what psychology terms "separation anxiety"—the fear of losing the bond to the parent as an individual.

Separation anxiety can take many forms, but it generally involves clinging to the parent, crying when the parent leaves, and behaving poorly for at least a short time while she or he is away. It can occur when a mother or father leaves the room for a few minutes or the home for hours, days, or weeks at a time.

Separation anxiety is a particularly common problem when the ongoing, day-to-day relationship between parent and child is suddenly altered by new demands that the parent be elsewhere on a regular basis: most notably, when a mother returns to work after caring for her infant child full-time.

Sometimes separation anxiety manifests itself as a fear of "outsiders," a category that may not only include strangers but also close relatives, like grandparents, who don't live in the home. Children wrestling with this type of separation anxiety aren't as much afraid of the outsider as they are of the possibility that she or he might come between them and their parents.

Not all children under the age of three go through *observable* periods of separation anxiety, but most likely all of them do, in fact, experience it to some degree from time to time. If your child seems troubled by it, rest assured that it is a normal response and try managing it in the following ways:

■ *Prepare in advance for separations.*
If you'll be away for several hours or more, inform your child well in advance when, why, and how you will be leaving. Spend your last ten or fifteen minutes at home with your child. Don't leave as soon as the

caretaker arrives; let your child get used to her or his presence—and connnection to you—before you go.

■ *Talk about what you'll do together when you return.*

This will give your child something pleasant to anticipate that's associated with your leaving. The more specific you can be about what you'll do, the better, because the image in your child's mind will be sharper. Just make sure that you live up to your promise and do so as soon as possible after you are reunited.

■ *Create a ritual way of leaving and returning.*

For example, say the same special "good-bye" phrase every time you leave (preferably the last thing you do) and "hello" phrase every time you return (preferably the first thing you do). The predictability and special attention associated with such a ritual will be reassuring to your child.

■ *Expect some initial distress.*

You can't hope to eliminate separation anxiety entirely. It's an important stage in your child's development of a more mature, less stressful attachment to you. Therefore, be careful about communicating to your child that separation anxiety is wrong, upsetting, or intolerable. Above all, don't be unduly concerned yourself if your child exhibits more (or less!) anxiety on a particular occasion than you had anticipated.

■ *Don't allow your own separation anxiety to feed the child's.*

Don't make too big a deal out of how much you'll miss your child. You may be teaching your child to lament the separation even more severely than she or he already does.

Parents are especially prone to experience separation anxiety of their own when the tables are turned and their child must first leave home for an extended period of time—for example, to go to day care or nursery school. Avoid making such a transition more difficult for your child by putting off leaving your child behind, oversentimentalizing the occasion, or behaving noticeably in a different manner from the way you normally behave.

■ *Prepare "strangers" for a potentially poor reception from your child.*

Talk to people who will be visiting your home—or taking care of your child—about your child's separation anxiety and the shyness and fearfulness it may cause. Encourage these visitors and caretakers to avoid sudden gestures or overly close contact (such as a kiss or hug) until the child invites it or initiates it.

■ *If you'll be separated for several days or more, make audiotapes or videotapes for your child.*

From time to time in your absence, these tapes can be played to reassure your child of your presence in the world and your continuing affection. Try reading aloud a favorite book, telling a family story, or talking about what you'll be doing while you're away.

■ *Practice miniseparations.*

One reason children in this age range love games like "now you see me, now you don't" or hide-and-seek is that they help them deal with their separation anxiety. They demonstrate that someone who "disappears" will in time "reappear."

In addition to such games, experiment with getting out of the house alone from time to time to perform short errands, leaving your child in the care of a neighbor, friend, or relative. The longer span of time that occurs between parent-child separations, the greater the anxiety will be when the next separation occurs.

CASE:

A Slice of the Other Life

Although Angie's father had always worked away from home during the weekdays, it wasn't until she was three years old that her mother began working in an office instead of at home. At first, the mother-and-daughter reunion at 5:00 P.M. was so happy and exciting for both of them that Angie didn't communicate the separation anxiety she felt during the day and her mother didn't suspect it. After a couple of weeks, however, Angie began exhibiting signs of sullenness and resentment at these reunions. Meanwhile, her reluctance to let her mother go in the morning was increasing rather than decreasing. It was clear to her mother that Angie was having problems accepting her absence.

Angie had visited her mother's office before, but only for a few minutes at a time. One evening, a television show gave Angie's mother an idea: If Angie could spend a sizable amount of time at the office every week or two, not only observing what her mother did there but also doing something there herself, it might help relieve her anxiety.

The following Saturday, Angie's mother brought Angie to her office. They were alone there, free to use their time as they wished. Angie's mother did some work of her own—routine work so that she could keep her eye on Angie—while Angie drew pictures and played with some of the safer office supplies and furniture. After two hours, they went out and had lunch together at a restaurant.

Angie's symptoms of separation anxiety quickly abated once she had developed a well-informed mental picture of her mother working at the office and in fact had "worked" there a few times herself. Angie realized that she could go to the office only on weekends, and only on those weekends that weren't otherwise busy. But with these occasional visits to anticipate, she was content to lead her independent day life from Monday through Friday.

8.
Discipline:
An Overview

In the context of child rearing, the word "discipline" still conjures up a Dickensian image of a stern, stiff-lipped adult shaking a hickory stick over an indignant, pouty-lipped child. The true meaning of the word is quite different. Discipline refers to the education of a novice (a "disciple"). Since a child is definitely a novice in life, the proper goal of discipline in child rearing is not *controlling* a child's behavior but *teaching* a child to control her or his own behavior.

In disciplining a child during the early years, adults need to remain ever aware that punishment in itself—or the threat of it—is a very poor deterrent to bad behavior. It's much more likely to breed resentment than to inspire good behavior. And although a resentful child may temporarily be a more cooperative child, she or he is almost certain to be a more estranged and devious one as well.

The first and foremost rule in disciplining a very young child is to be patient. Before you take any action, make sure you clarify in your own mind what you really want to accomplish as a result of that action.

For example, suppose you catch your child drawing on the wall with crayons. Your first thought may be: I want to put a stop to this right now! However, a moment's pause may help you appreciate that what you really want is to influence your child to respect family property and to associate the desire to draw with the right materials. If you scold your child too hastily or too harshly for making the walls dirty, you may thwart these goals. Knowing that drawing on the walls upsets you so much, your child may eventually do it again to strike back at you or, even worse, develop inhibitions about drawing or similar forms of creative self-expression.

A much better course of disciplinary action in this situation, given your goals, would to state strongly but more calmly that drawing *is* a good thing to do but that it is *not* good at all to draw on a wall.

Then you should make sure to involve your child in cleaning the wall and in imagining more appropriate drawing surfaces. Perhaps you'll find your child most enjoys drawing while standing up, in which case you can set up an easel for drawing or tape drawing paper to a special, out-of-the-way wall.

A different, more authoritative kind of disciplinary strategy is necessary to prevent your child from doing something dangerous. Suppose, for example, that you don't want your child to run into the street in front of your house. Your goal in this situation is not so much to encourage your child to behave in a more acceptable manner as it is to ensure that she or he does what you say. While you should certainly explain to your child *why* you want her or him to stay away from the street, your explanation alone may not bring about the result that you really want. The danger may be too theoretical for your child to appreciate; and if you make the danger too vivid, she or he may become unduly afraid of playing outdoors.

In this situation, it's better to insist earnestly that your child agree to the rule of not going into the street, thus making obedience rather than self-chosen behavior the focus of your discipline. The risk that your child may not obey you is too high to allow much leeway for failure, forgetfulness, or rebellion.

Besides underscoring the seriousness of a rule, you should repeat the rule often so that your child is sure to remember it. Creating a "rhyme" for a serious rule also helps. To keep your child from playing in the street, for example, you might formulate the rule "Keep your feet / Out of the street."

Assuming that you reserve such a disciplinary strategy—strict obedience to a rule—for circumstances that truly warrant it, you should have little difficulty getting your child to cooperate with it. She or he will realize that a demand so unusually strong must be very serious indeed. If you abuse this strategy by using it too often, it quickly becomes worthless.

Always taking time to consider the goals behind your disciplinary actions and commands will help you stay calm and collected during tense parent-and-child situations. It will also help you avoid mistreating your child unintentionally. Even the most conscientious parents can fall into the habit of issuing too many commands that are not at all in their child's interest but, rather, in their own. Consider, for example, a mother who tells her four-year-old daughter, "Hurry up and get ready," when she wants her child to accompany her on an errand. Is the mother acting in her daughter's interest or her own?

By itself, the mother's command is fairly innocuous, but it betrays a casual thoughtlessness that parents have to learn to keep in check, especially during moments when they are very angry with their child.

Parents can all too easily take for granted their love for, and authority over, their child. When this happens, they wind up confusing their wishes with what is best for their child. Meanwhile, their child winds up even more confused and possibly hurt and resentful as well.

For your own sake, or for the sake of your family, you may have to insist from time to time that your child do something that is not in her or his interest. Just be sure that you're aware of this fact when the occasion arises, that you reflect your awareness in your interaction with your child, that you offer a simple explanation for your request, and that you keep such occasions to a minimum. This way, your child will eventually learn to respect other people's interest as well as her or his own.

Here are some other ways to discipline very young children without causing counterproductive emotional problems:

■ *Be clear, consistent, and dependable in applying discipline.*
In many cases, the motive behind a very young child's misbehavior is a subconscious desire for order. The world as the child sees it is vastly mysterious and therefore threatening. To make matters worse, children at this age can't even depend on their own bodies or minds to do what they want them to do. Through their misbehavior, they cry out for their parents to set things right.

As a parent, it is your full-time responsibility to set firm standards of behavior for your child, to check periodically to make sure that your child understands and accepts those standards, and to function in a safely predictable way to maintain those standards. If you scream at your child for stealing cookies one day, only to smile indulgently when the same thing happens the next day, your child won't learn to control this behavior. Convinced that stealing sometimes might work, she or he will continue to leave the task of controlling to you.

If you live in a two-parent household, it's important for both you and your mate to use the same disciplinary style and to share disciplinary responsibilities in an equitable manner. Above all, one parent should never pass along the role of disciplinarian to the other parent, or bargain over who gets that role, in front of the child. Other people who may be responsible for disciplining your child, such as grandparents and baby-sitters, should be informed of the disciplinary measures you prefer and should be encouraged to use them.

■ *Never discipline children by physically striking them.*
Spanking or slapping a child is a signal that you've lost control of yourself. In essence, you're teaching a child that there are times when reason doesn't work and only brute force does. Out of fear, a child may temporarily respond to the physical assault with more acceptable

behavior. The net result is certain to be latent resentment, increased emotional estrangement from the attacker, and eventual retaliation in some form or another.

The bond between a parent and a very young child is so emotionally volatile and the interactions that typically occur between them so potentially stressful that even the kindest and most loving parents can sometimes be tempted to spank or slap their children. This is particularly true when a child does something reckless that scares a parent, such as running around with a knife or accidentally starting a fire. An isolated instance of spanking or slapping, regrettable as it may be, is forgivable. Repeated reliance on spanking or slapping as a disciplinary technique is not.

As soon as you feel the impulse to strike or grab your child, try some tension-reducing strategy like counting to ten or insisting that you and your child sit down and remain quiet for a few seconds. If you do strike or grab your child in a moment of strong emotion, be patient with both yourself and the child. Explain why you acted the way you did and apologize.

■ *Focus on the problem at hand, appealing to reason as much as possible.*

A common mistake in disciplining children when they've broken a rule or created a problem is to complain about *them* instead of the *situation*. When you catch your very young son tearing pages out of a book, resist the tendency to blurt out, "Bad boy!" or, "Why are you always getting into trouble!" Instead, tell (or remind) him that it's a rule not to tear pages out of books and secure (or resecure) his agreement to that rule. He should also be made to deal with the consequences of his act. Instead of punishing him by not letting him watch television, which won't seem logical to him, insist that he clean up the mess he has made.

A more subtle form of attacking the child rather than the problem is merely *commanding* the child, instead of *teaching* her or him, to do—or not to do—something. For example, if your daughter is tormenting the family cat, it's much more constructive to say, "The cat can get hurt when you grab its legs like that," than it is to yell, "Don't bother the cat!"

■ *When appropriate, use "time-out" as a disciplinary technique.*

There are inevitably going to be situations when a very young child simply will not stop misbehaving. Regardless of what the parent says or does, the child will continue whining, running around the room, or knocking things off shelves. Most likely, the child is seeking whatever attention she or he can get, even if it's negative. In this type of situation, time-out can be a very effective disciplinary strategy.

Time-out involves telling a misbehaving child to go to a specific, isolated place and stay there until ready to behave in a more acceptable manner. This not only removes the child from the situation that is inspiring bad behavior but also gives the child a chance to appreciate, at a self-regulated pace, what she or he has lost by the bad behavior, that is, the company of others.

For consistency's sake, the time-out place should always be the same—a specific chair in a quiet place, or the child's room. If the child tends to return not yet ready to behave, a timer should be set for a minimum-required time-out period. Try starting with one minute for each year of age. Don't go beyond a thirty-minute maximum. A "time out" period shouldn't be too long, or it loses its effectiveness.

■ *If possible, offer alternatives rather than simply saying no.*

Suppose, for example, that your child is drumming on one of your pans. If you don't want the pan to be used that way, offer a more appropriate alternative to a drum. If the noise bothers you, suggest that your child drum outside. Or you might try proposing another activity altogether, such as drawing or playing with blocks. Limit yourself to offering just *two* choices, however. Otherwise, your child may get confused.

■ *Try to mix praise with blame, good news with bad news.*

Very young children can't accept discipline gracefully or constructively unless they are confident that you still love them and that life isn't going to be miserable forever as a result of what has happened. Remember, from a very young child's perspective, whatever she or he has done seemed to be the right thing to do at the time. If you refute this, then the child starts doubting everything.

There are several ways you can give your child the reassurance she or he needs without defeating your disciplinary purpose:

> ■ Be careful not to overdramatize the damage that's been done. For example, if your child empties all your dresser drawers on the floor, don't say, "It will take me all day to put this room back together," when it won't.

> ■ Invoke the child's "better self" whenever she or he misbehaves, either to help ensure that the bad behavior isn't repeated (e.g., "You always keep your promises to me, so I know I can count on you not to fight with your cousin again") or to let your child know that she or he has not lost your approval altogether (e.g., "I'm proud of the nice way you helped me out

this morning, but we have a rule about not playing with the curtains").

■ Refer to something pleasant that your child can anticipate (e.g., "I want you to pick up these scraps, and then you can play with your blocks").

■ *Apologize whenever you have done something wrong.*

Part of setting a good example for your very young child is being sure to apologize when you realize that you've done something wrong in the course of administering discipline. This includes wrongdoings such as accusing your child unjustly, contributing to the problem, not giving your child sufficient opportunity to explain or rectify her or his behavior, or punishing your child too harshly.

The most effective apology relating to a disciplinary situation is one that is immediate, short, and simple. Also, it should stand by itself. It doesn't need to be accompanied by any special treat to assuage your guilt.

Giving Orders That Work

You can prevent many of the behavioral problems exhibited by very young children—and improve the emotional climate of your parent-child relationship—by changing the way in which you issue your commands. Here are some suggestions:

■ *Make sure that your child can—and does—listen to you.*

Minimize or eliminate possible distractions (such as television noise), talk to your child face-to-face, and ask your child to repeat what you've said so that you can be certain that it has been understood.

■ *Don't phrase your command as a question.*

If you say, "Would you please stop hammering the floor?," you're inviting your child to say, "No." It's better to be more assertive: "Please stop hammering the floor."

■ *Avoid phrasing your command as a favor.*

Sometimes you will want to enlist your child's cooperation in doing something that's strictly for your own benefit. However, try to limit the times when you refer to a command as a "favor." Children need to take it upon themselves to obey commands for their own benefit. Besides, if you make a practice of referring to commands as favors, your child may ultimately come to resent the imposition.

■ As often as possible, use the same particular tone of voice to issue commands.

Don't slip a command into your normal conversation with a very young child or experiment with a lot of indirect or cute ways of communicating a command. Be direct and use a tone of voice that is serious without being threatening.

■ Avoid issuing more than two commands at a time.

Very young children have a very limited attention span when it comes to conversations, not to mention a very limited tolerance for commands. If you stack several commands on top of each other, your child will feel overwhelmed. Even the child who can remember them all will most likely balk at fulfilling them.

■ If possible and appropriate, include an incentive in the command.

For example, instead of just saying, "It's time to get ready for bed," you could say, "It's time for you to go to bed, and then I can tell you a story"; or instead of just saying, "Please bring me that pot," you could say, "Please bring that pot to me so that I can start making your dinner." Avoid outright bribery. Also, be careful not to express yourself conditionally, for example, "If you'll pick up your clothes, we can start getting ready to go out." The use of "if" invites the child to comply or not to comply as she or he wishes.

■ Make sure that you stand behind your commands.

Don't let a child get away with refusing, forgetting, or deliberately failing to execute a command that you've given. Also, don't back down on the terms of a command unless your child offers very convincing reasons for you to do so. If your child absolutely refuses to cooperate, then you have no choice but to administer appropriate punishment.

How to Handle the "Gimmes" and the Grabs

Children under five can be very troublesome shopping companions, relentlessly begging for items that you don't want them to have or indiscriminately picking things off the shelves that catch their eye. As a result, what was intended to be a friendly outing together can turn into an emotionally exhausting tug-of-war for both of you.

Here are some suggestions for altering your child's unruly shopping behavior:

■ Discuss the trip with your child ahead of time (at least ten minutes before you leave).

Tell your child about what you're going to do together, what the experience will be like, and what kind of behavior you expect from her or him. This will give your child sufficient information and opportunity to get in the right mood.

■ Before you enter the store, agree on one special thing your child can buy and stick to that agreement.

To ensure that your child doesn't choose something inappropriate, you might want to ask her or him to select one among several stated options. Your child will feel more content to allow you to control the excursion knowing that she or he will derive specific and immediate gratification from it.

■ Play a game as you go through the store.

For example, give your child clues about what you want to buy next and ask her or him to guess what it is. Often the reason very young children are disruptive during a shopping trip is that they feel their parents are ignoring them.

■ Offer your child an unexpected treat when you sense restlessness.

Ideally, this treat will serve as a surprise reward for good behavior up to that point. If you're in a grocery store, consider offering your child something to be eaten during the rest of the time you are shopping.

■ *Give your child a specific amount of money to be spent as she or he wishes.*

This way, your child can feel independent, interested, and responsible instead of trapped, bored, and irresponsible. Whether or not this strategy is viable depends a great deal on how old, how careful, or how intellectually mature your child is. For a very young child, try simply stating the amount that can be spent. For an older child, try literally handing over the money.

■ *Engage your child as much as possible in helping you.*
Tell your child in advance what you want to get. Ask her or him to look for the next item you want. When the item has been located, ask your child to hand it to you. If both of you are legitimate shopping partners, your child will have a stronger emotional investment in making the experience a pleasant one.

Children age four through six may appreciate knowing how their parents make purchasing decisions. If so, their parents can simultaneously keep them occupied, foster their self-esteem, and educate them to be good consumers by involving them in choosing specific items: for example, the freshest fruit or the better of two different types of trash cans.

Managing Whining and Tantrums

The second year of a child's life is infamously known as the "terrible twos." At this age, children are just beginning to form independent identities and to realize that there can be an enormously frustrating gap between what they want of themselves, of their parents, and of the world and what they actually get.

To make matter worse, two-year-olds haven't yet mastered the language of adults. Unable to express in words exactly how they feel or to get the results they expect from the words they do use, they resort either to whining (a combination of "baby" crying and "adult" speaking) or to tantrums (a combination of "baby" helplessness and "adult" violence). In many cases, a frustrated child will employ both strategies, beginning with the milder one, whining, and building up to the more intense one, a tantrum—at which point the child quickly loses all fragile powers of self-control.

Unfortunately, this pattern of bad behavior doesn't come to an end when the child turns three. The typical reign of terror for whining lasts until the child is around three and a half years old, and the typical reign of terror for tantrums frequently lasts until the child is around four and a half years old. Thereafter, incidents of whining and tantrums still occur, but much more sporadically, unless the child is suffering some especially strong emotional disturbance.

Because whining and tantrums are motivated in the same way, they can be managed by parents in the same way. To say that they can be managed doesn't mean that they can *always* be stopped or even that they can *usually* be stopped. Like a spell of bad weather, a spell of whining or tantrum throwing often must be simply endured with as much equanimity as one can muster. Nevertheless, here is a practical six-step approach that can help tame the terror:

---

1. Investigate.
Make sure that your child's whining or crying isn't the result of fatigue, hunger, discomfort, or illness. If one of these factors does seem to be responsible, take appropriate action.

---

2. Distract.
A child in the grip of a whining jag or a tantrum needs your help to snap out of it. Try to interest your child in something that you know she or he likes, such as a beloved toy or game.

---

3. Ignore.
If there's no physical reason behind the bad behavior or if you can't distract your child, the best strategy is simply to ignore the behavior, no matter how difficult doing so may be. Eventually, your child will realize she or he is not getting any results from the whining or the tantrum and will stop. The more you ignore the behavior, the less inclined your child will be to resort to it, which is, after all, likely to be much more stressful to your child than to you.

---

4. Isolate.
Leave your child alone or insist that your child take time-out in a place specifically designated for that purpose (e.g., a quiet corner in the den or your child's room).

5. *Record.*

Keep a log of each time your child has a major whining fit or tantrum. You may discover that such behavior generally occurs at the same time of day, or in the context of the same type of activity. If so, you may be able to take action to forestall or eliminate future episodes of this behavior.

6. *Teach.*

Whenever possible—before, during, or after the incident of bad behavior—help your child learn more acceptable behavior for getting what she or he wants, or for passing the time when she or he is bored, sad, or out of sorts.

QUESTIONNAIRE:

Your Child's Self-Discipline

For each general situation listed below, rate your child's typical, overall behavior on a scale of 1 to 5: 1 indicating no discipline problems and 5 indicating a frequent occurrence of extremely defiant and unruly behavior. If you have difficulty completing this questionnaire or would first like to monitor your child's situational behavior more closely, photocopy this questionnaire and complete it at the end of a two-week or monthlong period of observation.

When you've completed the questionnaire, focus on the situations that you've rated 3 or higher and work on making them less troublesome. Take special note of any patterns that emerge, such as several poor ratings involving behavior when other people are around or compliance with requests. If you've given a rating of 3 or more to over twelve of the twenty-five situations listed, consider seeking professional help.

	PROBLEM FREQUENCY				
	low				high
1. During meals	1	2	3	4	5
2. While getting up in the morning	1	2	3	4	5
3. During the morning (in general)	1	2	3	4	5

	PROBLEM FREQUENCY				
	low				high
4. During the afternoon (in general)	1	2	3	4	5
5. During the evening (in general)	1	2	3	4	5
6. At bedtime	1	2	3	4	5
7. Overnight (while in bed)	1	2	3	4	5
8. While the television is on	1	2	3	4	5
9. While playing alone	1	2	3	4	5
10. While playing with other children	1	2	3	4	5
11. While alone with mother	1	2	3	4	5
12. While alone with father	1	2	3	4	5
13. While with a baby-sitter	1	2	3	4	5
14. While riding in the car	1	2	3	4	5
15. While visiting a public place	1	2	3	4	5
16. While getting dressed or undressed	1	2	3	4	5
17. During washing or bathing	1	2	3	4	5
18. While visitors are present	1	2	3	4	5
19. While visiting other homes	1	2	3	4	5
20. When asked to perform tasks	1	2	3	4	5
21. When you deny requests	1	2	3	4	5
22. When asked to change behavior or obey rules	1	2	3	4	5
23. While you're talking on the telephone	1	2	3	4	5
24. While you're focusing your affection on someone else (spouse, lover, other child, relative, best friend)	1	2	3	4	5
25. While you're absorbed in performing some task	1	2	3	4	5

CASE:

Nothing But the Truth

One hot summer afternoon, Debra and her best friend, Yvonne, took Cally, Debra's new five-year-old stepdaughter, to the zoo. After a couple of hours, Debra was exhausted. Cally, on the other hand, was still going strong. When Debra said, "It's time to go home," Cally started begging, "No, I don't want to go, I want to look at the lions." Reluctant to disappoint her step-daughter and risk jeopardizing their fragile relationship, Debra backed down and took Cally to the lion area.

Afterward, Debra again said, "It's time to go home," and met with further resistance. "No, no!" Cally pleaded. "We didn't see the baby chimp!" Completely frustrated, Debra snapped back, "Don't be a whiner, Cally. We've been here long enough. You either come with me, or I'm leaving you behind!" Cally plunked herself down on a nearby bench and pouted. Debra turned to Yvonne and asked in a low voice, "Now what do I do?"

Speaking from her own child-raising experiences, Yvonne replied, "Do what you'd do with me or anyone else. Be fair. Tell her what's really going on. Tell her you're tired, that you can come back some other time." Debra sat down next to Cally and admitted to her that she was tired. Cally jumped up and took her hand, and the three of them left the zoo with no more fuss.

CASE:

An Element of Surprise

Every now and then a parent can stop a tantrum in its tracks by resorting to some inspired zaniness as a distraction. Robby, age two and a half, was a frequent tantrum thrower. It usually worked to leave him alone—literally, by going into another room. But one Thanksgiving morning Robby burst into a major tantrum just as everyone was about to go to a family gathering across town. There wasn't any time to wait Robby out.

Acting on impulse, Robby's mother pulled her compact from her purse, put an arm firmly around his waist, and lightly powdered his hair and his stomach while making sounds like a bell: "Ring-a-ding-ding! Ring-a-ding-ding!" Dumbfounded, Robby abruptly ceased crying and thrashing around. In a few seconds, he was actually laughing at his mother's goofiness.

Who's the Boss?

Bob and Leslie were at their wits' end in dealing with their three-year-old son, Craig. He seemed to be a born dictator, constantly issuing orders according to his wishes: "Do this!" "Come here!" "Stop that!" "Not now!" Bob and Leslie were assertive people themselves, capable of admiring Craig's masterful spirit to some degree, but not in the tyrannical form it appeared to be assuming. Every moment in his company was turning into a battle of wills.

Finally, Bob and Leslie consulted with a child psychiatrist. With the latter's help, they formulated their frustrations into a few key questions: Why was Craig's behavior so combative? How could they tolerate it in the short term? How could they work to change Craig's behavior in the long term so it would be less obnoxious?

First, Bob, Leslie, and the psychiatrist discussed Craig's personal, family, and home-life history, especially his recent, day-to-day experiences. They established that their son had always been rather strong-willed, that there weren't any other noteworthy problems in his history or home life, and that his recent day-to-day experiences in themselves were not remarkably different from those of a "normal" three-year-old. Then the psychiatrist spent several hours getting to know Craig and his parents better, both as individuals and as a family group. Ultimately, they arrived at some answers to the key questions they had posed.

Why was Craig's behavior so combative? In essence, it is typical for three-year-olds to engage in battles of the will. It's a matter of testing and proving one's newly emerging strength to oneself and everyone else. In Craig's case, this development was compounded by his basic temperament, an assertive one that wasn't negative in itself but did require special handling. A contributing factor in his behavior was the basically assertive temperaments of his parents, who were naturally predisposed to view each troublesome interaction with Craig as a "win-lose" struggle.

How could Bob and Leslie tolerate Craig's behavior in the short term? Above all, they realized that they needed to learn more about child development at different ages so they could be more compassionate about the possible age-related strengths and weaknesses that were influencing their son's behavior. They also determined to prepare for each day more carefully. Their daily planning goal would be to avoid confrontational situations as much as possible and to maximize times when the three of them would be the most capable of enjoying each other's company.

How could they work to change Craig's behavior in the long term so that it would be less obnoxious? They decided that the best strategy was to "give in" gracefully to Craig's demands whenever possible—that is, when nothing really important was at stake. At the same time, they would gently make sure that Craig used polite language in his demands, like "please" and "thank you."

At times when it was necessary for Craig to cooperate with their wishes, Bob and Leslie would try not to *demand* cooperation, given Craig's unusually strong, combative nature. Instead, they would casually stage-manage the situation so that Craig would be maneuvered to cooperate without having to lose face. For example, instead of saying, "Get in the car, Craig, I want you to go to the store with me," in which case Craig would be challenged to refuse, they would say, "Okay, Craig, we're going to the store now" as they headed straight for the car, in which case Craig would be more inclined to follow along.

Also, Bob and Leslie made a special effort to leave Craig alone more frequently with a male baby-sitter—a teenager in the neighborhood who had earned their trust, who liked children, and who was very fair yet firm in dealing with them. An assertive child like Craig often profits from being around older kids and adults, especially of the same sex. They have the experience to temper the child's combativeness in a constructive manner, plus they provide a same-sex model for more mature interactive behavior.

At PCGC:
Treatment in a Family
Context

Children under six who have severe disciplinary or behavioral problems can't be separated from their parents for extensive treatment without suffering some degree of trauma. Further-more, a very young child's disciplinary and emotional problems are most effectively analyzed by examining that child in the context of her or his family life rather than in the context of an isolating, institutional testing.

One solution to these difficulties is to offer a "home-living" environment within the hospital or clinic: a place where the family can remain together and function as a family while the child's problems are being evaluated. This situation allows clinicians and treatment teams to witness the family culture in operation—either through "visits" or through one-way mir-ror observation—and to apply systematically a variety of in-terventions in a controlled environment.

In addition to severe disciplinary and behavioral problems, issues involving very young children that are appropriate for this kind of comprehensive on-site care include:

■ emotional complications relating to a chronic physical ill-ness;

■ psychosomatic disorders, such as asthma, gastrointestinal illness, or diabetes;

■ a situation where there are multiple patients within a single family.

PCGC has a "Family Apartment Unit Program" that offers this kind of clinical approach for very young children and their families needing intensive psychiatric evaluation and treat-ment in a therapeutic setting. The family as a whole literally moves into a two-room apartment (bedroom and living room/ dining and kitchen area) within the PCGC complex for profes-sional observation and intervention on a twenty-four-hour basis.

Prior to admission of the family, there are several assess-ment conferences with the family and the referring therapist to clarify how the program runs and how it might be useful and to arrange a schedule for the program that suits all in-dividuals involved. On arrival at the apartment for partici-pation in the program, the family inevitably has to mobilize its resources to cope with the novel circumstances. This effort in itself helps move the family toward positive change.

Once the family is fairly well established in the apartment, PCGC clinicians and treatment teams orchestrate therapeutic interventions to correspond with their observations. A "typi-cal" family therapy session is only one of many possible interventions aimed at reorganizing the way the family functions so that it as a whole and the child in particular can better manage the latter's problem. Other possibilities include testing (medical as well as psychological), education, conflict resolution, skill training, role-playing, and behavioral modification.

The primary considerations for discharge from PCGC's Family Apartment Unit Program are whether there has been a decrease in the child's symptoms and whether the family has begun to show itself capable of modifying those patterns of interaction that contribute to the child's problem. The overall goal in every case is for the family to learn how to take effective control of its own difficulties and how to make effective use of outside support systems.

Look for programs like PCGC's Family Apartment Unit Program in your area. If none exist, consult with your psychiatrist, psychologist, or mental-health professional about incorporating similar features into your child's therapy.

9.

Toilet Training

Few issues cause as much tension between parents and their very young children as toilet training. Fairly or unfairly, parents can't help but approach this disciplinary challenge not only as a test of their child's temperament and intelligence but also as a means of releasing them from singularly unpleasant and time-consuming cleanup responsibilities. No wonder there are so many misconceptions regarding when and how to meet this challenge!

Let's look at some of the major toilet-training myths and test them against reality:

■*Myth #1: There is a proper age at which to train a child to use a toilet.*

Children need to be both physically and cognitively ready for controlling elimination, and each child achieves this readiness at her or his own pace. Seldom does this occur before eighteen months of age, so attempting to train a child any earlier is almost certain to lead to frustration and conflict for all parties concerned. Most children are ready sometime between the ages of two and four.

■*Myth #2: You'll know for sure when to begin toilet training.*

Unfortunately, there is no one clear signal that all the brain-to-body connections have been made and all the emotional maturity has been developed that will enable your child to respond favorably to toilet training. You must make this judgment based on close observation of your child's daily behavior.

Among the clues that your child *may* be ready for toilet training are the following:

■ Your child indicates the need to eliminate, either verbally or nonverbally (e.g., by clutching self, going red in the face, crossing the legs), *in advance.*

■ Your child shows concern about her or his elimination habits or your reaction to them.

■ Your child chooses to watch—and perhaps imitate—your elimination habits.

■ Your child expresses discomfort about wearing diapers and/or eliminating in them.

■ Your child is independently capable of getting into, and out of, loose-fitting pants.

■ *Myth #3: There is one right way to toilet train a child.*

In each case, toilet training is essentially a trial-and-error proposition. Some children train quickly (e.g., in a couple of weeks); others don't. Some make steady progress; others go through several periods of retreat. Still others defy classification: All methods may seem to fail for months in a row, until suddenly the desired behavior falls into place.

Here are some general guidelines for toilet training your child:

■ Well before training starts, teach your child about the parts of the body involved in elimination and how they function. This teaching doesn't need to be elaborate and shouldn't be judgmental. It's simply a matter of helping your child learn more about her or his body on a casual, day-to-day basis. Your child should also become familiar with the toilet and the potty well before she or he is expected to use them.

■ Assist your child in self-training rather than merely imposing a training program. When your child gives a verbal or nonverbal clue of the need to eliminate, suggest that she or he do so in the potty. Try not to insist if you encounter strong resistance to this suggestion.

Children tend to be fairly predictable in their elimination habits (e.g., needing to move their bowels after eating breakfast). Take note of such patterns and help your child to prepare for easy use of the potty or toilet at appropriate times (e.g., by postponing diapering or suggesting that she or he sit on the potty at these times and play with a special potty-only toy). Don't compel a child to eliminate when she or he has not indicated a readiness.

■ Avoid dramatic reactions, one way or the other, to your child's training. Don't be overly enthusiastic when your child succeeds. Simply compliment her or him on being so grown up. Upon failure, suggest that the potty or toilet be tried the next time. These tempered reactions will keep your child from associating toilet training with volatile emotions.

As much as possible, try not to refer to success in using the potty or toilet as "good" and failure as "bad." Also, avoid labeling the products of elimination as "disgusting." These terms are judgmental and confuse the goal of training, which is not to learn new *values* but to master a new *skill*.

■*Myth #4: Children are forever traumatized by inappropriate toilet training.*

Daunting as it may seem to the parent at the time and despite popular folklore, toilet training is *not* the most significant determinant of a child's future psychological health. As long as the training is not abusive or linked to a stringent punishment-and-reward system, there shouldn't be any negative psychological aftereffects.

■*Myth #5: When bed-wetting occurs after toilet training, the cause is some emotional disturbance.*

Regardless of a child's emotional state, occasional, uncontrollable bed-wetting can persist beyond otherwise successful toilet training as late as seven years of age. Bed-wetting can also cease for long periods of time and then resume.

Bed-wetting

In most cases, a combination of factors are responsible for bed-wetting beyond toilet training: developmental (e.g., immature bladder capacity, often inherited and almost always outgrown); medical (due to such rare problems as a urinary tract infection); situational (e.g., overtiredness resulting in deeper sleep); and/or emotional (e.g., going to bed in a state of overexcitement or anxiety, which may stimulate bladder release).

Contrary to popular folklore, bed-wetting for children under seven is seldom strictly emotional in origin. And the emotions that do seem to be involved in certain bed-wetting cases are very generalized ones rather than specific emotions that can be associated with particular psychological issues.

If your very young child indicates that she or he is upset or ashamed by bed-wetting, offer gentle reassurance that such things happen and that no one is to blame. You might also tell the child that you will keep this incident a secret, since it is a private matter. Your child may be afraid that other members of the family will find out.

A Natural Transition

Rita sensed that her two-and-a-half-year-old son, Cruz, might be ready for toilet training when he told her that he didn't like his grandmother changing his diapers. That he even mentioned his diapers suggested to Rita that he might be interested in an alternative. She encouraged Cruz to become more familiar with the potty and to ask to use it whenever he felt the need, but this approach wasn't very successful. Rarely did Cruz ask to have his diaper removed so that he could go to the potty.

Finally, during a monthlong period when Rita was off work, she decided it was worth risking some messy moments to let Cruz have the full experience of life without diapers. She put him in training pants and hoped for the best. The first time urine ran down Cruz's leg, he was amazed and curious. The second time, he was plainly displeased. He began right away to be better at using the potty.

Nevertheless, Cruz didn't convert to the potty completely until the day when he spent an afternoon with his mother at a nearby playground. After an hour of swinging, climbing, and sliding, he was still eager for more. Then, suddenly, he had a bowel movement in his pants. He immediately realized, in a very visceral way, that this meant having to go home to clean up instead of playing. He never let such a thing happen again.

10.
Siblings:
Old and New

In all multichild households, there are inevitably major differences between the way parents see the relationships among their children and the way their very young children see them. Although parents can't help but nourish visions of their offspring as an essentially loving team or community, their very young children see themselves first and foremost as solitary beings. And while parents strive to remain always aware of each child's individual personality, needs, desires, and rights, their very young children are inclined to pull in the opposite direction—that is, to focus attention on their own specific personality, needs, desires, and rights. These widely divergent points of view make friction between very young children and their siblings especially difficult for parents to understand and manage.

First, let's consider the basic kinds of sibling conflicts that children under six experience. Then we can look at ways to deal with each one. The sibling conflicts most likely to affect children in this age range can be divided into three main categories:

1. The child argues with a sibling over a specific possession, judgment, or privilege.

This happens from time to time in every household with more than one child. The *apparent* cause of a particular argument may be gaining custody of a toy, occupying a specific sitting place, choosing a television program, defining the conditions of a game, establishing who is right, defending one's privacy, or simply gaining control of a parent's attention. A *hidden* cause of the argument may be one child's (or both children's) fatigue, hunger, or negative response to a temporarily stressful situation in the household (e.g., a visit by an outsider). An additional problem resulting from the argument may be physical violence, name-calling, or intense emotional frustration, manifesting itself in crying, withdrawal, or a tantrum.

2. The child is generally and consistently abusive to—or abused by—a sibling.

This situation is much less common than the one described above. It seldom gives rise to a two-party argument. Instead, one child is always the quick and clear perpetrator; the other, the victim.

Sometimes this is merely due to one child's being markedly more aggressive in temperament than the other. It may, however, be the result of a more specific issue. The perpetrator may be convinced that she or he continually receives an unfairly small or inferior share of possessions, privileges, or attention compared to the other child. Or the perpetrator may be reacting negatively to an ongoing stressful situation in the household, such as entrenched marital discord, by repeatedly taking out related frustrations on the easiest target.

3. The child fears being abandoned by the parents in favor of a new child.

It is quite common for a child under six years old to become upset at the prospect—or arrival—of a new brother or sister. This is especially true if she or he is an only child.

Normal symptoms of such a reaction (which is fundamentally an *adjustment* reaction, not a *denial* reaction) include recurring anxiety, moodiness, anger, withdrawal, and/or regression, a condition in which the child reverts to immature and even babyish behavior. Sometimes the child will take out ill feelings on the baby; other times, on the parent; much less often, on another child in the family. Almost always, however, the ill feelings have to do with a fear of losing the parents' affection, not with actual hatred for the baby.

Here are some suggestions for managing each of the above-mentioned categories of sibling conflict:

1. Your child argues with a sibling over a specific possession, judgment, or privilege.

■ Discuss the situation in the presence of both children.

If you actually witness the argument, you may want to intervene directly and immediately, depending on the age of the participants and the nature of the quarrel. For example, if your three-year-old daughter is unfairly bullying her two-year-old sister, you should gently but firmly clarify for both children's benefit what is right and wrong about the situation and then secure your three-year-old's promise to behave more fairly. Assuming your quarreling children are both in the four- to six-year-old range, you might be able to take the less authoritative role of moderator, assisting your children in discussing the problem with you and realizing for themselves what would be a fair solution.

If you don't witness the argument, be sure that both children come together in your presence before you begin to discuss what happened. Listen to each child in turn and then guide them to work out a problem-solving agreement in the most appropriate manner, according to the age and maturity of both children.

■ *If your children won't cooperate in discussing or resolving the problem, impose separation and time-out.*

Make sure that your children retire to—and remain in—separate rooms and that they have the time and tranquillity to think about what has happened. In some cases, this is an especially strong and instructive punishment. Difficult as it may be for a parent to appreciate, the two children may, in fact, have been expressing their enjoyment of being together by fighting. In such cases, the issue is not so much to get the two children to enjoy each other's company *more* but to get them to do so *in a more appropriate manner.*

■ *Keep track of the arguments that erupt between the two children and use this information to forestall, prevent, or manage future arguments.*

Among the items to monitor are when each argument happens, why it happens, what is going on in the life of each child at that time, what is going on in the life of the household at that time, what helps to resolve the argument, and what doesn't help.

2. Your child is generally and consistently abusive to—or abused by—a sibling.

In addition to applying the guidelines for the previous category to each particular incident, take the following steps:

■ *Examine your ongoing home life very carefully for any factor that may be causing or aggravating this situation.*

Among the questions you should ask yourself are the following: Am I giving each child an equal amount of high-quality, individual attention? Has the family been going through a difficult period of time lately (e.g., due to marital discord, tough work schedules, economic adversity, or prolonged and serious illness)? Has either child been going through a difficult period of time lately (e.g., due to a change in daily routine, a new stage in physical development, or new people in her or his daily environment)?

If you feel that any of these factors is causing or aggravating sibling conflict, then do what you can to diminish, remove, or alleviate its impact.

■ *Seek professional advice.*

Interpersonal behavior that is consistently negative can be a sign of a deeply rooted problem either in the emotional makeup of the child or in family dynamics. Even if it's not, the price of letting it continue for longer than a few months is just too great. It can jeopardize not only the future emotional health of the two children directly involved but also that of every family member.

3. Your child fears being abandoned by you in favor of a new child.

■ *Prepare your child in advance to have informed and realistic expectations about the newborn.*

Among the things to do are the following: Explain to your child how the baby was conceived, how the baby is going to develop, and what the baby will be like for the first few months after birth. Involve your child in some of the prenatal activities (e.g., weighing your child whenever you weigh yourself or shopping for baby goods). Try to let your child observe other newborns, preferably as you handle them, so that she or he will know what to expect and what not to expect.

Among the things *not* to do: Don't emphasize how much your child will enjoy the new baby, since this may not be the case. Don't characterize the baby as a "new playmate," since your child won't really be able to—and, in fact, should not—play with the baby for some time after the birth. Don't impress upon the child that you will need help in taking care of the baby, since she or he may not be capable of—or interested in—providing the help you really need.

■ *Spend additional time alone with your child in advance of the birth.*

This will reaffirm your child's place in your heart as well as in your daily schedule. Take advantage of this time to recall and review your child's personal history with the family. It will reinforce her or his sense of being forever special. Look at old baby photos together and reminisce about favorite experiences.

■ *Try to include your child in the excitement surrounding the baby's birth.*

If possible, arrange to have your child visit you and the newborn in the hospital or hospice (an alternative-health-care facility). Record the first meeting of the child and her or his new sibling with a photograph, movie, or tape. Give your child a present for now being a big sister or a big brother and encourage friends and relatives to give your child a present at the same time that they give a present to the new baby. (The two presents don't have to be equal in value.)

■ *As much as possible, avoid leaving your child alone with your new baby until the latter is around two years old.*

A child under six is very capable of unintentionally—or intentionally—hurting a younger child physically or emotionally, so it's best not to take any chances. Keep the two of them always in sight. Use a playpen whenever appropriate to guard your baby when the two of them are in the same room. Avail yourself of baby-sitters, day care, or nursery school to give your child appropriate time away from the baby and to give yourself appropriate time away from having to watch over the two of them at once. Also, try to stagger mealtimes, nap times, and bedtimes.

■ *Be sure to continue spending regular time alone with your child.*

Do things together that you've always done so that your child feels a sense of continuity. In addition, introduce new things to do so that your child feels newly stimulated by your relationship. While it's wise to devote a certain amount of time to activities that have nothing to do with the new baby, you might slowly interject appropriate baby-related projects, such as discussing with your child safe ways to interact with the baby.

CASE:

Like Baby, Like Mother

When four-and-a-half-year-old Diana was first told she was going to have a new sister or brother, she had only two questions: "How are babies made?" and "When will the baby be here?" For the next couple of months, she gave no signs of any reaction one way or another. Her parents kept reminding her that the baby was growing and would be there soon, but she didn't seem at all curious.

However, once her mother's pregnant state became visibly obvious, things changed. Formerly a very mature child for her age, she began regressing. The first indications were wetting her bed again—after eighteen months of no problems—and opting more often to crawl than to walk. Within a couple of weeks she was also demanding to be fed from a bottle and throwing an occasional tantrum when she didn't get her way.

Distressed as Diana's mother was by this behavior, she resisted the impulse to be angry at Diana for not acting her age.

Instead, she let her daughter do as she wished. She intervened only when absolutely necessary; and when she did, she treated Diana in about the same way she had when Diana had originally exhibited the behavior at a younger age.

Diana continued her regressive behavior for another three months, until about six weeks before the baby was due. Then, over the span of a single week, she did a complete turnabout. She began tending her favorite baby doll more solicitously than she ever had before, as if she were the new mother that her real mother was about to be. Her parents speculated that she had finally tired of living like an infant because it wasn't fun. Furthermore, it wasn't getting her the special attention she had imagined it might when she had observed her parents' eager anticipation of the new baby.

No longer did Diana wet her bed, crawl on the floor, feed from a bottle, or throw tantrums. Indeed, she played with her doll-child as if it were exhibiting those behaviors! When her new baby brother finally arrived home, she was behaving more maturely than she ever had, and the adjustment to her new sibling was much smoother than her parents had expected.

11.
Play

Play is the child's natural work. For very young children, it's their most valuable means of learning about themselves and the world around them. Powerless to do much more than *react* to adult supervision, they rely on playtime as their only opportunity to *act* as they wish; and this kind of self-determination is essential to their healthy development as human beings. Through play, children can teach themselves—safely, enjoyably, and instinctively—to appreciate their personal strengths and weaknesses, derive satisfaction from tasks and objects in their environment, and interact effectively with others.

In terms of emotional health, play offers very young children two particularly important benefits: First, it gives them a creative, instructive, and appropriate outlet for their feelings; second, it trains them to read the feelings of others and to respond to them in a socially acceptable manner.

Let's begin by considering how play functions as an emotional outlet. This process is observable in children as young as six months, when many babies first display an interest in peekaboo, a game that allows them to gain more control over the stress associated with a parent being "out of sight." A year or two later, children typically discharge feelings of anger, incompetence, and insecurity by building things with blocks and then tearing them down or by "acting out" such feelings in make-believe exchanges with dolls, stuffed animals, and action toys.

From around four or five years old, a child may start engaging in more violent forms of play: "pretend" fighting and even killing, especially boys. While such play may startle adult sensibilities, it is perfectly normal and even healthy for the children themselves. It guides them to discharge general feelings of hostility and vulnerability in a safely make-believe manner. Far from influencing children to become more belligerent in real life, "gunplay" (as such an activity is collectively called) can teach them to control their aggressive impulses. Psychologists often refer to this phenomenon as "reduction through symbolic play."

That aggressive play can be good for a child does not mean that parents should encourage it or refrain from regulating it when it becomes too rowdy. Nor does it mean that parents must ignore their own negative feelings about violence or war and play along with their children. Some children are more inclined toward this kind of activity—for all sorts of reasons—than others. Some are rowdier than others. And all of them need to get used to the fact that other people, including parents, are free to say yes or no when they're invited to play a particular game.

In your own household, the best strategy for coping with your child's occasional desire for violent play is first to make sure that she or he also has—or knows about—a number of interesting play options that are nonviolent. Then let your child play however she or he chooses, as long as it's safe and doesn't disturb others.

Here are some other suggestions regarding play:

■ *Give your child ample opportunities and resources for play, both alone and with others.*

As much as possible, build in regular, predictable times during your child's day when she or he is free to play alone. This will help your child become more independent. To increase your child's social skills, arrange regular, predictable "play dates" during the week with other children.

Also, do whatever you reasonably can to facilitate enjoyable play. Establish safe, roomy, and comfortable play areas in your home. Make sure to create play areas that you can easily observe as well as others that will allow each of you to have some degree of privacy. Help make sure that your child's toys are well organized so that different types are readily available for each given playtime. Take a variety of them along when you and your child are away from home in case a chance for play presents itself.

Play can be a wonderful solace when your child is emotionally troubled. Be alert for such times and gently lead your child by offering several attractive and appropriate play alternatives. For example, if your child feels neglected, you might propose playing together with dolls or playing Simon says—both very interactive games involving a great deal of personal attention.

■ *Regularly join your child in play.*

You and your child can develop a much closer bond if you know how to play together in a number of different ways and if you can depend on frequent play-together periods to communicate with each other—directly or indirectly. With this in mind, be sure to choose or devise a number of toys and games for your child that both of you are capable of enjoying.

■ *Be as patient as possible with your child's progress in mastering skills and learning to obey rules.*

Let your child take the lead, or have the feeling of taking it, when you play together. A child under six is often not emotionally equipped to handle losing very well, so be prepared to let your child win, even if it means allowing her or him to cheat. A certain amount of cheating may be necessary for your child to get through a game until she or he has acquired more proficiency, at which point the desire to cheat will most likely disappear.

■ *Tactfully help your child play well and gain maximum benefits from doing so.*

Without putting a damper on your child's fun, make her or him aware of the value of different games: what can be learned from them or how they can develop the body or mind. This information will help your child appreciate certain games more strongly. Then, when you play games with children, set a good example—and, if necessary, tailor the rules of the game—so that your child can derive maximum satisfaction from it.

Take care to play games with your child that suit her or his mood and the time of day. Relatively quiet games, for example, are more appropriate if your child is sad or listless or if it's almost bedtime. On the other hand, if your child is rambunctious and it's the middle of the afternoon, a more active game is appropriate.

At this stage in life, your child may have difficulty sharing toys with others or allowing them their fair turn. Gently establish what is right or nice as opposed to what is wrong or not nice and don't hesitate to intervene when necessary if your child is victimizing, or being victimized by, another child.

You might also try "practice sharing" rituals with your child, in which you ask to be given a toy, praise your child upon giving it to you, and then return it in a few seconds. However, don't expect your child to adopt more generous behavior very quickly and don't worry if she or he doesn't. It takes a considerable amount of time and experience for a child to recognize the value of sharing and fair play.

■ *Discreetly observe your child at play.*

Make a habit of watching your child play from time to time in a manner that doesn't attract attention. How or what your child plays can give you valuable insights into a host of current feelings. For example, your child may invent a frustrating scenario with a doll that you can relate to a specific troublesome scenario in her or his real life. Or your child may appear to have lost interest in some favorite toys, which could well signal a more complicated emotional conflict (such as separation anxiety). But even more important, routinely watching your child at play can tell you more about what she or he likes and dislikes. This knowledge will help you buy toys and plan playtimes that your child will enjoy and will ensure that you and your child have fun when you play together.

■ *Invite your child to bring a playful spirit to everyday activities.* Cleanup tasks, simple chores around the kitchen and yard, and daily rituals like bathtime can be made much more attractive and less stressful to your child if they are given a gamelike quality. Try accompanying such activities with playacting, sing-alongs, or follow-the-leader exercises. This kind of approach also allows your child to translate more easily into real life the skills acquired through play.

Group Games for the Early Years

Until kids are five or six years old, they are usually too self-centered to participate well in sustained games with other children. They lack the necessary concentration and cooperation skills, and they don't take losing gracefully. They do, however, love to play self-challenging games either in unison or by taking turns, especially if those games are structured around rhythm, repetition, or chanting.

Here are some specific group-game suggestions for different age ranges:

TWO TO THREE YEARS OLD

Children during these years are especially fond of games that exercise their newly emerging language and motor skills, like ring-around-a-rosy, mulberry bush, egg hunt, and follow the leader. As a rule, they are not yet emotionally mature enough for games with a strong acceptance-rejection theme (e.g., farmer in the dell, in which different players are chosen—or not chosen—to assume different roles).

THREE TO FIVE YEARS OLD

Children at this stage in their development enjoy a game that involves slightly more sophisticated motor skills. They are also emotionally mature enough for the game to include a mild degree of competition and/or acceptance-rejection. Ideal games of this nature include Simon says, hot and cold, London Bridge, bobbing for apples, pin the tail on the donkey, and musical chairs.

FIVE TO SIX YEARS OLD

By the time a child is age five or six, she or he is rapidly acquiring interpersonal skills and emotional resiliency. It's a good time for role-related games such as farmer in the dell, blindman's buff, hide-and-seek, cowboys and Indians, cops and robbers, relay racing, and leapfrog.

Imaginary Playmates

Anytime from age three and a half to age six, your child may go through one or more periods of having a make-believe friend: someone that your child openly includes in most daily activities and that you are entreated to accept as a real person. Annoying as it may be to put up with this ghostly companion, it is best to tolerate her or his presence in your child's life.

Creating an imaginary playmate at this stage in a child's development is a very constructive act. Not every child feels the need to invent such a figure, but those who do are definitely working toward better mental and emotional health.

On a strictly behavioral level, an imaginary playmate is a vehicle your child can use to try out new language and social skills and alleviate loneliness. On a deeper psychological level, an imaginary playmate functions as a valuable projection mechanism for different "selves" within your child. As two distinct entities, your child and her or his imaginary playmate can act out the "good" and the "bad" selves within your child's psyche, the "cowardly" and "brave" selves, or the "optimistic" and "pessimistic" selves, and so on. Through this two-part communication, your child can ultimately consolidate different aspects of her or his psyche into one strong personality.

Tolerating the fact that your child has an imaginary playmate doesn't mean you have to adopt the playmate as another
member of your household. Subconsciously, your child is aware
that the playmate exists for her or him alone. If you pretend
otherwise, you may turn the playmate into a kind of game
between you and your child, which not only interferes with
the true function of the playmate for the child alone but also
increases the potential length of time that the playmate will
hang around.

When an imaginary playmate comes to your home, try to
follow these guidelines:

■ Don't deny or make fun of the playmate.

This will only frustrate and humiliate your child, for whom
the playmate definitely has some sort of reality.

■ Always talk directly to your child instead of to the play-mate.

This strategy doesn't reject the existence of the playmate, but
it does make it clear that you can't see or hear the playmate.

■ Let the child take all initiatives with the playmate.

Don't mention the playmate unless your child does and don't
take the lead in acknowledging the playmate's existence (e.g.,
by setting a place for the playmate at the table without being
asked to do so).

■ Cater to the announced presence of the playmate only in a manner that suits you.

For example, if your child asks you to set another place at the
table, you can either do so—assuming it isn't inconvenient—
or you can simply ask your child to make other arrangements
for the playmate. If your child yells, "Look out! You're going
to bump into Sherman!," you can either move or say to your
child, "Please tell Sherman he'll have to get out of the way."

■ Make sure your child always assumes responsibility for the playmate's actions.

Often a child uses an imaginary playmate as a scapegoat. If
your child says, "I didn't do that. Sherman did!" say, "Then
tell Sherman that he was wrong and that you will take care
of it."

■ Minimize the need for an imaginary playmate by offer-ing your child alternative companionship.

The alternative companion might be yourself, a pet, or (with proper permission) your spouse, a sibling, a relative, or a friend (child or adult).

CASE:

Playing It Out

One of the major benefits of play for young children is that it allows them to channel unacceptable behaviors into games. Thus, they simultaneously eliminate a possible catalyst for real-life conflicts and add more fun to their play life.

At age fifteen months, Samantha was an inveterate pincher, poker, and puller. By far her favorite target was her mother. Attempts simply to punish this behavior weren't successful enough. Whenever Samantha pinched or poked her or pulled her hair, her mother would say, "No," and confine her to a playpen for several minutes; but it wasn't long before Samantha pinched, poked, or pulled again. The situation was generating a great deal of emotional stress for Samantha and her mother.

A magazine article about children's play gave Samantha's mother a new idea. Reinterpreting Samantha's behavior as an attempt to "connect" with her mother as well as an age-appropriate drive to exercise her powers of manipulation, Samantha's mother invented a game that might satisfy both purposes. She filled one of her easy-to-open purses with personal items that were small, safe, and expendable. Then, whenever Samantha exhibited the pinch-poke-pull behavior, her mother brought out the purse and gave it to her as a plaything.

As it happened, Samantha delighted in pulling everything out of her mother's purse and then putting everything back in again. Her mother also gave her the purse at other times so that she wouldn't associate it only with pinching, poking, and pulling. Sooner than her mother had thought possible, all pinching, poking, and pulling ceased.

12.
Transitional
Objects

The phrase may be fancy, but what it describes is usually the opposite. A common transitional object for a very young child is a threadbare blanket, an old stuffed teddy bear, or a bedraggled doll. It's an item that is especially beloved by the child because it provides a link to past moments of comfort and security, and so the child relies on its presence as she or he enters into new experiences. Disconcerted as many parents are by their two- to six-year-old child's clinging to a transitional object (especially when the object is ugly), the behavior itself is a positive sign of courage and resourcefulness.

Very young children exist in a state of ongoing dependence on other people. A certain degree of fear and disorientation is bound to occur when circumstances leave them relatively on their own. Such circumstances range from minor shifts in the daily schedule—like playing without supervision, riding in the car to unknown destinations, or going to bed at night—to major life-style changes—attending a day-care center, accepting a new baby into the family, or moving to another home.

Some children unaccountably take these shifts and changes in stride. Others respond with unruly behavior or stressful withdrawal. Those who choose to cope with the assistance of transitional objects occupy the middle ground. They are learning to control their negative reactions by reminding themselves of a "core" state of being that will survive the unsettling experience. This state is symbolized by the transitional object that the child literally carries from the secure realm of past experience into the comparatively insecure realm of the immediate or long-range future.

Here are some important points to keep in mind concerning transitional objects:

■*Don't criticize or tease your child regarding her or his dependence on a transitional object.*

A child who makes use of a transitional object is already trying to manage feelings of incompetence and vulnerability. Your criticism and teasing will simply aggravate these feelings and make your child feel embarrassed or ashamed.

■ *Consider offering your child a transitional object to help her or him manage emotionally trying experiences.*

For example, suppose your child expresses anxiety about going away from home for a family vacation. If a transitional object hasn't already been selected, try suggesting that she or he bring along a favorite toy or object as a special reminder of home.

Another strategy in this situation or a similar one (such as being separated from you for an extended period of time) is to give your child a gift to be used, if desired, as a transitional object. It isn't always necessary for it to have had a long history with the child. A gift coming from you, especially if it is something with which your child has seen you enjoy yourself, can have great symbolic value to her or him.

■*Avoid encouraging excessive reliance on transitional objects.*

A child can become overwhelmed with toys, stuffed animals, dolls, and other items that are somehow invested—overtly or subtly—with "special" meaning. It's okay to cooperate with your child's choice of transitional objects and to introduce an item as a possible transitional object in times of particular need. However, restrain yourself from routinely encouraging dependence on them. It may influence your child to put too much faith in symbolic support and too little faith in self-reliance.

■*Don't expect your child to appreciate, or cooperate with, your attempts to take care of the transitional object.*

Your child is likely to balk at having a transitional object cleaned or repaired. It's the sensual qualities that the object has acquired over time—the complex smell, the distinctive texture, the unique appearance—that contribute to its ability to work a reassuring magic. Your child probably won't even want you to notice or handle the object very much. After all, it represents something very personal and private to him or her.

Of course, if your child is distressed about the damaged condition of the object, you should certainly offer to repair or replace it. To ensure that all goes well, let your child be involved in the repair or replacement.

■ *When it does become necessary to wean your child away from a transitional object, do so gradually and tactfully.*

As your child becomes older, she or he may continue to keep a particular transitional object close at hand merely out of habit or sentimentality. While it's difficult to judge the precise time when your child has outgrown a genuine need for this object, you can intervene to start weaning your child away from it when you think such action is appropriate.

Avoid just taking the object away, whether or not your child is present. Instead, try to interest your child in something else. For example, if she or he clings to the object whenever you travel in the car, try substituting another toy for this purpose or playing a car game to divert attention from the toy.

Also, slowly withdraw your active cooperation in providing your child with this particular object. Don't automatically tell your child to get it when she or he seems out of sorts. Allow it to be forgotten when you leave home. If all else fails, gradually impose limits on its use.

■ *Allow the child to say good-bye to a transitional object in her or his own way.*

When you perceive that your child has ceased to rely on a particular item as a transitional object, don't call attention to the situation by complimenting your child for her or his independence or by engineering the sudden disappearance of the object. Also, leave it to your child to conduct any farewell ceremony (such as burying a disfigured doll or throwing away a hopelessly worn blanket). If your child doesn't take this approach, you shouldn't suggest it.

Just as your child privately elected to transform a certain item into a transitional object, she or he should have the private growth experience of laying it aside in her or his own way and time. Seeing the object still around, stripped of its former importance, can be a valuable reminder to your child of how much—and how successfully—she or he has matured.

Tension Tamers: Sucking and Rocking

A mere generation ago, parents did everything they could to discourage very young children from sucking their thumbs or rocking their heads back and forth. At best, parents considered these habits socially unacceptable and symptoms of possible maladjustment. At worst, they feared that pursuing these habits on a regular basis would cause physical damage. Now thumb sucking, head rocking, and like activities (such as ear clutching, hair twisting, and—sometimes—masturbation) are acknowledged for what they truly are: perfectly normal tension-releasing strategies that may not be pleasant to watch but are nevertheless harmless.

Thumb sucking, the most prevalent form of tension-releasing activity in very young children, can begin right after birth (in fact, it's been observed in the womb). During the first two years, it can occur at any time day or night, although the most popular time appears to be just before sleep, when the child uses it as a natural relaxation technique. After two years, most thumb sucking starts to taper off during the day, except at moments when the child is "compensating" for frustration, tiredness, or hunger. By age six, it all but disappears as other tension releasers (from nail biting and nose picking to vocalizing and playing) take its place.

Head rocking, the next most prevalent tension releaser, typically occurs only in bed and lasts for a much shorter period of time: until around age three, with brief, episodic lapses continuing for several years thereafter. Many infants enjoy banging their head rhythmically (and, thank goodness, softly) against the bars of their crib.

As a general rule, it's wise and safe to tolerate such tension-releasing habits and wait for them to pass as the child matures. Calling negative attention to them will only aggravate the discomfort that's causing the habit in the first place.

Here are some other, more specific guidelines:

■*If you find that thumb sucking upsets you too much, consider substituting a pacifier for the thumb.*

It's better than unintentionally taking out your irritation on your child. At first, gently remove your child's thumb from her or his mouth while simultaneously inserting the pacifier. After your child has become accustomed to the pacifier rather than the thumb, keep a pacifier handy at all times (or even an open box filled with pacifiers) so that either your child or you can conveniently insert a pacifier when needed. Conversely, if pacifier dependence disturbs you, consider helping your child use her or his thumb instead.

■ *If you're concerned about how strongly your child bangs her or his head against the crib bars, cushion the bars with cardboard.*

Cardboard is much softer than wood, metal, or plastic, but—unlike cloth or foam rubber—it will give your child a similarly satisfying "hard" surface to hit and "hard" noise to hear.

■ *As much as possible, minimize the causes for such tension releasers.*

Try to prevent your child from becoming unduly or overly frustrated, tired, or hungry. Always check out possible reasons *why* your child is crying or experiencing tension *before* leaving her or him to seek release via sucking or rocking. Your child may much prefer to be fed, put to sleep, or simply comforted.

13.

Storytelling

For as long as human beings have enjoyed the power of speech, storytelling—the face-to-face communication of a story—has enabled child and parent to come together and refresh themselves. From the child's point of view, it is a privileged opportunity to observe the parent closely and positively and to develop new understanding, appreciation, and trust. From the parent's point of view, it is an excellent means of recapturing a child's sense of wonder and of expressing care to a child in a nonauthoritarian manner.

As far as a child's emotional life is concerned, storytelling provides consolation, healing, and renewal in a number of unique and far-reaching ways. It gives children potent word pictures and symbols that they can use to understand and express their feelings. It suggests heroes and role models that they can ponder, imitate, and evaluate. It offers them creative insights into the emotional aspects of human behavior. And it exercises their powers of visual imagination, which is especially beneficial because very young minds often have trouble "seeing" the path into and out of an emotional crisis.

Kids today are immersed in an overtly visual world of television, computers, and video arcades. Even reading aloud to children usually directs them to what they can see on the surface: words and pictures in a book. Person-to-person storytelling stimulates the "mind's eye." The listener has the emotional freedom to envision a story as she or he chooses and the emotional safety of knowing that whatever may be imagined in this context, no matter how frightening, is only "real" in a very temporary, qualified, and experimental sense.

Most important of all, storytelling is compelling in its own right simply because it is fun both for the child and the parent. It associates speaking, listening, and being together with pleasure, and it serves as a "time apart" during the day that defuses troubles and strengthens hope.

Here are some suggestions for making storytelling an especially warm and rewarding activity:

■ *Have confidence in yourself as a storyteller.*

All of us have stories to tell: narratives that we loved as children; anecdotes about our family or circle of friends; plot lines we've picked up from books, television shows, movies, plays, musical comedies, and operas; tales about famous people, places, or events; and accounts of our own daily life. And all of us are capable of sharing stories with others.

If you're shy about storytelling with your child, the secret to confidence lies in preparation. Think in advance of a number of stories you might tell and keep your eyes and ears open for good ones you can borrow. Jot down notes about them to which you can refer from time to time. Practice telling stories to yourself before telling them to your child.

■ *Choose a good time for storytelling.*

The most advantageous circumstance for storytelling is during a regularly scheduled daily storytelling time, one to which you and your child can look forward. When storytelling is an organic part of each day, both of you will participate in it more naturally, with more cooperation and more mental and emotional absorption.

Bedtime is perhaps the most congenial time of all for storytelling. Many children need to achieve an emotional balance at the end of the day before they can fall asleep, and storytelling offers a means of realizing this balance. An alternative to bedtime is just before nap time.

Aside from a regularly scheduled storytelling time, consider telling a story whenever it's relatively quiet around the house and your child needs to be soothed, reassured, or perked up. Storytelling is also an emotionally restorative activity for a child who is sick, away from home, or forced to spend several minutes to a half hour waiting for something.

■ *Create a positive environment for storytelling.*

It's a good idea to establish one particular place in your home as the storytelling spot for non–bedtime stories. Whether or not you establish such a spot, make sure both you and your listener are comfortable and won't be distracted by other people or by outside noises. Dim lighting helps set the mood. Frequent eye contact with your listener will deepen her or his involvement in the story and allow you to gauge how it is being received as you go along.

■ *Give your storytelling session a ritual beginning and ending.*

This cues your listener to accept storytelling as a special event, apart from real-life events. To begin the session, suggest that you both close your eyes while you wait for a story to come to you, light a candle, sing a brief song, or "pluck" a story out of the air with your hands. If you're confident enough about your ability to spin any kind of story, begin by asking your child what kind of story she or he would like to hear. You can also use the same beginning phrase for each story: for example, the traditional "Once upon a time" or something more original like "This is a very special story that I call 'The Story of . . .' "

To end the session, try "reversing" the way you began it. Close your eyes and say good-bye to the story, blow out the candle, sing the brief song again, toss the story back into the air, and/or use a ritual closing line (e.g., ". . . and that is the way the story ends").

■ *Speak in a natural voice, trusting your story to inspire the right language and the right dramatic touches when they are appropriate.*

If you are too stagy when you're telling a story, it may seem forced and lifeless. Try not to speak in a voice that is unnaturally high or thin or in a rhythm that is overly fast or monotonous. And don't worry about whether you're using the right words or giving the story a truly polished recitation. Remember that you're not *performing*; you're *communicating*. You should have just as much fun telling the story as your child has listening to it.

■ *Consider telling a story that has a special bearing on an emotional conflict or crisis your child is experiencing.*

Telling a story can be a very safe and effective way of addressing your child's current emotional difficulties without embarrassing or frightening her or him. After all, a story is an independent entity with a life of its own; and your child remains free to accept it as such or, at her or his discretion, to connect what the story says with what is happening in real life.

When taking this approach to storytelling, be sure that the one you choose depicts a positive resolution. For example, if your child appears to be overcome with sorrow, anger, or guilt, try telling a story in which the hero goes through sorrow, anger, or guilt and emerges in better spirits. If your child seems to be experiencing jealousy or indignation, try one in which these emotions eventually disappear or are reversed rather than one in which the hero merely suffers as a result of these emotions.

Storytelling in general does not always have to involve "happy endings." Indeed, children can gain much wisdom and emotional fortitude from stories that present the unhappy side of life. But at a time when you're fairly certain that your child is wrestling with a particular negative emotion in real life, an upbeat story has a better chance of being consoling.

Choosing Age-Appropriate Stories

BIRTH TO ONE AND A HALF YEARS OLD

Storytelling can begin soon after birth. Although infants typically can't recognize voices and objects until around the ninth month and can't put words together to speak until around the sixteenth month, storytelling helps them become accustomed to the teller's voice and to identify that voice with a peaceful activity.

Storytelling to an infant also lays the groundwork for her or his receptivity to such similar experiences later in life. The infant listener learns to enjoy on a precognitive level the particular rhythmic cadence that inevitably distinguishes a special narrative from everyday chatter. Meanwhile, the teller gets valuable practice in storytelling.

Until your child is around one and a half years old, story content is essentially irrelevant. The act itself is what truly matters. Children this young do seem to appreciate stories that repeat sounds, phrases, and rhythmic patterns (which continues to be true for older children as well).

ONE AND A HALF TO THREE YEARS OLD

Between the ages of one and a half and two years, children typically start speaking on their own. At this point in your child's development, you can begin to form more logical, well-structured stories that enlist your child's understanding and encourage her or his efforts to become more involved in language.

From two to three years old, each child is a little Adam, fiercely bent on labeling everything her or his senses perceive in the immediate surroundings. Stories that name objects, define their function, and associate them with other objects are the most appropriate ones to tell. You can frame such a story by concentrating your attention on a single locale or a single group of items. For example, you may say, "In this room there is a ball, and the ball goes bounce, bounce, bounce. Mommy likes the ball, and the ball is red, and whoops, the ball rolls away. In this room there is also a door . . . ," and so forth. Accompanying the story with some pantomimed hand gestures will keep the listener's attention. Your child may even want to join in when you pantomime.

Stories that build on "What happens next?" are also interesting to children in this age range. Try building a story around what happens, step by step, during one of your own typical days, including the times when you are separated from your child. Be dramatic and imaginative in your rendition of what occurs.

Psychologically, this latter kind of story can be particularly beneficial. It may clear up disturbing mysteries in your child's mind about what goes on in your life. In any event, it reassures your child that when you do go away, you still think about her or him—and that whatever may happen during your day, you do ultimately return.

Another option is to spin a yarn about what might happen if the two of you—or just the child—were to go on a walk in the park, visit Grandmother, or perform some other fairly familiar activity. This helps your child be better prepared, intellectually and emotionally, when such experiences actually take place in the future.

THREE TO FOUR AND A HALF YEARS OLD

Newly capable of identifying some of the more basic emotions and of articulating major likes and dislikes, three-year-old children develop feelings of great intensity. They form very specific images in their minds and hearts of what they want and take the initiative in seeking out situations that have the potential of bringing them love, pleasure, and comfort.

You can now begin to weave more conventional story plots, keeping the narrative flow of events simple, active, and direct. "Goldilocks and the Three Bears" is an excellent example of such a story. It reflects a young child's search for "just the right thing" and, in addition, the child's recognition that things come in different sizes, including people.

Ordinary items that fascinate children of two to five years (and alternately inspire fear and attraction) include holes, puddles, cars, planes, trucks, birds, dogs, cats, squirrels, rain, snow, thunder, lightning, houses, shops, meals, and snacks. Story subjects that interest children in this age range tend to be extraordinary variations on these items: animals that behave like humans, weather that is particularly strong or magical, and so forth. An especially compelling story is one in which the hero (a reflection of the listener) is able to manipulate her or his environment in some wondrous way.

FOUR AND A HALF TO SIX YEARS OLD

Children in this age range are beginning to develop self-consciousness. As they interact more with other children and adults and venture more often away from home base, they become increasingly concerned with personality, social, and sexual differences. One major product of this concern is a new complication in their relationship with their parents: Sons tend to perceive their father as a rival for their mother's romantic interest, and daughters tend to regard their mother as a rival for their father's romantic interest.

Dealing emotionally with this perception as well as with their dawning recognition of adult-world problems like divorce, poverty, crime, and violence, children within this age range become passionately concerned about justice. The questions uppermost in their minds are How can this happen? Is it fair? Will I get what I deserve? Will others get what they deserve? How can things work out for the best?

This is the golden age range for classic fairy tales and folktales, which typically depict an individual triumphing over difficulties to gain fame, wealth, or romance and to restore moral order. The individual may be a princess (Snow White), a puppet (Pinocchio), or a pet (Puss-in-Boots). The difficulties may include a misfortune (the expulsion from an improverished home that Hansel and Gretel suffer), a malefactor (the sorceress who turns the prince into a frog), or a monster (the giant who lives at the top of Jack's beanstalk). Whatever the combination—retold or invented—the listener is provided with a "play" world within which she or he can mentally recast dramas from her or his own newly complex emotional life.

Suggestions for Reading Aloud

Reading stories aloud doesn't provide the emotional intimacy and creativity that face-to-face storytelling does, but it still serves many of the same therapeutic functions. In addition, it helps to acquaint children with the world of books, which can offer valuable private experiences of emotional release and consolation later in the child's life.

Listed below are suggested stories to read aloud that can assist a child in managing major emotional issues or situations occurring between the ages of two and a half and six. Your local librarian can make other recommendations.

Anger at Own Helplessness

Sara and the Door, Virginia A. Jensen (Reading, Mass.: Addison-Wesley, 1977). Ages two and a half.
Leo the Late Bloomer, Robert Kraus (New York: Scholastic, 1981). Ages four to six.

Anger at Parent

Daddy Is a Monster . . . Sometimes, John Steptoe (Philadelphia: Lippincott, 1980). Ages four to six.

Depression

Today Was a Terrible Day, Patricia R. Giff (New York: Viking, 1980). Ages four to six.

Jealousy Regarding a New Baby

Alex and the Baby, Mary Dickinsin (New York: Andre Deutsch, 1982). Ages three to six.
Nobody Asked Me If I Wanted a Baby Sister, M. Alexander (New York: Dial, 1971). Ages three to six.
That New Baby, S. Stein (New York: Walker, 1974). Ages three to six.

Jealousy Regarding a Peer

Jealousy, Eva Eriksson (New York: Carolrhoda, 1985). Ages three to six.

Sibling Conflicts

Sisters, David McPhail (New York: Harcourt, 1984). Ages three to six.

Separation Anxiety

First Pink Light, Eloise Greenfield (New York: Crowell, 1976). Ages three to six.

Divorce

Dinosaurs Divorce: A Guide for Changing Families, Laurene K. Brown and Marc Brown (Boston: Atlantic Monthly, 1986). Ages three to six.

Loneliness
Dear Phoebe, Sue Alexander (Boston: Little, Brown, 1984). Ages three to six.

Shyness
Fiona's Bee, Beverly Keller (New York: Coward-McCann, 1975). Ages four to six.

Hatred
The Hating Book, Charlotte Zolotow (New York: Harper, 1969). Ages four to six.

Toilet Training
Once Upon a Potty, Alona Frankel (New York: Barron's, 1980). Ages two to four (*note*: male and female versions available).

Death
The Dead Bird, M. W. Brown (New York: Dell, 1980). Ages two to four.
Pop's Secret, M. Townsend and R. Stern (Reading, Mass.: Addison-Wesley, 1980). Ages three to six.

Fear (General)
The Red Lion, Diane Wolkstein (New York: Crowell-Collier, 1977). Ages four to six.

Fear of Dogs
The Biggest, Meanest, Ugliest Dog in the Whole Wide World, Rebecca Jones (New York: Macmillan, 1982). Ages three to six.

Fear of Storms
Thunderstorm, Mary Szilagyi (New York: Bradbury Press, 1985). Ages three to six.

Nightmares
No Elephants Allowed, Deborah Robison (Boston: Houghton Mifflin, 1981). Ages three to six.

14.
Day Care

In just twenty-five years, day care has become a necessity for millions of American children. According to the most recent Census Bureau estimates (1988), over half of the kids now under five years old have working mothers and are dependent for care on nonrelatives during the day, compared with less than 30 percent in 1970. And while only 15 percent of such kids received day-care services in 1970, today almost 40 percent do: 15 percent in day-care centers and 24 percent in private homes (so called family-based day care).

These figures are almost certain to grow higher in the years to come as more and more women have no choice but to work. The same Census Bureau estimates reveal that two-thirds of all working women today—as opposed to one-third in 1970—are either the sole support of their family or have husbands who earn less than $15,000.

Given this trend, the main question regarding day care is no longer what it was in 1970—"Should I send my child to day care?" Now that day care has evolved into an unavoidable fact of life for so many Americans, the main question is "What effect will day care have on my child's emotional health?"

So far, experts have been unable to establish definitive answers to this question. The few authoritative follow-up tests that have been conducted on day-care children suggest that day care *in itself* is not noticeably positive or negative in its overall impact on the child's emotional health. Much more important, and ultimately decisive, is the relationship between parent and child, regardless of whether or not the child is in day care.

At the same time you are planning to send your child to day care, you should also plan to arrange your schedule so that the two of you will have especially close, joyful, and dependable periods of time together each day, however brief they may be. This will help ensure that you remain emotionally in tune with each other and that any problems that your child may be having—whether or not they involve day care—won't go unnoticed.

In addition, you should shop around for the best possible day-care service in your price range; and after you've enrolled your child in a day-care service, you should monitor her or his day-care life to make sure it is satisfactory. While tests may show that day care *in itself* has no discernible effect on a child's emotional well-being, these same tests also indicate that the *quality* of a specific day-care facility can make a significant difference.

Here are some steps you should take in choosing and monitoring a day-care service:

■*Familiarize yourself with state regulations concerning day care.*

Regrettably, there are no federal laws governing the care of small children. Instead, each state has its own regulations. Some have very strict licensing qualifications and procedures; others don't. Make sure any day-care service you're interviewing—or using—complies with the regulations in your state.

■ *Generate a large list of different kinds of day-care centers to visit.*

Comparison shopping makes for a better fit between child and service. Seek information on day-care centers as well as family-based day care. Besides recommendations from relatives and friends, check other sources, such as parent organizations, community service groups, and child welfare agencies.

Also, continue to keep your eyes and ears open for good-quality day-care centers and family-based day care even *after* you've enrolled your child in a particular service. You never know when you may have to change.

■*Ask about staff members' education, training, experience, and commitment.*

Some day-care services or staff members may be well qualified only to care for children in a particular age range—for example, three to five instead of one to three. Also, turnover is a big problem in day-care services. Other considerations aside, your child will be more emotionally secure at a day-care service if the staff has had a long-term history there and remains constant during your child's day-care life. Find out how long staff members have been at the service and how long they intend to stay.

■*Ask about the ratio of children to staff member.*

Good children-to-staff-member ratios are no more than four to one for infants under eighteen months old; five to one for children eighteen months to two years; eight to one for children two to three years; ten to one for children three to four years; and fifteen to one for children four to six years. Only a few states mandate ratios in these ranges. Some states allow up to twelve children of any age per staff member.

No matter what the ratios, your child will probably receive more emotionally satisfying individual attention in a service with a small number of children than in one with a large number of children. This means that a ratio of ten children to two staff members is preferable to a ratio of twenty children to four staff members.

■*Ask about their resources and daily program of activities.*
Make sure that your child will have plenty of opportunities for play and rest, a variety of playthings in good condition, and ample space to roam indoors and outdoors.

■*Ask about policies and procedures regarding discipline, safety, sickness, and visitation.*
Policies and procedures regarding discipline should be harmonious with those you have at home. The facilities should be fully "childproof" and hygienic. Parents should be free to visit the service at any time during the hours it is open.

■*Ask for references.*
Get the names and addresses or phone numbers of at least three families who relied on the service for an extensive period of time. Be sure to follow up on these references and to discuss any complaints you hear with the service itself.

■*Observe the day-care facility and personnel at work before you enroll your child.*
Check for the following:

> ■ How competent are staff members in dealing with children of different ages and temperaments?
>
> ■ How effective are staff members in giving care and encouragement to each individual child?
>
> ■ Do the various activities during the day seem well scheduled, well planned, and well run?
>
> ■ Do the children seem to like the staff members?
>
> ■ How safe and clean is the facility?
>
> ■ Is there plenty of well-equipped space for different types of individual and group activities?
>
> ■ How safely and effectively do staff members handle crises, such as illnesses, injuries, or emergency situations?

■How hygienically and efficiently do they change diapers? Illnesses commonly spread from one child to another in day care due to staff members not washing their hands or the station between changes.

■ *Visit the day-care facility from time to time while your child is in its care.*

Periodic firsthand observation for at least an hour each visit is the best way to tell if your child remains emotionally well adjusted to day-care life as time goes by. Try to be discreet during your visit, allowing staff members and your child to go about their usual routines without interference.

■ *Investigate possible sources for any unhappiness you or your child may have about the day-care service.*

It's better to be overly cautious than lax in this regard, for your own peace of mind, for your child's, and for the reputation of the service itself.

■ *Don't hesitate to change day-care services if you feel yours is unsatisfactory.*

Very young children are emotionally resilient enough to handle a switch in day-care services with little trouble, and it's much better to switch than to leave a child in a service that you don't wholeheartedly like.

Early Education: Yes or No?

As distinct from nursery schools, do academically enriched programs for preschoolers give them a head start toward scholastic success in life? Research to date offers no evidence that they do and suggests that an educationally enriched home life provides all the intellectual stimulation a very young child needs or can handle.

Children under six learn better through the type of spontaneous activity associated with play than they do through the controlled, pressurized format of adult-driven learning programs. The major reason has to do with brain development.

While many children under six may be capable of the type of rote learning required for performing simple math calculations and even reading words, most children in this age range still have a couple of years to go before they've developed the physical brain-cell connections necessary for the cognitive skills that underlie lasting academic intelligence. Among these skills are recognizing patterns, envisioning spaces, and sustaining an attention span. As a result, any academic gains that are made by a three- or four-year-old tend to be lost by the time the child is six, by which time "unschooled" peers can quickly catch up.

Another reason why children do not seem to benefit from preschool learning has to do with their emotional makeup. Expert observers have concluded that while very young children in academically enriched programs can derive personal satisfaction from pleasing their parents with what they've learned, they are also prone to be more anxious, less creative, and less positive toward "schooling" in general than children who are not in such programs.

Added to these potential problems is the often overlooked risk of failure. Children under six do not take losing well, and academically enriched programs inevitably set up standards that some children simply may not be able to achieve—or may not be able to reach at a desired rate. Such an inability to meet expectations can have a negative impact not only on the child's feelings but also on those of the parents, try as the latter might to be indifferent and accepting no matter how their child performs.

For all the disclaimers about the effectiveness or value of preschool educational programs, more testing still needs to be done before we can dismiss preschool education entirely. However, we do know enough now to say that parents should not assume that such programs are necessary in order for their child to live up to her or his intellectual potential, nor should parents push their child to cooperate with such programs if she or he seems resistant.

Other points to consider about preschool education are as follows:

■ *Guard against imposing your personal values and ambitions on your child.*

Granted, it's often very difficult to draw a line between what you would want for yourself and what is best for your child. Nevertheless, as far as academic matters go, try as much as possible to follow your child's lead.

First see what your child is *naturally* interested in doing or learning, then experiment with different ways to cultivate those interests. Being too quick to steer your child toward certain preconceived areas of—and approaches toward—learning may prevent you and your child from realizing her or his most promising talents.

■ *Expose your child to a variety of intellectually stimulating toys, resources, and activities.*

The very best things you can do at home to increase your child's love of knowledge are to read to, tell stories to, and talk seriously with your child about subjects that interest her or him. Also, treat your child frequently to short, educationally enriching excursions outside the home: for example, to a nature preserve, a science museum, a zoo, or a factory.

■ *Give your child many opportunities to interact with other people, including adults as well as children.*

Researchers have found that children attending preschool educational programs do seem to have better social skills than those who do not. In fact, some experts feel that the sheer interactivity among children, their peers, and their adult teachers that is built into these programs fuels a great deal of the learning that occurs.

There are a number of ways that you can provide your child with similarly interactive experiences. Attending a day-care service will give her or him a certain amount of exposure to other children and adults; but there are other measures you should consider instead of, or in addition to, day care. Set up regular times for your child to play with other children. Encourage your friends and relatives to spend time with your child. Include your child in your own group activities whenever appropriate.

When your child is three and a half to five years old and fairly mature in social situations, consider enrollment in a nursery school, which concentrates on developing a very young child's play and social skills. To choose a good nursery school for your child, follow the same basic procedures recommended here for choosing a good day-care center.

CASE:

"So Help Me, Harry!"

Jeff's son (now eight years old) had experienced several difficult weeks making the transition to day care: crying each morning before it was time to leave, clinging to whichever parent drove him to the day-care center, and acting withdrawn and resentful the first hour that he was back at home. After several visits to the center and interviews with staff members, Jeff had determined that the problem was separation anxiety.

To help make sure that his three-year-old daughter, Crystal, did not suffer as badly, Jeff decided to begin acclimating Crystal to the upcoming change in her routine about a month in advance. Gradually, day by day, Crystal spent more and more time with a baby-sitter. After two weeks, Jeff introduced a new ritual: telling a story to Crystal just before it was time for her to be with the baby-sitter. The very first story he told can be summarized as follows:

A little girl went out into the yard and found a beautiful little doll. After playing with the doll for a while and making it smile and laugh, she noticed that the doll was crying. The doll admitted that she belonged to another little girl who had lost her and that she didn't know how to get back home. The little girl said what her mother [like Crystal's mother] always said when she was stumped: "So help me, Harry!" All at once, a magical elf named Harry appeared and told the little girl who owned the doll and how to get in touch with this person.

Thereafter, the stories that Jeff told Crystal at this particular time of the day were always about Harry coming to help the little girl in various ways. Not only did these storytelling sessions enable Jeff and Crystal to enjoy each other's company just before a temporary separation, but also the running theme of the stories subconsciously gave Crystal confidence that she could call on her own "special power" to help her meet special challenges. By the time day care began, Crystal was used to being separated from her father, plus she actually looked forward to leaving home because that stage of the day began with a "So Help Me, Harry!" story.

15.
Psychotherapy

When children under six years old are going through a sustained period of moodiness or troublesome behavior, worried parents typically take solace in this favorite piece of popular wisdom on the subject: "Ignore it! The kid will outgrow it!" These words not only hold out hope; they also cater to the parents' instinctive and understandable wish to deny that their children might be seriously disturbed.

Sometimes this "ignore" policy turns out to be harmless. From birth to age six, children are developing so rapidly in every regard—physically and emotionally, intellectually and spiritually, socially and personally—that a certain number of transient, "phase-related" problems are inevitable.

In many cases, however, this policy runs counter to the best interests of the child or the family. Unfortunately, only time will tell whether ignoring a given problem is harmless or harmful.

Far better advice for parents is *never* to ignore a child's emotional difficulties, regardless of how young she or he may be. At the very least, a parent faced with such difficulties should be *extra* vigilant. On the one hand, the alert parent may get an unexpected opportunity to help the child resolve her or his problems in the quickest and most constructive manner. On the other hand, those problems may get much worse, either so suddenly that only an alert parent will be able to respond in time or so gradually that only an alert parent will be able to tell that it's happening.

In addition to being extra vigilant whenever a very young child is going through emotional difficulties, a parent should be ever mindful of her or his powers and limitations as far as child rearing is concerned. All on their own, parents can make an enormous, positive difference in how their very young children cope emotionally with the stresses and strains of daily life as well as with the pressures and pains of self-development. But there may come times when even the most competent parents are unable to read a child's distress signals, assist a child in overcoming her or his problems, or change a family situation that is causing or aggravating a child's problems. When these times come, parents shouldn't hesitate to seek professional help.

Parents commonly appreciate the fact that any emotional turmoil experienced by a very young child is also likely to affect the family as a whole. They have a much more difficult time accepting the possibility that their own personal problems as parents may actually be fueling that emotional turmoil in the first place. Mixed feelings of pride, shame, hope, fear, responsibility, and guilt interfere with this type of self-knowledge.

Parenting a very young child is one of the most challenging tasks an individual, or a couple, can undertake. First-time parents may find that the transition from an adult-oriented home life to a child-oriented home life is far more complicated and traumatic than they could ever have anticipated. Parents who already have children may have trouble balancing all the new demands on their time and attention while still preserving space for themselves, their marriage, and their other children.

And then there is the issue of the parent's personality versus the child's personality. Frequently, parents are doing all the "right" things, the child is developing "normally," and their life together is free of any "typical" cause for emotional disturbance. Nevertheless, the child's behavior clearly indicates distress. In such cases, the real problem may simply be a poor fit between the personality of the child and that of the parent. This possibility easily gets overlooked by parents of very young children, who erroneously assume that parent-child personality clashes can occur only when a child is older and more independent.

Parents must always keep in mind that a child has a very distinct personality from birth onward and that it may not be automatically compatible with the personalities of her or his parents. An unusually bold child may be confronted with an unusually cautious mother. A very playful father may be surprised by a very serious child. An exceptionally reserved couple may wind up with an exceptionally demonstrative child. Thus, both first-time and experienced parents may discover that a child presents them with specific, personality-related problems in addition to the general problems associated with parenting.

In any of these problematic parenting scenarios, the result can be doubts, resentments, anxieties, and frustrations that may easily lead to troublesome complications. Parents may unwittingly develop an overall child-rearing style that's inappropriately intense, casual, or erratic. Open conflicts may frequently break out between parent and child or between parent and parent.

Ultimately, as the parent-child relationship or the parent-parent relationship continues to be stressful, one or both of the parents may succumb to parental "burnout." Characterized by physical and emotional depression, parental burnout often leads to an involuntary carelessness that subtly undermines the psychological health of every individual in the family.

Just as it's perfectly normal for parents of very young children to have these problems, it should also be appropriate for parents experiencing such problems to consult a child psychologist, a child psychiatrist, or a social worker specializing in child and family psychotherapy. Such an individual is well qualified to assist both parents and children within a family in working through the causes and effects of their emotional problems.

Diagnostic techniques and treatments involving children under six years old vary considerably according to the specific situation. When the child is too young to talk, parental interviews are especially important. Parents are asked about their perceptions of their child and about their relationship with their child and with other family members, including their own parents.

To get a more intimate picture of how parents interact with their nonspeaking child, doctors or therapists also usually observe the parents playing with the child, bathing the child, feeding the child, and/or changing the child's diapers. Often doctors or therapists play with the child themselves to test how she or he responds to a stranger and to a variety of stimuli (such as different voices, expressions, and games). If it appears possible that a physical condition may be responsible for the child's behavior, then relevant medical tests are recommended.

When the child is old enough to talk, doctors and therapists often try "play therapy" in addition to age-appropriate variations of the procedures already mentioned. In play therapy, a child acts out emotions and discusses concerns in the contest of playing with dolls, toys, and games provided by the doctor or therapist.

Play therapy's indirect approach to eliciting a child's feelings and experiences avoids some of the problems that can arise in directly interviewing someone this young. Potential problems of this nature include the chance that the questions themselves might "lead" the responses; the risk that the child might be frightened by the dialogue; and the possibility that the child's replies might be inaccurate because of comprehension or communication difficulties or the child's wish to conceal the truth due to fear, guilt, or a desire to please.

Whatever complications may be involved in psychotherapy for a child under six, it is well worth considering if you are at an impasse in understanding or managing an emotional problem that your child has been exhibiting for several weeks on a fairly persistent basis. Many of the emotional problems that torment an individual at a later age have their origin in the early years of life. If these problems had been addressed when they were still in their initial stage of development, then years of needless suffering might have been avoided.

Here are some issues to consider in finding the right doctor or therapist for you, your child, and your family:

---

1. Before you begin your search, establish what you consider to be the problem you want addressed and the goal you want achieved.

First, write down your answers to the following five questions, bearing in mind that some of your answers may overlap.

a. What specific behaviors have I observed indicating that my child may be experiencing emotional turmoil? (To whatever extent possible, give dates, times of day, settings, and circumstantial surroundings.)

b. How would I define this emotional turmoil? (In other words, if you had to make a diagnosis, what would it be?)

c. What might be the cause(s) of this turmoil? (Include any speculations as well as any more conclusive opinions you may have—being careful to distinguish between these two categories.)

d. In what different ways has this emotional turmoil been bothersome or detrimental to my child, to me, and to other members of the family? (Be as specific as possible, as you were directed in answering question a.)

e. How have I tried to better the situation? (Indicate which methods have been at least partially successful and which have failed altogether).

Once you have answered all five questions to the best of your ability, write down a fairly succinct (one- or two-sentence) description of what you think the *problem* is. Next, write an equally succinct description of the *goal* that you want to achieve related to this problem: that is, what you would like to see happen *as a result* of psychotherapeutic intervention.

These statements, as well as the question-and-answer background material, will be enormously helpful to you in interviewing possible doctors or therapists. They will also be enormously helpful to the doctor or therapist you choose in her or his efforts to diagnose and treat your child successfully.

2. *Familiarize yourself with the major types of therapy that are available.*

The sheer variety of therapy labels is bewildering to the outsider: psychoanalytic (Freudian, Jungian, Adlerian, or otherwise), cognitive, behavioral, existential, Gestalt, transactional, reality-oriented, rational-emotive, and so on. However, for the purpose of interviewing potential doctors or therapists to work with a child under six years old, all you need is a very basic awareness of three broad categories of psychotherapy: psychodynamic therapy, behavioral therapy, and family-oriented therapy.

■ *Psychodynamic therapy* is geared toward getting the child to identify, understand, and self-manage her or his emotional problems. Because it depends heavily on effective verbal communication between the doctor or therapist and the child, it is not appropriate for children who have not begun to speak fairly fluently. (Usually this means children under four years old.) It also tends to be relatively long-term compared to the other categories of psychotherapy, often involving multiple sessions per week for up to a year or two.

■ *Behavioral therapy* is geared toward getting the child to change the way she or he behaves. Instead of focusing squarely on the causes of a particular problem, it concentrates on the symptoms. For example, it might help children learn to control their anger without necessarily getting them to appreciate why they get angry, to be less scared of nightmares regardless of whether they know about their possible source, or to interact more cooperatively with other people even if their feelings about them remain unresolved. It typically takes at least a few months of weekly or biweekly sessions before satisfactory results can be expected.

■ *Family-oriented therapy*, sometimes known as "systems therapy," is one of the types of therapy practiced at Philadelphia Child Guidance Center (PCGC) and the type that PCGC recommends most highly for children of any age, but especially for children under six years old. Drawing upon both psychodynamic therapy and behavioral therapy, family-oriented therapy is geared toward generating positive awareness and change in all aspects of the child's world: her or his own mind and behavior as well as the minds and behaviors of those people who directly influence her or his life. In comparison to the other therapies, it is much more adaptable to the situation at hand. Satisfactory results may be achieved in just one or two sessions or may take up to a year or two.

Use these very basic distinctions as beginning points for discussing with other people (such as knowledgeable advisers and potential doctors or therapists) the particular type or types of psychotherapy that may be appropriate to your unique situation. Also, investigate the literature about child psychotherapy that's available at local libraries and bookstores. The more informed you are about it—whatever form it may take—the more benefit you'll derive from the type of psychotherapy you finally choose, whatever it may be.

3. Familiarize yourself with the major types of doctors and therapists that are available.

The three most common practitioners of child-oriented psychotherapy are psychiatrists, psychologists, and social workers. Regardless of the specific title (e.g., "psychiatrist"), not all of these practitioners have special training or experience in treating children in particular as opposed to people in general. This is an important issue that you will want to investigate with individual practitioners that you interview.

Also, keep in mind that one type of practitioner, all else being equal, is not necessarily more or less desirable than another. Your final determination should be based on how appropriate the individual practitioner is, given the following factors: your child's problem, the goals you've established relating to that problem, the type of therapy you're interested in pursuing, your financial resources, and most important of all, the overall personalities of you and your child.

These warnings having been given, here are brief descriptions of each major type of practitioner:

■*Psychiatrists* are medical doctors (M.D.s), which means that they have had four years of medical school, one year of internship, and at least two years of residency training in psychiatry. In addition, virtually all child psychiatrists have had two-year fellowships in child psychiatry and are board certified.

One major advantage of a psychiatrist over other types of practitioners is that she or he can diagnose and prescribe treatment for physical problems that may be causing or aggravating a child's emotional problems. A possible disadvantage, depending on your particular situation, is that some psychiatrists (usually not *child* psychiatrists) are inclined to practice only psychodynamic forms of therapy.

■*Psychologists* have usually earned a doctorate (Ph.D.) in psychology, typically the result of five years of graduate training, including several supervised clinical programs and a year of formal internship. Most states also require postdoctoral experience before licensing. Some states, however, require only a master's degree (M.A.) to become a psychologist.

Although psychologists themselves cannot offer physical diagnosis and prescription, they almost always have close professional relationships with physicians whom they can recommend for such services. They are also likely to be more eclectic in their therapeutic style, although there is still a trend among psychologists to favor behavioral therapy.

■ *Social workers* have earned a master's degree in social work (M.S.W.), a process that involves two years of classes and fieldwork. In addition, some states require two or more years of postgraduate experience before licensing.

While social workers may not have had the extensive academic and clinical training that psychiatrists and psychologists have had, they are, as a rule, much more familiar with—and knowledgeable about—the home, community, and school environments of their clients. This background inclines them to practice family-oriented or systems-oriented therapy more than other types of therapy.

Another major issue to consider in choosing a particular type of doctor or therapist is whether the therapy will occur in a *private office* or a *clinic*. Other factors aside, therapy performed in clinics tends to be more multidimensional: a by-product of the fact that clinics are so often staffed with various types of doctors and therapists, who not only practice different kinds of therapy but also conduct different kinds of research projects.

---

4. Make a rough estimate of how much you can afford to spend on your child's therapy.

It may be impossible to put a price on a child's emotional well-being. However, it's quite possible to determine how much you can afford to spend for psychotherapy without making life much more difficult for yourself and your family—a situation that could only exacerbate your child's emotional problems.

You may have insurance that will cover some or all of the expenses directly incurred as a result of your child's therapy; but in the best of situations there are bound to be some hidden costs. Factor into your budget such possibilities as lost income for days off work, transportation and parking for therapy sessions, and baby-sitting care for other children while you are at the sessions.

In estimating how much you can afford for the therapy itself, take into account that private therapy is almost certain to be more expensive than therapy in a clinic. Also, clinics may offer lower fees if you accept therapy from a supervised student therapist or agree to participate in a research project (which typically means being observed, taped, and/or interviewed).

5. Seek several recommendations from a variety of qualified sources.

Ask relatives and friends who have benefited from the services of child psychiatrists, psychologists, or social workers for their opinions, but also seek leads from more experienced and disinterested parties, such as your pediatrician, family physician, and clergyperson. For the names of certified practitioners in your area, contact local and national mental-health and professional organizations (see Appendix for a list of suggestions).

6. Interview different doctors and therapists thoroughly about their credentials, areas of expertise, and therapeutic techniques.

Among the specific questions you should ask are the following:

■ What is your educational and training background (see issue 3)?

■ Are you board certified? By whom?

■ With what professional organizations are you affiliated (see Appendix for a list)?

■ How long have you practiced in your current capacity?

■ What is your general or preferred style of therapy (see issue 2)?

■ What are your areas of special expertise?

■ How much work have you done with children who are the same age as my child?

■ How much work have you done with the type of problem(s) my child is having (see issue 1)?

■ Would you feel committed to achieving the goal I have in mind (see issue 1)?

■ What kinds of services can I expect from you toward meeting this goal?

■ What kinds of commitment and cooperation would you expect from me and my family in the course of my child's therapy?

■ How, and at what rate, will you keep me informed of the progress my child is making in therapy?

■ How much time do you estimate the therapy might take?

■ How much will it cost, will my insurance or medical assistance help pay the cost, and are there ways to reduce the cost (see issue 4)?

7. *Make sure that you choose a doctor or therapist who respects you and with whom you are comfortable.*

Some doctors or therapists may unintentionally cause you to feel guilty or incompetent, in which case you should look for someone else. The doctor or therapist you select should be a person who inspires you to feel good about yourself: *re*moralized instead of *de*moralized.

Your answer to each of the following questions should be yes both during your initial interview with a doctor or therapist and throughout the time that the therapy itself is in progress:

■ Does the doctor or therapist take into account *your* theories, opinions, and concerns as well as her or his own?

■ Does the interaction you have with the doctor or therapist seem like a dialogue rather than a monologue on the doctor's or therapist's part?

■ Does the doctor or therapist seem genuinely interested in you and your situation (evidenced by her or his paying close attention to you, maintaining fairly consistent eye contact with you, and regularly soliciting your comments and reactions)?

■ Does the doctor or therapist seem genuinely interested in your child and her or his problems?

■ Does the doctor or therapist make sure that you understand what she or he is doing and saying?

■ Does the doctor or therapist answer all of your questions promptly, thoughtfully, and to the best of her or his ability?

■ Do you leave the doctor's or therapist's company feeling clear about the direction that your child's case will be taking?

■ Do you leave the doctor's or therapist's company feeling generally stronger rather than weaker?

Possible Symptoms of Emotional Problems: Birth to Age Six

BIRTH TO SIX MONTHS

■ failure to put on weight or develop physically within "normal" parameters

■ indifference to feeding

■ poor eye contact and indifference to human voice and play

■ persistent sleep disturbance (apart from colic-related sleep loss or simply not sleeping through the night)

■ hypersensitivity to sights and sounds

■ ticlike movements of face and hands

■ rumination (swallowing regurgitated foods)

SIX MONTHS TO ONE YEAR

■ persistent self-injurious behavior (other than "normal" rocking and head banging)

■ lack of any discernible pattern in sleeping and eating

■ failure to imitate sounds and gestures

■ persistent lack of appropriate emotional response to surprises, fearful situations, or pleasurable stimuli

■ generalized apathy

■ persistent lack of distress when confronted with strangers

■ significant delays in "normal" cognitive and motor development

ONE TO TWO YEARS

■ withdrawn behavior

■ excessive rocking and posturing

■ persistent lack of distress when separated from parents

■ excessive distractibility

■ frequent irritability that does not respond to calming efforts (apart from occasional tantrums)

■ night wandering

TWO TO THREE YEARS

■ persistent fearfulness

■ failure to make efforts to talk

■ inability to play in any focused manner for ten minutes at a time

■ intense and ongoing sibling conflict

■ hyperactivity

■ persistent and excessive aggressiveness

■ slow recovery from angry outbursts

■ severe and prolonged reaction to separation from parents

THREE TO SIX YEARS

■ frequent incidents of self-punishing or self-injurious behavior

■ frequent and severe conflicts with other children

■ persistent withdrawal from other children

■ general inability to follow rules or directions

■ persistent refusal to talk

■ sudden, noticeable, and long-lasting declines in general self-confidence, attentiveness, or interest

■ persistent depression

Special Diagnoses: Children Under Six

MENTAL RETARDATION

Mental retardation is a very general descriptive term applied to any child who exhibits these two characteristics: (1) an intelligence quotient (IQ) that is *significantly* below normal; (2) *considerable* problems in adapting to everyday life. Retardation in very young children may be complicated by physical problems, such as difficulty in hearing, seeing, or speaking. It may also be complicated by emotional problems, such as ongoing frustration, anxiety, withdrawal, or rebellion. These emotional problems can be associated either with the retarded child's awareness of her or his retardation (most retarded children recognize that they are different from "normal" children) or with her or his general lack of coping abilities.

Mild mental retardation is frequently difficult to diagnose before a child reaches age three, the earliest time at which a reliable IQ test can be administered. In some cases, however, mental retardation is so profound that a diagnosis can be made much sooner. A child may fail completely to reach cognitive, behavioral, and emotional milestones in her or his development, much less to meet them within the "normal" parameters set by experts in child development.

The leading physical cause of mental retardation is *Down syndrome*, a genetic disorder that is also one of the most common birth defects. Today the chance of an American woman's giving birth to a Down child is about 1 in 1,500 when she is under twenty-four, increasing to about 1 in 100 by the time she is forty. Characterized by distinctive facial features—eye folds that make the eyes look slanted, sunken cheekbones, and a protruding tongue—as well as by other physical characteristics, like poor muscle tone, Down syndrome can almost always be diagnosed at birth.

Contrary to popular misconceptions, most mentally retarded children, including children affected by Down syndrome, can learn a great deal, can maintain emotional stability, and, as adults, can lead relatively independent lives. Most important, they can enjoy their lives as much as anyone else. For the most part, they do not require permanent institutionalization; and federal law guarantees them educational as well as other services at public expense.

A very comprehensive evaluation is vital in assessing a retarded child's true developmental and educational potential. Such an evaluation is almost certain to coordinate consultation with a number of different specialists in neurology, hearing, speech, vision, physical therapy, or special education as well as in psychiatry. It's best to perform this evaluation as early in the child's life as possible. The earlier parents know about the very particular nature of their child's retardation, and the earlier they expose their child to intervention programs, the greater the opportunity to effect positive change in her or his physical and emotional well-being.

AUTISM

Autism is a developmental disorder characterized mainly by a child's persistent and severe lack of responsiveness to others as well as severe language problems. The actual cause is unknown. Typically, an autistic child is one who doesn't cuddle, make eye contact, speak, or even make gestures or facial expressions to communicate feelings.

Autism almost always manifests itself within the first three years of a child's life. In addition to the symptoms already mentioned, psychotherapists look for one or more of the following signs:

■ a tendency toward unusual and repetitive movements, such as arm flapping, rigid posturing, stomping, and spinning (older children may develop bizarre and complex rituals associated with bedtime or mealtime);

■ speech oddities, such as persistent "singsong" or monotonous talk;

■ extreme responses to normal occurrences, such as an inconsolable panic reaction to a doorbell ringing;

■ extreme attachment to, or avoidance of, particular objects in the environment, such as a fan, a shoe, or a table;

■ routine self-mutilating behavior, such as cutting oneself with scissors or knives.

Autistic children can usually be helped to lead more "normal" and independent lives with the combination of a more structured environment and proper teaching, training, and motivation. Depending on the particular range of symptoms, sedative or tranquilizing drugs may also be prescribed. Some autistic children can be fully rehabilitated, but many bear some traces of the disorder throughout their lives.

Besides working directly with the autistic child, psychotherapists can help the family as a whole resolve the stress that's commonly associated with having an autistic family member living in the same household. Unlike a child with Down syndrome, who often manifests a happy and loving personality, an autistic child doesn't automatically invite tolerance and compassion. The illness is simply too alien for most people to appreciate. Psychotherapists enable individual family members, regardless of their age, not only to understand autism but also to deal effectively with problem situations the autistic child may create and support her or his progress toward a more emotionally fulfilling life.

ATTENTION-DEFICIT HYPERACTIVITY DISORDER

By far the most common psychiatric disorder of childhood, with an overall prevalence rate of 5 percent, attention-deficit hyperactivity disorder (ADHD) may not be discovered or diagnosed until a child is of school age. At that point, it manifests itself fairly unmistakably as a combination of restlessness, noisiness, an inability to sit still or concentrate, poor socialization, and poor scholastic performance. Nevertheless, the disorder has its roots in much earlier stages of a child's development. In fact, one of the commonly accepted criteria for a professional diagnosis of ADHD is that there must have been indications of the disorder *prior* to school age.

The causes of ADHD are generally biochemical in nature. In infants and toddlers, ADHD manifests itself in excessive crying, sleeping problems, feeding difficulties, and a host of other "troublesome behaviors," including, possibly, colic. In children from three to six years old, it usually shows up as excessive motor activity, difficulty paying attention or listening, aggressiveness, and an extremely short attention span.

Psychotherapists who suspect ADHD from a very young child's history will recommend a medical evaluation to determine if there may be some alternative explanation for her or his symptoms: for example, a hearing impairment, hyperthyroidism, a seizure-related condition, or an allergy. If ADHD does seem to be the source of the child's problems, then the psychotherapist helps the child and the family develop coping strategies—for example, procedures that will keep the child focused on individual tasks as they present themselves and help the child pace her- or himself through the performance of each task in an appropriate manner. In cases in which a diagnosis of ADHD is indisputable, medication may also be prescribed.

At PCGC:
Preschool At-Risk
Program

Families in which there is a history of mental illness, substance abuse, or child abuse often require special assistance. Parents need to develop better parenting skills through building their level of confidence and comfort in dealing with their children. Children need to receive the particular care and education that will enable them to overcome their problems and live more competent lives.

PCGC's Preschool At-Risk Program helps families who fall into the above-mentioned "at risk" categories. Children in the program are drawn from the preschool population and are referred to the program by teachers and caretakers as well as by the Social Work Department of The Children's Hospital of Philadelphia and the Child Development Department of Children's Seashore House.

Specifically, the program offers the following services:

EVALUATIONS

Each child is given a psychoeducational assessment to determine levels of functioning, and home visits are conducted to assess how well the family functions. From these assessments, an individual program plan is developed. If appropriate, other, more specialized assessments are performed by psychologists, psychiatrists, and/or speech therapists.

CLASSROOM WORK

The work in the program's special classroom format involves the family as a whole and integrates family therapy with educational activities. The three main objectives of the classroom approach are as follows:

1. to create learning tasks that are relevant to the child's developmental level, parental concerns, and issues involving parent-child interactions;

2. to devise successful interpersonal transactions that draw upon and reinforce parental competence;

3. to assist parents in changing their child's behavior and in helping her or him develop cognitive, intellectual, and social skills.

FAMILY THERAPY

This service is provided by a preschool therapist in the program. The therapist meets with families on a weekly basis, either alone, in concert with a psychoeducational therapist, or in the context of the program's classroom.

PARENT SUPPORT GROUP

The parent support group offers an opportunity for parents in the program to come together and discuss general issues related to raising young children as well as specific issues that they are addressing in family therapy or the classroom. By asking questions of one another, sharing experiences, and extending advice, group members come to feel less alienated and more involved in a network of concerned parents. The result is a living, evolving resource that any member can tap: for personal relief, for crisis-related information, for baby-sitting, or for family socializing.

Aside from these services, the Preschool At-Risk Program also features several outreach components:

■ A Community Involvement Team (consisting of a psychoeducational specialist and a program therapist) periodically visits families in their home environment. There the team assists families in applying the knowledge they acquired through family therapy and/or the classroom, evaluating the progress they have made in managing difficulties, and identifying any further needs.

■ A model program developed by the Preschool At-Risk Program helps integrate specialized preschool services (e.g., speech therapy) with normal preschool programs, such as Head Start. The effect of this "mainstreaming" is a reduction of the psychologically damaging segregation and isolation that at-risk children with special needs must otherwise endure.

■ The Preschool At-Risk Program coordinates its services with many existing human services agencies and volunteer groups to better serve the parents and children in the program. It also maintains a very strong collaborative relationship with The Children's Hospital of Philadelphia.

If your child, or a child you know, may benefit from a program of this type, consult a local mental-health organization. There may be a similar program in your area.

The Early Years: Selected Terms and Concepts

acting out   indirectly expressing emotional conflicts—or "forbidden feelings"—through negative behavior. Such behavior is typically overdramatic and designed to attract attention. It may or may not be overtly self-punishing or injurious to others. For example, a child who feels rejected by a parent may "act out" that feeling by refusing to speak to that parent, constantly trying to distract the parent, talking back, or picking fights with a sibling who appears to be getting more attention.

affective disorder   also known as *emotional disorder* or *mood disorder*, a specifically defined psychological illness relating to the emotions (e.g., *attention-deficit hyperactivity disorder*). Generally, such a disorder is apparent in the problematic manner in which a child physically displays emotions (hence, the root "affect"). The disorder may also have a physical cause.

attachment   the emotional bond between parent and child. Most often the term is used in reference to the child's bond to the mother, although attachment is a two-way street and also forms between child and father.

Attachment between child and mother is uniquely strong because of the latter's role in childbearing and early caretaking. Conditioned to seek closeness with the mother, the child may suffer emotional difficulties if deprived of maternal affection or if that affection becomes overly demanding.

attention-deficit hyperactivity disorder   an affective disorder involving certain severe and interrelated behavioral problems, such as chronic restlessness, an inability to concentrate or finish tasks, and poor listening skills. In most cases, the disorder is not detected until the child enters school and experiences academic difficulties.

autism   a developmental disorder characterized by a persistent and severe lack of responsiveness to others as well as severe language problems.

behavior modeling   a therapeutic technique by means of which the child is taught or encouraged to replace negative behaviors with more positive ones. The teaching or encouraging process involves modifying the way that each parent or caretaker interacts with the child so that the child learns by example or direct experience (e.g., a reward system) to behave more constructively.

conduct disorder   a psychological problem manifested in chronic, excessively unruly behaviors, such as stealing, running away, lying, or setting fires.

defiance   more technically known as *oppositional behavior*, defiance refers to any act on the part of a child that is intentionally designed to challenge parental authority. Common examples include saying no, refusing to perform assigned tasks, and deliberately withdrawing from meals and other prearranged family activities.

distractibility   a problematic behavior involving a limited ability to concentrate on a single activity for an appropriate amount of time. Distractibility can be a sign of underlying anxiety, or it can lead to anxiety. It can also be a symptom of *attention-deficit hyperactivity disorder.*

dysfunctional   as opposed to *functional*, a term used to describe a personality or family unit that does not operate effectively or satisfactorily to meet day-to-day life challenges. In some cases, there is apparent effectiveness or satisfaction, but achieving it causes underlying psychological damage. In other cases, the personality or family unit is clearly having problems that pose a threat to its survival.

This term is sociological in origin and is rapidly losing currency in the field of psychology. Many therapists consider it too negative and abstract to be useful diagnostically.

emotional disorder   (see *affective disorder*)

extroversion   a generally outgoing attitude toward the world at large. First defined by Carl Jung, extroversion is also associated with a relatively strong interest in social interactions and concrete realities and a relatively weak interest in self-contained activities and abstract thought.

Extroversion is assumed to be an inborn personality trait that is neither positive nor negative in essence and that can be modified only slightly by experience or conditioning. The opposite quality is *introversion*.

functional   (see *dysfunctional*)

identification   a means of bolstering one's own self-image by associating it with someone else's self-image, either consciously or unconsciously. For a child in the early years, the most common form of identification is with the same-sex parent. However, the object of identification can be anyone—regardless of sex or age—who possesses physical, psychological, or social qualities that the identifier admires or considers absent or deficient in her or his personal identity.

In most cases, the process of identification is a normal and healthy stage in the child's self-development. The form it takes varies according to the individual and may or may not be detectable on the surface. Most often, it involves spending a lot of time around the object of identification, mimicking that person's behavior or extending unqualified devotion and service to that person.

individuation   in the philosophy of Carl Jung, the long process by which a child evolves from being totally dependent on others, emotionally and socially, to being a separate and successful individual with a unique, self-sustaining psychological makeup.

introversion   a generally inward-looking attitude toward the world at large. First defined by Carl Jung, introversion is also associated with a relatively strong interest in self-contained activities and abstract thought and a relatively mild interest in social interactions and concrete realities.

Introversion is assumed to be an inborn personality trait that is neither positive nor negative in essence and that can be modified only slightly by experience or conditioning. The opposite quality is *extroversion*.

maladaptation   also known as *maladjustment*, this term refers to a child's inability to react in a calm, effective, or successful manner either to a single life change or to the demands of life in general.

maladjustment   (see *maladaptation*)

mood disorder   (see *affective disorder*)

oppositional behavior   (see *defiance*)

other-directed behavior   individual actions that are oriented toward other people: for example, seeking attention, initiating and responding to interactions, expressing hostility. Therapists often explore whether a child has a healthy, age-appropriate balance of other-directed behavior and its opposite, *self-directed behavior.*

overanxious disorder   a psychological problem manifesting itself in chronic, generalized, and often irrational feelings of fear, apprehension, and misgiving. There may also be physical symptoms, such as frequent headaches and stomachaches.

overcorrection   a negative effect of the parent-child relationship in which the discipline or punishment imposed on a child's conduct—or the child's "reforming" response to discipline or punishment—exceeds appropriate limits.

phobia   an excessive and persistent fear of particular people, things, or situations. (Precise targets vary from individual to individual.) Phobias are fairly common among children in their early years. Most often they are transitory and not indicative of any serious psychological problem.

projection   an unconscious, self-protecting measure in which a child denies negative, forbidden, or unpleasant feelings and instead attributes them to someone else. In most cases, the person upon whom the child projects such negative feelings is the trigger for them. For example, a child who is angry at Mother may unconsciously reclaim her or his innocence by believing instead that Mother is angry at her or him.

psychopathology   the study of mental illnesses. The term "pathology" refers to a disease or a disorder, as opposed to a less severe problem.

repression   a means of emotional self-protection in which traumatic thoughts or memories are automatically relegated to the unconscious mind and forgotten by the conscious mind. In older children, thoughts or memories that are merely unpleasant may also be repressed, along with traumatic thoughts or memories.

resilience   a child's ability to adapt effectively to change or recover effectively from a crisis. Children that have more resilient emotional natures are likelier to be healthier psychologically.

self-directed behavior individual actions that are oriented around the self: for example, solitary play or self-punishment. Therapists often explore whether a child has a healthy, age-appropriate balance of self-directed behavior and its opposite, *other-directed behavior*.

temperament a child's inborn character, which forms the basis of the later-developing personality. Generally speaking, an individual temperament involves a certain combination of behavioral dispositions that can be modified only slightly by later experience. For example, a child may be temperamentally predisposed toward *extroversion* or *introversion*.

"Temperament" is a very loosely defined term. Various schools of psychological thought differ over which emotional characteristics are primarily a matter of temperament, as opposed to being primarily a matter of acquired personality.

withdrawal a child's willful separation, emotionally or physically, from an event or person that is somehow distressing. In most cases involving very young children, withdrawal is a temporary delaying tactic rather than a more entrenched, long-term, and far-reaching posture. For example, a very young child who is angry with a parent or perceives the parent as being angry with her or him may withdraw from that parent for a while but will quickly abandon such behavior once the feeling or perception passes or is alleviated.

Part Two: The Middle Years

AGE SIX TO AGE THIRTEEN

Part Two:
The
Middle
Years
AGE SIX TO AGE THIRTEEN

Introduction

The transition from being a preschool child to being a school-age child can be likened to that amphibious period in evolutionary history when animals first began living on land as well as in water. From age six to age thirteen, human beings live in a privileged middle phase between babyhood, when they are physically and intellectually underdeveloped and completely dependent on their parents, and puberty, when they so dramatically enter the final stage of their maturing process and their dependence on their parents.

From a child's perspective, the middle period of childhood is an especially glorious time of first discovering all the wonders of kinship, friendship, education, and life itself. However, the middle years are also especially vulnerable ones, filled with all sorts of intimidating new duties and challenges.

A child in the middle years is forced to engage in a balancing act she or he didn't have to perform during the early years. Within the family, the child at this stage of life is expected to assume more and more responsibility for doing chores, for meeting her or his personal needs, and for managing many of her or his interpersonal problems with siblings and other relatives. At school, the child is faced with the task of developing more and more proficiency in numerous, different academic areas. Among peers, the child must play increasingly more sophisticated social games in order to achieve and retain popularity and self-esteem.

All the while that a child during the middle years is compelled to perform this balancing act, she or he is also coming to terms with the beauties and terrors of society at large. If personal experiences of the outside world don't expose a child to poverty, crime, violence, injustice, or catastrophe, then television will. The result of such exposure can, at times, be emotionally devastating. And there's always the frightening possibility that the child will fall victim to the worst ills of the outside world by running away or experimenting with drugs or alcohol or having dangerous sexual encounters.

Nevertheless, the middle years of childhood in most cases constitute the golden age of childhood, an era of emotional awakening, growth, and engagement that is exciting in itself and lays the foundation for a rich and rewarding life as an adult. To help ensure your child's emotional well-being throughout this period, keep in mind these basic truths:

1. The maintenance of a good ongoing dialogue between parent and child during the middle years is vital to the latter's emotional health.

A school-age child is intensely involved in developing verbal communication skills; they should be tapped to enhance the quality of the parent-child relationship. Make it easy and comfortable for your child to express experiences and feelings to you by initiating conversations with her or him on a frequent, regular, and dependable basis. Be an active listener whenever your child is speaking to you and withhold judgment about what is communicated whenever possible.

Conversations with your children are your single best source of information about their emotional state of being and the factors contributing to it. But perhaps even more important, these conversations help them put experiences and feelings into perspective so that they can be appreciated more fully and constructively.

2. A child in the middle years needs to be granted a certain amount of independence, even if it entails a certain amount of risk.

However much you may want to protect your school-age child from any physical, emotional, or social harm, you need to allow your child some freedom to discover her or his capabilities and limitations and to learn from mistakes and misfortunes. The more carefully—and discreetly—you observe your child and the more effectively you consult with other knowledgeable people about your child, the better equipped you will be to make difficult decisions regarding how much independence to grant her or him in specific situations.

3. A child in the middle years thrives on praise and support.

A school-age child is constantly being critiqued for shortcomings in school, games, friendships, personal conduct, and chore performance. This barrage of criticism needs to be offset by sincere and hearty praise whenever it's appropriate. Your child also needs to be confident that you will always be there if your help is needed or requested.

The material presented in this section of the book will assist you in maintaining an emotionally supportive and helpful relationship with your school-age child. It is organized as follows:

1. SEXUALITY *(Page 170)*

■ milestones in sexual development, curiosity, and activity and emotional issues associated with those milestones

■ how to prevent, and cope with, sexual abuse in the middle years

■ how to cope with puberty

■ what to expect in terms of gender-related behavior and how to avoid harmful gender stereotypes in raising your child

2. FEAR *(Page 186)*

■ how fears develop in very young children; how to recognize them and how to manage them

■ a timetable of common fears at different ages

3. DISCIPLINE *(Page 194)*

■ common disciplinary challenges, emotional issues associated with them, and general guidelines for handling them successfully

■ guidelines for evaluating problem behavior and its emotional causes and effects

■ at PCGC: treatment in a family context

4. CHORES *(Page 206)*

■ how to assign and supervise chores in a manner that avoids emotional stress and strain

■ guidelines for determining whether or not to "bribe" a school-age child to perform chores

5. RUNNING AWAY *(Page 214)*

■ how to discourage or prevent your child from running away

■ how to cope with running away when—and after—it happens

6. DEPRESSION AND STRESS *(Page 217)*

■ causes and effects of depression and stress in school-age children

■ how to prevent, manage, and overcome common problems associated with depression and stress

■ timetable of major stress issues during the middle years

■ guidelines for evaluating the existence and extent of depression or stress in a school-age child's life

■ how to help a child cope with a family move

■ how to help a child cope with serious illness

■ at PCGC: seasonal affective disorder

■ at PCGC: pain management for school-age children

7. LYING AND STEALING *(Page 234)*

■ the causes and effects of lying and stealing in the life of a school-age child

■ how to cope with lying and stealing when it happens

8. SIBLING RIVALRY *(Page 238)*

■ how and why sibling rivalry develops

■ how to prevent and manage sibling rivalry

9. DIVORCE *(Page 243)*

■ how to announce and explain a divorce to school-age children

■ how to help a school-age child cope emotionally with a divorce while it's in progress

■ how to help a school-age child cope emotionally with parental dating and remarriage

10. THE ADOPTED CHILD *(Page 249)*

■ the causes and effects of common emotional problems associated with being an adopted child

■ how to talk with a school-age child about her or his adopted status

■ how to help a school-age child cope with adoption-related emotional problems

11. SCHOOL *(Page 254)*

■ the causes and effects of common emotional problems associated with school life

■ how to help your child avoid or cope with school-related emotional problems

■ guidelines for evaluating whether or not it may be beneficial for a school-age child's emotional health to repeat or skip a grade

12. FRIENDSHIP *(Page 260)*

■ common problems associated with a school-age child's friendships and how to cope with these problems

■ guidelines for evaluating whether a school-age child may be overly shy or aggressive

■ how bully-victim relationships develop and how to help potential bullies or potential victims avoid, or defuse, such relationships

13. TELEVISION *(Page 270)*

■ the positive and negative emotional effects of television viewing on school-age children

■ how to manage your child's television viewing so that it doesn't interfere with her or his emotional well-being

14. PSYCHOTHERAPY *(Page 274)*

■ how to determine if your school-age child might need psychotherapy

■ how to choose the appropriate therapy and a doctor/therapist

■ the meaning behind special diagnoses: attention-deficit hyperactivity disorder and learning disabilities

■ at PCGC: ADHD evaluation and treatment

The Middle Years: An Emotional Time Line

Although it's difficult to define what is "normal" in the year-to-year emotional life of a school-age child, here are some very broad guidelines:

SIX TO SEVEN YEARS

■ tends to exhibit extremes of emotional responses: for example, exuberant delight instead of a quiet joy or hysterical crying instead of simple sadness

■ is very susceptible to having hurt feelings

■ may exhibit "school phobia," a fear of going to school that can lead to feigned or psychosomatic illness

■ quarrels with parents—especially mother—as a means of discharging separation anxiety associated with starting school life or of testing parent-child relationship in this new school-oriented stage of life

■ forms multiple, relatively superficial, and relatively short-lasting relationships with peers

■ engages in "sex play" to satisfy curiosity about genitals

■ frequently initiates sibling rivalry

■ occasionally resorts to lying or stealing as a coping mechanism or a means of rebellion

SEVEN TO NINE YEARS

■ exhibits much more emotional equilibrium than previously, although at age eight may go through a recurrence of extreme emotional reactions and quarrels with parents

■ experiences both fear and rational concern related to possible dangers lurking in the outside world: crime, violence, catastrophe

■ becomes interested in sex talk and sex jokes and is curious about the mechanics of reproduction

■ develops crushes on peers

■ handles competitive play—and losing—pretty well

■ worries about failure in academic performance

■ assumes more responsibility for own acts instead of blaming others

■ fears being wrong or being humiliated

NINE TO ELEVEN YEARS

■ is generally happy and content

■ relies more and more on peers as opposed to parents for evaluation, approval, and direction

■ forms "puppy love" relationships with peers

■ develops much more mature relationships with siblings

■ exhibits concern over issues of justness and fairness

■ seeks and develops a "best friend" relationship

■ worries about the possibility of parents' fighting, divorcing, losing their jobs, becoming ill, or dying

ELEVEN TO THIRTEEN YEARS (EARLY ADOLESCENCE)

■ becomes very self-conscious and sensitive about physical development, physical health, and sexuality

■ fears losing possessions, popularity, or status

■ develops more and more romantic attachments with peers

■ occasionally loses patience with siblings and parents as they increasingly interfere with personal, peer-related interactions and ambitions

■ seeks and develops a close circle of friends for social support

■ frequently exhibits moodiness and irritability

Psychosomatic Illness

By definition, a psychosomatic illness is a genuine physical illness that has psychological, as well as biological, causes (*psycho*: the Greek root for mind; *soma*: the Greek root for body). More technically, such an illness is known as a *psychophysiological disorder*. As a rule, when the underlying physiological problem is effectively addressed, the physical symptoms of the illness are greatly alleviated and may even disappear.

The body and the mind are so interconnected that almost any illness can be said to have a psychosomatic component. However, certain stress-sensitive illnesses are commonly thought to be especially psychosomatic in nature, such as ulcers, headaches, stomachaches, asthma, high blood pressure, skin rashes or blemishes, and allergies.

Several factors besides exposure to stress increase the tendency of a child to suffer from illnesses that are especially psychosomatic in nature. One factor involves the "built-in" reactivity of the child's nervous system. Some individuals are born with nervous systems that produce strong responses to outside stimuli; some are not. The "high reactors" experience stronger responses to outside stimuli, which can make them basically shy (an unconscious defense against possible stress) as well as predispose them toward psychosomatic illnesses.

Another factor predisposing a child to psychosomatic illness can be the vulnerability of a particular organ or system in the child's body. Due to heredity or a prior illness, a child may have impaired lungs, a quirky digestive system, or any number of physiological weaknesses that render her or him more susceptible to stress-related physical problems.

Finally, a major factor affecting psychosomatic reactions in children during the middle years involves what they are taught—directly or indirectly—about the connection between stress and illness in particular and emotional health and physical health in general. A school-age child's mental/emotional life interacts with her or his physiological life very closely—much more closely than adults can usually appreciate.

For example, a child who receives loving attention only when not feeling well can eventually "learn" how to be sick more easily and more often. So can the child who is automatically allowed to stay home from school whenever she or he doesn't feel well and the child who is prompted to fear certain physical illnesses without being given sufficient understanding of them or practical guidance on how to avoid or manage them.

Alternatively, a child who regularly experiences caring and comforting love, whether healthy or ill, is less likely to respond to occasional neglect with illness. A child who is always encouraged to communicate openly about physical and emotional feelings, knowing that her or his parents are concerned about these feelings, is less likely to express displeasure with school—or with anything else—through physical symptoms. And a child who receives an ongoing, commonsense education about stress triggers and physical illnesses is better equipped to avoid or manage them.

Cognitive Development

Separate from, but interrelated with, a child's emotional development is her or his cognitive development. The expression "cognitive development" refers to a child's ability to perceive, think, and remember. As such, it is more closely associated with intellectual capabilities than with psychological makeup.

How a child feels is bound to affect how she or he perceives, thinks, and remembers—and vice versa. However, the particular cause-and-effect relationship between a child's cognitive and emotional development depends on biological and social variables and differs greatly from individual to individual. Therefore, any useful picture of such a relationship in the case of a specific child can only be drawn in the context of comprehensive therapeutic treatment.

Among the many theories concerning cognitive development in children, that of the French psychologist Jean Piaget is the most popular. It divides a child's cognitive development during the early years into two distinct, age-related stages that can be described as follows:

1. Sensory-motor thinking

This stage is associated with infancy. The child acquires the ability to identify and remember different facets of the physical world (e.g., faces, sounds, toys, smells, foods). The child also learns to connect certain perceptions with certain physical actions (e.g., judging distances, moving within a given set of physical parameters, anticipating the course of simple gestures and events).

2. Intuitive and representational thinking

This stage is associated with toddlers and preschoolers. The child acquires language skills, recognizes major differences in individual points of view, formulates simple stories, ideas, or plans, and develops an understanding of basic time-and-space concepts.

During the middle years (ages six to thirteen), a child goes through the *concrete operations* stage of cognitive development, during which she or he develops logic and the ability to perform core intellectual activities, for example, reading, writing, computing, and experimenting. Thereafter—that is, through adolescence and adulthood—an individual is involved in the *formal operations* stage of cognitive development, during which she or he refines intellectual capabilities and learns to conceptualize more and more philosophically.

At PCGC: Psychological Testing in the Middle Years

Mental-health professionals, physicians, school personnel, and other specialists frequently make decisions that have a profound influence on children during their middle years. Historically, psychological testing has been a widely used and valued method for providing such professionals with the proper information to make those decisions.

Psychological testing is generally employed to determine individual differences and needs by providing specifics about a school-age child's abilities, strengths, personality style, and emotional functioning. It is also helpful in evaluating the actual or potential effects on school-age children of significant situational events, such as moving to a new home, coping with a serious illness, or going through a parental divorce.

For children between the ages of six and thirteen, psychological testing provides data about intellectual capacities, problem-solving strategies, neuropsychological processing, and personality styles. In addition, academic achievement is tested in order to assess the possible presence of learning disorders. Tests that PCGC frequently recommends or uses for personality analysis include the Rorschach test (recently rejuvenated and rendered more useful by a research-based scoring system), the Thematic Apperception Test, and Sentence Completion Tests.

The experience of PCGC has shown that the more the family is informed about the testing and involved in the testing process, the more useful the evaluation is to them. Therefore, PCGC employs and advocates the following testing process:

■ The first step in the process is to help the child understand the purpose of the testing. For example, it is counterproductive to tell six- or seven-year-old children that they are "going to play some games." Instead, they should be told, in a manner that they can understand and appreciate, that they are going to find out how best their minds work so that family and school situations can be made better for them.

■ Before the testing itself begins, the psychologist or test administrator meets with the child and parents to identify the reasons why testing is being sought, obtain relevant background history, address any initial questions or concerns the child and parents have, and explain the testing process.

■ It helps to have between two and four short, separate testing sessions rather than one long one. That way, fatigue factors are minimized, and a fuller range of the child's accomplishments and capabilities can be tested.

■ When testing is completed, the results are discussed with the family and the child.

For more information about psychological testing of school-age children, consult your physician, school counselor, or a local mental-health agency.

1.

Sexuality

Sigmund Freud referred to the years between age six and age eleven as the "latency period." He believed that a child within this age range is relatively unconcerned with sexual matters and that any such interest is much more likely to be motivated by scientific curiosity than by romantic or erotic feelings.

Today experts debate about whether Freud was accurate in describing this age span as sexually "latent." Nevertheless, it certainly *appears* that a child's sexuality causes much less emotional turmoil during the middle years than it does in the years immediately before and after.

From approximately age four to age six, when children are first becoming consciously aware of sexual roles and sexual activities, they typically endure an intense romantic attraction to their parent of the opposite sex (or, in the absence of this parent, to some other adult of the opposite sex who plays a major role in their life). In response to this powerful attraction, they also experience a strong feeling of competitiveness and even anger focused on the parent of the same sex (or toward anyone romantically interested in their love object).

In the case of boys, Freud called this phenomenon an Oedipus complex, after the legendary Greek hero and supposed orphan who unknowingly killed his father and married his mother. In the case of girls, he called it an Electra complex, after the daughter of the Greek King Agamemnon, who killed her mother out of love for her father.

Whatever modern experts may label this phenomenon, most of them agree with Freud that it's a growth experience characterized by great emotional upheaval. They also agree that the middle years represent a stabilizing recovery period, during which children form more rational and practical partnerships with their parents and other adults they love. The more effectively parents learn to manage sex-related issues associated with the middle years, the better these partnerships develop.

At the other extreme from the middle years is adolescence. The very word suggests an era of newly emerging sexuality, at frequent and dramatic odds with the individual's ongoing family dependence, social immaturity, and personal lack of self-confidence.

Compared to the average teenager's life, the average school-age kid's life is decidedly more peaceful in terms of sex-related matters. But how much turmoil individual children actually experience when they are teenagers depends to a great extent on how successfully their parents prepare them for adolescence during their middle years.

In issues having to do with a school-age child's sexuality, your major contribution will be educational. As an educator, your biggest challenge will be discussing the emotions and ethics that are associated with sexuality. It's not an easy task by any means, but it's an essential one if your child is to mature into a healthy, satisfied, and morally decent adult.

When you converse with your child about the emotions and ethics associated with sex, you have little choice but to let your conscience be your guide and hope for the best. Awkward though it may be to describe to your child the mechanics of sexual intercourse, menstruation, conception, pregnancy, and birth, at least you can speak with a more or less scientific detachment. When it comes to talking with your child about sexual feelings and responsibilities, you must speak from your heart. Only through a very sensitive and compassionate dialogue can you communicate to your child how to exercise safety, self-control, and regard for others in sexual situations—and why.

Take advantage of every opportunity that your school-age child gives you to talk about sexuality; in these discussions, always try to interrelate the mechanical aspects of sex with its emotional and ethical aspects. Also, be alert for signs that your child may require such a talk, even though she or he may not be forthcoming about the need. Possible signs of this nature include making flip or erroneous statements about sex, introducing sexual content into solitary or group play, and expressing noticeable interest in sex-related songs, television programs, or printed matter.

Here are some additional tips for discussing, and dealing with, your school-age child's sexuality:

■ *Discuss sex in a manner that is appropriate to your child's age and to the situation at hand.*

Many parents have a rough-draft "sex lecture" in reserve for just that moment when their school-age child comes to them and says, "Tell me about sex." While it's a good idea to anticipate what your child may want and need to know about sex and to prepare yourself accordingly, you don't want to intimidate, embarrass, or bore your child with stiff, out-of-the-ordinary lecturelike material. And while most school-age children occasionally do come to their parents with sex-related questions, it's a rare child who ever bluntly says, "Tell me about sex."

Whether your child introduces the subject of sex or you bring it up, conduct any discussion in a natural, informal manner. Don't feel you have to go into details (e.g., about how reproduction works) unless your child seems interested. A six-year-old child may be old enough, and attentive enough, only to grasp the fact that "Daddy's penis puts a seed into Mommy's vagina." By contrast, a ten-year-old child is generally intelligent enough—and curious enough—to learn the whole basic process, from conception and fertilization to birth.

In addition to being appropriately responsive to your child's questions about sex, you also need to take the initiative in informing your child about certain sex-related matters. Your child needs to be told about such subjects as not masturbating in public, respecting other people's privacy (particularly in regard to sex play with peers), and avoiding situations that could lead to being sexually abused or sexually abusive. Don't wait for your child to say something if you feel the time is right.

Generally, the earlier you talk with your child about sex, the better. However elementary your initial discussions of it may be, they pave the way for easier, more productive discussions later on.

Children develop more self-consciousness the older they get, and so it becomes more difficult with each passing year to start talking about sex. A child over ten years old may conceal ignorance about sex in a desire to appear more sophisticated. By the time a child is sexually active, which could be as early as age eleven, she or he is bound to be acutely uncomfortable, if not downright resistant, to having any sort of discussion about sex with her or his parents.

■ *Avoid being preachy.*

You *do* need to give your child guidance in handling sexual desires and sexual pressures in a responsible manner. You *do not* need to scare your child about sex or issue threats about what will happen if your child doesn't do what you'd like her or him to do. This latter approach to such an extremely sensitive area of your child's life can only be counterproductive, inspiring possible resentment and rebellion in your child's teenage years.

■ *Relate sexual matters to everyday life.*

The best way to avoid appearing as if you're giving a lecture about sex instead of simply talking about it is to connect what you are saying with what your child has witnessed or experienced in the real world. Using specific references in this way also helps your child apply what you've said constructively to her or his own life.

For example, in talking about the love and responsibility associated with having a sexual relationship, you might allude to a recent wedding that your child attended, to the recent birth of a baby that she or he remembers, or to the lyrics in a song that your child likes. This enables her or him to think of these matters in a more respectful and understanding light. Of course, given this same discussion, you might also refer to your own relationship with your spouse or to your child's own birth, depending on how comfortable you and your listener are about discussing such personal topics.

In this type of conversation, as in any conversation relating to sex, never worry about putting ideas into your child's head. You can safely assume that more ideas—and more potentially troublesome ones—are already there than you can possibly match.

■ Don't tease your child about her or his sexual or affectionate interests.

A crush or a case of puppy love is a serious business for your school-age child. Through this kind of emotional attachment, a child learns to recognize and cope with all sorts of feelings related to her or his sexuality, including tenderness, yearning, devotion, despair, possessiveness, and jealousy. Dismissing or trivializing such an experience can not only rob it of its educational value but also cause significant emotional turmoil.

When your school-age child develops a romantic attraction to someone else, even a celebrity that your child has little chance of ever meeting, try to provide the freedom for your child to indulge in the attraction without comment from you. Step in only if the indulgence seems to be taking up too much of your child's time and energy or if it's creating serious problems for the love object (which is unlikely, because such attractions are usually nurtured in private).

■ Handle incidents of sex play calmly and sensitively.

While "show me" or "doctor" games are much more prevalent among preschoolers, children between the ages of six and ten may play them from time to time, even with members of the same sex. By far the most likely motive for such games is simple curiosity rather than erotic interests, just as it is for preschoolers.

Over the age of ten, children are typically too self-conscious to play sex games with members of the opposite sex. However, isolated incidents of sex games with members of the same sex are relatively common up to puberty and, like similar sex games at an earlier age, do not necessarily indicate that the children involved are gay.

If you catch your school-age child engaging in sex play or hear that your child has engaged in it, avoid overreacting. Instead, speak frankly and firmly with your child about the matter, advising that such activity is not appropriate and making sure she or he knows about sex and sexual responsibility. The mere fact that you've discovered what your child has done will probably embarrass her or him enough to put an end to future sex play.

Naturally, if a particular incident of sex play includes actual intercourse, abuse, or injury, you need to take stronger disciplinary action, perhaps in concert with the parents of the other child involved. Just remember at all times that your child is extremely vulnerable to becoming emotionally upset whenever her or his sexuality is at issue. With this in mind, do everything possible to help your child (1) retain her or his dignity and (2) *want* to behave more appropriately.

■ *Steer your child away from using sexual terms as swear words.*
Most children go through periods of using sexual terms as expletives or attention getters. Whenever you overhear their use, calmly let your child know that she or he is using the particular sex-related word or expression in a wrong and offensive manner. If necessary, explain exactly what the word or expression means. In any event, assure your child's promise not to misuse that particular word or expression, or any other word or expression relating to sex, in the future.

■ *Always indicate that you trust your child to handle sexual situations in a responsible manner.*
The most powerful incentive your child can have for behaving in a sexually responsible manner is your trust and positive expectations. Never permit your child to think that she or he is incapable of good behavior or that you don't have much faith in her or his judgment in sexual matters.

In situations when you do need to discipline your child for sexual misconduct, take special pains to criticize the act itself, not your child. And in any discussion you have with your child about sex, communicate your confidence in her or him to successfully manage any sex-related difficulties.

A Timetable for Sexuality: The Middle Years

Few aspects of a school-age child's emotional life vary more from child to child than sexual feelings and behaviors. Despite the enormous peer pressure on school-age children to regard and act out their sexuality in a certain manner, year after year individual kids may secretly harbor their own distinctive attitudes and pursue their own unique interests.

Nevertheless, here's a schedule describing how a child *commonly* manifests her or his sexuality at different ages during the middle years:

SIX TO SEVEN YEARS

■ efforts at strengthening personal identity through embracing gender stereotypes both in play activities and real life

■ claims to dislike peers of the opposite sex

■ heterosexual sex play to satisfy curiosity about genitals

■ interest in babies and how they are produced

■ crushes on adults (such as teachers and friends of the family)

SEVEN TO NINE YEARS

■ use of sex-related language to swear and to attract attention

■ waning of sex play

■ self-consciousness about nudity

■ dawning of prurient interest in sex

■ crushes on nonreciprocating peers

NINE TO ELEVEN YEARS

■ renewal of efforts to embrace gender stereotypes and claims to dislike the opposite sex

■ use of smutty jokes and gestures

■ drawing of naked figures and sex-related images

- increased scientific interest in sexuality and reproduction

- crushes on peers of same sex (sometimes reciprocated)

- same-sex sex play

- puppy love with peers of the opposite sex

ELEVEN TO THIRTEEN YEARS

- increased capacity for romantic attachments to peers

- increased self-consciousness about nudity

- sexual teasing, aimed both at members of the same sex and members of the opposite sex

- interest in pornography

- crushes on adults (such as celebrities)

- possible beginning of puberty

- possible beginning of sexual activity

Sexual Abuse in the Middle Years

Beginning around age six, a child is socially mature enough to associate "wrongness" with even the gentlest sexual fondling by someone else. Accompanying this sensation are all sorts of potentially traumatic emotions: feelings of fear, powerlessness, guilt, dirtiness, and worthlessness. Thus, *any* action on the part of someone else that is intentionally aimed at engaging a six- to ten-year-old child in sexual activity or is designed to sexually stimulate that child can be considered a sexually abusive act.

Sometimes abused school-age children manifest their negative emotions in a psychological way right after the abuse, for example, in nightmares or in excessive panic at being left alone. At other times, the emotions lie dormant until later in life, perhaps puberty, when the child more fully realizes what has happened. At this point, the buried emotions tend to surface behaviorally as well as psychologically. Besides having low self-esteem, the formerly abused child may reject sex altogether, seek sex compulsively, or become a sexual abuser her- or himself. Indeed, a high percentage of known abusers were abused as children.

If the sexual abuser is someone the school-age child knows and trusts, the possibility for trauma is compounded. Trapped between her or his regard for this person and the negative emotions already mentioned, the abused child may develop life-crippling feelings of betrayal, mistrust, and anger. If the abuser is a member of the family, the abused child may also feel jealousy, shame, or hatred in relationship to other family members.

Other situational factors influence how great the psychological aftermath of sexual abuse may be for a school-age child. Assuming abusive episodes occurred repeatedly over an extensive period of time or frequently over a short period of time, the emotional damage is more likely to be severe and long-lasting. The same holds true if there were multiple perpetrators of abuse, if the abuse involved coercion, terrorizing, or pain, or if the abuser enforced secrecy.

On the positive side, effective parental response to the sexual abuse of a school-age child can do much to minimize and even eliminate many of the damaging emotional and behavioral consequences of the abuse, no matter how severe it was. Parents can also do a great deal to help prevent such abuse in the first place or to put an end to it before it gets worse.

Here are some important steps to follow relating to the sexual abuse of children in their middle years:

■ *Make sure that your child is well informed about sex.*
Knowledge that links the mechanics of sexual activity to appropriate sex-related emotions, situations, and responsibilities will help your child recognize and prevent sexual abuse when it threatens to happen. In the event that sexual abuse should take place anyway, this knowledge will help your child understand what has happened and discuss it with you and other people who can assist her or him to recover from it. The earlier this ongoing process of sexual education begins, the better. If you're not sure how to manage the specifics of such a dialogue, seek advice from some trustworthy, knowledgeable person who knows your child (such as a teacher or clergyperson) or, better still, a child psychologist or psychiatrist.

■ *Advise your child when—and how—to reject physical contact.*

Assuming your child is relatively well informed about sex, considering her or his age, you can caution your child about letting other people take liberties with her or his body. You don't want to bring up abuse possibilities and strategies *every* time you discuss sex or you'll be encouraging your child to think of it as something scary in itself. But you do *occasionally* want to talk about abuse when you can work it naturally into the conversation.

First and foremost, your child should know that her or his body is private, especially the sexual areas. Then tell your child that whenever someone touches her or him in a way that feels "funny," "strange," or "not nice," she or he should immediately say no, get away from that person, and talk to you about the matter as soon as possible.

Don't worry if your child possibly misjudges innocent gestures from family members and friends. Any harm done by such misjudgments is easily remedied compared to the harm that can be done if your child reserves judgment.

■ *Be alert for signs that your child has been sexually abused.*

Among these signs are the following:

■ inexplicable bruises or scratches, especially in the genital area;

■ sudden preoccupation with sex or with her or his body;

■ sudden preoccupation with sexual themes in games, language, or drawings;

■ dramatic increase in nightmares and fearful episodes (especially a fear of being left alone);

■ dramatic loss of spiritedness and self-esteem; and

■ inexplicable incidents of self-punishment.

If you observe any of the signs and suspect child abuse, express your concern to your child about her or his physical and emotional condition. Then give your child the chance to talk about anything that's bothering her or him without forcing the issue and without putting words into her or his mouth.

■ *Take seriously and pursue any reference your child makes to having been sexually abused.*

If your child makes any comment that indicates to you that she or he may have been sexually molested, give her or him your full attention and calmly but firmly encourage her or him to tell you more. Regard as truthful anything about sexual abuse that your child says to you. The odds that she or he would lie about such a disturbing matter are extremely small.

■ *Allow your child every freedom and opportunity to discuss incidents of sexual abuse as she or he chooses, without pressure.*

Don't badger your child into talking when you meet resistance and don't attach limits or cautionary terms to what your child can say. It's very difficult for children to speak about sexual abuse and you don't want to risk inadvertently causing them to refuse to speak at all.

Letting your child discuss what happened whenever—and however—she or he chooses accomplishes two important functions: It helps your child discharge her or his bad feelings about the incident, and it gives you special insights into your child's mechanisms for processing emotions.

■ *Calmly and firmly reassure your child about her or his personal worth and safety.*

Tell your child that the abuse was not her or his fault and has no effect on her or his value as a person. Also, don't forget to commend your child's bravery, honesty, and virtue in bringing the abuse to your attention.

As soon as possible, let your child know in no uncertain terms that you will do everything in your power to ensure that she or he is safe from being abused again. More than anything else at the moment, your child needs to hear you make this commitment in order to be convinced that she or he has been right to confide in you.

■ *Contact the proper authorities immediately.*

You need to honor your pledge of safety to your child by making sure you have every possible support when and if it is needed. If the suspected abuse has occurred *within* the family, contact your local Child Protection Agency. If it has occurred *outside* the family, contact your local police department or district attorney's office.

Anyone reporting to these agencies in good faith is immune

from prosecution. They will advise you about what steps you can, or should, take next.

■ *Take your child for a physical exam and a psychological evaluation.*

A visit to a medical doctor is always a good idea in cases of child abuse. Even when there are no outward signs of physical abuse, a medical examination can make certain that there is no internal physical damage or sexually transmitted disease. It can also alleviate any doubts as to the child's medical or physical condition that may emerge later on in life.

Also, since a child between the ages of six and thirteen is old enough to know that there was something wrong in what happened, it's always a good idea to get a psychological evaluation from a qualified doctor or therapist. Even if the child appears to be handling the situation pretty well, you want to do everything possible to identify any underlying psychological trauma connected with the abuse and to forestall any future development of abuse-related emotional problems.

Coping with Puberty

Puberty, the emergence of secondary sexual characteristics, can occur anytime between the ages of nine and fifteen. For females, the onset of menstruation usually takes place between twelve and fourteen years old; for males, fertility occurs between thirteen and fifteen years old.

The emotional stress directly caused by *hormonal changes* during puberty has been greatly exaggerated in popular mythology. Far more significant is the emotional stress triggered by *social issues* accompanying puberty. With all the changes they're experiencing in their bodies, children going through puberty can become very worried about peer reaction. And because their self-esteem is so wrapped up in how their peers regard them, this worry can't help but affect how they feel about themselves personally.

Puberty-related problems are more prevalent—and more severe—when puberty comes earlier than the norm. For a girl, this might be anytime between the ages of nine and twelve; for a boy, between the ages of eleven and thirteen. What makes early puberty more troublesome for the children going through it is that they are even more at odds with their peers, thus increasing the chances that they'll feel like outsiders.

A girl experiencing early puberty typically suffers much more than a boy, again for social reasons. Western culture tends to encourage boys to become men as soon as possible and, once they have, to revel in their virility. Girls, on the other hand, are taught to prize innocence, sweetness, and virginity—all characteristics of prepubescent children. Womanhood is associated not so much with power as it is with onerous hygiene matters attending menstruation, along with greater vulnerability and an unwelcome need to be especially circumspect in behavior. Illegitimate and unfair as such biases are, parents can't ignore their continuing prevalence in, and impact on, society as a whole.

Here are some guidelines for helping your child adjust to puberty, whenever it comes and regardless of how it is received by the social world outside your family:

■ *Don't tease your child about puberty.*

Remember that your child is acutely sensitive about the image she or he is projecting to other people during this period of change. She or he can easily, and unpredictably, misinterpret even the most well meaning jests about her or his newly emerging identity. And she or he can be very skillful at concealing any hurt you may have caused.

■ *Don't assume that puberty automatically means your child is more mature mentally, emotionally, or socially.*

Your child will have enough problems simply coming to terms with puberty. Don't expect her or him to take on more adult behaviors and responsibilities right away. Society at large doesn't even treat an idividual as an adult until she or he is twenty-one years old. Instead, allow your child to mature at approximately the same rate as she or he did prior to puberty.

■ *Assist your child in developing self-esteem and social poise.*

Without being pushy, make an extra effort to encourage your child to engage in *solitary* activities that she or he performs well and that give her or him gratification. Doing so will help your child maintain an ongoing sense of competency, value, and pleasure as her or his body and social image changes.

Simultaneously, and again without being pushy, help your child seek information, instruction, and experiences that will enhance *social* skills. For example, you might try interesting her or him in reading young-adult-oriented books or periodicals, taking athletic lessons, attending summer camp, or participating in a young-adult environmental action project or hobby club.

■ *Treat puberty as a cause for joy.*

Take pride in the fact that your child has reached puberty and let her or him know that you feel proud. In discussing puberty with your child, present it as a desirable and positive stage of growth—linked with beauty, power, and a rich new range of feelings.

QUESTIONS AND ANSWERS

GENDER STEREOTYPES

■ *In what ways are children in the middle years inclined to exhibit gender stereotypes?*

One of the major stereotypes associated with females is that they are inherently more sensitive and caring toward others than males. There is no scientific evidence that such traits are inborn; however, there is overwhelming experiential evidence that female behavior does generally conform to the stereotype.

Girls who are age six or older are mentally capable of appreciating the fact that they may someday bear children. Along with this appreciation comes a natural predilection toward "mothering" and caretaking. Thus, while females may not be genetically programmed to be more interested than males in interpersonal relationships and more compassionate than males while in them, school-age girls inevitably do tend to exhibit such characteristics.

In the wake of this basic gender dissimilarity follows a host of other more or less inevitable differences. Around the ages of six through eight, boys tend to discharge their aggressive or anxious feelings through combative games (such as gunplay). Girls, by contrast, tend to discharge similar feelings through role-playing games (such as "doll-baby" or "house") or within the context of their ongoing relationships with others (e.g., by teasing, arguing, or verbally manipulating). This doesn't mean that boys don't also play house or girls cops and robbers occasionally. It simply points to a *tendency* that has the appearance of inevitability.

Around the ages of nine through twelve, both boys and girls tend to discharge their aggressive or anxious feelings within the context of their ongoing relationships with others, but they do so in stereotypically different ways. Girls tend to discuss such feelings relatively openly among each other or to work them into what is otherwise a fairly cooperative dialogue. Boys, however, tend to hide such feelings, translating them instead into efforts aimed either at dominating relationships or maintaining a safe personal distance within relationships.

Aside from these rather entrenched gender stereotypes, there are others that are commonly enacted by school-age children much more voluntarily and that have much less validity. These stereotypes are mythologies about masculinity and femininity that are perpetuated by our culture; and because the latter is male dominated, they tend to present a biased image of females as submissive.

Among these culturally imposed stereotypes regarding a child's emotional life are the following:

■ Girls are naturally disposed to behave well and obey rules; boys are not.

■ Boys like sports; girls do not.

■ Girls enjoy dressing and grooming themselves; boys do not.

■ Boys prefer doing chores outside the house; girls, inside.

■ Girls are inclined to be afraid and to cry; boys are not.

■ Boys derive satisfaction from working with their hands; girls do not.

■ Girls need to express and receive a great deal of affection; boys do not.

■ Boys are emotionally tough; girls are not.

■ *How harmful is it for children to indulge in stereotypical behavior?*

Adapting to a *stereotype* is always potentially harmful in the sense that it replaces behaving according to one's *personal* identity and the *personal* identity of others. Some stereotypes may arguably be more harmful than others. For example, the stereotype that boys do not cry may cause more pain in the life of a school-age boy than the notion that boys prefer working outdoors rather than indoors. However, there is no such thing as a *good* stereotype.

By definition, a stereotype is a simplified, standardized image of a particular subject. To regard individuals, or categories of individuals (such as gender groups), in a simplified or standardized manner is always to diminish them. And to behave in accordance with a stereotype is always suspect, making it even more difficult to distinguish where one's own identity ends and a robotlike identity imposed on one by the outside world begins.

In the case of school-age children, however, some allowances for stereotypical attitudes and behaviors relating to gender need to be made. Children in the middle years are just beginning to develop self-sufficient social skills. Having relatively weak personal identities due to their continuing dependence on their parents and wanting to relate to each other as quickly, easily, and thoroughly as possible, they are irresistibly drawn toward imitating the gender stereotypes they see all around them. This grants them a certain measure of emotionally healthy security.

More to the point, demanding that a child forsake *all* stereotypical attitudes and behaviors during this formative stage in their lives can cause more emotional stress than its worth. Although it is definitely a good idea to steer children away from stereotypical attitudes and behaviors, such a policy works best when you reserve serious educational or disciplinary intervention for occasions when it's especially necessary: for example, when your child has hurt someone else's feelings or has stated a belief that is patently untrue.

Always remember that your child's attitudes and behaviors during the years between six and thirteen are largely experimental. As long as you set a good example as parents and do what you reasonably can to help your child appreciate the difference between gender stereotypes and personal realities, she or he will most likely outgrow a great deal of the predilection toward gender stereotypes.

■ What specific things can parents do to discourage stereotypical behavior in their children?

Aside from stepping in tactfully whenever your child has done or said something that is particularly offensive, here are some other things you can do:

■ Don't make general statements that suggest gender stereotypes, like "Be a man!" or "Girls don't carry on like that."

■ Avoid setting up stereotypes—directly or indirectly—in parenting your child. In two-parent households, fathers and mothers should share, and occasionally swap, caretaking tasks. In one-parent households, every effort should be made to involve an adult of the opposite sex in some of the caretaking tasks.

■ Use television programs, movies, news stories, and everyday incidents as contexts for discussing sexism.

■ Try interesting your child in points of view or activities that counter gender stereotypes. For example, expose your son to ballet; and if he shows interest, follow through with lessons. Or shoot baskets with your daughter; if she shows interest, find a basketball team for her to join.

■ Assuming your child is relatively indifferent, resist the tendency to buy clothes, toys, furniture, or personal items for her or him that conform to gender stereotypes (e.g., caveman T-shirts, toy trucks, rustic bunk beds, and tiger-striped notebooks for boys, as opposed to flowered T-shirts, dolls, canopied beds, and kitten-print notebooks for girls).

■ Assuming your child is otherwise happy and healthy, don't succumb to stereotypical attitudes and behaviors yourself by worrying about your child's "masculinity" or "femininity" or by pushing her or him to conform more closely to a stereotype of either. Let your child find her or his own way in this highly sensitive area of emotional life.

Allowing your child this kind of happy and healthy emotional freedom means being no more disturbed by homosexual crushes, sex play, and puppy love than you are by heterosexual crushes, sex play, and puppy love. A child's affectional experimentation during this age range should not be taken as a sign of her or his basic sexual orientation. Even more important, a child shouldn't be forced to regard homosexual feelings, let alone a homosexual orientation, as intrinsically negative.

2.
Fear

Compared to the early years, the middle years in a child's emotional life are much less plagued by fears and phobias. The school-age child possesses more knowledge about what fear is and how it develops and is more experienced in dealing with specific fears. This knowledge and experience enable the child to confront and process typical fears during the middle years fairly effectively, at least on a subconscious level.

On the other hand, when school-age children *do* have seriously disturbing fears, they are much more likely to hide them from their parents than are younger children. The same desire to appear more mature that helps school-age children get over their fears can also make them ashamed to reveal them.

Concealment of fear is especially common in the case of boys, who can be very sensitive to the notion that it is "unmanly" to be fearful, much less to express such an emotion. Concealment is also common in the case of boys and girls who are highly success oriented. In their minds, to admit to being fearful is to acknowledge failure of some sort.

Contributing to this potential information gap between parent and school-age child is that the child is no longer at home and observable as much as she or he was during preschool years. Thus, it is easier for parents not only to miss literally seeing their child suffer from a given fear but also to lose some of their "sixth sense" insight into their child's emotional frame of reference.

Along with the estrangement from their child, parents must also cope with alienation from the world she or he inhabits. Once children begin school and therefore enter into a comparatively active interpersonal life with peers and adults outside the home, a far greater percentage of their fears tend to be social in nature. Primarily, they worry about being unacceptable, humiliated, or left out vis-à-vis the outside community.

While these school-age "social fears" may not be as emotionally devastating as the comparatively life-and-death personal fears of pre-school years, they can still be immensely distressing and potentially harmful to the child's long-term emotional health. A school-age child may be intellectually capable of recognizing when fears are out of proportion, but prevailing circumstances may not give the child the time, space, energy, or incentive to exercise this capability. Instead, she or he may live on with the fear to the point that it becomes second nature, subtly coloring everything she or he does.

Unfortunately, from a parent's perspective, many social fears never get displayed at home. Indeed, home can become a refuge from them— a place where they don't have to be indulged. And so the fears may fester far longer than is appropriate, adversely affecting the child and the family without the parents realizing what they are actually up against.

Of course, a school-age child also remains subject to fears that take place at home. In addition to such personal ones as fear of the dark or of illness, they include variations of the social fears: the fear of being unacceptable, humiliated, or left out in regard to the family in general or to a particular member of the family.

Often these home-based fears may be quite evident and fairly easy to pinpoint. For example, a six-year-old boy who is afraid of the dark may scream at night about shadows on the wall, or an eight-year-old girl who fears a loss of parental love may cling to her parents and raise a fuss whenever they leave her behind. In these cases, the cause-and-effect progression is rather obvious.

At other times, it may be apparent that the child fears *something*, even if the precise nature of that fear can't be identified. For example, a ten-year-old boy who shuns visiting his grandparents on their farm may be afraid of them, their hired hand, crossing the high bridge on the way to the farm, the horses on the farm, or any combination of the above.

However, even home-based fears may remain entirely private and undetectable to the casual observer. A school-age child can be ex-tremely protective of her or his personal dignity. This may lead the child to do everything possible to avoid either revealing the true na-ture of a fear or being in situations in which she or he may unwittingly betray that fear in the presence of others.

The key to helping a school-age child manage fears in a timely and appropriate manner is to remain as informed as possible about what is going on in her or his life. Without making your child feel that you are invading her or his privacy, maintain regular communication with other adults who are witnesses to her or his day-to-day life: teachers, caretakers, and parents of your child's friends. These individuals can provide you with valuable clues about fears that your child may have, and they can serve as valuable allies in helping your child overcome those fears.

Most important, cultivate a relationship with your child that makes it easier for you to spot fears and more comfortable for your child to talk with you about them. This requires somewhat of a balancing act between treating your child as an independent person and as your dependent. You need not only to give your child a certain amount of freedom to endure fears without you but also to make sure that your child isn't burdened with more fear than she or he can properly handle.

Here are some suggestions for helping your school-age child discuss and manage her or his fears:

■ Be more of a listener than a talker.

The single most important thing you can do for your fearful child is to be a good listener. It will give you a much better understanding of what's bothering her or him and why.

Children have their own, often roundabout way of getting to the heart of the matter in conversation. Unless you give them a full opportunity to express themselves without cutting them off or putting words in their mouth, you may jump to the wrong conclusions about the nature of their fear. Worse, you may discourage them from confiding in you in the future.

To be a good listener, practice these three behaviors:

1. Concentrate on being receptive to what your child has to say instead of thinking about what you are going to say—or do—in response. Stay focused on both the actual words she or he is using and the nonverbal communication that accompanies them, such as facial expressions, body movements, posture, and eye contact.

2. Wait until your child has clearly finished saying all that she or he has to say before making any comments of your own, even if it means putting up with long, silent pauses in the conversation.

3. Periodically paraphrase what your child has said, both to make sure you've understood it correctly and to encourge your child to elaborate.

For example, suppose your child says, "I'm afraid to play ball with those guys. They're too rough." You might paraphrase this statement by saying, "So you think you might get hurt if you play ball with these guys." Your child may respond by saying, "Yes! They push and shove and run into people." Or your child may say, "Well, if I do something wrong, they yell at me." Either response moves both of you closer to the real truth about the fear.

■ *Acknowledge the pain that your child's fear is causing her or him to feel.*

Whether or not you think your child's fear is justifiable, let your child know that you understand that she or he is troubled. If appropriate, you might acknowledge that you, too, are sometimes fearful of the same situation.

■ *Assist your child in putting her or his fear into perspective.*

Begin by getting your child to express each fear-related incident in as much detail as possible (without suffering undue discomfort) so that these incidents are fully realistic in both of your minds. Then ask her or him to compare these incidents, using such questions as:

What was the worst incident to handle? Why?

What was the easiest incident to handle? Why?

The answers to these questions may give you leads regarding the main factors contributing to the fear and how to deal with it.

Another strategy to consider is to ask your child to compare this fear to other fears—real and/or hypothetical. You might also ask your child to rate this fear according to a certain scale, such as a one-to-ten scale on a mutually generated scale of awfulness. This latter activity can even inject some healthy humor into the situation—by no means to belittle your child but certainly to diminish the impact of the fear on your child.

■ *Steer your child toward facing and outgrowing her or his fear in step-by-step stages.*

After you've discussed the fear itself in sufficient depth to satisfy both of you, be sure to discuss what can be done to manage it. This discussion should be both soothing and pragmatic.

Solicit suggestions first. If your child doesn't have any suggestions to offer, then put forward your own suggestions in such a manner that she or he is free to choose among them. Before you finish your discussion, you should agree on *some* strategy and timetable, even if it's very general.

Assuming your child doesn't voluntarily propose tackling the fear head-on and right away, the best way to approach overcoming the fear is slowly but surely. Suggest an appropriate first step toward getting over the fear and get your child to agree to take that step.

For example, if your child fears heights, you might consider a picnic together near some not-so-high overlook. If your child fears failing at school, you might consider helping her or him concentrate on doing a particular assignment well, mastering a particular subject, or completing a special project that will earn special recognition. Then proceed from this initial plateau to others, being careful to let your child set the pace.

In the event that the two of you can't develop a general strategy for tackling a particular fear, try setting up an open-ended self-evaluation instrument. Your child can then use it with or without your collaboration, according to her or his preference and to your need to know how she or he is progressing.

For younger kids during the middle years (ages six to nine), this instrument may consist of a graph marking out individual days or weeks. As time goes by, your child can affix different-colored stars to particular days or weeks, according to how well the fear was managed: gold for no fear at all, silver for a little fear, red for a lot of fear, or any other system that seems appropriate.

For older kids (ages nine through twelve), a more sophisticated program can be set up: for example, a series of standard questions relating to fear management that can be answered in writing each week. Sample questions might include the following:

- How many times did I have this fear during the past week?

- How would I list them, in order of how bad they were (number 1 being the worst)?

- For each time, what was the fear like, and how did I handle it?

- For each time, how might I have handled this fear better?

- What did I learn this week about my fear and about how to handle it?

■ Be especially patient and optimistic about your child's progress in dealing with her or his fear.
You should definitely encourage your child to confront and master her or his fears. You should perhaps even nudge your child gently and tactfully toward doing so if she or he seems to be stuck in a pattern of denial or avoidance. However, don't be too insistent if she or he refuses to follow through on your encouragement and nudging.

The more your child takes it upon her- or himself to conquer the fear, the better. Too much pressure from you can easily backfire, making her or him even more anxious and hopeless in regard to the fear.

Try at all times to pull rather than push. Express confidence in your child's ability to work through the fear; praise all efforts made and reward each victory.

As a general rule, allow your child several weeks to learn to cope with the fear, assuming it isn't causing too much disruption in the life of your child, you, or your family. Be available to provide solace or help if your child requests it, but otherwise play the more or less passive role of an observer.

When a fear persists at about the same level of severity for longer than a couple of months, more direct intervention is warranted. Perhaps there are seriously disturbing emotional issues underlying the fear. If you have reason to believe that this is the case, consider getting a professional evaluation and, possibly, professional help.

■ *Set a good example.*

School-age children expect to be taught how to do things. Often the basis for a school-age child's fear—or a major catalyst for that fear—is ignorance: What can happen to me in this situation? What's the best thing to do to get through this situation?

As a parent, you are the most influential teacher. Let your child watch you managing situations that she or he fears. Don't just give advice; literally show your child how to act out that advice. For example, if your child fears the ocean, offer ample opportunity to see you swimming in the ocean: first, near the shore in relatively calm water, and later, farther out from shore among bigger waves.

In addition to this kind of specifically targeted behavior modeling, try as hard as possible to exhibit self-confidence and bravery whenever your child is around, regardless of the situation at hand. It's also a good idea to arrange occasions when your child can observe you demonstrating bravery in the course of performing activities that you enjoy (e.g., playing basketball, painting on a ladder, or taking an active part in a social gathering).

Sometimes even setting a good example might not go all the way toward getting your child to overcome her or his fear. This is especially true in cases involving a fear of failure.

Suppose, for example, that your child remains afraid of ice-skating no matter how well you demonstrate that there is little to fear. It may be much easier for your child to overcome this fear if you entrust her or him to an expert coach, away from your watchful eyes. It isn't that your example didn't help; it's just that your child has an additional problem besides fear of ice-skating: namely, fear of embarrassment and of disappointing you.

A Timetable for Fears

Children during the middle years typically experience different types of fears at different stages in their physical, cognitive, and emotional development. Among the most prevalent age-appropriate fears are the following:

SIX TO SEVEN YEARS

■ strange, loud, or abrupt noises (e.g., animal noises, telephone and alarm ringing, wind and thunder sounds)

■ ghosts, witches, and other "supernatural" beings

■ bodily injury

■ separation from parents and being lost

■ being alone at night (and having nightmares or visitations from "evil" creatures)

■ going to school (so-called school phobia)

■ physical harm from, or rejection by, specific individuals at school

SEVEN TO EIGHT YEARS

■ the dark and dark places (such as closets, attics, and basements)

■ real-life catastrophes suggested by television, the movies, and books (e.g., kidnapping, floods, fires, nuclear attack)

■ not being liked

■ being late for school or left out of school or family events

■ physical harm from, or rejection by, specific individuals at school

EIGHT TO NINE YEARS

■ personal humiliation

■ failure in school or play

■ being caught in a lie or misdeed

■ being the victim of physical violence (either from known people or from strangers; either deliberately or randomly motivated)

■ parents fighting, separating, or being hurt

NINE TO ELEVEN YEARS

■ failure in school or sports

■ becoming sick

- specific animals (especially animals larger than humans or those known to attack them)
- heights and sensations of "vertigo" (e.g., dizziness)
- sinister people (e.g., killers and molesters)

ELEVEN TO THIRTEEN YEARS

- failure in school, sports, or social popularity
- looking and acting "strange"
- death or life-threatening illness or disease
- sex (attracting others, repelling others, being attacked)
- being fooled or "brainwashed"
- losing possessions, being robbed

3.
Discipline

Most parents of "difficult" preschoolers secretly look forward to the school-age years as a well-deserved era of calm after the storm. They assume that their children will be more amenable to reason in matters of discipline and that the schooling experience itself will teach them better self-control and more appropriate behaviors in addition to academic knowledge.

In reality, parents of preschoolers are well justified in harboring such hopes. But in their eagerness to envision the new *positive* possibilities that can accompany this stage of a child's life, they tend to overlook the new *negative* ones.

The school-age years are, indeed, generally characterized by a more sophisticated dialogue between parent and child relating to acceptable versus nonacceptable behavior. And the schooling experience typically helps socialize children and make them more responsible for their own conduct and success in life. However, the same mental and emotional growth that enables school-age children to be more *mature* in their conversations and behaviors also emboldens them to be more *devious* in their conversations and behaviors.

In disciplining your child between the ages of six and thirteen, keep in mind that she or he is going through a period of frequent and often intense criticism affecting every aspect of life. This criticism ranges from formal grades on intellectual performance to informal peer evaluations of her or his desirability as a playmate or companion to family judgments about what kind of individual she or he is turning out to be: mentally, physically, morally, and emotionally.

Furthermore, this criticism is no longer tempered by the kinds of indulgent smiles and gushes that a preschooler so easily inspires, even when misbehaving. Instead, the school-age child is expected to act like an adult-in-training—someone who is now a serious individual in her or his own right and who is accountable for every failing.

In order to adjust to this climate of criticism and then to live within it, the school-age child develops many different coping mechanisms. Among the most prevalent is what is known in psychological terms as "acting out" behavior: that is, "undisciplined" behavior prompted by an overpowering need to relieve anxiety, express displeasure, rebel against control, or simply cry out for help.

Thus, while a specific act of bad, incompetent, or inappropriate behavior may have a simple explanation, it may also have a very complicated one. And while conversation with your child may help you understand misbehavior, it may also set up a smoke screen. In a conscious or subconscious effort at self-defense, your child can now use her or his emerging verbal and social skills to mislead you whenever such a strategy seems necessary.

For example, a school-age boy who persists in damaging the furniture when he plays in the house, despite repeated parental discipline, may have legitimate difficulty in managing his basic exuberance. On the other hand, he may be wrecking the furniture as an indirect means of attacking his parents' "unacceptable" bedtime rules. In the latter case, whether or not he realizes his true motivation, he may blame the damage on a sibling or on an innocent accident.

Similarly, a school-age girl who continually fails to learn better table manners may sincerely have a problem concentrating on manners amid other mealtime distractions. Alternatively, she may be refusing to use good table manners just to have the final say in *some* aspect of her life, even if it isn't a very important one. Whatever the case, she may try to thwart her parents' disciplinary efforts by feigning incompetence, lack of hunger, or illness.

Given these two key factors in the lives of school-age children—(1) the amount of criticism typically directed toward them and (2) the potential complexity and elusiveness of their real motives for misbehavior—parents of school-age children need to be especially discriminating in deciding *when* and *how* to manage individual disciplinary issues. In more colloquial terms, they need to make sure they look before they leap.

This overall approach to discipline involves a great amount of patience and observation. You need to reserve criticism and disciplinary action for especially serious situations, letting minor annoyances and infractions pass without comment. Any school-age child can easily suffer emotional turmoil from too many "dos" and "don'ts," no matter how gently these "dos" and "don'ts" are offered.

Moreover, you need to avoid jumping to conclusions about what has occurred and why. Respect the fact that life has become more complicated for your school-age child and allow her or him the benefit of the doubt whenever possible, as well as every opportunity to express and explain her or his feelings. Remember that ultimate responsibility—and reward—as a parent is not to discipline your child but to help your child discipline her- or himself.

Here are some additional guidelines for managing disciplinary matters involving your school-age child:

■ *Be as specific as possible about what you want—or don't want—your child to do.*

School-age children tend to hold parents to their exact words, so your
directives and rules should be very clear. It isn't enough to tell a
seven-year-old, "I want you to be on your best behavior when we visit
Aunt Marian." Instead, the seven-year-old needs a few specific examples of what constitutes "good" as opposed to "bad" behavior. Although children are likely to tune out long-winded descriptions and
explanations, they do need specific images to use in controlling their
behavior.

Besides making sure that children know *what* you expect of them,
you should also make sure they know *how* to meet those expectations.
Whenever possible, teach them various ways in which they can control
their "unacceptable" behavior, or change it, and still derive personal
satisfaction.

Finally, give the reasons behind your requests and check to make
sure your child understands and accepts those reasons. The more a
school-age child buys into *why* a certain command or rule is being
issued, the more likely she or he is to cooperate with that command
or rule.

It isn't always easy to communciate reasons to be a "newly" rational
child without opening up a prolonged debate. Again, patience is a
necessity. The long-term benefit, however, far outweighs the short-
term effort.

For convenience' sake every parent of a school-age child occasionally resorts to demanding obedience strictly "because I say so." Just
try to keep these occasions to a bare minimum. If you don't, your "say-
so" starts losing its effectiveness.

■ *Be honest about the possible difficulty or unpleasantness in- volved in what you want your child to do.*

Don't seduce your child into following a certain rule or performing a
certain task by sugarcoating the consequences. Once your child finds
out the truth, she or he will cease to trust you. Instead, anticipate
any problems your child is likely to have with the rule or task and
acknowledge those problems up front. Obviously you don't want to
belabor these problems. But you also don't want to leave your child
unprepared and possibly unwilling to overcome them as well as suspicious ever after of your judgment in such matters.

For example, suppose you want your child to be home from playing
each day by five in the afternoon so that she or he is off the streets

during rush hour and has plenty of time to get ready for dinner. After communicating this rule to your child and your reasons for making it, let her or him know that you're aware of how hard it can be to stop playing when you're having fun—but that you believe you can count on her or him to do these things even if they aren't easy.

■ *Criticize your child's behavior, not your child.*

When your child does something wrong, don't imply that she or he is "wrong." Instead, stay focused on the particular incident at hand and why the behavior is unacceptable.

For example, if your child throws something at you in anger, resist the temptation to yell something like "You're being a real monster today." Instead, say in a more controlled voice, "That's a very wrong thing to do," and lead her or him to understand *why*.

Children in the middle years are very sensitive about their self-worth and can be devastated by even the mildest criticism directed—intentionally or unintentionally—toward who they are. Whatever they may have done, it somehow seemed right to them at the time. Their misperception needs to be corrected; they don't need to be "corrected" as individuals.

■ *Don't permit discussions involving misbehavior to escalate into arguments.*

Every time you're obligated to confront your child about something "wrong" that's been done, give her or him a chance to tell you about it before you drop the matter entirely or administer punishment. Listen carefully to what your child says, without interrupting, and make sure that you understand her or his version of what happened. This can give you valuable insights into the nature of your child's ongoing emotional life as well as into the particular episode at hand.

In these discussions, also be alert to your child's *nonverbal* communication. For example, if your child avoids eye contact or fidgets excessively, it could be a sign that she or he is fearful, lying, or hiding something. Assuming that you suspect such is the case, question your child tactfully, opening up every opportunity for some information to be volunteered.

Keep discussions relatively short and simple. School-age children can be very clever at extending a dialogue, either to press their point or to forestall punishment, but a child is not yet your intellectual equal. You can't expect to reason out everything, nor can you always come to full agreement about all the issues involved in the incident.

Once you feel that you have given your child a fair chance to talk and that you have adequate knowledge about what has happened and why, bring the conversation to a close. Then make a more or less "formal" and "final" announcement of how you interpret what has happened and, if appropriate, the consequences of what she or he has or hasn't done.

■ *Make any punishment fit the misdemeanor.*

In many cases, your criticism and apparent disappointment may be sufficient punishment. Certainly this should be your goal. However, in those cases in which stronger discipline seems warranted, make every effort to relate the punishment to the particular wrongdoing.

For example, if your child creates a mess, assign her or him the job of cleaning it up. If that's not possible, suggest some other chore. If a child strikes another child, insist that she or he apologize to that child and then remain alone and quiet in her or his room for an appropriate amount of time. If a child fails to do homework or chores because she or he was watching television, don't allow any viewing for an appropriate period of time.

This strategy not only appeals to a school-age child's need for logic and justice in life but also teaches responsibility for the consequences of specific actions. If you rely on a fixed, limited repertoire of punishments—for example, consistently either denying television privileges or "grounding" your child, no matter what the offense—your child will gradually learn to tolerate such punishments (whether or not she or he lets you know it), and they will lose their deterrent power. Even worse, you will be teaching your child to see the misbehavior-punishment cycle as a ritual game that is played between the two of you.

Whenever you are disciplining a child, try to remain in firm control of your temper, your words, and your actions. Your authoritative demeanor will not only help you manage disciplinary matters as efficiently as possible without negative emotional repercussions but also set a powerful example of self-control for your child.

■ *Try never to spank or strike your child.*

Resorting to physical violence gives children a very negative example of what to do when one is losing control of her or his emotions. It also automatically provokes fear and resentment. Children have little choice but to suppress most, if not all, of this fear and resentment—a development that threatens their long-term, overall emotional well-being and damages their relationship with you.

Despite being aware of the repercussions, even the most well-meaning parents can, on occasion, get carried away and strike or spank their child, especially if they themselves received this type of discipline when they were children. In the event that you do strike or spank your child, immediately offer her or him a calm but sincere apology and proceed with another, more constructive form of punishment.

Then forgive yourself and renew your personal commitment not to let a similar loss of self-control happen again.

■ *Try to give your child more positive than negative feedback.*

The best way to motivate your child to behave well and strengthen the effectiveness of any discipline you're compelled to administer from time to time is to make sure that you *praise* more often than you *criticize* your child. Be on the lookout for commendable behavior and comment on it. At the same time, ignore behavior that isn't commendable as much as you can.

You may also try to assist your child in those activities during which she or he is most inclined to exhibit appropriate behavior or perform exceptionally well. Your child's self-esteem will be bolstered, and you will have more opportunities to bestow praise upon her or him. This technique is particularly advisable if your child is experiencing major discpline or self-confidence problems in some other aspect of her or his life.

■ *As much as possible and appropriate, coordinate your own disciplinary policies with others that your child may experience.*

Talk with all of your child's teachers about their specific disciplinary policies in the classroom as well as the general ones of the school. Also, let each of your child's teachers know about your disciplinary policies at home. Work out a "compromise" policy that helps ensure that your child's disciplinary problems are handled in a consistent manner, whether they crop up at home or in school.

It's also a good idea to inform other caretakers of your child—babysitters, relatives, or friends—about your preferred ways of administering discipline. This helps prevent your child from being treated too leniently or too abusively when you aren't there to supervise.

In addition, regularly interview your child's teachers and caretakers at some length about how your child behaves in their presence. Often disciplinary problems only arise, or disappear, in a particular interpersonal or environmental context.

If you find out that your child misbehaves when she or he is away from you, try to arrange a meeting that includes you, your child, and the teacher or caretaker who encounters this misbehavior. At this meeting, present to the child what you've been told in a loving and nonthreatening manner, ask for her or his reaction, and then discuss the problem and how to manage it, giving priority in the discussion to your child's comments and suggestions.

If such a meeting can't be arranged, then tactfully bring up the issue with your child by yourself. In the event that she or he persists in denying the accusation, take a hypothetical approach (i.e., "Supposing someone did act this way . . .") and briefly discuss the problem and the possible solutions.

Assuming you discover that your child misbehaves only in your presence, it's more diplomatic to talk about the issue with your child by yourself rather than including the teacher or caretaker who made the problem known to you. Again, be very supportive and nonthreatening and solicit your child's comment on how the situation might be improved.

■ Set a good example.

To a school-age child, an adult's word is only as good as her or his deed; and a school-age child is keenly observant regarding adult deeds. Anytime you and your child are together, make a special effort to practice what you preach and to be obedient to rules (including those imposed by outside authorities, such as speed limits, crossing signals, and litter laws).

QUESTIONNAIRE:

Problem Behavior in the Middle Years

Here is a two-part questionnaire you can use for two purposes:

1. to begin making distinctions between more serious and less serious discipline problems in your school-age child's life; and

2. to begin making possible connections between your school-age child's discipline problems and emotional issues contributing to, or resulting from, those problems.

First, complete "Part A: Discipline Problems," rating the degree of each problem on a scale of 1 to 5, with 5 being the most severe rating. (*Note:* Some of the listed problems overlap in certain situations.) Next, complete "Part B: Emotional Issues," rating each issue in the same manner. Then make a list of all the problems in Part A that you've rated 4 or 5 and a separate list of all of the issues in Part B that you've rated 4 or 5. Finally, draw any cause-and-effect relationships that seem relevant to you between items on your Part A, 4 or 5 rating list and items on your Part B, 4 or 5 rating list.

If you have rated ten or more items 4 or 5 in either of the original lists, then your child may be suffering from serious emotional problems. If you think this may be the case, consider seeking professional help.

PART A: DISCIPLINE PROBLEMS

1. Doesn't obey rules	1	2	3	4	5
2. Doesn't play cooperatively with siblings	1	2	3	4	5
3. Doesn't play cooperatively with peers	1	2	3	4	5
4. Creates disturbances when other adults are present	1	2	3	4	5
5. Bullies siblings or peers	1	2	3	4	5
6. Talks back to parents	1	2	3	4	5
7. Talks back to adults other than parents	1	2	3	4	5
8. Destroys property	1	2	3	4	5
9. Lies or refuses to tell the truth	1	2	3	4	5
10. Steals	1	2	3	4	5
11. Doesn't clean up own messes	1	2	3	4	5
12. Picks quarrels	1	2	3	4	5
13. Uses offensive language	1	2	3	4	5
14. Strikes out physically at others	1	2	3	4	5
15. Expresses displeasure or resentment when asked to do something	1	2	3	4	5
16. Refuses to do something when asked	1	2	3	4	5
17. Fails to do something after agreeing to do it	1	2	3	4	5
18. Blames other people for own actions	1	2	3	4	5
19. Acts disturbingly immature	1	2	3	4	5
20. Gets into fights	1	2	3	4	5

PART B: EMOTIONAL ISSUES

1. Feelings get hurt	1	2	3	4	5
2. Acts in a shy manner	1	2	3	4	5
3. Acts in an aggressive manner	1	2	3	4	5
4. Worries	1	2	3	4	5
5. Exhibits fear	1	2	3	4	5
6. Gets distracted	1	2	3	4	5
7. Seems restless	1	2	3	4	5
8. Overreacts	1	2	3	4	5
9. Goes through major mood changes	1	2	3	4	5

10. Gets frustrated performing tasks	1	2	3	4	5
11. Acts possessively toward parent	1	2	3	4	5
12. Avoids parent	1	2	3	4	5
13. Avoids sibling	1	2	3	4	5
14. Avoids peers in general	1	2	3	4	5
15. Avoids particular peer	1	2	3	4	5
16. Exhibits disappointment	1	2	3	4	5
17. Exhibits boredom	1	2	3	4	5
18. Is unable to sustain relationships	1	2	3	4	5
19. Exhibits hostility	1	2	3	4	5
20. Exhibits unhappiness	1	2	3	4	5

CASE:

The Mother Tester

Danny was a bright, sensitive, loving child until he reached age eight. Almost overnight, it seemed to his mother, Susan, as if he'd been secretly appointed her special persecutor.

Whenever Susan needed to correct Danny's behavior, he screamed, "I hate you. You're the meanest mother on Earth." If she was forced to deny him something, he shrieked, "You don't love me. You don't let me have anything I really want." And yet he constantly followed her around and complained bitterly on those few occasions during the week when she tried to have some moments to herself.

Susan knew from her reading and her conversations with friends that eight-year-olds are inclined to fight with their mothers and thereby act out their own frustrations regarding dependence and control. But Danny's nonstop rebelliousness was taking too much of a toll on her time and energy, not to mention on their relationship. Was something else bothering Danny, Susan wondered, or was this simply a very intense version of the "crazy eights"?

After discussing Danny with his teacher, his baby-sitter, and other adults in the family and observing Danny's day-to-day life more closely for a couple of weeks, Susan was convinced that her son's only significant problem lay in his relationship with her. Therefore, she resolved to improve that relationship as much as possible. Together with her husband, Joe, she devised a two-part plan.

The first part of Susan's plan was to arrange Danny's schedule so that the two of them spent much more time apart from each other, at least for a few weeks. Fortunately, Danny and Joe got along with each other beautifully, and Joe was willing and able to double the time that he took charge of Danny. Even better, this time included many more hours away from home for Danny so that both Danny and his mother could have a complete and refreshing break from each other.

The other part of Susan's plan was to improve the quality of the time that she and Danny did spend together. As often as she could during these times, she gave Danny her undivided attention. She made sure to express her affection for Danny frequently and to engage him in activities that they could both enjoy, such as playing computer and card games, watching television, flying kites in the park, and raking leaves.

Soon after Susan inaugurated her two-part plan, Danny's behavior started changing for the better. He continued to attack Susan verbally from time to time. But when he did, she took it much more in stride, which, in turn, sent a message to Danny that his attack strategy wasn't really accomplishing anything.

By his ninth birthday, Danny had recovered from being an eight-year-old "rebel with a cause." Susan's plan had not eliminated that necessary stage in Danny's emotional growth, nor had it made her job as a mother any less demanding. However, her plan had made that growth period for Danny much less painful and her job as a mother much more rewarding.

At PCGC: Treatment in a Family Context

School-age children who have severe disciplinary or behavioral problems can't be separated from their parents for extensive treatment without suffering some degree of trauma. Furthermore, these disciplinary and emotional problems are most effectively analyzed by examining that child in the context of her or his family life rather than in the context of an isolating, institutional testing.

One solution to these difficulties is to offer a "home living" environment within the hospital or clinic: a place where the family can remain together, and function as a family, while the child's problems are being evaluated. This situation allows clinicians and treatment teams to witness the family culture in operation—either through "visits" or through one-way-mirror observations—and to apply systematically a variety of interventions in a controlled environment.

In addition to severe disciplinary and behavioral problems, issues involving school-age children that are appropriate for this kind of comprehensive, on-site care include:

■ emotional complications relating to a chronic physical illness;

■ psychosomatic disorders, such as asthma, gastrointestinal illness, or diabetes;

■ problems related to eating (including obesity and such eating disorders as anorexia or bulimia);

■ school phobia;

■ severe depression and/or suicidal behavior;

■ persistent attempts to run away;

■ a situation in which there are multiple patients within a single family.

PCGC has a Family Apartment Unit Program that offers this kind of clinical approach for school-age children and their families needing intensive psychiatric evaluation and treatment in a therapeutic setting. The family as a whole literally moves into a two-room apartment (bedroom and living room/dining and kitchen area) within the PCGC complex for professional observation and intervention on a twenty-four-hour basis.

Prior to admission of the family, there are several assessment conferences with the family and the referring therapist to clarify how the program runs and how it might be useful and to arrange a schedule for the program that suits all individuals involved. On arrival at the apartment for participation in the program, the family inevitably has to mobilize its resources to cope with the novel circumstances. This mobilization effort in itself helps to move the family toward positive change.

Once the family is fairly well established in the apartment, PCGC clinicians and treatment teams orchestrate therapeutic interventions to correspond with their observations. A "typical" family therapy session is only one of many possible interventions aimed at reorganizing the way the family functions so that it as a whole and the child in particular can better manage the latter's problem. Other possibilities include testing (medical as well as psychological), education, conflict resolution, skill training, role-playing, and behavioral modification.

The primary considerations for discharge from PCGC's Family Apartment Unit Program are whether there has been a decrease in the child's symptoms and whether the family has begun to show itself capable of modifying those patterns of interaction that have contributed to the child's problem. The overall goal in every case is for the family to learn how to take effective control of its own difficulties and how to make effective use of the outside support systems.

Check with local mental health organizations to find out if there are similar programs in your area. If not, discuss with your psychiatrist, psychologist, or mental-health professional ways to incorporate similar features into your child's therapy.

4.

Chores

G iving school-age kids chores to do at home helps them teach themselves the ways, means, and virtues of behaving responsibly. The long-term result is a lowering of stress and a heightening of self-esteem. As a bonus, performing chores instills in kids a greater appreciation for their parents' efforts at setting up and maintaining a harmonious home environment.

Some six- to twelve-year-olds take naturally to chores. They may see performing chores as a kind of adult "game," as an emotionally satisfying way of imposing order on chaos, as a source of "instant pride" and gratification, or as an extension of their love for their home and their parents. A child who falls into this category should be directed toward some of the more complicated and rewarding household activities that go beyond mere chore performance, such as cooking, gardening, car maintenance, home repair, or home decorating.

A child who expresses a sincere enthusiasm and talent for one of these activities can become an apprentice as well as a chore doer. Be careful not to force matters. Instead, keep a keen eye on your child's interests, follow her or his lead, and put everything on a voluntary basis. In the meantime, your child should still have a certain number of required chores.

Regrettably, most children between the ages of six and thirteen do not fit the above description. For numerous reasons, including simple lack of interest, they do not tend to take to chores naturally. However, if they receive firm policies, firm direction, and firm monitoring from their parents, they can learn to perform chores not only skillfully and dependably but also enjoyably.

Most children in their middle years have no choice but to participate in personal and home maintenance if the household is to function smoothly. This is especially true in the case of households with one parent or two working parents. Unless the participation is organized into clear, well-conceived, and mutually agreed-upon task assignments, it will forever give rise to disappointments, resentment, misunderstandings, quarrels, and animosities.

Assigning chores and making sure that they are performed can be an emotional battleground in itself. Parents can easily find themselves turning into dictators, at which point children inevitably cast themselves as defiant—and self-righteous—rebels.

Here are guidelines for managing chore assignments so that there is a minimum of stress and strain:

■ *Create with your child a schedule of chores that she or he needs to perform on a regular basis.*

Work together with your child to make this schedule so that both of you have input. Be as specific as you reasonably can, including days and time frames for performing individual tasks. When the schedule is finished, copy it over so that it's very neat and official looking and post it in a highly visible place in the home. You might even want to include spaces on the list for marking off each time a task has been completed.

The actual number of chores—and the duration of each one—should be tailored to fit the age of the child and the amount of free time the child has: not so many that completing all the chores satisfactorily becomes a hardship and not so few that no real sacrifice is involved. Start low and adjust the list every few months—adding, subtracting, or changing—if and when the situation seems to warrant it.

Ideally, there should be one or more tasks that the child needs to do, and that a parent can monitor, on a daily basis. "Two or three days" seems like a much longer period of time to a six- to twelve-year-old child than it does to an adult, and you don't want too much time to pass during which your child feels as if she or he has no household responsibilities. Examples of daily tasks a school-age child might perform include picking up toys and other objects from the family-room floor, setting the table, making sure that certain wastebaskets are emptied, or feeding the family pet.

■ *Assign chores that make your child feel that she or he is making an important contribution to family life.*

In addition to personally meaningful responsibilities like "clean your room," the list should include some family-oriented tasks like "wash the dishes," "clean the inside of the car," or "bind papers for recycling." Some of these tasks should be ones that the child performs completely independent of anyone else.

Be sure to solicit suggestions for family-oriented tasks from your child. You may be surprised at the number that she or he has observed or feels capable of undertaking.

Always try to let your child do any job that she or he volunteers to do, even if it means revising your normal method of doing it. Your child's spirit of initiative should be encouraged whenever possible.

If your child wants to take on a chore that you think is beyond her or his capabilities, try breaking it down into parts and giving your child one of them to do. Add parts as competence is acquired. Again, you may be surprised at your child's capabilities, given the right opportunity.

■ *Assign chores that suit your child's interests, temperament, and skills.*

Any task that your child enjoys doing will be better performed and therefore more rewarding to both you and her or him. Keep your eyes open for tasks, or parts of tasks, that might fit this category. Your child may not come up with many suggestions of her or his own, partly because she or he is not as familiar as you are with the full range of chores that need to be done.

■ *Assign some chores that you and your child can perform together.*

Working together is a wonderful way of getting to know each other better, of learning to interact more cooperatively, and of building stronger emotional bonds. Most of the chores you assign should be those that can be done without your help, but one or two could be done together. Start with easy chores—ones that allow you plenty of freedom to chat and even to play around—and then progress to those that are more complicated—ones that your child may not even be capable of tackling without your being there.

Exercise special patience with your child in these situations. Remember that your goal is not only to finish the task successfully but also to develop a good, long-term partnership. If performing a certain chore together doesn't work out after you've given it a sufficient trial, tactfully bring the experiment to an end, wait a while (a few weeks or more), and try performing another chore together: one that you feel has a better chance.

■ *Make sure that your child understands how best to perform each chore.*

Before officially assigning a task to your child, make sure she or he knows how to do it, when to do it, why it needs to be done, and what you expect as a result. Children don't respond well to lengthy directions, so be as clear and concise as you can without leaving any room for misunderstanding.

■ *As much as possible, don't do chores yourself that your child fails to do.*

Let your child see the consequences of her or his negligence. For example, if she or he forgets to set the table, keep the meal waiting until the task is accomplished. If your child doesn't empty the waste-baskets, let them overflow as long as you can until your child empties them. If your child doesn't pick up her or his toys, leave them on the floor (sliding them out of traffic paths) until she or he collects them.

■ Establish, and stick to, appropriate procedures and penalties for not doing chores.

At the time you first establish what chores your child is to perform, you should also tell her or him the penalty policy for nonperformance of chores. This policy should be general and flexible enough so that individual penalties can fit specific situations.

For example, you might agree on a policy of "losing time for play, television, or other personal activities." Then, assuming there comes a time when your child plays outdoors instead of doing a chore, you might ground your child for a day or require her or him to spend a certain amount of time alone in her or his room.

Make certain that your child pays an appropriate penalty, if warranted, *every time* she or he fails to perform a task, in accordance with your original understanding. And try to enforce the penalty as soon as possible after the nonperformance, preferably within a day or two.

As a general rule, it's not advisable to punish children by cutting or withholding their allowance. In the first place, it inclines them to associate doing chores with earning money instead of doing them purely for their own sake and/or for the good of the family. In the second place, being without their regular amount of money may put them at a serious and unfair disadvantage, causing them, for example, to miss a worthwhile outing with friends or to make up the shortfall by stealing, lying, or cheating.

However, if your child's misbehavior involves money (e.g., breaking a window that must be repaired), then it may well be appropriate to ask your child to pay for part, or all, of the damage. This can be done in a lump sum or in installments.

At the same time that you set up a penalty policy, you also need to establish procedures for those occasions when your child has a time conflict affecting chore performance. In cases when your child knows in advance that she or he may not—or will not—be able to do her or his chores, she or he could be required to renegotiate the chore time with you, volunteer to do some other chore at a more convenient time, or find a replacement to do the chore.

In emergency situations, when there's a good reason why the chores can't be done and advance notice can't be given, your child should be required to do everything within reason to let you know about the situation as soon as possible.

To Bribe or Not to Bribe?

A major dilemma for every parent of a school-age child is whether or not to barter money, possessions, or privileges in exchange for the child's good behavior or successful task performance. If the question doesn't first occur to the parent, it will eventually be raised by the child. And if such a bartering system prevails in the outside, adult world, why shouldn't it prevail inside the home, between parent and child?

On the one hand, this type of reward system in the home eliminates the need to wrangle over such issues as "Why should I?" School-age children are generally quite eager to strike bargains that offer them tangible benefits. If they should ultimately fail to meet their end of the bargain, the punishment is built in: They don't get the reward. Thus, a lot of time and emotionally draining energy is saved for both parent and child.

On the other hand, this type of reward system sets up a highly questionable value system. Children learn to sell their good behavior and chore-doing skills instead of offering them freely out of a sense of love, self-satisfaction, and personal responsibility. Given this "sell" mentality, the price for good behavior and chore-doing skills is bound to go up as time goes on. The result is a situation in which children can arbitrarily pick or choose when and how to be good or to do chores on their own terms—a situation filled with emotionally upsetting booby traps for parent and child alike.

Unfortunately, there is no black-and-white answer to the bribery question. What works between adults in the outside world is not *always* applicable to the parent-and-child situation inside the home, where the child is most definitely dependent on the parent both financially and in terms of the child's moral education.

However, *sometimes* what works in the outside world *is* applicable and even appropriate. Occasionally you do need to bargain with your child to achieve more than what is normally expected and your child does need to learn the positive aspects of how bargaining works in the real world.

Here are some tips for determining whether or not to bribe as well as how and what to bribe when doing so seems appropriate:

■ *Above all, save bribery for very special situations.*

Don't apply it to regular chores but to one-time tasks that are unusually time consuming or undesirable. Also, allow a generous amount of time to lapse between bribe situations: at least two weeks for a six- to eight-year-old and at least a month for a nine- to twelve-year-old.

Try never to offer a bribe merely for good behavior. This strategy undermines your ability to influence your child's behavior under any circumstances *without* offering some tangible incentive.

In cases in which exceptionally good behavior is desired, you might try incorporating some task into the period during which the good behavior is to be exercised. For example, if you want to help make sure that your seven-year-old behaves well at a large family gathering, you might offer to pay your child to watch over one of the younger children there—an assignment that would include the direction not to engage in roughhousing, monopolizing adult attention, or wandering out of sight. Nevertheless, it would be much better in the long run if you could forgo bribery and give your child a chance to live up to your expectations.

■ *Retain control of what the bribe is to be.*

Don't ask your child what she or he would like in exchange for doing something. You might get an answer that you don't want! Offer the child a specific bribe of your own choice at the same time that you present the assignment.

Depending on the situation, your child's emotional maturity, and the relationship you have with her or him, you might allow a small margin for bargaining *after* you've presented your offer. But know your limit ahead of time and stick to it, even if the assignment ultimately goes unaccepted. It's better to lose out one or two times than to succumb to a policy that makes you fail on a regular basis.

■ *Make the reward modest and specific.*

Your child should be encouraged to work for the reward in itself and not *according to its value*. For this reason, it's not necessary or even advisable that the reward be exactly commensurate with the task from an adult-world point of view. It should simply be something that you know your child would like regardless of whether it is attached to task performance.

Be conservative in what you offer. Don't verbally set up

equations between the reward and the task (e.g., "I think this task is worth a trip to the zoo"). Instead, refer to the bribe as a treat that you are offering as a special, appreciative gesture for doing something above and beyond normal requirements. And try not to create a pattern of bribery that indirectly sets up a value scale for different types of tasks.

Also, your bribe should be something that is well defined and therefore easily visualized. This makes for a much more powerful incentive. Avoid relatively vague bribes like "I'll buy you something at the store" (what? when?) or "I'll look the job over after you're done and decide." You might be paving the way for disappointment and discouragement.

The best bribes are nonmonetary ones. They not only make for more appealing mental pictures but also don't lend themselves as easily to creating a cut-and-dried value system. Try offering specific privileges, outings, or goods. If you do offer money, offer a fixed amount, not increments per parts of the job or a sliding scale.

It's best to avoid bartering with official rules and procedures involving chores, allowance, bedtimes, television hours, and so on. A bribe should involve something entirely outside—and in addition to—the normal, assured, and reassuring scheme of things.

■ *If possible, make the reward appropriate to the request.*
While you don't want to set up a *value equation* between a task and a bribe, it helps if you can draw a *logical connection* between a task and a bribe. For example, if you want the garage cleaned out, you might promise an excursion by car. If you want the room where you watch television cleaned up, you might offer to rent a video for that night. If you want the kitchen floor mopped and waxed, you might propose making a special snack or meal. This way, the child can truly enjoy the fruits of her or his labor.

■ *Provide the reward as soon as possible after it is earned.*
To children in the middle years, more than a week away is a very long time. Live up to your end of the bargain promptly, being careful to wait until the entire task is completed. Also, don't offer the reward in advance. It may ultimately not be earned!

■ *Occasionally give surprise rewards for exceptional task performance.*
After children have been especially diligent in performing

their assigned chores over an extended period of time, it's appropriate to surprise them with some sort of tangible acknowledgment that you've noticed, and are pleased by, what they've done. A surprise reward is even more appropriate when children take it upon themselves to perform a nonrequired task or when they perform an exceptionally onerous task at your request without getting a bribe.

In these situations, the best reward is arranging to do something special together that you both enjoy, such as fishing, going out to eat, visiting an amusement park, or taking in a movie. Ideally, this treat will be just for you and your child, independent of other children in the family (unless they also have the same record of exceptional performance, and everyone can enjoy the event and each other's company during the event).

5.
Running Away

The image of a school-age child defiantly insisting that she or he will run away from home and be self-sufficient is a popular piece of Americana, inspiring amusement for parents and romantic adventure for children. The reality, however, is frightening both from the child's and the parent's point of view.

Even if a would-be runaway only pretends to make good on this threat by hiding somewhere or by fleeing to a friend's or relative's home, the emotional effect on the family of such a dramatic gesture can be very painful. The would-be runaway must forcibly confront just how isolated, dependent, and powerless she or he is, while the parent, in addition to being worried about her or his child, can't help but feel personally rejected, humiliated, and frustrated.

Once a child who has threatened to leave home actually takes to the streets, with or without any serious intentions, her or his life itself is at risk. The child's anger, hurt, and confusion make her or him exceptionally accident-prone. They also make her or him exceptionally vulnerable to suggestion and coercion; and tragically, the streets are becoming more and more populated by molesters, criminals, and opportunists who are dangerously clever at suggesting and coercing.

To prevent runaway threats from occurring or to manage them when they do occur, follow these recommendations:

■ *Keep arguments from escalating into verbal fights.*
Most threats to run away emerge in the context of heated arguments between parent and child, when the child feels she or he has no other ammunition to use. Therefore, guard against arguing to the point where you and your child are deliberately intimidating each other. If you feel things getting out of hand, stop speaking, pause, and suggest that you both take time to cool down—at least a few minutes—before resuming the conversation.

■ *Never directly or indirectly present leaving home as an option.*
Resist any temptation to dare your child to leave home or to tease your child about being incapable of surviving away from the family.

Always make it clear that you want your child to live at home because you love her or him, not just because you are responsible for her or his welfare.

Also, be careful not to draw a strong, dramatic line between home and the outside world in your child's imagination. In conversations or outright arguments with your child, try never to use provocative phrases like "As long as you're living under my roof, you'll do what I say" or "Once you get out on your own, you're free to do whatever you want; but until then, you have to abide by the rules." These kinds of remarks are, in effect, offering your child a very risky choice.

■ *Always take seriously any threat your child makes to run away.*
In the vast majority of situations, a child who threatens to run away doesn't really want to leave home. Instead, she or he feels rejected or out of place at home. The threat to run away is simply a cry for recognition, love, and acceptance. If you dismiss this threat in your language or behavior, your child may feel not only doubly ignored but also doubly pressured to follow through on the threat or else lose face entirely.

For these reasons, never ridicule, deny, or treat casually any threat that your child makes about running away. Let your child know immediately, in a calm but firm voice, that you don't want her or him to run away, that it would make you very unhappy, and that you will do everything you can not to let it happen—or, if it does happen, anyway, to bring her or him back.

■ *Offer your child options to running away.*
If, during the course of day-to-day family life, you sense that your child is contemplating running away or feels in any way "crowded" or burdensome at home, take appropriate action to make her or his life within the family more satisfying. Assuming your child seems to desire more privacy, you might arrange matters so that she or he can be alone and undisturbed for a certain period of time each day or can have a room of her or his own. Assuming your child seems to desire more attention, you might give her or him a leadership role in a particular family activity.

In situations when your child literally threatens to run away, ask her or him if there isn't some other possible solution. If your child isn't forthcoming with alternatives, you might suggest getting away from each other for a while. Perhaps your child could visit a relative or a friend whose parents you know and trust.

■ *Don't hesitate to search for your child as soon as you discover that she or he has run away.*
Frequently, parents of runaways will convince themselves not to take action immediately but to allow their absent child a little time to let

off some steam. This strategy may be well intentioned, but it's too risky. Minute by minute, as a runaway child imagines that no one cares, her or his emotional well-being suffers. And while most runaways in this age range voluntarily return home safe and sound within twenty-four hours, the physical dangers any runaway might encounter during this time period are horrendous. Thus, it's *never* advisable to wait before trying to find your runaway child and bring her or him back home.

■ *When your child returns from running away, express your love for her or him and your pleasure that she or he is back.*
Your priority in this situation is to convince your child that returning home is in her or his best interest and to prevent her or him from turning around and running away all over again.

Remember that the typical runaway is motivated by a feeling of rejection. Reassure your child that she or he is *not* being rejected, whatever other problems both of you may be having.

■ *As much as possible, avoid punishing your child for the act of running away.*
Most likely, your child's embarrassment at having failed to remain independent and regret at having caused you so much trouble are punishment enough, although you may not see any evidence of this for a few days. Regard the incident itself as a plea for more understanding from you and act accordingly in addressing any problems or disciplinary issues that might have led to it. You may even consider having a little celebration in honor of your child's coming home.

■ *Encourage your child to have confidential relationships with other adults whom you trust.*
Children need help in understanding their parents, and the most valuable support can come from adults outside the immediate family. Far from diminishing your personal intimacy with, and authority over, your child, a close relationship between your child and another adult will actually enhance that intimacy and authority. Even more to the point, that adult will serve as a safe refuge during times when you and your child are temporarily at odds with each other so that she or he won't feel compelled simply to run away.

6.
Depression and Stress

The extra agitation of the nervous system that we call stress is inescapable for school-age children as well as for adults. In fact, a fully realized human life is inconceivable *without* it. Far from being just toxic to the emotions, making us feel frustrated, insecure, and overwrought, stress can also be a tonic—spicing life with added interest, enthusiasm, and drama.

In other words, stress in itself isn't a problem, although it may be a response to a negative situation in the environment. The real problem lies in stress *management*. And for a child in the middle years, effectively managing stress often requires parental help.

In contrast to stress, depression is an emotional illness, always characterized by feelings of hopelessness and helplessness. Like sadness, it is generally triggered by stress and, in turn, generally produces stress of its own. Unlike sadness, however, it's a psychologically paralyzed state of being that can last for several months, or longer, at a time.

Until very recently, experts assumed that depression, being much more serious in nature than sadness, could only afflict adolescents and adults, who are intellectually much more mature than children. Clinical research has since overturned this assumption. Experts now say that about 10 percent of all children suffer serious depression during their middle years—almost two-thirds the rate for adults—and that in either stage of life depression has no proven link with intellectual development. Thus, in addition to helping their school-age children control stress, parents must also be prepared to help them manage depression.

Intellectual development aside, some school-age children do seem basically more vulnerable than others to stress and, further along the stress continuum, to depression. Whether or not this quality is related to the sensitivity of their nervous systems, as some neurologists have suggested, it does seem to be constitutional in nature rather than environmental. In very deprived and abusive home (or homeless) situations and in very affluent and loving homes, the child population between the ages of six and thirteen exhibits the same spectrum of vulnerability.

At one end of this spectrum are kids who react quickly, resiliently, and resourcefully to whatever happens—good or bad. When their birthday makes them the center of attention, they're happy, poised, eager to have fun, and anxious to see that others are happy. When they receive bad news, they respond appropriately and shrug it off as best they can. When others attack them, they discharge their anger by counterattacking, but only as much as necessary to defend themselves.

At the other end of the spectrum are kids whose reaction to good or bad events is prolonged, noticeably out of proportion, and counterproductive. During their birthday celebrations, they're either very shy and embarrassed or overly excited, causing discomfort for both themselves and their guests. When bad news comes, they're either unreasonably silent or uncontrollably emotional. When they're under attack, they either withdraw immediately or counterattack with unwarranted brutality and vindictiveness.

Most school-age children are in the middle third of the spectrum—sometimes very vulnerable to stress or depression, sometimes not. That your child is more inclined to be vulnerable doesn't mean that she or he is less emotionally healthy or more emotionally disadvantaged than stronger peers. A special vulnerability to stress and depression may render an individual particularly good at fighting for justice, caring for others, appreciative of beauty, or able to foresee—and forestall—catastrophes.

No matter how your school-age child is constitutionally equipped to *receive* stress in general, you must always be ready to help your child *manage* specific incidents of stress—and, if stress should turn from bad to worse, specific incidents of depression. The best thing you can do is to make the most of every opportunity that comes along, big or small, for you and your child to enjoy each other. It not only gives your child a reservoir of happiness and high self-regard from which to draw in emergencies but also brings the two of you closer so that your child is more likely to seek help from you when it's needed.

Here are other important steps to follow:

■ *Anticipate situations when your child may experience stress or depression and prepare for them accordingly.*
Certain easily foreseeable events are guaranteed to be stressful to children and may even give rise to depression as a direct consequence of the stress or as a counterbalancing aftereffect. Among such events are a stay in the hospital, the start or the end of the school year, a

scheduled visit by a relative, a planned family move, a major holiday, or the birth of a sibling. To prepare for such an event, you can begin well in advance to talk with your child so that she or he goes through it with reasonably informed expectations and to orchestrate it so that it isn't too unsettling.

Other events, equally guaranteed to be stressful, are more difficult, but still possible, to anticipate. It's all a matter of personal judgment. For example, it may or may not be appropriate to anticipate the death of a close relative who is very sick. When your child joins a ball team, it may or may not be appropriate to anticipate that she or he will not perform well.

You have less scope to prepare your child for these more hypothetical events, but you can still make sure that they don't catch him or her completely by surprise. To avoid scaring your child unnecessarily, take advantage of moments in your normal conversations to bring up such possibilities in a sensitive and constructive manner.

■ *Be alert for symptoms that your child may be going through excessive stress or depression.*
The universe of symptoms associated with stress and depression is basically the same. But the possible symptoms involved in a particular case of stress or depression can vary considerably from child to child.

Emotionally, these symptoms include fear, dejection, boredom, moodiness, irritability, rage, anger, or overexcitement. Behaviorally, they include any radical change in conduct, from unusual withdrawal to unusual belligerence, or from unusual placidity to unusual twitchiness and teeth clenching. Psychosomatically, they include otherwise inexplicable stomachaches, headaches, or changes in sleeping pattern or appetite.

Whether a particular constellation of symptoms indicates stress or depression is determined by how pronounced and sustained the symptoms are. In some cases, a child's symptoms may go unnoticed or ignored while they're in their "stress stage," thus increasing the odds that the child will develop a full-blown depression: a psychological condition that is much more likely to command attention.

For a school-age child experiencing stress, the symptoms usually diminish, if they don't disappear altogether, within a few days after they first appear. In severe cases of stress, they may last as long as two months; but during that period they are intermittent rather than persistent.

On the other hand, a school-age child is not clinically considered depressed until the symptoms have lasted longer than two months without significant interruption or diminution. And the extent to which the depression *might* last is entirely open-ended.

The bottom line is that stress is much less intense and much easier to treat than depression, which makes it imperative that parents do what they reasonably can to spot and alleviate the stress symptoms quickly and efficiently.

■ *Whenever your child seems troubled, be an especially good listener and observer.*

Encourage sharing of feelings by engaging your child in supportive conversations. Often children can overcome their stress or depression simply by talking it out.

A supportive conversation does not require that you judge or resolve your child's feelings. Such reactions—or their prospect—might inhibit your child from unburdening her or his soul to you. Instead, this type of conversation requires you to be especially attentive to what your child says, only offering commentary that helps her or him be more forthcoming.

During such talks, demonstrate to your child that you sympathize with an emotionally painful dilemma by *reflecting* her or his feelings. From time to time, nod affirmatively to indicate that you understand what your child is saying, paraphrase key statements, and adopt facial expressions, phrases, and vocal tones that are compatible with those that your child is using.

Reflecting your child's feelings does not mean that you condone them; rather, that you realize and appreciate the significant impact these feelings have on your child's life.

In addition to being a good listener at times when your child is overly stressed or depressed, you also need to be a good observer. Frequently the real cause of a child's emotional problems is masked—intentionally or unintentionally—by outward behavior.

For example, a child who is very upset over the loss of a parent, either through death or divorce, may subconsciously choose to be unusually aggressive or hyperactive rather than to wallow in grief, as one might expect. Similarly, a child who is mercilessly teased about being fat by classmates may resort to abnormal overeating rather than to a more "logical" strategy of self-starvation.

When your child is behaving in a strange manner, try to observe her or him in a variety of different settings on various occasions before jumping to conclusions as to the reasons for the behavior. Also, elicit from other adults in your child's world, discreetly and confidentially, their observations.

■ *Identify what can be done to make your child feel better.*

Once you understand *how* your child is feeling and, to some degree, *why* she or he is feeling that way, solicit her or his suggestions about what can be done to alleviate these feelings or change the situation that is causing them. Be sure to give your child some time to think about possible suggestions and ask for recommendations concerning what your child and what you—or others—can do.

If your child is unable to come up with any ideas or if those she or he voices are inappropriate, then try generating some of your own. Again, give yourself time to think about the most practical and potentially effective strategies for the particular situation at hand and include ideas concerning what your child and you or others can do.

Ideas for overcoming stress or depression tend to fall into two categories: They're either remedies or distractions. Remedies involve learning to live with, or through, the situation that is causing the stress or depression. Distractions involve diverting one's mind away from preoccupation with the cause of stress or depression. In many cases, a combination of remedies and distractions is appropriate.

For example, a child's grief for a parent who has died may be remedied (if not cured) by some sort of formal ceremony in which the child is able to say a personal good-bye to the parent: a special hour of reminiscence with the surviving parent, a gravesite visit, or a careful packing away of the deceased parent's favorite belongings. On the other hand, the same child may also be distracted from grief by going on an especially happy outing with the surviving parent, becoming involved in a new group activity, or getting a new pet.

Assuming a child is subjected to the stress of being teased about her or his weight, some remedies might be to teach the child a few good-natured "comeback" lines and to help the child follow a diet and exercise program that will trim off extra flab. Some distractions might be to lead the child to appreciate her or his admirable qualities and engage the child in activities that bolster self-esteem.

■*Avoid indirectly fostering stress and depression through overprotecting or pressuring your child.*

Children during the middle years need room to experiment with difficult life situations so that they can work out those coping strategies that best suit their individual personalities, wishes, and ambitions. It is this effort that puts them in touch with their personal genius and builds character for facing the yet more independent and complicated world of adolescence.

Although you should always be especially solicitous regarding your school-age child's emotional well-being when she or he is actually suffering from stress or depression, don't make it a habit to run interference between your child and any situation that might upset her or him. Your task as a caring parent is to *assist* your child in managing stress or depression, not to manage it yourself.

On the other hand, don't set up overly high expectations for your child regarding her or his abilities to accomplish demanding tasks, to handle difficult situations, or to meet certain standards of maturity. These expectations in themselves often cause a child to experience stress or depression.

A Timetable for Stress

Listed below are situations that are *particularly* stressful for different age groups during the middle years, although a child of *any* age during the middle years can experience *any* of the stressors cited here, regardless of the specific age group listing under which it appears.

Note that stress can result from positive situations as well as negative ones. Also note that certain individual stressors evolve and change character as a child gets older.

For example, a six- to nine-year-old's concern about rules can turn into a more sophisticated concern about responsibilities between the ages of nine and eleven. Similarly, a nine- to eleven-year-old's desire to have the same things that her or his peers have can mature into a concern about overall popularity between the ages of eleven and thirteen.

SIX TO NINE YEARS

- fighting with parents
- parents fighting with each other
- making new friends
- fighting with friends
- being teased or embarrassed
- feeling jealous and/or envious
- being ignored
- rules (remembering, obeying, or breaking)
- not getting the permission or opportunity to do things she or he feels capable of doing
- beginning school
- mother's pregnancy and/or birth or adoption of sibling
- holidays

NINE TO ELEVEN YEARS

- fighting with parents
- parents fighting with each other
- making new friends
- fighting with friends
- family move
- school tests and grades
- money and buying decisions
- games and sports
- feeling overwhelmed with responsibilities (chores, homework, after-school activities)
- having clothes and possessions like the ones that friends have
- trying to be on time
- vacation (away from school or away from home)

ELEVEN TO THIRTEEN YEARS (EARLY ADOLESCENCE)

- family move
- change in family's standard of living (better or worse)
- parents fighting, separating, or divorcing
- school tests and grades
- money and buying decisions
- games and sports
- physical appearance
- sex-related feelings and body changes
- drugs (avoiding, choosing, or taking)
- school, community, and athletic awards, honors, and recognition (winning them or not)
- popularity with peers (having it or not)
- being treated, and treating others, fairly

Depression Questionnaire

The following questionnaire is adapted from instruments used by child psychiatrists and psychologists to determine whether a school-age child might be suffering from depression. It is designed to be completed by the child, but it can also be used by parents for their own rough evaluations of their child's overall emotional state.

For each numbered statement, a check is placed in the column that best describes the child's life over the past few months. A completed questionnaire with a substantial number of checks (over eight), indicating frequent negative experiences or emotions, is a possible indicator of depression.

	most times	sometimes	never
1. I like doing things now as much as I always have.	____	____	____
2. I have problems sleeping.	____	____	____
3. I feel sad.	____	____	____
4. I have lots of energy.	____	____	____
5. I enjoy being with my family.	____	____	____
6. I get picked on by other kids.	____	____	____
7. I feel like crying.	____	____	____
8. I feel proud of what I do.	____	____	____
9. I like playing with other kids.	____	____	____
10. I enjoy eating at mealtimes.	____	____	____
11. I feel angry.	____	____	____
12. I want to get away from people.	____	____	____
13. I get bored.	____	____	____
14. I look forward to things now as much as I always have.	____	____	____
15. I think people like me.	____	____	____
16. I feel happy.	____	____	____
17. I don't feel like doing things.	____	____	____
18. I feel lonesome.	____	____	____
19. I feel I can take care of things.	____	____	____
20. I don't feel very good.	____	____	____
21. I have a lot of fun.	____	____	____

22. I have bad dreams.   _____   _____   _____
23. I feel like giving up.   _____   _____   _____
24. I enjoy my friends now as much as I always have.   _____   _____   _____
25. I am easy to cheer up.   _____   _____   _____

Coping with Family Moves

One of the most stressful and depressing events commonly faced by school-age children is a family move. In most cases, such a move involves relocating to another community and therefore a different school district. From the child's perspective, vital friendships are interrupted, reassuring routines are broken, and a beloved home base is lost.

Perhaps most disturbing of all, however, is a far more subtle issue that seldom gets acknowledged by either party in the move, the parent or the school-age child. While adjusting to the move, the school-age child must once again depend on her or his parents almost totally for emotional security, just at a stage of life when she or he was starting to develop more personal independence.

The result of this kind of setback in the child's emotional life can be a passive "giving up" to boredom, a regression to immaturity, or a rebelliousness designed to express some sort of personal power, even if it's negative. And the older the school-age child is, the worse this reaction tends to be, given the growing value a school-age child places on independence.

To make the period of transition in a family easier on the emotions of your school-age child, try following these suggestions:

■ *Make sure your child knows about the move—and the reasons behind the move—well in advance of the moving day.*

The earlier your child is told about the move, the more time to adjust to the change. And the more carefully you explain all the positive reasons for moving, the easier it will be for your child to think of the change as desirable.

Be specific about the time and circumstances surrounding the actual moving day so that it comes across to your child as a well-planned, easily envisioned, and inevitable event. Also, include among your announced reasons for moving specific factors that can appeal to your child: for example, a larger bedroom, a bedroom of her or his own, a bigger yard for playing, a better school, closer proximity to favorite relatives or to favorite recreational areas.

Don't be disappointed if your child doesn't mirror your enthusiasm for the move right away. What's important is not that your child is "sold" on the move but that she or he has some attractive images to ponder that are directly associated with the move.

■ *Acknowledge the difficulties associated with the move and indicate your faith that they will be overcome.*

Your child needs to know that you understand what a shock the move might be to her or his personal universe. Allow her or him to express freely and fully any anxious feelings about the move and indicate that they are natural, given the circumstances. Then make it clear to your child that you'll do whatever you can to make the move more positive and that you have confidence in her or his coping abilities and future happiness.

■ *Involve your child in learning more about where you are going to move.*

Share maps, photographs, newspapers, and stories with your child that will foster a familiarity with your new place of residence. If possible, make numerous visits there in advance of moving day so that she or he can begin to develop favorite sights and experiences associated with your new home.

■ *Give your child special tasks during the move.*

Put your child in charge of certain age-appropriate aspects of the move, such as packing and labeling all the household tools, finding sturdy boxes in the neighborhood, compiling a list of all the people to whom to say good-bye, or unpacking certain specific boxes in the new home. These responsibilities will help your child feel more as if she or he is helping to make the move happen.

■ *Once you've moved into your new home, get involved with your child in family-oriented activities sponsored by the school, the community, or local organizations.*

In doing so, you will not only be exposing your child to potential new friends and pleasurable pastimes, you will also be setting an example for your child of how to enter into a new situation and make the most of it. Start by checking out the PTA, scouting organizations, church or synagogue groups, and lists of family-oriented activities in local newspapers.

Coping with Serious Illness

School-age children who have a chronic health problem, such as asthma, epilepsy, diabetes, or sickle-cell anemia, or who are suffering from a long-term illness, such as severe mononucleosis, nerve paralysis, hepatitis, or leukemia, have special emotional needs. Besides worrying more than their peers about their physical well-being, they must also go through the psychological turmoil associated with not being able to live a fuller life, like their healthier peers.

A younger child during the middle years often subconsciously assumes that her or his illness is some sort of punishment for being bad. An older child during the same period tends to be angry with her or his parents and physicians for not being able to deal with the illness more successfully. And a child of any age during the middle years is likely to experience despair, a lack of self-confidence, and mixed feelings of attraction and repulsion toward being pampered or being paid any sort of attention at all.

You can help your child cope with stress, depression, and other emotional turmoil that can accompany a serious illness by doing the following things:

■ *Make sure both you and your child are as well informed as possible about the illness and what it means.*

Ask your child's medical-care team for full information about her or his condition, including detailed directions regarding what your child can do, should do, and should not do given the condition. Stick to professional judgments in deciding what rules will govern your child's behavior and daily life, taking care not to be either excessively cautious or permissive. It's also a good idea to read about your child's condition in reputable medical books and to talk about the condition with others—doctors, parents, or victims—who are informed about that condition. However, it is *not* a good idea to take for granted anything you read or hear about your child's condition from someone who is not closely involved in her or his treatment.

Always bear in mind that each case of a serious illness is different. Before you act on anything you read or hear about your child's condition, verify it with her or his medical team.

■ *Avoid making your child feel vulnerable or exceptional.*
The more your child is able to feel competent and normal, the more positive her or his self-image will be and, therefore, the greater her or his sense of emotional security. Refer to your child's medical problems only when absolutely necessary. Otherwise, remain focused on her or his strengths as an individual and her or his natural and social evolution as a school-age kid.

■ *Encourage your child to engage in activities that will develop self-confidence and self-esteem.*
School-age children with serious illnesses frequently have a lot of "rest time" on their hands. Guide your child in using such time constructively by turning her or his interests and talents into hobbies and skills.

Also, seek opportunities for your child to enjoy and display skill mastery in the company of others. Depending on your child's particular skills and the nature of the illness, appropriate opportunities may include participating on athletic teams, in game or hobby clubs, in school or fair competitions, in choirs, bands, or orchestras, or in informal play sessions with other children.

■ *Get outside support for both you and your child.*
If your child's illness is serious, then it's important to line up people to whom you can turn for help in a crisis. Check out local support groups both for victims of illness and for their families.

Consider going to a family-oriented psychiatrist or psychologist for an evaluation of your child's emotional response to being ill. This initial contact can pave the way for future help whenever you and/or your child are experiencing difficulties in coping with the illness.

At PCGC: Seasonal Affective Disorder

Seasonal affective disorder, or SAD, is a form of depression that is attributed to seasonal changes in natural light, as registered on the retina and processed in the brain. Other factors, such as wintertime temperature and humidity changes, may also be involved in SAD, but less is known about how they might operate. Also, some people experience decreased alertness, increased sleepiness, and sustained depression in *summer* instead of winter, a condition called reverse SAD. This latter condition, far less prevalent than SAD itself, may be related to a latent summer-hibernation drive in the victim's brain, like the one that is activated in many animals during hot and dry seasons.

Most people barely register *any* major, season-related changes in their emotional state aside from holiday-related ups and downs or occasional bouts of "spring fever." However, many live throughout each winter with noticeably strong symptoms of depression, including children as young as six years old (so far the earliest age at which SAD symptoms have been clinically detectable).

The Mood, Sleep, and Seasonality Program at PCGC studies how child and adolescent depression relates to the seasons and what long-term effects such depression may have on its sufferers. The program has established that adolescents with SAD regularly exhibit various combinations of the following symptoms during the winter months:

■ extreme tiredness and listlessness;

■ appetite changes: most often an *increase* in appetite (possibly as the result of winter-triggered carbohydrate-craving obesity syndrome [COS]);

■ frequent irritability and negativity;

■ persistent and pronounced sadness;

■ difficulty in concentrating, often accompanied by a slowness in thinking and causing a downward trend in school performance;

■ sleep changes: either too much or too little;

■ withdrawal from family and peer social activities.

According to what the Mood, Sleep, and Seasonality Program has learned to date, school-age SAD is typically not as intense as adolescent SAD, which, in turn, is inclined to be less severe than adult SAD. The implication is that an untreated case of SAD worsens over time and that early intervention—especially if it occurs during the victim's middle childhood—can make a significant difference in the victim's lifelong emotional state.

A child is referred to PCGC's Mood, Sleep, and Seasonality Program by her or his parents and/or teachers. A psychiatrist then assesses the various biological, psychological, environmental, and family elements that may be contributing to the child's apparently season-related depression. One such element may be heredity. Both SAD and other forms of extreme seasonal mood and energy variation tend to occur in family groups; and family members from different generations may go through persistent seasonal mood changes of differing intensities.

Ultimately, the program psychiatrist arrives at a specific diagnosis, which may point to season-related depression but not SAD itself. Then the psychiatrist outlines a treatment plan tailored to the particular needs of the child and family.

Among the most successful treatments for SAD is phototherapy, which involves daily exposure for approximately an hour or more (depending on the case) to banks of high-intensity light. This type of exposure has worked to counteract many of the effects of SAD in approximately 80 percent of the patients admitted to the program.

If you have reason to believe that SAD may be affecting your school-age child, discuss the possibility with your psychiatrist, psychologist, or mental-health professional. She or he may be able to arrange for diagnosis and treatment.

At PCGC:
Pain Management for
School-Age Children

Compared to all that we know about the emotional and physiological factors relating to *adult* pain, there is a surprising
lack of information and education about the emotional and
physiological factors relating to *children*'s pain. As a result,
many misconceptions exist, such as the false notions that children do not feel pain as intensely as adults and that they are
essentially incapable of managing the pain they do feel.

The best way for hospitals and clinics to help child patients
and their families cope more intelligently with severe or
chronic pain is to coordinate medical, psychological, nursing,
physical therapy, and technological resources into an integrated treatment plan. Increasingly, hospitals and clinics are
aiming in this direction.

The guiding philosophy of this kind of "pain management"
is to minimize the child's pain as much as possible while at
the same time increasing her or his ability to function. For
example, in the Pain Management Program conducted by The
Children's Hospital of Philadelphia and PCGC, a so-called pain
management team of professionals is assigned to each case.
To treat the physical aspects of pain, physicians on these teams
rely on new medications, old medications used in new ways,
and innovative techniques in administering medications. To
address the psychological aspects of pain, psychiatrists and
psychologists on these teams rely on various nonmedical methods to help the child cope with pain and the family manage
stress factors associated with it. Among these nonmedical
methods are the following:

ACTIVE LISTENING

Children in pain often feel that other pepole—especially
adults—are incapable of understanding or appreciating what
they are going through. Team members always exercise active
listening skills when they are working with a child, and they
teach family members and caretakers to do the same. The main
active listening skills are as follows:

■ establishing trust with the child;

■ encouraging the child to talk openly about painful experiences;

■ not interrupting or "speaking for" the child;

■ never questioning what the child says about her or his pain;

■ demonstrating that you understand and respect what the child has said.

BIOFEEDBACK

Using a computer, child patients are able to see or hear their own physiological reaction to pain. This helps them put the pain into a more realistic perspective and inspires them to work effectively toward reducing it.

For example, a girl with chronic leg pain can attach computer-connected electrodes to her leg and then engage in relaxation techniques aimed at easing her leg pain. As these techniques change the level of her skin conductivity, thus indicating a relaxation of her leg pain, she sees the change registered by the computer: A train appears on the screen and runs downhill on a track. Through this kind of activity she learns to direct her attention more and more toward *controlling* her physiological reactions instead of just *expressing* her discomfort.

SELF-HYPNOSIS AND RELAXATION

Many techniques exist for teaching a child how to relax, including deep muscle relaxation or visual imagery. The techniques chosen for a specific case depend on the age of the patient and the nature of the pain.

Take, for instance, the relatively extreme case of a boy with cancer who is frightened of bone-marrow aspirations. His anxiety makes the procedure even more painful than it normally is. To alleviate the anxiety, the boy can be taught to visualize a line running from the back of his neck to the place on his body where he feels the pain and then to imagine that he himself is turning the wire on and off. Eventually, he can learn to "let go" of his pain when the wire is "off" and thereby tolerate the temporary procedure with much less discomfort.

PAIN DIARY

A pain diary is a written account—often supplemented with drawings, charts, or graphs—of when and where the pain occurs, what seems to precipitate the pain, and how intense the pain is (e.g., on a "pain is . . ." scale of "slight," "bad," "very bad," or "awful"). By helping a child keep such an account, family members can assist themselves and their child in gaining a more tangible understanding of the pain and thereby have more control over pain-related experiences.

FAMILY COUNSELING

Counseling for some or all of the child's family members can help ease ongoing or intermittent tensions that may be contributing to the child's pain. In addition, such counseling can teach family members how to cope with the personal and interpersonal difficulties caused specifically by the illness as well as how to assist the child in coping more effectively with the pain, given the overall family situation at hand.

Look for hospitals or clinics in your area that provide pain management programs similar to the program described above. If none is available, consult your physician or mental-health professional about creating a similar kind of treatment plan for your child.

7.
Lying and Stealing

Children over the age of six are definitely old enough to know when they are lying or stealing and, what's more important, that both are wrong. Nevertheless, even the most well behaved and morally sensitive child may occasionally resort to such behavior. The possible rationales for it during a child's middle years are numerous; and the tendency toward rationalization during these years is very strong and can easily turn irresistible, depending on the circumstances.

Among the major reasons why a school-age child is tempted to lie or steal are the following:

■ The child is trying to get even for a perceived injustice. For example, she or he may steal a sibling's prized possession upon feeling that the latter has been unfairly overbearing, or circulate a vicious lie about a friend if she or he feels betrayed by that friend.

■ The child is trying to avoid something undesirable. For example, a sick child may lie and feign illness in order to prevent having to put up with an unwanted therapy, or a child may steal money rather than go through the humiliating ordeal of begging for it and then lie in order to escape punishment.

■ The child is testing people for their reactions. For example, a child may tell a teacher lies about her or his home life in order to learn more about the latter's capacity to be fooled or attitude toward a certain issue (the subject of the lie). Or the child may steal a playmate's hat just to see how she or he behaves without it.

■ The child is attempting to prove her or his daring. For example, a child may steal a garden tool from a garage simply to prove that she or he isn't really afraid of an intimidating neighbor, or may lie in the presence of other kids who know the truth simply to impress them with her or his bravado.

■ The child is trying to get more attention. For example, a child may steal a bracelet her or his mother is sure to miss as an indirect means of forcing some sort of interaction with her, even if it is negative, or may lie about being ill in order to elicit more hands-on care and sympathy.

Assuming you handle your school-age child's early episodes of lying or stealing in a forthright, loving, and effective manner, she or he should outgrow this type of behavior fairly quickly. Try following these guidelines:

■ *Be sure that you and your child agree that lying and stealing are not to be tolerated.*

It's one thing for your child to realize that lying and stealing are wrong; it's quite another for her or him to understand *why* these activities are wrong and to make a personal commitment not to lie or steal based on that understanding.

In addition to reminding your child from time to time, directly or indirectly, that you disapprove of lying and stealing, ascertain whether she or he also does. Also, probe, when appropriate, to make certain that your child appreciates *why* lying and stealing are wrong.

■ *Take any instance of lying and stealing seriously.*

You shouldn't berate or punish your child too severely for lying or stealing, because occasional incidents of this kind of behavior are to be expected in this age range. At the same time, you shouldn't let an instance of it pass unmentioned or—even worse—be treated as a harmless prank.

Discuss every case of lying or stealing with your child as it comes to your attention, being careful not to criticize your child her- or himself but rather what she or he did. Give your child a full opportunity to account for any wrongdoing and guide her or him toward appreciating the gravity of the matter.

■ *Help your child figure out more acceptable ways she or he might have behaved instead of resorting to lying or stealing.*

Often children lie or steal because they can't think of any other way to behave in order to achieve their desired goal. For example, a child may lie to a relative in order to avoid having to spend time alone with her or him. Try role-playing such situations with your child so that she or he can learn more acceptable behaviors.

■ *Cooperate with your child to work out any restitution for the lie or the theft.*

Your child should assume responsibility for her or his wrongdoings and do whatever possible to make up for them, but this doesn't mean you can't help. For example, don't hesitate to accompany your child on an apology mission if she or he asks you to do so, and consider helping your child replace any object that she or he has stolen if doing so all alone would be particularly difficult.

■ *Never allow your child to profit from lying or stealing.*

Insist that your child forgo any advantage gained—directly or indirectly—as a result of the lie or the theft. Under no circumstances should you allow your child to "get away" with a lie if it's at all possible to correct it with the truth, nor should you allow a stolen object to be kept.

■ *Avoid harsh punishments for lying or stealing and don't suggest to your child that you no longer trust her or him.*

In cases when the lie or the theft is not very damaging, you should be fairly quick to forgive. If a child is made to appreciate the wrongness of what she or he has done and also makes restitution for the lie or the theft, she or he should not have to go through any further punishment. In cases of especially damaging lies or thefts, you might want to add some temporary, mild form of punishment simply to underscore the seriousness of the incident.

Whatever the situation, never permit your child to feel that the damage is irreparable or that she or he will forever suffer the consequences of having lied or stolen. You don't want your child to give up trying to be good or to develop such a bad self-image that she or he starts having serious emotional problems.

CASE:

A Plea to Play

Carl begged his parents to let him join the neighborhood touch football team, but they refused. At nine years old, Carl would have been the youngest member of the team, which consisted of ten- and eleven-year-olds, and his parents were concerned that he might get hurt. A very obedient son, Carl was forced to accept their judgment, albeit not with the best of spirits.

It was shortly afterward that Carl's parents first began missing some of their personal possessions. His father somehow lost or misplaced his harmonica. The crystal swan that usually sat on his mother's bureau suddenly disappeared. One day, when his mother made a rare trip to the attic to look for an old photo album, she discovered the two objects and several other stolen items of little practical value tucked away in a battered old suitcase. She knew only Carl could have taken them.

When she confronted Carl about her discovery, he at first denied stealing the objects, but he eventually broke down and confessed. He apologized profusely and swore to his mother that he had just taken the objects because he liked them so much and wanted to have them all to himself. He seemed so contrite that his mother accepted his account and forgave him, even though she remained perplexed about why such a basically good child would suddenly resort to stealing.

Later, Carl's fourth-grade teacher called his mother in for a special conference and informed her that Carl had been caught stealing small, fairly insignificant items from her desk and from those of some of the other students. Distraught, his mother told his teacher about the thefts at home. His teacher then asked, "Has Carl been upset about anything lately? Is there any reason that he might be feeling unhappy, or angry, or lost?"

Carl's mother recalled the time that Carl had been so disappointed at not being allowed to play football with the other boys in the neighborhood. Convinced that Carl's frustration over this decision—one with which he had been unable, rationally and emotionally, to agree—might be driving him to retaliate by stealing, his teacher suggested that his parents talk with the school athletic director about the appropriateness of letting Carl play on the team.

After the athletic director, well acquainted with Carl and his physical capabilities, advised Carl's parents that it would be all right for him to play with the team, they gave their permission. Carl was overjoyed, and no further incidents of stealing occurred.

8.

Sibling Rivalry

Tensions, arguments, and outright fights between siblings are inevitable, no matter how mild mannered or basically compatible the two individuals may be. In fact, two siblings involved in a "normal" relationship may spend up to half their time in conflict with one another. It is part of a necessarily slow and complex process of learning how to get along together in a polite, responsible, and mutually satisfying manner.

The phrase "sibling rivalry" refers to especially significant contests of will that occur during this process. Rivalry situations stand out from others that are conflict-related not only because they tend to be more intense but also because they so often serve as contexts for a child to express more deep-seated emotional needs that may or may not have anything to do with a sibling.

On the surface, a child engaged in a rivalry struggle with a sibling is vying with that sibling for a specific right, honor, power, or possession. Beneath the surface, however, the child may be seeking more parental attention, acting out anger at a friend, or trying to compensate for a failure at school. Dealing effectively as a parent with sibling rivalry demands being sensitive both to surface issues and to possible underlying issues.

Sibling-rivalry situations occur most frequently with a child between the ages of six and nine. They typically involve fights relating to dominance (e.g., determining who gets to set the rules for a game) or to the possession, division, or sharing of tangible items (e.g., determining who gets to play with the video games).

A younger sibling within this age range typically initiates a rivalry battle indirectly by teasing or aggravating an older sibling into open retaliation. An older child within this age range typically provokes a rivalry battle by "bossing" a younger sibling beyond the usual limits that are more or less accepted by both of them.

Between the ages of nine and thirteen, sibling-rivalry contests are usually much less frequent and much less bothersome, although rivalry in itself can still be a major factor in the relationship between two siblings. Rivalry battles within this age range commonly relate to more intangible issues, such as recognition (e.g., establishing who performs a certain skill better) or fairness (e.g., determining whether one sibling's rights, privileges, and responsibilities are appropriate in comparison with those of another sibling).

Whether or not two siblings are two brothers, two sisters, or brother and sister doesn't appear to make much difference in the quality or frequency of their sibling-rivalry contests. However, sibling rivalry between a brother and a sister can take on a gender-related dimension. A brother, for example, may justly or unjustly accuse his sister of receiving kinder treatment simply because she's a girl, or a sister may justly or unjustly accuse her brother of being allowed more freedom simply because he's a boy. Parents faced with this kind of dilemma need to examine carefully whether their own parenting style or behavior as individuals may be partly responsible for such accusations. If it appears that this may be true, then the parents need to amend their parenting style or their behavior as individuals so that it is less conducive to sexism.

Here are some other tips for parents who need help in managing sibling rivalry:

■ *Try to give each child a similar amount of attention.*
Bear in mind that one of the most potent catalysts of sibling rivalry is a desire to attract parental attention. Take care to spend time individually with each of your children on a frequent, regular, and dependable basis.

Giving your children a *similar* amount of individual attention does not necessarily mean always giving them an *equal* amount. Although equality of attention is an ideal goal, there are certain specific circumstances or occasions that warrant giving one child more attention than another.

For example, if one child is seriously ill physically or emotionally, most of the parents' available time may rightfully have to be spent caring for her or him. In such a case, the parents should explain the circumstances to each other child and continue to give each one some amount of individual attention every day, even if it's only for a few moments. Then, at the earliest possible opportunity, the parents should do something special with each other child individually.

Another example of a time when strict equality of individual attention is not appropriate is a child's birthday. On this day, the birthday celebrant should definitely be the center of attention, but the parents should also make the day special for the other children by involving them in the celebration plans and activities and by giving them small gifts as reminders that they, too, are loved and remembered.

■ *Give clear guidelines to all your children regarding each child's respective possessions, privileges, and rights.*

Make sure that every child knows who "owns" what, who is entitled to which age-appropriate privileges, and what rights each child has in common with the others (such as the right of privacy). As much as possible, make such declarations in the presence of all your children so that there is no chance for one child to plead ignorance to another.

Also, let your children know how you expect them to interact with each other. Tell them, for example, that you do not want any physical abuse or name-calling.

■ *Don't compare one child to another.*

As much as possible, avoid making statements to your child like "Why aren't you as nice to your grandmother as your brother is?" or "If your sister can get ready for school all by herself, so can you." Also, avoid letting your child overhear you saying to someone else things like "Robert was a real quiet baby, but Mac was a terror" or "Jamie has the looks, and Wendy has the brains." These kinds of comparisons can easily give rise to taunts and resentment between children. Instead, help your children appreciate their differences in a noncompetitive manner.

■ *As much as possible, allow your child to settle their own conflicts.*

One of the most troublesome and unsavory aspects of sibling rivalry is tattling, which usually puts a parent in the position of taking one child's side against another without the benefit of knowing what really happened. As much as possible, resist cooperating with the tattler. Instead, make it clear that you expect your children to work out their own differences.

In order to assist your children in handling their rivalry conflicts, take every opportunity to teach them good problem-solving strategies. Any such strategy should include both children first taking a moment or two to cool down and then reasoning out a decision that is mutually satisfactory.

Of course, school-age children are not always capable of reasoning out problems they have with their siblings, so you have to be prepared to allow a certain percentage of them to remain unresolved for an indefinite period of time. Try to intervene only when they are clearly undermining a child's emotional health or the proper functioning of family life.

■ *Encourage positive sibling interactions.*

Guide your children toward playing cooperatively, in a manner that is appropriate to their respective ages. Remember that a child is generally not ready for roughhouse games or strongly competitive games until around age eight.

Try involving your children in performing chores cooperatively. This might help them learn to have more patience with each other and to appreciate each other's capabilities and limitations. When your children work especially well together in accomplishing a certain task, be sure to praise them for their cooperation.

Meanwhile, periodically engage your children in activities that they can enjoy in each other's company, such as camping trips or visits to the zoo. Shared memories of good times make powerful bonds between siblings.

Finally, reinforce those moments when your children demonstrate love for each other. A younger child often feels very proud of an older sibling, and an older one often feels very protective toward a younger one. Subtly support such feelings and make them more memorable for both children.

■ *Encourage each child to develop an independent life.*

One of the best ways to reduce the frequency and intensity of sibling-rivalry situations is to make it possible for each child to have a personally rewarding life of her or his own. Help each child realize her or his own interests and talents. Then give each one time and space for cultivating those talents and interests and insist that your other children do the same.

CASE:

Putting a Stop to Fights

Nine-year-old Cassie and seven-year-old Warren bickered, argued, or fought together almost every day. Concerned about the frequency of this type of behavior, their parents secretly kept track of when, where, how, and why it occurred over a period of two weeks.

The parents discovered that Cassie and Warren most often quarreled at times when both parents were nearby and that these particular squabbles inevitably featured screaming and/ or other loud noises as well as "stagy" pleas for justice. It seemed clear to the parents that the children were fighting in order to get their attention. Sure enough, when the parents paid them no heed at such times and instead gave them more consideration when they behaved well, the incidence of fighting dropped considerably.

Nevertheless, during long car trips Cassie and Warren would still wind up fighting. It was as if they knew that their parents were a captive audience in such a situation. Finally, the parents hit upon a solution. Before the next long car trip, they told their kids that they would stop the car if the kids started quarreling.

After an hour of traveling, Warren and Cassie began fighting, and their father, who was driving at the time, pulled over to the side of the road and parked. He gave no reason for doing so; he simply waited until the kids quieted down. Then he started up again. Rarely again did he ever have to stop during a car trip.

9.
Divorce

At its very best, divorce is still traumatic. And it's especially so for children during the middle years. Having outgrown the almost total self-centeredness of the preschool years, kids between the ages of six and thirteen increasingly identify with their parents, relying on them for their own sense of self and turning to them as models of rational, adult behavior. Thus, a breakup of their parents' marriage throws their whole world and their whole future development as individuals into doubt.

To add to this trauma, a school-age child is just learning to be independent from home life, a condition thrust upon the child when her or his formal schooling began. The threat to home life implicit in any divorce disturbs this learning process. Suddenly, the child reverts to a longing for the stable, all-nourishing home environment she or he knew as an infant and suffers pangs of anger, fear, and resentment that such an environment no longer exists. The child may even feel guilt about having contributed to the dissolution of the family by having "left home" for school.

If you are contemplating a divorce or going through one, consider these ways to prevent, alleviate, or resolve much of that doubt for your child:

■ *Don't pretend that the divorce is "good" and don't expect your child to appreciate your rationale for the divorce.*

A divorce needs to be presented to school-age children as a fact of life—a firm and final decision that has been made by the two adults involved. Therefore, guard against talking to your school-age child about the possibility of a divorce. Instead, wait until divorce is a certainty and then announce it to your child as soon as you reasonably can—preferably together with your spouse.

From the child's point of view, a divorce can't help but seem like a negative development. With this in mind, don't confuse your child or discredit her or his sorrowful feelings by trying to convince her or him that your divorce is a positive development. Acknowledge that the divorce is bad news but that you're hoping that all of you will try to get through it as best you can.

Also, don't express your reasons for the divorce as if it were something that was strictly a logical matter, that is, something that you could conceivably be reasoned out of doing. Instead, describe the divorce as the only alternative you have given the fact that the two of you have too many irreconcilable differences and are no longer able to live with each other.

■ *Avoid assigning blame for the divorce or criticizing the other party in your child's presence.*

Beyond any other consideration, your child needs to maintain positive images of both parents in order to feel good about her- or himself. Resist the temptation to "expose" the other parent's character flaws or misbehavior to your child or to vent your anger or disappointment on the other parent in conversations with your child.

It may be necessary to inform your child about unpleasant facts leading to the divorce decision. For example, you or your spouse may have developed another, very serious romantic relationship or created serious legal or financial problems that made the marriage no longer tenable. Giving your child this information may be the only way you can spare her or him the pain of learning these facts later in a negative way or the feeling of having been deceived once the facts become known.

If it is necessary to communicate unpleasant facts that led to your divorce decision, present them as calmly and simply as you can. Remember always to cast disapproval on the deed, not the person.

■ *Reassure your child that she or he did not cause the divorce and will continue to be loved and tended by both parents.*

Frequently remind your child of these facts during the transition process. Also, try to give your child more specific images of *how* she or he will receive each parent's love and attention in the future: for example, when, how, and how often she or he will be in contact with the noncustodial parent.

Also, the more you and your divorcing partner can join together in doing things with your child—before, during, and after the divorce—the better. It helps convince your child that her or his welfare can transcend the individual differences her or his parents have. Just make sure that these occasions of togetherness can and do take place without any outbreaks of open hostility. Also, be careful not to feed your child's wish that you and your divorcing partner might get back together sometime in the future.

■ *Don't put your child on the spot by involving her or him in divorce-related decisions.*

Your child shouldn't be forced, directly or indirectly, to choose one parent over the other. This type of decision making inevitably results in loyalty conflicts that could cause long-term emotional problems for your child.

With your child's welfare uppermost in your minds and with the understanding that she or he needs both parents actively involved in her or his life, you and your divorcing partner should make all decisions relating to child custody, child visitation, and division of parenting responsibilities. Don't turn your child into a consultant, judge, or jury.

■ *Keep your child informed about divorce-related events and decisions in a timely and frank manner.*

One of the worst fears a school-age child can have about a divorce is to feel left out of the event entirely. Talk with your child at regular intervals during the divorce process about what has happened, what's happening currently, and what's going to happen.

In these talks, try to remain fairly calm, but don't be afraid to let your child know—very briefly and undramatically—that you yourself are worried, depressed, or confused. It prepares your child for moments when you won't be functioning quite as smoothly as before, and it may create an opportunity to talk about her or his own divorce-related emotional problems.

■ *As much as possible, avoid making changes in your child's normal routines.*

The more your child's day-to-day life remains familiar, comfortable, and predictable, the more reassured she or he will be about the safety and happiness of life in the future, despite the divorce. Try to put off making any major changes in your child's life, whether they are divorce related or not, until after she or he has had at least a few months to adjust to the divorce itself.

■ *Allow your child full freedom to express her or his feelings both to you and to other trusted adults.*

Always make time to ask your child how she or he is doing from time to time during the divorce process and to listen nonjudgmentally to your child's fears, worries, grievances, and complaints. However, don't pressure your child to communicate if she or he isn't forthcoming. In many divorce situations, children simply don't have much to say, and you don't want to scare or depress them unnecessarily.

It can also be very helpful for school-age children to be able to discuss the divorce with other adults—relatives and friends who can be trusted to be honest, fair, and reassuring. Tactfully encourage such discussions by arranging for your child to have some time alone with adults you trust. Just be sure to prepare the adults for these talks. Keep them informed about the divorce itself so that they won't be inclined to pump your child for information, and give them guidelines for talking about divorce-related issues so that they won't, for example, wind up casting blame on anyone or setting up false expectations.

Helping Kids Handle Parental Dating and Remarriage

There are three main reasons why school-age children are very likely to have difficulties accepting the romantic lives of their divorced parents.

1. Children between the ages of six and thirteen are typically not mature enough to appreciate the need of adults for peer companionship, much less their desire for sexual gratification.

2. They are typically too dependent on their parents' time and energy not to feel that it's a sacrifice to allow their parents the personal freedom for a romantic life.

3. They are typically identifying with their parents very strongly and can therefore easily be disturbed by aspects of their parents' lives that they cannot—and often don't want to—share.

If you are a divorced parent of a school-age child and are concerned about the emotional effects on your child of your dating or remarrying, here are some guidelines for making such situations more pleasurable for all parties involved:

■ *Wait until you know your new romantic interest fairly well before arranging for her or him and your child to spend time together.*

You don't have to go out of your way to avoid any meeting at all between the person you are dating and your child. However, it is a good idea not to throw them together socially until you yourself are comfortable with your date and have a reasonably well informed idea of how your date and your child will get along.

Above all, avoid leaving your child alone with your date until you know her or him very well and until after you, your date, and your child have spent time together on numerous occasions. Your child may feel very shy and awkward at being left alone with your date while she or he is still a comparative stranger, and this shyness or awkwardness can easily translate into displeasure or even fear.

■ *Allow your child to get used to this person gradually, at her or his own pace.*

Avoid communicating—or even forming—high expectations about how your child and your date will respond to each other. School-age children are typically very guarded in forming a new relationship with an adult; and as such a relationship develops, they often resort to brief periods of false behavior— for example, mock flirtation or mock rejection—in order to try out their new acquaintance's reactions.

As a parent, you need to respond to your child's *apparent* feelings about your date in a calm and constructive manner. Just don't jump to conclusions about her or his *true* feelings regarding your date. Be patient and allow them to emerge in their own way and their own time.

Part of being patient is allowing your child certain emotionally important freedoms. Don't insist that your child be friends with your date, act a certain way, or call your date by a certain name. And continue to allow your child this freedom even if your date ultimately becomes your child's stepparent.

■ *Keep your child informed about your relationship but don't force your child to make decisions about it.*

While your child will definitely appreciate your sharing basic information about your ongoing romantic relationships (information that's appropriate to her or his age as a listener), it won't make your child feel important if you ask for permission to date or marry someone. It will simply add to her or his anxiety about the situation. Be responsible to yourself and your family for your own romantic relationships and respect the fact that your child is your dependent, not your partner.

■ *Involve your child in your marriage plans in an appropriate manner.*

Announce your marriage intentions to your child as soon as possible and make sure that there is a sufficient "adjustment time" between this announcement and the wedding—at least a month. Then give your child mutually agreeable roles to play in preparing for and participating in the wedding and making any physical arrangements necessary for setting up a new household.

During the weeks immediately before and after the wedding, take care to maintain regular, dependable hours of private time for just you and your child. This will help ensure that your child doesn't feel as if she or he were losing you to your new spouse. Also, reserve a similar amount of private time for just you and your partner so that she or he won't feel slighted by the attention you pay your child. The honeymoon itself, for example, should definitely *not* include your child, even if this means postponing it until arrangements can be made for your child's care while you are away.

■ *Seek agreement with your new spouse on child-rearing policies.*

Coordinating with your spouse ahead of time on child-rearing policies reduces the odds that your child will be distressed by parental quarrels in her or his name or different messages from each parent. As much as possible, your child-rearing policies should be the same *after* your marriage as they were *before* so that your child can feel more comfortable with this new phase of family life.

10.

The Adopted Child

The earlier a child is told that she or he is adopted, the better. Parents can begin to refer to their child's adopted status from the moment they begin talking to their child, in casual remarks like "I'm so glad we adopted you!" As their child matures, so can the references to the adoption.

If, instead, parents withhold this vital piece of information for any length of time at all, the child may view the adoption as a shameful thing when she or he is finally told about it. Otherwise, she or he may reason, why was the adoption kept a secret?

Unfortunately, many parents do put off telling their child that she or he is adopted until she or he has reached school age. Because their child is then considered "just old enough" for formal education, these parents apparently assume that she or he is also "just old enough" to understand what "adopted" really means.

In fact, waiting until a child is of school age to talk about her or his adopted status is *not* advisable. Far from being the best time for a child to deal with the fact that she or he was adopted, the middle years are perhaps the worst.

From all the evidence we have, preschoolers remain fairly untroubled by the knowledge that they were adopted. During the years between six and thirteen, however, the situation can be very different. Children who have known about their adopted status since babyhood are inclined to be much more bothered by it during this age span. And children who are just learning about their adopted status during this age period are inclined to be even more upset.

Researchers testing both adopted and biological children of all ages are unable to distinguish one group from the other psychologically until around the age of six, at which point adopted children as a group do begin showing more signs of emotional trouble than do biological children. Common symptoms of such trouble include depression, withdrawal, aggression, hyperactivity, and/or defiance, and they remain noticeably more prevalent among adopted children than biological children until adolescence, when the two groups of children again become less psychologically distinguishable.

Why should concern about having been adopted manifest itself so much more strongly during a child's middle years than during the early years of adolescence? There are three basic reasons for this phenomenon:

1. Compared to the average preschooler, the average school-age child has much more peer contact and is therefore much more distressed about being different. The adopted school-age child is keenly aware that most peers live with their biological parents, and her or his imagination may very well interpret this difference as being far more significant than it actually is.

By adolescence, the school-age child is less likely to read as much meaning into the difference. She or he may still want to resemble her or his most valued peers, but this desire for resemblance is less involved with the family relationships of those peers.

2. The average school-age child is just learning to view the world rationally and logically, and so the adopted school-age child is inevitably led to speculate about *why* she or he was put up for adoption. Among the questions that typically torment such a child are the following:

■ Was I rejected because I wasn't sufficiently smart or attractive?

■ Were my real parents evil or careless people who wanted nothing to do with raising a child?

■ Was the adoption itself the tragic result of an accident, a misunderstanding, or even a crime?

These kinds of speculation can stir up intense feelings of abandonment, grief, loneliness, resentment, and guilt—feelings that are easier for an adolescent to ignore, manage, or overcome.

3. School-age children are deeply involved in establishing more mature, person-to-person relationships with their parents. They identify with them, imitate them, test personal differences against them, bargain with them, and seek common ground with them.

These activities are much more problematic for a school-age child who is adopted. The adopted child can always attribute incompatibilities with her or his parents to the fact that she or he is not their biological child, and such incompatibilities inevitably seem more threatening and more difficult to resolve.

By the time adopted children are teenagers, they, like most teenagers, are not so bothered about being different from their parents.

They're more concerned about person-to-person relationships with their peers. When they do show concern about their biological parents versus their adoptive ones, it's usually a matter of curiosity. They may want to know the identity of their biological parents or even to track them down; but this desire is more intellectual than emotional in nature.

This doesn't preclude the fact that some adopted children have a lifelong and deep-seated longing to find out about, or reconnect with, their biological parents. As a rule, however, such children will express this desire in relatively plain terms to their adopted parents.

If you have not yet told your school-age child that she or he is adopted, then by all means do so as soon and as positively as possible. Unfortunate as the timing may be, it is better for your child to know about her or his adopted status sooner rather than later.

Make a special, private occasion out of the announcement and explain your delay in telling your child about the adoption in terms of your wish to demonstrate your own parental love during her or his early years, *not* in terms of her or his inability during those years to understand or accept the news.

Whether or not you have waited to tell your child about being adopted, here are some ways to help her or him deal with her or his adopted status during the especially sensitive middle years of childhood:

■ *Always refer to the adoption itself, and to the status of being an adopted child, in positive terms.*
Whatever you know—or don't know—about the circumstances leading to your child's availability for adoption, reassure your child that she or he was loved by her or his biological parents and that they were doing what they thought was best for her or his welfare. Also, describe your first meeting with your child in loving detail, emphasizing the pleasure that you felt and that your child expressed.

In regard to the status of being adopted, make sure your child realizes that your decision to adopt her or him came from the heart and was based on your feelings about her or him as a person. Then point out her or his special qualities as an individual, especially those that are unique to her or him, and how much you love these qualities.

■ *Don't deny the fact that being an adopted child is different from being a biological one.*
You should certainly communicate to your adopted child that you love her or him just as much as if she or he were your biological child— and if there are biological children in the family, just as much as you

love them. However, avoid belittling your child's feelings that her or his situation is different from that of a biological child.

For example, adopted children often worry about whether their biological heritage is compatible with, or as fortunate as, the heritage of their adoptive parents. They also often worry about their biological parents showing up unexpectedly and taking them away from their adoptive mother and father. These worries should be addressed and alleviated, but they shouldn't be treated as if they were foolish or unwarranted.

Invite your adopted child to discuss any feelings of difference in more detail. Help her or him deal with them but don't imply that there is anything "wrong" with having them. Remember that your child is the first and foremost authority on how she or he feels. And unless you yourself were adopted, your child knows a great deal more about how it feels.

Your adopted child needs to know that you can accept and appreciate her or his sense of things even though you aren't biologically related. Contradicting your child's genuine impressions of difference will only create even more feelings of alienation.

■ *Don't expect your child to resolve all troublesome feelings about being adopted.*

People who are adopted often describe the knowledge that they are adopted as a wound that never completely heals. Be prepared for your school-age adopted child to exhibit occasional age-appropriate symptoms of this wound, such as the following:

> ■ accusations that you are not her or his "real" parent (including, possibly, allegations that she or he has been kidnapped by you);
>
> ■ exceptional problems getting along with siblings, especially if they are your biological children;
>
> ■ fantasies about being reunited with, or rescued by, her or his biological parents;
>
> ■ refusal to cooperate in family activities;
>
> ■ unusual shyness around relatives;
>
> ■ overly—or inappropriately—intense emotional reaction to television shows, movies, stories, or pictures featuring parent-and-child relationships.

■ *Prepare family and friends to deal with your child's adoption-related concerns in a comfortable and constructive manner.*

Let them know everything that your child knows about the adoption.

Also, let them know how you'd like them to respond if your child expresses to them any concerns about being adopted.

Another adult, especially a close friend who is not a blood relative of a parent, can be an especially helpful confidant and role model for an adopted child. Like the child, this person is not biologically linked to the family but is nevertheless an integral part of it.

Encourage all such relationships between your adopted child and appropriate adults in your circle of close family members and friends. One or more of these "special" relationships could prove invaluable in giving your insecure child a stronger sense of connection to the world around her or him.

■ *Consider seeking professional help if your child's adoption-related concerns are seriously interfering with her or his well-being or that of the family.*

If your child exhibits frequent symptoms of distress about her or his adopted status for longer than a month, it could be a sign of deeply rooted emotional problems, some of which may not even be directly related to the adoption. If you believe this may be the case, don't hesitate to seek professional help.

Professional help for the family may be advisable if you feel that you and/or other members of your family are suffering unduly as a result of your child's adoption-related concerns. Evidence of such suffering would include a month or more of any of the following situations:

■ frequent episodes of intense sibling rivalry;

■ profound and unshakable parental anxiety about the adopted child's emotional state;

■ consistent disruption of family gatherings due to the actions—or withdrawal—of the adopted child.

11.

School

When school enters a child's universe, it has an overwhelming impact. The educational experience in itself accounts for only a part of that impact. At least equally significant is that the child begins to lead an emotionally demanding double life upon attending school.

At home, the school-age child is a clearly dependent, beloved, and secure family member; but at school the situation is different. There the child is a relatively independent class member who must work to earn approval from peers and teachers in order to feel accepted and secure.

Most of the time children are able to make the transition from one life to the other remarkably well. The emotional support, self-esteem, and intimate knowledge of human behavior that they derive from family life help them achieve their personal objectives in school life both academically and socially.

However, when a child's home life and school life are not in harmony with each other, the side effects can be devastating emotionally. Problems at school can easily create trouble at home, and vice versa. The child forced to go back and forth from one troubled life to another is doubly vulnerable to anxiety, depression, frustration, anger, fear, and despair.

For example, a child upset by tension among family members may be distracted from her or his lessons in school. This could result in poor academic performance, which might exacerbate tensions between the child and her or his parents. Or the same child might start taking out her or his frustrations with family members on her or his teachers and peers, thus causing behavior problems at school that the parents must ultimately address.

Another example of trouble transferring from one life to another is the possible dilemma of a child who experiences problems at school— either academically or socially—while at the same time enjoying a comparatively happy home life. The child may go through a long period of concealing any school-related problems from her or his parents, thus creating a rift between parent and child that can't help but widen as long as the deception continues. Or the child may react to school-related problems by being rebellious, withdrawn, or generally out of sorts at home—a reaction she or he can't afford to display at school.

As the parent of a school-age child, you need to make every effort to ensure that your child's home life and school life are in productive harmony with each other. Here are suggestions to help you meet that goal:

■ *Encourage your child to talk about school life at home.*

Don't just confine your expression of interest to a routine, open-ended greeting like "How was your day at school?" Occasionally each week, at quiet times when there is little risk of distraction, initiate a more in depth conversation about school.

Keep track of specific names, events, and details your child has told you so that you can refer to them as a means of initiating such conversations. Also, be sure to inquire about your child's classmates, social activities, and teacher(s) as well as about academic subjects.

■ *Consult your child's teacher regularly and frequently about academic, behavioral, and social matters.*

Whenever you feel that you don't know what's happening in your child's school life or that she or he is having school-related problems or that her or his life at school might shed some light on problems at home, don't hesitate to set up a parent-teacher conference. In fact, it's a good idea to consult with your child's teacher at least every couple of months, even if there are no specific issues prompting such a consultation.

During any consultation—whether it's for a specific reason or simply for a general "checkup"—always express to the teacher that you are willing to do anything that will help benefit your child's school life. If serious disagreements develop between you and the teacher, make every effort to resolve them peacefully, even if it means conferring jointly with the school principal. Otherwise, you may be inadvertently putting your child in an extremely awkward position—torn between loyalty to you and allegiance to a teacher.

■ *Keep informed about your child's curriculum, school, and school system.*

You want to make sure not only that you know what's going on in your child's school life but also that you have a sound basis for evaluating whether or not your child is receiving a high-quality education in a supportive environment. Attend all school-sponsored meetings and those conducted by parent-teacher organizations. Also, routinely read about your school and school system in local periodicals.

In these meetings and readings as well as in conferences with your child's teacher, seek specific information about what your child is learning and how it is being taught. Other issues to explore are teacher qualifications, classroom and school disciplinary policies, and counseling services and educational options that are available to your child.

■ Help your child do homework without actually doing it yourself.

Set up with your child a specific time when homework should be done (such as one hour after dinner) and enforce the routine. It will help develop good study habits. Show an interest in the schoolwork that your child is assigned to do at home and make sure that she or he has space and materials to do the work to the best of her or his ability. However, if your child comes to you with specific questions about the work, help her or him discover the answers independently instead of simply supplying the answers.

■ Avoid tying grades for academic performance to a strong punishment-and-reward system.

Your child should learn to regard success in academic performance as its own reward and failure as its own punishment. It's good to express pleasure when a child does particularly well in school and occasionally to celebrate. It's also appropriate to express caring concern when a child does particularly poorly in school and, if circumstances warrant it, to insist that more attention to schoolwork take precedence over other activities. However, try as much as possible not to set up a rigid routine of rewards and punishments: for example, a half hour more TV watching a night for good grades or a half hour less for bad ones. The routine in itself can easily become a source of emotional conflict.

■ Help motivate your child to be interested in what is being taught in school.

Begin with what already interests your child and draw connections between it and school subjects. You might, for example, try turning your child's love of movies into an enthusiasm for reading by giving her or him a book related to a favorite movie; or you might try turning your child's fondness for games into a love for research challenges in general.

In addition, look for subtle opportunities to apply school knowledge to practical activities at home. For example, involve your child in applying mathematical skills to cooking from recipes or buying paint for covering a certain area of space.

■*Make a special effort to maintain a stable, supportive home environment during major turning points in your child's school life.*

Occasions like the first few months of school life, the beginning and end of each school year, and the transition from elementary school to middle school or junior high are particularly stressful times for children. Try as much as possible to avoid major changes or problems at home during these periods. The resulting calm in your child's home life will help her or him handle more effectively the turbulence in her or his school life.

Repeating and Skipping Grades

What can parents and teachers do when a child just doesn't seem to be compatible with other children in her or his chronologically assigned grade level? One possibility is to assign the child to a grade level that is likely to be more appropriate, even though virtually all the children in that grade level are a different age.

If the child is socially and/or intellectually more advanced than her or his age peers, it may be helpful to skip a grade (technically known as a "double promotion"). If the child is socially or intellectually less advanced, it may be helpful to repeat a grade.

However, changing a child's grade level is not always beneficial in such situations. It may even make matters worse. A relatively slow child may suffer even more loss of self-esteem and motivation if forced to be "one year behind" chronological peers for the rest of school life. Inevitably, much of the repeated year will be made up of material the child has already learned, which may only increase the child's boredom and dissatisfaction with school.

A good student who skips a grade may feel physically, socially, and emotionally "one year behind" classmates at the new grade level for the rest of the school year, which could significantly reduce the student's former initiative and pride. Inevitably, she or he will miss important academic material in that "lost" year.

On the other hand, a poorly performing student who gets an extra year to catch up—academically, socially, and emotionally—may turn into a competent or even an outstanding student and remain so for the rest of her or his school life. A student who skips a year may have been rescued from stagnating at a grade level that would have offered insufficient intellectual challenges.

Before allowing your child to step out of sequence from her or his "regular" grade level, consider the following important issues.

REPEATING A GRADE

■ Is your child experiencing difficulties in *every* academic subject or just in some of them? If your child is doing fine in just one area, there's reason to hope that she or he is capable of improving in the other areas with special assistance, thus reducing the argument for holding her or him back a grade.

■ In addition to poor academic performance, is your child less mature socially or emotionally than most other children in her or his present grade level? If not, then the case for holding her or him back a grade is much weaker.

■ Has your child's teacher carefully analyzed her or his educational needs and offered an informed opinion about why she or he has academic problems—and, possibly, social and emotional problems as well? Don't agree to let your child repeat a grade unless such an analysis has been made to your satisfaction.

■ Does your child know all the reasons why she or he may have to repeat a grade? Have you allowed your child to express her or his feelings about the possibility of repeating a grade? Have you and your child's teachers informed her or him about all the potential problems and opportunities associated with such a step? If the answer to any of these questions is no, don't allow any action to be taken. Should your child be—or become—adamantly opposed to repeating a grade, the chances are almost nil that the strategy will be helpful.

■ Can you fully support the decision to have your child repeat a grade, and are you prepared to give your child the extra attention and assistance that may be required to adjust to such a transition? If not, then rethink the situation.

SKIPPING A GRADE

■ Is your child more advanced in *all* academic areas relative to other children in her or his chronologically assigned grade level? And is she or he so advanced in these areas that she or he can be a top achiever in the new grade level? If the answer to either of these questions is no, then skipping a grade may create academic problems as well as, or instead of, academic progress. Explore other options for intellectual challenge.

■ In addition to being academically more advanced than other children her or his age, is your child more mature socially and emotionally? If not, then it's highly questionable that she or he will adjust well to the higher grade level.

■ Is your child physically smaller or less developed than most other children her or his age level? If so, then your child is likely to feel grotesquely out of place among children in a higher grade level. Such a feeling can have a very damaging effect on your child academically, socially, and emotionally.

■ Does your child know all the reasons why she or he is considered eligible to skip a grade? Has your child been given every chance to express her or his feelings about the idea? And has your child been fully informed about the possible problems and opportunities involved in such a move? Don't take any action unless the answer to all these questions is yes.

■ Do you firmly believe that your child's skipping a grade is the best action to take given her or his situation, and are you prepared to offer your child the extra attention and assistance that such a move may require? If the answer to either of these questions is no, pursue some other alternative.

12.
Friendship

Friendships during the school-age years can be a great source of emotional strength not only at the time but also later in life. Through such early experiments in intimacy, children develop self-awareness, self-confidence, and self-esteem. In addition, they learn to rely on human relationships as vehicles for reaching beyond the self to enlarge and enrich one's frame of reference. Thus, friendships help carry them through emotional crises and conflicts in their ongoing lives that might otherwise cause lingering psychological problems.

By contrast, children who remain friendless during their school years are more likely to develop negative, compensatory behaviors that actually trigger emotional crises and conflicts. Specifically, children suffering from loneliness during their middle years are more susceptible—then or later—to academic failure, eating disorders, substance abuse, sex-related troubles, and even suicidal thoughts than their more sociable peers are.

Typically, school-age children between the ages of six and nine form relatively casual friendships with a number of children. Many of these friendships subsist on the basis of a single activity. For example, a seven-year-old girl may have one friend for ice-skating, another for riding bikes, and a third with whom to eat lunch at school. There may be several "multiactivity" friends (neighborhood kids tend to fall into this category) with whom a child in this age range spends a great deal of time; but, generally, personal allegiances to these friends are fairly simple and nondemanding. It's not unusual for friendships of any type to come and go in a matter of a few months.

Around the time a child reaches age nine, friendship becomes a far more serious enterprise. By then a child has been socializing enough with her or his peers to appreciate the value of having close, dependable allies. Even more significant, a child this old is emotionally mature enough to empathize with peers and is therefore more interested in sharing thoughts and feelings with particularly compatible friends than a younger child is.

As a result, a school-age child over nine years old usually seeks, or possesses, an intense and demanding relationship with one special friend of the same sex, the so-called best friend. This relationship may remain a vital source of pleasure and pain for years, since the child feeds it, is fed by it, and frets about it. In general, all friendships will tend to be more complex and more long-lasting than earlier ones were.

The specific reasons why a school-age child makes, or doesn't make, friends vary from child to child and include a wide range of purely situational factors, such as the nature of the child's home life and personal interests. However, children who have ongoing difficulty making friends tend to fall into one of two categories: those who are too shy or those who are overly aggressive. It's dangerous to make too many assumptions based on such tendencies, for shyness and aggression in themselves may not be problems at all. They may even be assets in making friends. It's the extremes of those traits that cause problems. An excessively aggressive child can easily turn into a bully; a very shy one can easily turn into a bully's target.

Whether they are overly shy, overly aggressive, or just plain friendless, not all isolated children suffer from loneliness, nor do all children suffering from it go on to experience emotionally troubled lives. In some cases, isolated or lonely children evolve into exceptionally resourceful and creative people, perhaps because their solitary state challenged them to excel.

Nevertheless, as a parent, you should do what you reasonably can to foster your child's social skills and opportunities, providing her or him every chance to enjoy the undeniable benefits of healthy peer friendships. You should also be prepared to deal effectively with the emotional pain that friends—or a lack of them—can cause your child.

Here are some guidelines:

■ *Be especially cautious about intervening in your child's social life.*
As much as possible, grant your child the emotional growth experience of finding her or his own ways of making friends and of dealing with rejection. Friendship is one area of life in which a child wants, needs, and should receive a certain amount of independence and privacy.

Also, don't jump to conclusions about your child's social life—or apparent lack of it. This includes making hasty judgments that your child is not getting along with friends, is suffering from not having them, or is involved in "undesirable" friendships.

Before acting on any serious concerns you may have, check your impressions against those of other adults who are knowledgeable about your child, including her or his teacher. Your vision of the situation may easily be very selective, biased, or misinformed.

You might also ask your child's siblings discreet and casual questions about your child's friendships, if you think it would help. Just be very careful not to put your child in an awkward or embarrassing situation by doing so.

■ *Encourage your child to talk about her or his friendships.*

Your best source of information about your child's friendships, and the first one you should consult, is your child her- or himself. Make it easy for your child to talk about friends—or about life without them. You can do this by expressing your interest regularly and casually, withholding your personal judgments, recalling specific names and events that your child has mentioned previously, and sharing appropriate memories of your own past and present friendships.

These conversations can be just as helpful to your child as they are to you. They provide a forum for expressing and thereby realizing true feelings about particular friendships or about not having the kinds of friendships she or he may want.

■ *Help your child understand social cues and behaviors.*

Children often have difficulty relating well to their peers because they don't know how to read the verbal and nonverbal signals that people commonly use to indicate their feelings. For example, some children don't realize that a playmate's mild teasing may be a sign of interest and even affection rather than dislike. And some children unintentionally alienate a favorably disposed playmate by continuing to seek the playmate's company after she or he has indirectly expressed a desire to be alone for a while.

Take advantage of every opportunity to educate your child in a casual manner regarding the social meaning of particular behaviors. One way of doing this is to offer nonthreatening commentary on peer-related incidents your child tells you about or to make instructive side remarks about interpersonal scenes that both you and your child witness either in real life or on television.

■ *Teach your child basic rules regarding how to handle social situations successfully.*

Your child should be told—and made to understand—that grabbing, whining, tattling, bullying, lying, and stealing are *not* socially rewarding behaviors. And your child should also know what behaviors *are* socially rewarding: sharing, cooperating, being trustworthy and dependable, respecting other people's bodies and property, showing concern for other people's problems, and helping other people enjoy themselves.

In addition, take appropriate opportunities to talk with your child about the basic elements of conflict resolution: stating what one wants, listening to what the other one wants, negotiating peacefully, and working out a compromise. Role-playing with your child is one of the best ways to communicate these basic elements, so be alert for specific, real-life situations to role-play that come to your attention (e.g., disagreements or fights that your child tells you about).

■ *Help your child become involved in peer-group activities.*

Try interesting your child in joining a sports team, a scouting group, a hobby club, or a community action group. Also, take your child to places and events where there will be other children with whom to socialize, such as a park, a beach, a fair, a neighborhood gathering, a group picnic, an amusement park, an environmental center, a children's theater production, or a holiday-related public event.

■ *Make sure that your child receives loving one-on-one attention at home.*

The depressing or anxiety-producing effects of having trouble with friends or of having no friends at all can be greatly alleviated if a child feels that she or he has warm, supportive, and entertaining relationships with other family members. Over time, such relationships can also help a socially awkward child develop the confidence and skills needed to form more satisfying friendships with peers.

How to Tell: Excessively Shy? Overly Aggressive?

Signs that a child may be extremely *shy* include any combination of the following symptoms lasting longer than two months:

■ repeated refusal to participate in peer activities;

■ consistent lack of reference, or disparaging reference, to peers in conversations;

■ repeated incidents of being victimized by other children (taken advantage of, taunted, hit);

■ apparent preference for being left alone;

■ recurring episodes of excessive clinging to parents;

■ persistent fearfulness or depression.

Signs that a child may be excessively *aggressive* include any combination of the following symptoms lasting longer than two months:

■ repeated incidents of victimizing other children (taking advantage of, taunting, hitting);

■ consistent inability to be alone;

■ repeated episodes of angry screaming or tantrums;

■ persistent defiance of parents and other authority figures;

■ numerous acts of physical destruction or stealing.

The Bully and the Bullied

Teasing and being teased is an inalienable part of any school-age friendship. So is fighting, which means sometimes losing and sometimes winning. However, a bully and her or his victim are locked into a relationship that is primarily, if not entirely, characterized by teasing or fighting, with one kid always dominating the other.

Sometimes the two individuals involved in the bully-victim relationship mistakenly think of it as a friendship—and so might their peers, their teachers, and their parents. At other times, the two individuals—and everyone else who observes them closely—have no illusions that the relationship is anything more than a vicious and decidedly unfriendly game.

Curiously enough, school-age bullies and their victims tend to gravitate toward each other. Bullies tend to be aggressive people by nature who subconsciously seek someone on whom they can vent their general anger, fear, and frustration. Victims, on the other hand, tend to be shy people by nature who subconsciously seek someone to punish them for being (in their own opinion) generally weak, inferior, or incompetent. Thus, while a bully-victim relationship may *appear* to be one-sided, with the bully always being responsible, in fact it usually takes two kids to make a bully and two to make a victim.

If you suspect that your child is bullying, or is being bullied by, another child, here are some ways to help break up the bully-victim relationship:

BULLY

■ Educate your child about the rights of other children.
Don't just assume that your child already knows the difference between right and wrong in matters of social conduct. Help her or him empathize with peers, especially those to whom she or he seems especially insensitive. In conversations with your child about these people, encourage her or him to imagine how they must feel, what they must want, and what they deserve.

■ Set clear and firm rules regarding the social behavior you expect.
Tell her or him that any abusive behavior toward another child—such as picking a fight, teasing beyond the limits of fairness, threatening serious harm, or damaging personal property—is not allowed. Also, establish punishments for such behavior (such as "grounding") and stick to them.

One of the most effective punishments for a child who bullies others is to impose isolation in a quiet environment. Usually, this kind of child dislikes being alone and still, which accounts to some degree for her or his aggressive interactions with others. Being forced to spend time alone and still not only punishes the child but also works in the long run to make the child more capable of self-control.

■ Make a special effort to teach your child acceptable behaviors for getting what she or he wants.
This involves teaching your child, as palatably as you can, the benefits and techniques of negotiating with other people instead of strong-arming them. Take advantage of spontaneous incidents in day-to-day life to make important points. Also, try role-playing situations that your child has encountered or is about to confront, letting your child take turns playing both roles. Role-playing is particularly effective with school-age girls, whose bullying tends to be more verbal than that of boys.

■ Involve your child in "safe" activities where she or he can have fun with others in a polite and constructive manner.
The more practice your child has in getting along with others without resorting to bullying, the better equipped she or he will be to avoid it whenever the impulse strikes. The trick is to steer your child toward situations in which interaction with others will be directly, or indirectly, moderated.

Encourage your child's participation in family gatherings and supervised outings and sports activities (which are often effective in channeling an aggressive child's excess energy). The presence of adults during such activities will help discourage the would-be bully; as a result, she or he will learn to derive more pleasure from being cooperative.

■ *Keep track of your child's bullying offenses and note any patterns.*

You may discover, for example, that your child is most likely to bully other children whenever there's a stressful situation in the family or when experiencing a personal crisis, such as a failure at school or the beginning of a new enterprise. This kind of information can help you prevent, alleviate, or respond to episodes of bullying more successfully.

■ *Set a good example.*

Make sure that you aren't indirectly teaching your child to bully by doing it yourself. And, when appropriate, let your child see you gracefully allowing others to have their way.

■ *Be sure to praise your child's good behavior.*

Frequently, children resort to bullying when they are not getting any attention. If you consistently make a special effort to commend your child for behaving in a polite, cooperative, or compassionate manner, she or he won't need to seek attention through bullying.

VICTIM

■ *Explain to your child that the bully is a troubled person.*

Often the victim of a bully is unable to comprehend why the bully behaves the way she or he does. Sometimes the victim can only conclude that she or he deserves to be bullied and that the bully is in some way a superior person. Tell your child that a bully is an unhappy child and that this unhappiness makes her or him want to hurt other people, which is not fair.

■ *Teach your child "the best way" to cope with a bully.*

You don't want your child to respond to a bully in kind, thereby only escalating the potential danger of the situation, nor do you want your child to have to cower in terror every time she or he is bullied. The proper strategy lies in the middle ground: While refusing to let the bully bother you, look the bully straight in the eye, tell her or him to stop, and then walk away from the situation in a firm and dignified manner. Even though this strategy may not always work, you should let your child know that it is the "best way" to try to get the bully to stop.

Practice role-playing variations of this basic strategy with your child, taking turns playing each role. In relationships where assuming the middle ground seems especially difficult or risky, advise your child to stay away from the bully whenever it's convenient to do so.

■ *Encourage your child to talk about her or his relationships, especially those with bullies.*

These conversations will help both you and your child put the bullying into perspective. Be sure to tell your child that if the bully ever resorts to physical violence, then she or he should immediately report the incident to a responsible adult (teacher or parent).

■ *Engage your child in activities, especially interpersonal ones, that will help build self-esteem.*

The victim of a bully needs to bolster her or his self-confidence. Encourage participation in fun activities that make her or him feel safe and competent but also involve a certain amount of self-assertion: games, sports, hobbies, contests, and/or community services.

■ *Praise your child for any acts of skill mastery, personal achievement, courage, or leadership.*

This kind of feedback helps alleviate the fear and self-contempt that a bully can inspire. Just make sure that your praise is sincere and not extravagant.

When a child is praised for such acts in the presence of a bully (or, for that matter, when a bully is praised for good behavior in the presence of her or his victim), much of the interpersonal chemistry that creates a bully-victim relationship may be neutralized. No longer do the roles seem so clear-cut.

Interpersonal Versus Intrapersonal Intelligence

Child psychologists and psychiatrists often speak of a child's "*inter*personal" as opposed to "*intra*personal" intelligence. Interpersonal intelligence refers to a child's knowledge and skills involving social relationships. By contrast, intrapersonal intelligence refers to a child's knowledge and skills involving her or his own inner self, independent of the outside world.

A child with a high degree of interpersonal intelligence is one who understands the dynamics of making and keeping friends, who can figure out how to lead others, and who is adept at cooperating, compromising, and resolving conflicts within a group context. Interpersonal intelligence tends to be acquired by extensive socialization in a variety of contexts, such as assuming an active role in a large family, engaging in different types of play and competition with various friends, and performing tasks in concert with other individuals and work teams.

A child with a high degree of intrapersonal intelligence is one who is adept at cultivating self-knowledge as well as knowledge for the sake of personal development, who is capable of self-entertaiment (i.e., enjoying solitude) for extended periods of time, and who can identify and formulate her or his personal needs, motivations, and feelings apart from those of others.

Every child has some degree of both types of intelligence, but most children become more intelligent in one of these two ways than in the other. Typically, a child who is extroverted by nature will wind up having a better-developed interpersonal intelligence; one who is introverted by nature will wind up having a better-developed intrapersonal intelligence.

As a result, extroverted children often suffer psychological problems because of a deficiency in intrapersonal intelligence (i.e., a lack of knowing their "inner selves"). Introverted children generally have the opposite problem: They suffer psychological problems because of a deficiency in interpersonal intelligence (i.e., a lack of knowing how to interact effectively with others).

When such imbalances are first detected by parents or educators, they are often treated inappropriately. Simply pressuring an apparent bookworm into joining a soccer team so that she or he will become more interpersonally intelligent could easily backfire. The bookworm may experience so much unpleasantness and even trauma playing soccer that she or he will retreat even further into books. The same kind of thing might happen if a soccer lover is forced to read the complete works of Shakespeare to become more intrapersonally intelligent. The soccer-lover's dislike of reading may instead be reinforced.

Much can be done to correct a troubled child's imbalance in interpersonal versus intrapersonal intelligence, but it must be done carefully, with full respect for the child's personal capabilities and vulnerabilities. Fortunately, most psychologists and psychiatrists are well qualified to assist individual children (along with their parents, teachers, and caretakers) in identifying the particular training methods and experiences that will most help them develop the type of intelligence they lack.

13.
Television

Aside from school and family, no human institution has a greater impact than television on the life of a child during the middle years. Experts estimate that American children between the ages of six and thirteen spend an average of three and a half hours a day watching TV. Not only does TV give them a considerable amount of their day-to-day entertainment and information, it also plays a major role in shaping their attitudes, behaviors, and value systems.

It is this latter fact that worries many parents and educators. Their principal questions:

■ How emotionally healthy can it be for children to spend so much of their time watching TV, since it's such a passive activity and such a large proportion of TV fare is violent?

■ Does watching TV stifle a child's imagination and creativity by keeping her or him from engaging in more constructive leisure-time activities, like reading, conversing, playing games, and simply daydreaming? Or does it actually stimulate a child's imagination and creativity in ways that these other activities cannot?

■ Does watching violence on TV inspire a child to be cruel in real life? Or does it provide a vicarious means for the child to discharge the negative emotions that she or he already harbors so that she or he is less likely to be violent in real life?

For the most part, clear answers to these questions are elusive. While watching television is undeniably a passive activity, which can, indeed, result in physical and emotional lethargy, it can also be a very calming activity, encouraging otherwise restless and unruly children to relax and pay attention. And while watching television certainly does detract from the time kids spend engaging in other activities that are mentally and emotionally enriching, it is not necessarily time lost. In addition to broadening their knowledge by watching newscasts, documentaries, and informational programming, kids can exercise their minds and emotions by becoming involved in television dramas, comedies, and movies.

Nevertheless, child psychiatrists and psychologists who have studied the effects of TV violence on children are becoming more and more convinced that they are mainly negative. Specifically, they are concerned about the following tendencies:

■ Children are likely to mimic the violence they see on television, either playfully or seriously.

■ Children are inclined to identify with particular victims or victimizers and to carry these identifications into real-life situations.

■ Children can become desensitized to the horror of brutality after witnessing so many violent images.

■ Children can reach the point where they regard violence as an acceptable mode of behavior, perhaps even a way to solve their problems.

By following the suggestions listed below, you can help control the amount of TV violence to which your child is exposed as well as help prevent TV viewing in general from absorbing too much of your child's time and energy:

■ ***Don't permit your child to watch TV programs that are offensive.***
As much as practical, help your child plan in advance which programs will be watched, making sure to avoid programs that you think might be too violent, sexually suggestive, or stressful. If you aren't involved in the advance planning, then ask your child what programs she or he is going to watch that day and screen—either in advance or while it's being watched—any program that concerns you.

If you discover your child watching a television program that you think is too violent, sexually suggestive, or stressful, express your concern and ask your child to choose another program or another activity besides watching TV. Be firm and don't hesitate to change the channel or turn off the TV yourself if your child refuses to do so.

■ ***Help your child distinguish between events on TV and those in real life.***
When you and your child witness an offensive act of violence on TV, be sure to draw attention to the fact that the "act" is staged and involves actors and props. Clarify anything that isn't realistic about the situation. For example, victims of television violence typically appear to recover more often—and much faster—than victims of real-life violence.

Also, when appropriate, take care to distinguish between nonviolent situations depicted on TV and their real-life counterparts. For example, if your children cite a sitcom parent as being funnier and wiser than you are, point out that sitcom parents don't really live with their TV children, that they have a team of writers giving them lines, and that they get to rehearse the same situation numerous times until they get it right.

■ *Set limits and conditions regarding the hours per day your child can watch TV.*

Given the total amount of time in a typical school-age child's day, three and a half hours of watching television is excessive, leaving very little time for homework, chores, reading, solitary play, or interaction with others. One hour—or, on special occasions, two hours—is a much more appropriate time limit; and *no* TV viewing should be permitted if it means that there won't be time to do chores or homework.

Whatever time limit you set, be specific about it and include time your child spends watching television with other family members as part of her or his personal time allotment. You may also want to set a time span within which TV viewing must fall (e.g., between 7:00 and 9:00 P.M.). Any special extensions should be negotiated in advance and involve a particular program that has special merit.

The clearer and more firmly enforced your TV rules are, the better they will work. Because watching TV is such a passive activity, it's very easy for an hour to drift into two or three. And rules governing TV can become ineffective if you permit too much leeway or bargaining. For these reasons, it's important to be very sparing about using extra hours of TV watching as a reward.

On the other hand, remember that your goal is *not* necessarily to allow as little TV watching as possible. It can be very beneficial to your child, providing not only entertainment and information but also a field of reference to be shared with peers. Instead of discrediting TV altogether, your goal is to keep certain programs from having a negative impact on your child's life and to prevent TV watching in general from overwhelming her or his leisure time.

■ *Suggest and/or arrange activities for your child to replace television watching.*

Just cutting off your child's TV-viewing hours without proposing alternative activities can be counterproductive. If there is nothing else to do, the child may miss TV so much that she or he will come to value it even more.

In addition to suggesting that your child play with a toy, pursue a hobby, or do something else alone that is pleasurable, try proposing fun activities that you can engage in together. For example, you might play games, bake cookies, or go for a walk.

■ *From time to time, experiment with a "no TV" night.*

When it seems appropriate—that is, when there's nothing on TV that's especially interesting and you can propose an alternative activity— try declaring a "no TV" night. Make sure you refer to this night deliberately as a "no TV" night so that your child feels a sense of achievement in simply not watching TV. A particularly appropriate time is after you've had one or more nights of extended TV watching.

■ *Reform your own bad TV habits.*

Set a good example of TV viewing by adopting these policies yourself:

■ Never leave the TV set on without watching it.

■ Avoid watching violent programming, at least while your child is at home.

■ Avoid doing other things in front of the TV set, thus implying that TV makes a good "background" activity.

■ Try cutting down on the number of hours per day that you watch TV.

■ Do other things with your visitors besides always watching TV.

■ Let your children see you choosing specific programs in advance rather than simply channel hopping to find the best program on the air.

14.

Psychotherapy

The middle years of a child's life are normally characterized by all sorts of trial-and-error experiences in living and therefore all sorts of transitory crises, problems, fears, misbehaviors, and mistakes. Thus, whenever a school-age child appears to be experiencing emotional stress, it can be very difficult for parents to determine objectively whether psychotherapeutic help is necessary.

Perhaps the best way for you, as a parent, to approach any such determination in the case of your child is to make a separate evaluation of each of the four main areas of your child's world: home, school, social life, and personal life. If there seem to have been serious problems lasting for several months in more than one area, then a professional evaluation of your child's overall emotional state may be advisable.

Among the issues to consider in each separate area of your child's world are the following:

HOME

■ Do you and your child frequently quarrel? Why? How intense are these quarrels? How well does your child recover from them? Do you repeatedly quarrel over the same issue without making much progress? Why?

■ Does your child frequently quarrel with his or her siblings? Why? How intense are the quarrels? How well does your child recover from them? What effect do they have on her or his siblings? Why? Do they repeatedly quarrel over the same issue without making much progress? Why?

■ Is your child consistently unhappy and withdrawn at home? Why? Does this behavior interfere with family life? How?

■ Does your child consistently avoid one or more members of the family in particular? Why? How does this avoidance affect the person or persons who are avoided?

■ Has your child's behavior at home undergone any significant and lasting change for the worse recently? How so? Why?

SCHOOL

■ Is your child's academic performance consistently poor? How so? Why?

■ Does your child repeatedly exhibit behavior problems at school? How so? Why?

■ Does your child frequently express unhappiness about school? How so? Why?

■ Has your child's behavior at school recently undergone any significant and lasting change for the worse? How so? Why?

SOCIAL LIFE

■ Does your child frequently quarrel with peers? Why? How intense are the quarrels? How well does your child recover from them? What effect do they have on peers? Are the quarrels repeatedly over the same issue without any progress being made? Why?

■ Does your child consistently avoid peer contact? Why? Are there particular peers that she or he avoids? Why?

■ Does your child frequently express fear, dissatisfaction, and anger regarding peer relationships? How so? Why?

■ Does your child appear to suffer from a lack of friends? How so? Why does she or he lack friends?

PERSONAL LIFE

■ Does your child frequently express boredom or an inability to find things to do? How well does she or he handle such situations?

■ Does your child appear to suffer from a lack of self-esteem? How so? Why?

■ Does your child engage in any self-punishing behavior or in solitary activities that appear to you to be unhealthy or unsavory? How so? Why?

■ Does your child appear to suffer from a lack of interests or initiative? How so? Why?

If you have reason to believe that your child's emotional health should be evaluated by a professional, don't hesitate to take action. The sooner you arrange for the evaluation, the better the chances are that you can catch any problems before they become even more serious. The evaluation itself may or may not reveal the need for actual psychotherapy.

As a rule, psychotherapeutic interventions involving school-age children are relatively brief and pragmatic. Individual sessions typically last from forty-five minutes to two hours. In some cases, one or two sessions may be sufficient. For example, a concerned parent may simply need professional reassurance that her or his child's psychological development is progressing normally or professional advice on strategies and activities that will foster more satisfying parent-child relations. In other cases, effective intervention may require weekly or biweekly sessions for several months. Specific goals for psychotherapy of school-age children generally include helping parents interpret their child's emotional state more accurately, increasing the quality and quantity of a child's—and a family's—social supports, and assisting family members in coping more productively with stressors outside the family.

Case-by-case diagnostic techniques and treatments involving children between the ages of six and thirteen vary considerably according to the specific situation. Generally speaking, parental interviews are always a major part of the process. Parents are asked about their perceptions of their child and about their relationship with her or him and with other family members, including their own parents.

In addition to parental interviews, doctors and therapists rely on "play therapy" and direct interviews with the child. In play therapy, a child acts out or discusses her or his emotions and concerns in the context of playing with toys and games provided by the doctor or therapist.

Play therapy's indirect approach to eliciting a child's feelings and experiences avoids some of the problems that can arise in directly interviewing someone this young. Potential problems of this nature include: the chance that the questions themselves might "lead" the responses; the risk that the child might be frightened by the dialogue; and the possibility that the child's replies might be inaccurate because of comprehension or communication difficulties or the child's wish to conceal the truth due to fear, guilt, or a desire to please.

Here are some issues to consider in finding the right doctor or therapist, and the right type of therapy, for you, your child, and your family:

1. Before you begin your search, establish what you consider to

be the problem that you want addressed and the goal that you want achieved.

First, write down your answers to the following five questions, bearing in mind that some of your answers may overlap:

a. What specific behaviors have I observed indicating that my child may be experiencing emotional turmoil? (To whatever extent possible, give dates, times of day, settings, and circumstantial surroundings.)

b. How would I define this emotional turmoil? (In other words, if you had to make a diagnosis, what would it be?)

c. What might be the cause(s) of this turmoil? (Include any speculations and conclusive opinions you may have, being careful to distinguish between the two categories.)

d. In what different ways has this emotional turmoil been bothersome or detrimental to my child, to me, and to other members of the family? (Be as specific as possible, as you were directed to be in answering question a.)

e. How have I tried to better the situation? (Indicate which methods have been at least partially successful and which have failed altogether.)

Once you have answered all five questions to the best of your ability, write down a fairly succinct (one- or two-sentence) description of what you think the *problem* is. Next, write an equally succinct description of the *goal* that you want to achieve related to this problem: that is, what you would like to see happen *as a result* of psychotherapeutic intervention.

These statements, as well as the question-and-answer background material, will be enormously helpful to you in interviewing possible doctors or therapists. They will also be enormously helpful to the doctor or therapist you choose in her or his efforts to diagnose and treat your child successfully.

2. Familiarize yourself with the major types of therapy that are available.

The sheer variety of therapy labels is bewildering to the outsider: psychoanalytic (Freudian, Jungian, Adlerian, or otherwise), cognitive, behavioral, existential, Gestalt, transactional, reality-oriented, rational-emotive, and so on. However, for the purpose of interviewing potential doctors or therapists to work with a child between the ages of six and thirteen, all you need is a very basic awareness of three broad categories of psychotherapy: psychodynamic therapy, behavioral therapy, and family-oriented therapy. Let's consider each category individually:

■ *Psychodynamic therapy* is geared toward getting the child to identify, understand, and self-manage her or his emotional problems. It depends heavily on effective verbal communication between the doctor or therapist and the child, so it may not be appropriate for younger children in this age range, who may not be very fluent in verbal communication. It also tends to be relatively long-term compared to other categories of psychotherapy, often involving multiple sessions per week up to a year or two.

■ *Behavioral therapy* is geared toward getting the child to change the way she or he behaves. Instead of focusing squarely on the causes of a particular problem, it concentrates on the symptoms. For example, it might help children learn to control their anger without necessarily getting them to appreciate why they get angry, to be less scared of nightmares regardless of whether they know about their possible source, or to interact more cooperatively with other people even if their feelings about them remain unresolved. It typically takes at least a few months of weekly or biweekly sessions before satisfactory results can be expected.

■ *Family-oriented therapy*, sometimes known as "systems therapy," is one of the types of therapy practiced at Philadelphia Child Guidance Center (PCGC) and the type that PCGC recommends most highly for children of any age. Drawing upon both psychodynamic therapy and behavioral therapy, family-oriented therapy is geared toward generating positive awareness and change in all aspects of the child's world: her or his own mind and behavior as well as the minds and behaviors of those people who directly influence her or his life. In comparison to other therapies, it is much more adaptable to the situation at hand. Satisfactory results may be achieved in just one or two sessions or may take up to a year or two.

Use these very basic distinctions as starting points for discussing with other people (such as knowledgeable advisers and potential doctors or therapists) the particular type or types of psychotherapy that may be appropriate for your unique situation. Also, investigate the literature about child psychotherapy that's available at local libraries and bookstores. The more informed you are about child psychotherapy—whatever form it may take—the more benefit you'll derive from the type you finally choose, whatever it may be.

3. Familiarize yourself with the major types of doctors and therapists that are available.

The three most common practitioners of child-oriented psychotherapy are psychiatrists, psychologists, and social workers. Regardless of the specific title (e.g., "child psychiatrist"), not all of these practitioners have special training or experience in treating children in particular as opposed to people in general. This is an important issue that you will want to investigate with individual practitioners that you interview.

Also, keep in mind that one type of practitioner, all else being equal, is not necessarily more or less desirable than another. Your final determination should be based on how appropriate the individual practitioner is, given the following factors: your child's problem, the goals you've established relating to that problem, the type of therapy you're interested in pursuing, your financial resources, and most important of all, the overall personalities of you and your child.

These warnings having been given, here are brief descriptions of each major type of practitioner.

■ *Psychiatrists* are medical doctors (M.D.s), which means that they have had four years of medical school, one year of internship, and at least two years of residency training in psychiatry. In addition, virtually all child psychiatrists have had two-year fellowships in child psychiatry and are board certified.

One major advantage of a psychiatrist over other types of practitioners is that he or she can diagnose and prescribe treatment for physical problems that may be causing or aggravating a child's emotional problems. A possible disadvantage, depending on your particular situation, is that some psychiatrists (usually not *child* psychiatrists) are inclined to practice only psychodynamic forms of therapy.

■ *Psychologists* have usually earned a doctorate (Ph.D.) in psychology, typically the result of five years of graduate training, including several supervised clinical programs and a year of formal internship. Most states also require postdoctoral experience before licensing. Some states, however, require only a master's degree (M.A.) to become a psychologist.

Although psychologists themselves cannot offer physical diagnosis and prescription, they almost always have close professional relationships with M.D.s whom they can recommend for such services. They are also likely to be more eclectic in their therapeutic style, although there is still a trend among psychologists to favor behavioral therapy.

■ *Social workers* have earned a master's degree in social work (M.S.W.), a process that involves two years of classes and fieldwork.

In addition, some states require two or more years of postgraduate experience before licensing.

While social workers may not have had the extensive academic and clinical training that psychiatrists and psychologists have had, they are, as a rule, much more familiar with—and knowledgeable about— the home, community, and school environments of their clients. This background inclines them to favor family-oriented or systems-oriented therapy over other types of therapy.

Another major issue to consider in choosing a particular type of doctor or therapist is whether the therapy will occur in a *private office* or a *clinic*. Other factors aside, therapy performed in a clinic tends to be more multidimensional: a by-product of the fact that clinics are so often staffed with different types of doctors and therapists, who not only practice different types of therapy but also conduct different kinds of research projects.

4. *Make a rough estimate of how much you can afford to spend on your child's therapy.*
It may be impossible to put a price on a child's emotional well-being. However, it's quite possible to determine how much you can afford to spend for psychotherapy without making life much more difficult for yourself and your family—a situation that could only exacerbate your child's emotional problems.

You may have insurance that will cover some or all of the expenses directly incurred as a result of your child's therapy; but in the best of situations there are bound to be some hidden costs. Factor into your budget such possibilities as lost income for days off work, transportation and parking for therapy sessions, and baby-sitting care for other children while you are at the sessions.

In estimating how much you can afford, take into account that private therapy is almost certain to be more expensive than therapy in a clinic. Also, clinics may offer lower fees if you accept therapy from a supervised student therapist or agree to participate in a research project (which typically means being observed, taped, and/or interviewed).

5. *Seek several recommendations from a variety of qualified sources.*
Ask relatives and friends who have benefited from the services of child psychiatrists, psychologists, or social workers for their opinions, but also seek leads from more experienced and disinterested parties, such as your pediatrician, family physician, and clergyperson. For the names of certified practitioners in your area, contact the local and

national mental-health and professional organizations (see Appendix for a list of suggestions).

6. Interview different doctors and therapists thoroughly about their credentials, areas of expertise, and therapeutic techniques.

Among the specific questions you should ask are the following:

■ What is your educational and training background (see issue 3)?

■ Are you board certified? By whom?

■ With what professional organizations are you affiliated (see Appendix for a list)?

■ How long have you practiced in your current capacity?

■ What is your general or preferred style of therapy (see issue 2)?

■ What are your areas of special expertise?

■ How much work have you done with children who are the same age as my child?

■ How much work have you done with the type of problem(s) my child is having (see issue 1)?

■ Would you feel committed to achieving the goal I have in mind (see issue 1)?

■ What kinds of services can I expect from you toward meeting this goal?

■ What kinds of commitment and cooperation would you expect from me and my family in the course of my child's therapy?

■ How, and at what rate, will you keep me informed of the progress my child is making in therapy?

■ How much time do you estimate the therapy might take?

■ How much will it cost, will my insurance or medical assistance help pay the cost, and are there ways to reduce the cost (see issue 4)?

7. Make sure that you choose a doctor or therapist who respects you and with whom you are comfortable.

Some doctors or therapists may unintentionally inspire you to feel guilty or incompetent, in which case you should look for someone else. The doctor or therapist you select should be a person who inspires you to feel good about yourself: *re*moralized instead of *de*moralized.

Your answer to each of the following questions should be yes both during your initial interview with a doctor or therapist and throughout the time that the therapy itself is in progress:

■ Does the doctor or therapist take into account *your* theories, opinions, and concerns as well as her or his own?

■ Does the interaction you have with the doctor or therapist seem like a dialogue rather than a monologue on the doctor's or therapist's part?

■ Does the doctor or therapist seem genuinely interested in you and your situation (evidenced by her or his paying close attention to you, maintaining fairly consistent eye contact with you, and regularly soliciting your comments and reactions)?

■ Does the doctor or therapist seem genuinely interested in your child and her or his problems?

■ Does the doctor or therapist make sure that you understand what she or he is doing and saying?

■ Does the doctor or therapist answer all of your questions promptly, thoughtfully, and to the best of her or his ability?

■ Do you leave the doctor's or therapist's company feeling clear about the direction that your child's case will be taking?

■ Do you leave the doctor's or therapist's company feeling generally stronger rather than weaker?

Special Diagnoses: Children in the Middle Years

ATTENTION-DEFICIT HYPERACTIVITY DISORDER

Attention-deficit hyperactivity disorder (ADHD) is the most common psychiatric disorder of childhood, with an overall prevalence rate of 5 percent. It manifests itself most clearly in school as a persistent combination of restlessness, noisiness, an inability to sit still or concentrate, poor socialization, and poor scholastic performance. However, ADHD affects all aspects of a child's life, not just her or his school life, and the victim usually exhibits some signs of ADHD even before school age.

Psychotherapists who suspect ADHD from a child's history will recommend a medical evaluation to determine if there may be some alternative explanation for her or his symptoms: for example, a hearing impairment, hyperthyroidism, a seizure-related condition, and/or an allergy. If ADHD does seem to be the source of the child's problems, then the psychotherapist assists the child and the family in developing coping strategies: for example, procedures that will keep the child focused on individual tasks as they present themselves and help pace the child through the performance of each task in an appropriate manner. When a diagnosis of ADHD is severe and indisputable, tranquilizing medication may also be prescribed.

LEARNING DISABILITIES

A school-age child suffering from a learning disability typically tries hard to follow instructions in school, concentrate on performing well, and complete all assignments in a timely manner. Nevertheless, she or he routinely fails to master assignments and falls far behind other classmates.

Although the precise cause of learning disabilities is not known for sure, it is generally believed that they result from a complication in the nervous system that adversely affects the brain's ability to receive, process, and/or communicate information. Some learning-disabled children also suffer from ADHD, which may be the cause of their particular disability. Overall, learning disabilities affect approximately 15 percent of otherwise capable school-age children.

A psychotherapist who suspects that a child suffers from a learning disability will arrange for appropriate testing with school professionals as well as other specialists. Among the possible treatment procedures for a learning disability are placement in a special class or school, speech or language therapy, and/or parent-driven programs for helping the child cope with the disability, make the most of her or his learning potential, and develop more self-confidence and initiative.

At PCGC:
ADHD Evaluation and
Treatment

Attention-deficit hyperactivity disorder (ADHD) is one of the most widely researched subjects in child psychology. And yet in many respects it remains a perplexing mystery, with much disagreement among experts about what it is, what causes it, and how it should be treated.

This confusion stems primarily from the fact that each case of ADHD is different. Some sufferers have no other apparent problem than a high degree of distractibility. Others have a whole constellation of problems, including severe personality and learning disorders. As a result, each child with ADHD must be considered apart from all the others, and each evaluation and treatment strategy must be custom-tailored.

The Evaluation and Treatment Program, a joint project of The Children's Hospital of Philadelphia, Children's Seahorse House, and PCGC, serves as an example of how to facilitate effective individual-based evaluation and treatment of ADHD. Children from ages five to fourteen are enrolled by referral.

The therapeutic approach of the program is multimodal. Pediatricians, psychologists, psychiatrists, and social workers form a team that works along with the child and her or his parents to maximize the child's chances for successful management of ADHD. One team member initiates the diagnosis and remains the "case manager," coordinating the various psychological, educational, and medical assessments that are deemed necessary and any treatment interventions that are indicated by those assessments.

The diagnostic phase of the program begins with a consultation between the case manager, the parents, and the child. The next step usually involves the completion of questionnaires by the child's parents and teachers aimed at determining the *general* scope and severity of the child's ADHD problem. For example, one of the most frequently used and revealing questionnaires is the Conners Teacher Rating Scale, which directs the evaluator to gauge symptoms like "restlessness" according to four degrees: "not at all," "just a little," "pretty much," and "very much."

Additional diagnostic strategies are employed in the program to arrive at a more *specific* picture of the child's ADHD problem. A pediatrician takes a detailed developmental history and conducts a lengthy physical examination; a psychologist performs one or both of the following observational studies:

■ direct observation of the child's behavior at school: in the classroom and/or on the playground;

■ direct observation of the child (via a one-way mirror) during a simulated work or play experience set up at the clinic.

To determine the extent to which learning difficulties are—or may be—involved in the case, the psychologist also administers various tests to measure the child's intelligence quotient and intellectual achievements as well as her or his abilities to control impulsivity, to concentrate, to organize her or his thoughts, and to utilize her or his memory. If psychological problems are apparent, if the family is experiencing significant conflicts, or if medication seems indicated, an extensive psychiatric evaluation is conducted. Essentially, this evaluation determines the potential or existing impact of anxiety, depression, anger, or other emotional disturbances not only on the child's ADHD itself but also on the child's ability to respond to ADHD therapy.

Specific treatment of ADHD advised by the program varies according to the case at hand. In some cases, medical management is indicated. The most common medication used to treat ADHD is Ritalin, a trade name for the stimulant methylphenidate. Alternative stimulants that may be prescribed are Dexedrine (dextroamphetamine) and Cylert (pemoline). In low dosages, these drugs enhance attention without causing an increase in motor activity.

Other ADHD cases in which medical management is indicated call for an antidepressant instead of a stimulant. The antidepressants most often prescribed for ADHD are known as tricyclic antidepressants (TCAs): namely, Tofranil or Janimine (both imipramine) and Norpramin or Pertofrane (both desipramine).

Whether or not medical management is indicated, ADHD treatment supervised by the program always consists of three integrated components: behavioral management, family counseling, and educational counseling:

■ *Behavioral management* refers to the administration of techniques by parents and teachers to change the child's ADHD-related behavior for the better. Specifically, the aim is to get the child to alter or eliminate undesirable behaviors and to adopt or increase wanted behaviors by applying a system of rewards, skills training, and environmental manipulation.

■ *Family counseling* is geared toward the promotion of healthy family interactions in general and toward the promotion of effective coping with the child's ADHD in particular. Usually it involves a series of psychotherapeutic sessions in which all members of the family participate jointly.

■ *Educational counseling* involves working with parents, teachers, and in some cases, special agencies and institutions, to make sure that the ADHD-afflicted child receives the kind of instructional, informational, and intellectual training from which she or he can best benefit.

For more information about ADHD in general, see *A Parent's Guide to Attention Deficit Disorders* by Lisa J. Bain (a Delta book, New York: Bantam Doubleday Dell Publishing, 1991). This practical book is based on the ADHD-related experience of pediatricians, psychiatrists, psychologists, neurologists, and social workers associated with PCGC, The Children's Hospital of Philadelphia, and the Children's Seashore House.

The Middle Years: Selected Terms and Concepts

acting out   indirectly expressing emotional conflicts—or "forbidden feelings"—through negative behavior. Such behavior is typically overdramatic and designed to attract attention. It may or may not be overtly self-punishing or injurious to others. For example, a child who feels rejected by a parent may "act out" that feeling by refusing to speak to that parent, constantly trying to distract the parent, or picking fights with a sibling who appears to be getting more attention.

adjustment disorder   a psychological illness characterized by a child's failure to respond effectively to change or to recover effectively from a crisis.

affective disorder   also known as *emotional disorder* and *mood disorder*, a specifically defined psychological illness relating to the emotions (e.g., *adjustment disorder*). Generally, such a disorder is apparent in the problematic manner in which a child physically displays her or his emotions (hence, the root "affect"). The disorder may also have a physical cause.

attachment   the emotional bond between parent and child. Most often the term is used in reference to the child's bond to the mother, although attachment is a two-way street and also forms between child and father.

   Attachment between child and mother is uniquely strong because of the latter's role in childbearing and early caretaking. Conditioned to seek closeness with the mother, the child may suffer emotional difficulties if deprived of maternal affections or if that affection becomes overly demanding.

attention-deficit hyperactivity disorder   psychiatric disorder characterized by persistent restlessness, noisiness, inability to concentrate, poor socialization, and poor scholastic performance.

behavior modeling   a therapeutic technique by means of which the child is taught or encouraged to replace negative behaviors with more positive ones. The teaching or encouraging process involves modifying the way each parent or caretaker interacts with the child so that the child learns by example or direct experience (e.g., a reward system) to behave more constructively.

bipolar disorder   also known as *manic-depressive disorder*, a psychological illness characterized by extreme mood swings back and forth between depression and elation. Each mood phase lasts for an indeterminate amount of time, varying from individual to individual and from episode to episode. The disorder has a biological basis and can often be controlled by medication.

compliance   the tendency to respond effectively—both in emotional and behavioral terms—to scheduling arrangements, rules, and discipline.

conduct disorder a psychological problem manifested in chronic, excessively unruly behaviors, such as stealing, running away, lying, or setting fires.

conflict resolution a therapeutic technique in which a child is assisted in alleviating or managing chronic interpersonal conflict. Often group therapy is involved, bringing together the child with the other person or persons involved in the conflict. The therapy may also, or alternatively, feature one-on-one teaching, whereby the child learns general strategies for handling interpersonal conflicts more effectively.

defense mechanism according to Sigmund Freud's terminology, a means unconsciously and automatically employed by the psyche to avoid emotional pain, such as *projection* or *repression*.

defiance more technically known as *oppositional behavior*, a term that refers to any act of a child that is intentionally designed to challenge parental authority. Common examples include saying no, refusing to perform assigned tasks, and deliberately withdrawing from meals and other prearranged family activities.

depression more technically known as *unipolar disorder*, a term that refers to a distinct psychological illness characterized by chronic apathy, hopelessness, and fatigue—physical as well as emotional.

distractibility a problematic behavior involving a limited ability to concentrate on a single activity for an appropriate amount of time. Distractibility can be a sign of underlying anxiety, or it can lead to anxiety. It can also be a symptom of attention-deficit hyperactivity disorder (see pages 282–83 in this section).

dysfunctional as opposed to *functional*, a term used to describe a personality or family unit that does not operate effectively or satisfactorily to meet day-to-day life challenges. In some cases, there is apparent effectiveness or satisfaction, but achieving it causes underlying psychological damage. In other cases, the personality or family unit is clearly having problems that pose a threat to its survival.

This term is sociological in origin and is rapidly losing currency in the field of psychology. Many therapists consider it too negative and abstract to be useful diagnostically.

eating disorder   a psychological illness manifested by chronic, abnormal eating behavior. Among the most common eating disorders are "anorexia nervosa," in which the child starves her- or himself, and "bulimia," in which the child binges on food and then vomits to purge her- or himself. Eating disorders of this nature are relatively rare among children in the middle years. Instead, they tend to manifest themselves during adolescence.

Electra complex   according to Sigmund Freud's philosophy, the natural psychological drive in a young girl to compete with her mother for her father's attention and affection. In other words, the father is perceived as a romantic ideal whose presence is constantly desired, while the mother is perceived as a rival, an unwanted presence.

Typically, a young girl experiences the Electra complex between the ages of three and six. Sometimes, however, its effects may linger until age eight. The counterpart of the Electra complex for young boys is the *Oedipus complex*.

emotional disorder   (see *affective disorder*)

empathy   the emotional and social ability of a child to respond effectively, with compassion and without self-interest, to the pains and needs of another human being. A child can demonstrate isolated instances of empathy from a very early age, especially in connection with parent, sibling, or loved one. However, the overall capacity to feel, sustain, and enact empathy is relatively limited until around ages six to eight, by which time the child has had sufficient social experience to develop such a capacity.

extroversion   a generally outgoing attitude toward the world at large. First defined by Carl Jung, extroversion is also associated with a relatively strong interest in social interactions and concrete realities and a relatively weak interest in self-contained activities and abstract thought.

Extroversion is assumed to be an inborn personality trait that is neither positive nor negative in essence and that can be modified only slightly by experience or conditioning. The opposite quality is *introversion*.

functional   (see *dysfunctional*)

impulsivity   a child's persistent and inappropriate pattern of acting spontaneously according to personal desires without thinking of the consequences. It may be a sign of an underlying psychological problem. It may also be a symptom of attention-deficit hyperactivity disorder.

individuation in the philosophy of Carl Jung, the long process by which a child evolves from being totally dependent on others—emotionally, intellectually, and socially—to being a separate and successful individual with a unique, self-sustaining psychological makeup.

introversion a generally inward looking attitude toward the world at large. First defined by Carl Jung, introversion is also associated with a relatively strong interest in self-contained activities and abstract thought and a relatively mild interest in social interactions and concrete realities.

Introversion is assumed to be an inborn personality trait that is neither positive nor negative in essence and can be modified only slightly by experience or conditioning. The opposite quality is *extroversion.*

latency according to Sigmund Freud's philosophy, the period between six and ten, when a child is relatively free from psychological upheavals having to do with sexual development. For this reason, a child during latency is considered to be more emotionally stable in general than during her or his earlier or later years.

maladaption also known as *maladjustment*, this term refers to a child's inability to respond in a calm, effective, or successful manner either to a single life change or to the demands of life in general.

maladjustment (see *maladaption*)

manic-depressive disorder (see *bipolar disorder*)

medical intervention in most cases, the use of medication (e.g., tranquilizing drugs) to alleviate the cause or symptoms of a psychological problem.

mood disorder (see *affective disorder*)

nature versus nurture an expression referring to the concept that some of a child's psychological traits are primarily inborn (i.e., "natural") and others are primarily acquired through upbringing (i.e., "nurturing"). Different schools of thought assign different "nature versus nurture" ratios to the development of individual psychological traits.

neurosis as opposed to the more serious condition *psychosis*, a psychological problem that still allows the victim to maintain reasonably good contact with reality and to perform intellectually and socially in a reasonably acceptable manner.

This term does not refer to a specific illness. Therefore, it is technically not accurate to say that a child is suffering from a "neurosis." Because of this fact, the term is rapidly being replaced by the expression "neurotic process" (e.g., "If treatment is not applied, this child's emotional problem could trigger a neurotic process").

obsessive behavior   a pattern of applying excessively intense and perhaps ritualized concentration to the performance of a specific task (e.g., hand washing). Often the child's preoccupation with a particular task appears to be fanatical—a desperate quest for certainty or perfection. If the behavior persists over an extended period of time, it could be a sign of an underlying psychological problem.

Oedipus complex   according to Sigmund Freud's philosophy, the natural psychological drive in a young boy to compete with his father for his mother's attention and affection. In other words, the mother is perceived as a romantic ideal whose presence is constantly desired, while the father is perceived as a rival and unwanted presence.

Typically, a young boy experiences the Oedipus complex between the ages of three and six. Sometimes, however, its effects may linger until age eight. The counterpart of the Oedipus complex for young girls is called the *Electra complex.*

oppositional behavior   (see *defiance*)

other-directed behavior   individual actions that are oriented toward other people: for example, seeking their attention, initiating and responding to interactions, expressing hostility. Therapists often explore whether a child has a healthy, age-appropriate balance of other-directed behavior and its opposite, *self-directed behavior.*

overanxious disorder   a psychological problem manifesting itself in chronic, generalized, and often irrational feelings of fear, apprehension, and misgiving. There may also be physical symptoms, such as frequent headaches and stomachaches.

overcorrection   a negative effect of the parent-child relationship in which the discipline or punishment imposed on a child's conduct—or the child's "reforming" response to discipline or punishment—exceeds appropriate limits.

pathology   (see *psychopathology*)

phobia an excessive and persistent fear of particular people, things, or situations. (Precise targets vary from individual to individual.) Phobias are fairly common among children in the middle years. Most often they are transitory and not indicative of any serious psychological problem.

projection an unconscious, self-protecting measure in which a child denies negative, forbidden, or unpleasant feelings and instead attributes them to someone else. In most cases, the person upon whom the child projects such negative feelings is the trigger for them. For example, a child who is angry at Mother may unconsciously reclaim her or his innocence by believing instead that Mother is angry with her or him.

psychoanalysis as opposed to the broader term *psychotherapy*, a mode of diagnosing and treating a child's psychological problems through one-on-one therapist-patient dialogue. There are many different schools of psychoanalysis, each based on a particular philosophy regarding how the psyche functions.

Because of its reliance on verbal and cognitive skills, psychoanalysis is more often applied to adolescents and adults than to children in their middle years. The latter group is more often diagnosed and treated by means of therapies in which the whole family participates or in which the object is *behavior modeling* rather than intellectual understanding.

psychopathology the study of mental illnesses. The term *pathology* refers to a disease or a disorder, as opposed to a less severe problem.

psychosis as opposed to the less serious condition *neurosis*, a psychological problem that often or continuously prevents the victim from maintaining reasonably good contact with reality or performing intellectually and socially in a reasonably acceptable manner.

A particular psychotic disorder may be either psychological or biological in origin or both. Among the distinctive indicators that an emotional problem is psychotic rather than neurotic are the presence of delusions (irrational beliefs) or hallucinations (distorted perceptions).

psychotherapy a professional method of treating emotional problems and *affective disorders*. Psychotherapy can take a number of different forms, such as *psychoanalysis*, or varying therapies designed to provide appropriate *behavior modeling*.

repression a means of emotional self-protection in which traumatic or unpleasant thoughts or memories are automatically relegated to the unconscious mind and forgotten by the conscious mind.

resilience a child's ability to adapt effectively to change or recover effectively from a crisis. The more resilient a child's emotional nature is, the psychologically healthier she or he is.

resistance in the context of psychotherapy, a child's conscious or unconscious refusal to cooperate with the therapist or the therapy.

self-directed behavior individual actions that are oriented around the self: for example, solitary play or self-punishment. Therapists often explore whether a child has a healthy, age-appropriate balance of self-directed behavior and its opposite, *other-directed behavior.*

unipolar disorder (see *depression*)

withdrawal a child's willful separation, emotionally or physically, from an event or person that is somehow distressing. Long-term withdrawal, or an ever-widening pattern of withdrawal, can be a sign of an underlying psychological problem.

Part Three:
Adolescence
AGE THIRTEEN TO AGE TWENTY

Introduction

L ife during adolescence is rife with paradoxes. The word *adolescence* itself means "to be in the process of becoming adult," which signifies that a teenager has no fixed characteristics or identity. Instead, she or he is a transitional being, a changeling, who progresses through various and unpredictably shifting degrees of being part child, part adult, and part in-between. Although studies indicate that most teenagers are not *seriously* troubled despite popular opinion that they are, the potential for emotional turbulence is ever-present.

One major paradox of adolescence involves the nature of a teenager's emotional dependence on her or his parents. While typical, self-absorbed adolescents are always craving personal freedom from their parents, they still want—and need—their love just as much as ever.

All too easily teenagers can feel as if they are no longer cute, little, helpless, or even innocent enough to attract such love. And all too easily parents assume that their teenage children don't like to be "babied" with the same old expressions of love. This latter assumption may or may not be true; but in either case, the sad result is that many parents become inhibited about expressing their love to their teenage children in *any* direct manner, which only makes their children feel all the more unloved.

Another major paradox of adolescence has to do with the powerful conflict between rationality and irrationality in the teenage psyche. For long periods of time during a child's adolescence, it can appear as if two equally strong internal forces—order and chaos—are wrestling for control of all words and actions, with neither force very often winning a decisive victory.

On the "order" side, teenagers are intensely concerned with understanding *why* things are as they are, from the way society in general operates to the way their parents run their particular household. They'll argue social and family policies fiercely and doggedly, with an apparent reverence for logic, reason, and clarity that can often make them appear far more mature and judicious than they really are.

On the "chaos" side, teenagers are predisposed to experiment more creatively from time to time with their emerging adulthood, testing the limits of the pleasures and pains that it has to offer. On many occasions, this tendency can lead to an impulsive disregard of reason, rules, or responsibilities for the sake of establishing and feeling one's own individuality. Sometimes this tendency can lead even further toward a deliberate and outright defiance of what is right or logical— perhaps even a reckless act of thrill seeking that may end in disaster.

Yet another major paradox of adolescence involves the *rate* at which teenagers evolve from being immature children into being mature adults. This rate varies not only *among* individual teenagers in a group but also *within* each individual teenager, according to which particular aspects of his or her life are under consideration.

In some respects, a teenager can appear to grow up very fast, especially one in today's world. Within a few short years after puberty, most contemporary adolescent boys and girls are copying adult dress and behaviors fairly successfully, carrying on active sex lives, and earning enough money to buy themselves a significant amount of financial independence, at least as far as their day-to-day personal and social activities are concerned.

In other respects, today's teenagers are postponing their final coming of age further and further into the future, prolonging residence at home and/or overall dependence on their parents until after they have earned a college degree, achieved job security, or found someone with whom to start a family, or a life, of their own. Indeed, it's not at all uncommon today for individuals to remain emotionally dependent or "childlike" in their relationship with their parents until well into their twenties and even thirties.

In trying to work through these paradoxes to raise your adolescent child more effectively, here are some essential points to remember:

1. During your child's adolescence, you should expect and accept a certain rise in the amount of emotional difficulties.

In the case of most children, the so-called middle years between age six and puberty are less emotionally turbulent for parent and child alike than the early years between birth and age six. Regrettably, this trend doesn't usually continue beyond the middle years into adolescence. Instead, the onset of adolescence, with its dramatic physical and social changes, initiates a return of sorts to the stormier emotional climate associated with the early years of childhood.

During turbulent adolescence, your perfectly "normal" child may do many things that will make you feel worried, ashamed, fearful, helpless, angry, or guilty. Here's just a sampling of various types of "normal" teenage problems that have distressing emotional causes and effects:

■ spending most of the time at home, silent and withdrawn;

■ driving a car around without a license;

■ treating adults in general with distrust and disrespect;

■ stealing money from wallets and private stashes;

■ attacking, quarreling with, and rejecting parents on very personal grounds, especially the "same sex" parent;

■ lying about activities and whereabouts;

■ defying household rules and family standards of decency;

■ staying out all night, whereabouts unknown;

■ shoplifting;

■ refusing to go anywhere with the family;

■ abusing drugs;

■ skipping school for extended periods of time;

■ running away;

■ tormenting younger children;

■ engaging in promiscuous sex.

Clearly some of these problems are more alarming than others, at least on the surface. Nevertheless, *all* of them are common among teenagers—regardless of sex, race, family status, moral upbringing, socioeconomic class, or geographic area. And although a child's emotional and behavioral history before becoming a teenager will have a strong impact on how she or he progresses through adolescence, so will all the new physical, social, and emotional challenges that are unique to adolescence and, to a great degree, unpredictable.

Because of these facts, no parent of a teenager can afford to dismiss any one of the above-mentioned problems as "inconceivable" or "intolerable" in the case of her or his child. Instead, every parent of a teenager must be somewhat prepared in advance to handle all of these problems so that she or he won't be completely at a loss if any one of them—or more—should arise.

When you, as a parent, are faced with such concerns, the key to maintaining your authority and sanity is to put each difficult situation involving your teenage child into its proper perspective. Accept what you can afford to accept—for your own sake, your child's sake, and your family's sake—whenever it's possible to do so. Reserve serious criticisms, disciplinary actions, or rescue attempts for situations that truly warrant them, based on your own informed and practical judgment.

---

2. *Your teenage child depends on you to be emotionally calm, steady, and strong*.

With so many emotional ups and downs and twists and turns going on in their lives, teenagers appreciate getting a sense of proportion from their parents, whether they openly acknowledge it or not. But such a sense is only one of the things teenagers are seeking from their parents.

Observing how any adult—but especially a parent—maintains a strong, emotionally secure center through good times and bad actually inspires teenagers to try to do the same thing themselves. By consciously and/or unconsciously imitating such models of mature steadiness, teenagers develop a more consistent, responsible, and balanced feeling for who they are and how they're getting along in life.

As the parent of a teenager, try to remain as composed and consistent as possible in your parenting style, particularly during difficult parent-child encounters. Don't let conversational negotiations degenerate into heated arguments. Above all, guard against taking out your personal anxieties and frustrations on your child by doing unto your child the same types of upsetting things that she or he does unto you.

---

3. *Throughout your child's adolescence, you should work together toward achieving a more mature and mutually independent parent-child relationship*.

Often parents of a teenager suffer consciously or subconsciously from a reluctance to yield *any* of their parental authority. They fear not only that their child might founder if they begin withdrawing their support and control but also that they might thereby start losing their child altogether.

In fact, an adolescent child's growth as an emotionally healthy and independent human being depends on a gradual giving up of parental authority so that the child can eventually manage and assume full responsibility for her or his own life and activities. In this process, parents don't *lose* their children. Instead, they let their children *loose* so that they can be free to form more mature and mutually rewarding relationships with everyone in their lives, including their parents.

As the parent of a teenage child, you need to appreciate these facts and use them as the basis for developing a flexible and less authoritarian parenting style. It's for your own good as well as that of your child.

Be alert for opportunities to trust your teenage child with new freedoms and responsibilities. Share with your child new, more adult-oriented interests and activities, as appropriate. Allow your child to experiment with new, less child-oriented ways of interacting or socializing with you in particular and with the family in general. And help your child lay the groundwork, block by block, for a new, satisfying, and self-reliant future life apart from you and the family.

4. *Your child never outgrows the need for your love, care, and respect*.

Although children may demand and deserve an increasing amount of independence from direct parental supervision and control as they progress through their teenage years, they will always need their parents to love them, to be concerned about their welfare, and to hold them in high regard. From these parental gifts they derive a great deal of their ongoing emotional security and sense of self-worth.

Always make sure that your teenage child realizes your love, care, and respect for her or him regardless of what she or he may do. In criticizing or disciplining your teenage child, be careful to focus your disapproval on the offending *act*, not on your *child* her- or himself. And occasionally go out of your way to express positive feelings about your child in ways that are appropriate to her or his current age and sensibilities.

This section of the book offers guidelines that assist you in helping your child enjoy the pleasures and endure the pain that commonly accompanies adolescence. It is organized as follows:

1. SEXUALITY *(Page 308)*

■ what to expect in terms of sexual activity during adolescence

■ how to help a teenage child be sexually safe and responsible

■ how to deal with problems associated with a teenager's sexual behavior

■ how to prevent, and cope with, sexual abuse: in the event that the teenager is the would-be or actual victim, and in the event that the teenager is the would-be or actual abuser

■ how to help a gay teenage child

■ at PCGC: treating teenage sex offenders

2. POPULARITY *(Page 324)*

■ why popularity—or the lack of it—is such an important issue for teenagers

■ how to prevent, manage, and overcome problems associated with popularity or the lack thereof

■ guidelines for responding to a teenager's desire for cosmetic surgery

3. DEPRESSION *(Page 333)*

■ causes and effects of depression in teenage children

■ how to prevent, manage, and overcome problems associated with teenage depression

■ how to detect and prevent a teenager's intention to commit suicide and what to do in the aftermath of a suicide attempt

■ at PCGC: the onset of adulthood

■ at PCGC: seasonal affective disorder

4. DISCIPLINE *(Page 348)*

■ common disciplinary challenges presented by teenagers; emotional issues associated with those challenges

■ how to handle major teenage disciplinary problems

5. SUBSTANCE ABUSE *(Page 356)*

■ common causes and effects of teenage abuse of controlled substances, including specific attention to the four most abused varieties: (1) alcohol, (2) amphetamines and barbiturates, (3) marijuana, and (4) cocaine

■ possible dangers associated with the use of specific drugs

■ how to detect whether a teenager is abusing drugs

■ how to help a teenager avoid, manage, and overcome substance-abuse problems

■ specific resources to contact for help in dealing with teenage substance abuse

6. RUNNING AWAY *(Page 366)*

■ why teenagers run away

■ how to detect whether a teenager is planning to run away

■ how to discourage or prevent a teenager from running away

■ how to cope with running away when—and after—it happens

7. OVEREATING *(Page 373)*

■ common causes and effects of teenage obesity and overeating

■ how to prevent, manage, and overcome teenage overeating problems

■ At PCGC: helping obese teenagers

8. PSYCHOTHERAPY *(Page 381)*

■ how to determine if a teenager might need psychotherapy

■ how to choose an appropriate therapy and an appropriate doctor/ therapist

■ the meaning behind special diagnoses: depression, anorexia nervosa, and bulimia

Psychosomatic Illness

By definition, a psychosomatic illness is a genuine physical illness that has psychological as well as biological causes (*psycho*: the Greek root for mind; *soma*: the Greek root for body). More technically, such an illness is known as a *psychophysiological disorder*. As a rule, when the underlying psychological problem is effectively addressed, the physical symptoms of the illness are greatly alleviated and may even disappear.

The body and the mind are so interconnected that almost any illness can be said to have a psychosomatic component. However, certain stress-sensitive illnesses are commonly thought to be especially psychosomatic in nature, such as ulcers, headaches, stomachaches, asthma, high blood pressure, allergies, and skin rashes or blemishes (including acne).

Adolescence is a period of emotional and physical growth

characterized by all sorts of new stress factors that have direct physical correlations. Among these factors are major and frequently unpredictable changes in body image; the onset of powerful new sexual feelings; and the demand for new or enhanced physical competencies (e.g., work skills, driving skills, athletic skills, and life-management skills).

Given all these new stress factors and their direct physical correlations, an adolescent is very likely to manifest new psychosomatic illnesses. She or he might also, or alternatively, experience the resurgence of former psychosomatic illnesses—even those that have not appeared since early childhood (something that often happens with asthma).

It's important for the parent of an adolescent who is troubled by such an illness to realize that the illness is real, not imaginary. However much you or your child may be creating stress that is contributing to the illness, neither of you is to blame for the illness itself. Instead, it is a natural process, and there are various ways that it can be successfully treated.

One of the most effective ways to manage or even cure many forms of psychosomatic illnesses involves biofeedback training. The sufferer is taught to recognize the link between emotions and physical symptoms, sometimes with the aid of computerized technology. Then behavior modification is employed to give the sufferer an increasing amount of control over the link. This behavior modification addresses both the emotions themselves and the physical reactions they help to produce.

Whenever you suspect that emotional factors may be contributing to your teenage child's illness, it's wise for you and your child to consult not only with a medical doctor but also with a psychologist or psychiatrist. This qualified professional can help both of you to "unlearn" patterns of transferring emotional stress to the body that might otherwise remain unconscious and unappreciated.

Autonomy Versus Intimacy

In referring to an adolescent child, psychologists, and psychiatrists will often speak of the child's psychological capacity to be either *autonomous* (i.e., independent and self-reliant) or *intimate* (i.e., closely involved with another individual and dependent on her or him for emotional security). In general, this is known as the *autonomy versus intimacy* issue.

Depending on the situation at hand, the healthy adolescent is capable of achieving either autonomy or intimacy in an appropriate manner and with a minimum amount of difficulty. For example, a normal adolescent who spends increasing amounts of time with an agreeable companion will most likely develop an intimate friendship with that companion. Should the friendship dissolve either through irreconcilable differences or separation, the adolescent will be upset for a while but will will soon recover and enjoy life on her or his own until the time comes when a new friendship evolves. Similar patterns will develop with romantic partners, older mentors, or younger children that the adolescent takes care of.

By contrast, emotionally disturbed adolescents may suffer severe difficulties being either autonomous or intimate, or they may assume autonomy or intimacy in a distinctly inappropriate way. For example, emotionally troubled adolescents may be unable to express their true feelings to their best friend. Indeed, they may not be able to form close friendships at all. Or they may become overly dependent emotionally on a mere acquaintance. When a relationship breaks up, they may be devastated and lonely for an alarmingly long period of time. Or they may toss off friendships and love affairs with a nonchalance that is bewildering to everyone around them.

If you suspect that your adolescent child has persistent difficulties forming intimate attachments or being independent—or problems in both areas—consider discussing the situation with a qualified professional. Such problems are better addressed early in your child's "adult" life than later.

At PCGC: Psychological Testing in Adolescence

Mental-health professionals, physicians, school personnel, and other specialists frequently make decisions that have a profound influence on teenage children. Historically, psychological testing has been a widely used and valued method for providing such professionals with the proper information to make those decisions.

Psychological testing is generally employed to determine individual differences and needs by providing specifics about a teenage child's abilities, strengths, personality style, and emotional functioning. It is also helpful in evaluating the actual or potential effects on teenagers of significant situational events, such as moving to a new home, coping with a serious illness, making the transition from junior high or middle school to high school, or going through a parental divorce.

For adolescents, psychological testing provides data about intellectual capacities, problem-solving strategies, neuropsychological processing, and personality organization. In addition, academic achievements are tested in order to assess the possible presence of learning disorders. Tests that PCGC frequently recommends or uses for personality evaluation include the Rorschach test (recently rejuvenated and rendered more useful by a research-based scoring system), the Thematic Apperception Test, Sentence Completion Tests, and (for adolescents age sixteen and older) the Minnesota Multiphasic Personality Inventory.

The experience of PCGC has shown that the more the family is informed about the testing and involved in the testing process, the more useful the evaluation is to them. Therefore, PCGC employs and advocates the following testing process:

■ The first step in the process is to help the child understand and appreciate the positive purpose of the testing: that is, to identify internal and external factors that may make living and learning easier for her or him.

■ Before the testing itself begins, the psychologist or test administrator meets with the child and parents to identify the reasons why testing is being sought, obtain relevant background history, address any initial questions or concerns the child and parents have, and explain the testing process.

■ It helps to have between two and four short, separate testing sessions rather than one long one. That way, fatigue factors are minimized, and a fuller range of the child's accomplishments and capabilities can be tested.

■ When testing is completed, the results are discussed with the family and the child.

For more information about psychological testing of adolescents, consult your physician, school counselor, or a local mental-health agency.

1.

Sexuality

The past twenty years have worked a revolutionary change in what it means to be a teenager, and by far the biggest impact has been in the area of sexuality. Thanks to medical and nutritional advances, teenagers today mature physically about two years earlier than their parents did, and the world within which this maturing process takes place harbors an unprecedented range of sex-related opportunities and dangers.

Sexual activity among teenagers today is less stigmatized and much easier to come by than it was for teenagers a mere generation ago. Therefore, it also begins at an earlier age and is more prevalent with each passing year. According to most expert polls and estimates, the majority of teenagers—males and females—are having regular sex (at least two or three times a month) by the time they are in eleventh grade.

At the same time, the potential risks involved in teenage sexual activity has escalated dramatically. One of the fastest-rising risk groups for acquired immune deficiency syndrome (AIDS) is teenagers. To date, no one has been known to recover after being infected with the HIV virus that leads to AIDS, and the average postinfection life span is four years.

Since 1989, according to the federal Centers for Disease Control in Atlanta, the number of reported cases of HIV infection among American teenagers has been doubling every fourteen months, with a much higher rate of heterosexual transmission than among adults. And while the current volume of teenage cases accounts for only 1 percent of the national total, about 20 percent of the latter are people in their early twenties. Many, if not most, of these people with AIDS in their early twenties are very likely to have contracted the infection—and, even more horrifying, to have spread it—unknowingly during their teenage years.

Besides the risk of AIDS during the teenage years, there's also the risk of other sexually transmitted diseases (STDs). The teenage rate for gonorrhea and syphilis, the most familiar STDs of the past, hasn't changed much in a generation. This is mainly because the ever-increasing numbers of gonorrhea and syphilis cases over the past twenty years have been detected and cured very early in their development, thus putting a limit on the spread.

However, the teenage rate of chlamydia, a little-known virus twenty years ago, has skyrocketed to become the most common STD in this age group. Currently it affects an estimated 25 percent of female teens and 15 percent of male teens.

Chlamydia is much more difficult to detect than gonorrhea and syphilis because it is more often asymptomatic—that is, the victim has no basis for suspecting that she or he is infected. Only about 20 percent of female teenagers infected with chlamydia actually suffer such physical indicators as abdominal pain, nausea, and/or a low fever. And an even smaller percentage of males afflicted with chlamydia actually suffer such physical indicators as painful urination or a runny discharge from the penis. Yet even in cases of chlamydia in which no symptoms present themselves, the long-range result can be sterility and/or widespread damage to the reproductive system and abdominal cavity.

Finally, there is the age-old problem of unwanted or inappropriate teenage pregnancy, which occurs more frequently today than it ever has in American history. The wider distribution and use of birth-control measures in recent years has simply failed to keep pace with the amount—and impulsiveness—of teenage sexual activity. Right now, one out of ten girls between the ages of fifteen and nineteen becomes pregnant, and half of the pregnancies result in childbirth. Each of these statistics represents a twofold jump over twenty years ago, and the situation shows every sign of getting worse with each passing year.

Emotionally speaking, the current, unprecedented increase in adolescent sexual opportunities and problems can subject the typical teenager to a much wilder roller-coaster ride than her or his parents experienced when they were teenagers. Because sexual activity is more commonplace among today's teenagers, so is the pressure to have sex and, if one becomes sexually active, to be a good sexual performer and to craft a personally satisfying sex life. Because the risk of contracting AIDS or chlamydia is much higher, so is the potential for fear, hysteria, and hostility. And because the odds of becoming a reluctant teenage mother or father are steadily increasing, so is the potential for life-crippling feelings of anger, guilt, and hopelessness.

To make the sex-related roller-coaster ride emotionally smoother for your teenager, try following these important guidelines:

■ *Educate yourself about sex-related issues that may affect your teenager*.

Always bear in mind that the situation you yourself faced as a teenager is *not* the same one that a teenage child today faces. Among the issues to become—and remain—informed about are the following:

> ■ sexual and romantic mores and customs among contemporary teenagers in general as well as among teenagers in your specific community;

> ■ sex-education programs that your child encounters or are available to your child at school, at religious organizations, or within the community;

> ■ birth-control options and resources;

> ■ options and resources available to teenage mothers- and fathers-to-be;

> ■ information regarding the transmission, prevention, and treatment of STDs, especially AIDS and chlamydia.

■ *Share with your child your own values regarding sex in general and your anxieties and preferences regarding her or his sexual life in particular.*

Be very honest and let your child know about your personal beliefs relating to romance and sex, your concerns relating to her or his romantic and/or sexual life, and how you would prefer that she or he behave. Don't keep your child guessing about where you stand and don't assume a guise of being more liberal—or more conservative—than you really are. In parent-to-child communication about sex, insincerity and a lack of candor can have disastrous consequences.

At the same time that you let your child know your feelings regarding her or his sex life, be careful not to translate these feelings into demands. Issuing ultimatums to your child regarding permissible attitudes and beliefs—whether they pertain to sex or to anything else—is inappropriate and potentially very harmful. It denies your child's rights to privacy and self-determination, leaves no room to disagree with you, and encourages secrecy and deception about what is really happening in case such knowledge might alienate you.

■ *Make sure that your child is informed about how to avoid common problems associated with sexual pressure or sexual activity.*

One of the biggest mistakes parents make with their teenage children is to advise them *what* problems to avoid without going one step further to advise *how* to avoid them. Through casual conversations, personal demonstrations, or even role-playing, try to encourage or even help your teenage child devise ways to do the following:

■ turn down unwanted sexual advances in a manner that best suits her or his personality and the situation at hand;

■ display a romantic interest in someone else in a respectful, nonintimidating manner;

■ recognize and respect someone else's rejection of her or his advances;

■ convey romantic feelings and expectations to her or his partner openly and honestly instead of letting them fester inside and misleading the partner;

■ elicit the romantic feelings and expectations of her or his partner in direct conversation instead of guessing them and being misled;

■ negotiate dating activities that are mutually agreeable as well as reasonably safe and responsible (e.g., that don't involve a high risk of being stranded somewhere or of winding up in unwanted company);

■ establish terms of intimacy with her or his partner that are physically safe, responsible, and respectful of both parties (if not abstention from sex, then the practice of safer sex).

■ *Encourage your child to be open with you about her or his feelings, attitudes, romantic interests, and relationships.*
Ask open-ended questions about your child's social life, that is, questions that invite casual, general discussion rather than a specific answer or a simple yes or no. For example, "What kind of relationship would you like to have with a boy?" or "Tell me about Mary—how are things going?" Listen calmly and nonjudgmentally to whatever your child tells you.

Above all, don't trivialize your child's romantic feelings no matter how humorous or absurd they may seem to you. For example, children in their early teens often develop strong crushes, usually on someone who is decidedly unattainable, such as a media star, a married teacher, or the much older sibling of a friend. Later, they may form seemingly obsessive attachments to individuals they barely know. However superficial or fantastical such feelings may appear to you, they are very real and important to your child. Indeed, they help her or him to experiment in a relatively safe context with a wide range of emotions and behaviors associated with love and sex.

An excellent way to maintain good communication with your child about romance, dating, and sex is to volunteer your own related experiences as a teenager whenever and however it is appropriate to do so. Offering such stories in a purely conversational manner can help your child better manage her or his own romantic or sexual life as well as bring you and your child closer together.

■*Negotiate reasonable and clear policies with your child regarding her or his dating practices.*

Although it may not be advisable—or even possible—to force your beliefs about sex onto your child, it's very important to come to an agreement about practical matters associated with dating. Together with your child, set fair and workable policies regarding the following:

■ how and when you are to be informed about dates;

■ how and when you are to meet the people your child dates;

■ how many nights a week—and what nights—it is appropriate for your child to date;

■ how late at night your child can stay out on a date;

■ which dating spots and situations you consider to be "off limits";

■ what steps your child should be prepared to take during a date if an emergency or an undesirable situation arises (e.g., demanding to be taken home, calling home, calling a trusted friend or relative, getting a cab ride home, calling the police).

■*Avoid always being negative when you talk about sex-related matters.*

Keep track of the times that you talk about sex-related matters with your child and make sure that these discussions don't repeatedly involve disparagements, warnings, fears, or prohibitions. A significant proportion of sex-related discussions with your child should be positive or at the very least neutral.

If, instead, your discussions are consistently negative, you may be sending a message to your child that you will categorically reject any positive or alternative sex-related feelings or information that she or he has to communicate. This kind of message is sure to inhibit your child from talking about sex at all and ultimately from valuing anything you have to say about sex.

■*Whenever you and your child are talking about sex, be sure attention is paid to its emotional as well as its physical aspects.*

Your child needs to learn that any sexual involvement with another person has emotional repercussions for both partners. Help your child realize and appreciate this dimension of sexuality by referring to it every time you discuss sex.

Give your child a sense not only of the different emotions—pleasant and unpleasant—that she or he might experience in the course of various relationship scenarios but also of the feelings that her or his partner might experience. Impress upon your child that along with sexual desire comes the responsibility to manage that desire in a mature and thoughtful way and to ensure that the emotional well-being of both participants is respected and protected.

Sexual Abuse in the Teenage Years

In the popular imagination, "child sexual abuse" is taken to refer to the molestation of prepubescent children. It's commonly thought that postpubescent children are physically, intellectually, socially, and emotionally so much more mature that they are far less likely to get into abusive situations, or if they do, to suffer from them.

In fact, the dramatic physical changes brought on by puberty are *not* accompanied by equally dramatic intellectual, social, or emotional changes. The latter changes take place at a much slower pace. Meanwhile, the postpubescent child, still insecure, unsophisticated, and dependent on others, remains vulnerable to the same types of abusive incidents and behavior patterns that are inflicted on prepubescent children.

According to the American Academy of Child and Adolescent Psychiatry, one out of every four females and one out of every ten males suffers sexual abuse before reaching the age of eighteen. And roughly half of the abuse victims at any given time are teenagers.

It's true that most cases of a teenage child being abused involve a long history of abuse by the same individual, often a family member, beginning well before the child entered puberty. But whether a child first encounters abuse *before* or *after* puberty, its emotional effects are the same in kind, and they can be similarly devastating in intensity. Aside from a confusing mixture of shame, guilt, fear, mistrust, anger, and hate, the victim is likely to develop a general and abiding sense of personal worthlessness. In a teenager, this feeling can easily lead either to sexual promiscuity or sexual frigidity.

Tragically, postpubescent children sometimes become perpetrators of sexual abuse of younger children. Most often the victim is a brother, sister, cousin, or child of a neighbor or friend: someone whom they encounter—and abuse—on a regular basis. Many of these teenage abusers were abused themselves as younger children, which helps to explain their behavior. Others were never abused but are tormented by various types of psychological problems, such as emotional abuse or deprivation at home or an overwhelming sense of personal failure and humiliation at school.

Listed below are separate sets of guidelines to follow relating to sex-abuse situations: "ABUSED," if you have reason to suspect that your teenage child is a victim of sexual abuse, and "ABUSER," if you have reason to suspect that your teenage child has sexually abused another child.

ABUSED

■ *Pay attention to signs that your child may have suffered sexual abuse.*

Among these signs are the following:

■ inexplicable bruises, scratches, or physical injuries;

■ depression or withdrawal from family or friends;

■ atypical aggressiveness and rage;

■ unusual avoidance of a particular individual or social situation;

■ dramatic change in attitude toward, or interest in, sex-related matters;

■ secretiveness;

■ uncharacteristic risk taking or suicidal behavior.

■ *Encourage your child to converse freely with you about any problem relating to sex abuse that she or he may be having.*

As much as possible, remain calm and allow your child a full opportunity to discuss not only her or his experiences but also how she or he *feels* about them. Don't interrupt with your own reactions or judgments until your child has fully spoken.

Always take any indication of sexual abuse very seriously. Assure your child that you believe her or him and that you understand her or his feelings about the situation.

■ *Reassure your child of her or his value as a human being.*

Children who have been sexually abused suffer from severely damaged self-esteem. Let your abused child know that you love her or him very much and that you are very proud of her or him for having the courage to talk to you about the abuse. Tell your child that whatever she or he has gone through is not her or his fault but the fault of the abuser.

Also, reassure your child about her or his future safety. Promise that you will do everything you can to make sure that the abuse doesn't happen again.

■ *Contact the proper authorities immediately.*

Before acting on your own to confront the abuser, get in touch with the proper authorities. They can help you plan the most effective strategy for making sure that the abuser never bothers your child—or another child—again; and they can offer such advice without requiring you to press charges or to face prosecution.

If the suspected abuse has occurred *within* the family, contact your local Child Protection Agency. If the suspected abuse has occurred *outside* the family, contact your local police department or district attorney's office.

■ *Arrange for your child to be examined physically and emotionally.*

Even an apparently mild form of sexual abuse can have serious physical and emotional consequences. As soon as possible, arrange for your child to see a physician for a medical checkup and a psychologist, psychiatrist, or qualified mental-health professional for an emotional evaluation.

ABUSER

■ *Be alert for signs that your child may be sexually abusing another child.*

Among these signs are the following:

■ unusual or problematic association with a younger child (e.g., your child spending a lot more time with a younger child than is customary, or consistently making the younger child cry);

■ seductiveness toward younger children;

■ secretiveness, especially in concert with a younger child;

■ estrangement from, and/or hostility toward, peers and adults;

■ excessive prurience or preoccupation with sexual matters;

■ possession of large amounts of pornography, especially depicting or describing forced sex and/or sex with younger children;

■ general aggressiveness toward others, with episodes of particular aggressiveness toward younger children;

■ marked increase in lying, stealing, or other forms of prohibited conduct.

■ Ask your child about suspicious situations in a manner that encourages honesty and disclosure.

Confront your child honestly and seriously with any reasons you have to believe that she or he may be abusing another child. Then help your child be straightforward with you by being a good, patient, and (for the time being) nonjudgmental listener.

Don't play games with your child by withholding information to see if she or he will corroborate it. This type of strategy only invites mistrust and resentment. Instead, be honest, direct, and concerned without being hostile.

When your child has finished telling you what she or he has to say and it's time for you to express your feelings about the matter, try not to lose your composure. Remember to direct all censure toward the bad *act* your child has committed, not toward your *child* her- or himself.

■ Set rules and adopt measures aimed at preventing your child from getting into a potentially abusive situation.

As much as possible, keep your child away from children she or he may be inclined to victimize or from situations that may invite seduction or abuse. Instead of leaving your child alone for extended periods of time, arrange for her or him to be supervised.

If you've established that there is someone in particular that your child has been sexually abusing, it is incumbent upon you to inform the parents of that child. Armed with such information, they can get medical and psychological care for their child and help you prevent your child from committing further acts of abuse.

Before you talk with the parents, it may be helpful to consult a qualified authority in child sexual abuse about how best to handle this type of exceptionally sensitive communication, given the particular situation and personalities involved. A consultation of this type will also give you additional courage and support for performing such a personally painful task.

■ Help your child learn better self-control and more acceptable interpersonal behavior.

Through conversations, carefully supervised social events, and even role-playing of specific real-life situations, help your child develop more respect for the rights of others and more skill at expressing her or his feelings in a respectable manner.

Assist your child in identifying and practicing better ways of achieving personal satisfaction in her or his relationships with others, such as working with others on a project, playing team sports, going with others to entertainment events, or competing against others for a particular honor. Encourage your child to use her or his *positive* interests and personality traits to form more lasting and mutually beneficial friendships with peers.

■ Seek professional help for your child.

Without question, a child who abuses another child sexually is suffering deep-rooted emotional problems. Her or his parents can use all the help they can get to address those problems as well as to come to terms with their personal feelings of outrage, guilt, shame, and disappointment.

If you are convinced that your child has been—or could be—sexually abusing children, don't hesitate to confer with a psychiatrist, psychologist, or other qualified mental-health professional. This person can evaluate your child's emotional health, work with her or him on specific psychological problems, and help you cope with your own pain and parental responsibilities under the circumstances.

Helping Your Gay Teenager

Being gay is typically not something that a teenager can accept without a certain amount of inner turmoil. There may be serious, if misguided, doubts: for example, "Am I gay because I love my best friend?" There may be denial: for example, "I'm just going through a strange phase right now." In fact, however, the prevailing estimate is that one out of every ten teenagers is genuinely homosexual, with an equal rate of incidence for males and females.

Homosexuality in itself is not a psychological illness, nor is it a matter of choice, except, perhaps, in the case of isolated acts of sexual experimentation. Rather, it is an affectional and erotic orientation toward the same sex, one that is as fundamental to a homosexual's psyche as an erotic orientation toward the opposite sex is to a heterosexual's psyche.

Unfortunately, society at large, being 90 percent heterosexual, subjects homosexuals to a considerable amount of discrimination and persecution. It can be very difficult for parents of a gay teenager to accept the fact that their child is so different from them and so vulnerable to the prejudices of others. But refuting, bemoaning, or rejecting their child's homosexual feelings will only add to their child's adjustment problems.

If your child appears to be gay or reveals her or his homosexual feelings to you, here are some guidelines for dealing with the situation rationally, sensitively, and constructively:

■ *If you have good reason to believe that your child is gay or is concerned about the possibility of being gay, don't be afraid to initiate conversation on the topic.*

It's better to bring the issue out into the open than to let it fester. Make your initial inquiries very tactful, general, and open-ended. Ideally, use questions that can't be—and don't have to be—answered with a simple yes or no.

Depending on the circumstances, a very impersonal approach might be better: for example, "Many people develop strong, sexual attractions toward members of their own sex. How do you feel about this?" Or you may decide that the circumstances warrant a more personal approach: for example, "There's something I want us to talk about so that we can be closer to each other. Do you ever have sexual feelings toward (boys/girls)?"

Try to avoid using phrases like "Are you gay?" Instead, ask, "Do you have sexual feelings toward (boys/girls)?" Adolescents in particular—and people in general—occasionally have such feelings without being predominantly gay. Either way, it's important not to label your child "gay," or for that matter, "straight." Let your child come to understand, and declare, her or his own sexual identity.

In fact, throughout this initial conversation, try hard to be a listener rather than a talker. And don't push things if your child isn't forthcoming. At least you've opened up the subject for discussion; you—or your child—can pick it up again later.

■ Don't attack your child or your child's feelings.

Given the way society stigmatizes homosexuality, teenagers who suspect or know that they are homosexual are automatically susceptible to self-loathing, self-denial, depression, and suicidal impulses. However unresolved your private feelings may be, avoid inflicting even more emotional burdens on your child than she or he may already be carrying.

■ Keep the lines of communication open.

Most gay teenagers don't feel comfortable discussing their homosexuality with anyone, much less with a parent—at least until they themselves have sorted out their initial confusion about it. The resulting social isolation that gay teenagers suffer can be detrimental to this sorting-out process as well as devastating to their overall emotional well-being.

The more patient, nonjudgmental, and supportive you can be regarding your child and her or his highly sensitive sexual feelings and the more willing you are to listen whenever your child needs to talk about those feelings, the better it is for her or his psychological health. Avoid saying anything that makes your child feel rejected, makes you appear repulsed, or inhibits or precludes future discussions.

■ Reassure your child of your love and of her or his value as a human being.

Gay teenagers shouldn't be made to feel that their entire identity as individuals is defined by their sexual orientation. Nor should their parents withhold from them any demonstrations of love and regard until such a time as they "give up" being homosexual or resolve any confusion they may have about their sexuality one way or the other.

Such misguided strategies can only do harm, convincing gay

teenagers that they are sexual freaks who may never be able to lead a worthwhile life. Instead, convince your child that she or he is loved and valued, and fully capable of having a fulfilling life, regardless of her or his sexual orientation.

■ *Avoid blaming yourself, someone else, or some situation for your child's homosexuality.*

No one knows what "causes" homosexuality. Quite likely it is just as rooted in biology and interpersonal chemistry as is heterosexuality.

Certainly no expert has ever been able to prove that an individual's homosexuality was the result of her or his mother or father being overly domineering, overly affectionate, overly distant, or otherwise at fault. Nor has it ever been established that casual experimentation with homosexuality transformed an otherwise straight individual into a gay one.

Furthermore, homosexuality is not, in itself, "blameworthy" except from a prejudicial point of view. Rather than worrying about what has caused—or is causing—your child to be or feel homosexual, accept the fact that your child is who she or he is, and feels what she or he feels, independent of who you are and how you feel.

Bear in mind that your role as a parent is to help your child become more self-aware and responsible so that she or he can lead a personally satisfying and productive life. You can't assume responsibility for your child's sexual orientation, but you can help your child come to terms with that orientation.

■ *Seek the support of sympathetic groups for your child and yourself.*

Contact local gay and lesbian organizations and encourage your child to do the same. Many areas have groups specifically designed to assist parents of homosexuals. (One major national group with many local chapters is called Parents and Friends of Lesbians and Gays [PFLAG].)

Whatever attitudes and emotions you and your child have toward homosexuality, both of you should be as well-informed about it as possible. And given the threat of social ostracism and gay bashing, you and your child should also have as substantial a network of potential supporters as possible.

CASE:

The Mother-Daughter Transfer

Four years after her divorce, Michele was going through another period of domestic warfare, this time with her thirteen-year-old daughter, Jody. The catalyst for the warfare was boys: Jody wanted to start dating them, they wanted to start dating Jody, and Michele was standing in their way.

"You're not old enough to date," Michele pronounced, and that was that as far as she was concerned. Jody, however, had some very powerful arguments on her side. Most of her close friends had already begun dating with their parents' permission, and these were parents whose opinions Michele had often admired and invoked in conversations with Jody.

In all other child-raising matters involving rules and rights, Michele had been remarkably successful. From time to time Jody would initially rebel against a particular policy, but in every case she soon acknowledged the wisdom of that policy and cooperated with it.

This time was dramatically different. For the past two months Jody had been actively fighting Michele to lift her ban on dating; instead of diminishing in intensity, the fights were getting steadily worse and worse. After an especially ugly shouting match, they agreed to seek help from a family therapist.

Michele discovered that she was going through a common experience for a parent of a just-datable teenager, namely, being haunted by ghosts from the past: the ghost of one's own just-datable teenage self and the ghosts of one's own parents at that time. The more Michele examined her nay-saying behavior with Jody, the more she realized that she had been automatically reenacting her own and her parents' fears about males and about love when she herself first began dating. Subconsciously, these fears now seemed even more justified to her in hindsight, given the trauma of her recent divorce.

The therapist explained to Michele that almost all parents occasionally project their own childhood experiences, perceptions, and sensibilities onto their children and occasionally lapse, against their will, into the same parenting style that their parents modeled for them. However, the tendency to do so can be much stronger and much more unconscious when their children reach dating age. Suddenly, the parents are subject to all sorts of mixed emotions. These emotions include not only *fear* (regarding possible harm to, as well as possible loss of control over, their child) but also *jealousy* (aimed at anyone who might capture their child's affections), *envy* (aimed at their child, whose youthful adventures are just beginning), and *grief* (regarding the upcoming "loss" of their child's innocence).

Understanding these psychological dynamics in her relationship with Jody helped Michele be more realistic about the dating issue. She could see that the real question facing her was not *whether* Jody should date but *how* Jody should date. Thereafter, Michele was much less overbearing in her conversations with Jody about dating. And while it was some time before Jody actually began dating, the fights over it ceased almost immediately.

At PCGC:
Treating Teenage Sex Offenders

Many teenage sex offenders were victims of sexual abuse themselves when they were younger. Indeed, psychiatrists and psychologists now consider that a personal history of sexual abuse is one of the most common factors influencing a teenage child to abuse other children in a similar way. Treating teenage sexual offenders thus becomes a matter of interrupting a destructive, sex-related cyclical pattern in the offender's behavior.

But effective therapy for teenage sex offenders doesn't stop there. It must also address other destructive cyclic patterns in the offender's behavior so that the offender learns to manage each interdependent aspect of her or his personal life more maturely and successfully. This comprehensive approach to therapy, administered relatively early in the offender's life, greatly reduces the risk that she or he will continue to create— or suffer—serious sex-related problems of any type during the rest of adolescence and adulthood.

Finally, effective therapy for teenage sex offenders needs to address the manner in which the teenager's environment contributes or reacts to the offensive behavior. Besides involving the teenager's parent(s) or parental substitute(s) and other family members, effective therapy may have to extend to the teenager's friends, teachers, school administrators, and personnel from other agencies that already have—or could have—a significant impact on the teenager's life.

One example of this type of comprehensive approach to therapy is PCGC's Adolescent Sex Offender Treatment Program. A five-person treatment team, including a child psychiatrist and a clinical psychologist, works directly with each client to develop appropriate strategies for eliminating the offending behavior. It also works both directly and indirectly with the offender's family and community to set up and support these strategies.

Specific treatments administered by the program include individual counseling, family therapy sessions, group meetings for the offenders, and group meetings for the parents, or parent substitutes, of offenders. Other services available on an as-needed basis are psychiatric consultation, medication clinic, and psychological evaluation.

All treatments in the program focus on the client's sexuality but deal with other relevant issues as well. For example, the group meetings address socialization issues, such as peer relationships, school problems, and preparation for employment and independence. Family therapy concentrates on supporting parental competence in handling the child's inappropriate behaviors through the restructuring of family roles and relationships and the development of more effective family management skills.

Families of teenage sex abusers often initiate their own referral to the PCGC's Adolescent Sex Offender Program. Other referrals come from the state's Department of Human Services, mental-health centers, and individual professionals in the mental-health field.

If your child, or a child you know, might benefit from this type of program, ask your psychiatrist, psychologist, or mental-health professional whether a similar program exists in your area. If not, seek therapy that has the potential of involving family members and community members.

2.

Popularity

It's not difficult for parents to appreciate a teenage child's interest in being popular among peers of the same sex. What's difficult for them to appreciate is that a teenage child can so often place a higher value on the opinions of friends than on the opinions of her or his parents—or, for that matter, of society as a whole. Just for the sake of being popular within a special group, a basically sensible teenager may willingly and enthusiastically engage in foolish, harmful, and even criminal behavior.

For the vast majority of children between the ages of thirteen and twenty, male or female, peer approval is enormously important. During the eighth and ninth grades in particular, it can be the single most valued factor in a child's life. The reason for this does not lie as much in the desire for friendships in themselves as it does in the desire to be an accepted member of a group.

Caught in an awkward transition period between childhood and adulthood, teenagers are psychologically insecure as individuals—much more so than during the so-called latency period that extends roughly from age six to age twelve. Membership in a specific group of peers brings with it a precious feeling of being worthy as a person, having social power, and belonging somewhere in the world outside the family.

In fact, being popular is such a major issue for teenagers in general that it's often a sign of emotional problems if an individual teenager is *not* a fiercely involved member of a particular group of peers. This doesn't mean that a teenager who is solitary by nature or circumstance can't still be emotionally healthy; but such an individual is definitely the exception rather than the rule.

Most teenagers who are not a part of a "pack" suffer a great deal of emotional distress, not from being unpopular per se but from experiencing specific incidents of subtle or blatant rejection. In many cases, a teenager's preexisting emotional problems, such as extreme shyness or aggressiveness, inspire rejection by her or his peers, and so the rejected teenager winds up becoming doubly troubled.

As far as experts have been able to determine, the desire to be popular is just as intense in teenage boys as it is in teenage girls. However, there are some minor, gender-related distinctions.

Western culture permits—and on certain occasions, such as social gatherings, even expects—females to be more expressive and demonstrative than males regarding their friendships. Thus, in comparison to their male counterparts, teenage girls tend to *appear* more enthusiastic and effusive during times when they are secure about their popularity and more depressed and antagonistic when they are insecure about it.

Moreover, peer bonding among teenagers usually manifests itself in different ways, according to whether the group is all male or all female. Teenage girls tend to reinforce their group identity by trying to *look like each other*. Teenage boys in a group might find themselves imitating each other in appearance, but such occasions are much less frequent and considerably less meaningful than they are for girls. After all, the total range of culturally acceptable appearance possibilities for males of any age is relatively narrow as opposed to the total range for females. In contrast to teenage girls, teenage boys tend to derive a stronger sense of group identity simply by *hanging around each other*.

One popularity-related characteristic that is common to both teenage boys and teenage girls is a strong preference for keeping the world of friends and that of home as separate as possible. This makes it extremely challenging for parents to get a good working sense of what is actually happening in their teenage child's social life outside the home. Even the most honest and family-oriented teenagers will occasionally resort to secrecy and misrepresentation when it comes to talking to their parents about their friends.

Teenagers have a right—and a need—to be granted a certain measure of privacy in conducting their peer relationships. It enables them to test their independent capacity to get along with others and to experiment with attitudes, behaviors, and pursuits that differ from the ones prevailing in the home environment. Thus, parents of a teenager have to accept the fact that some sort of information gap will always exist between them and their child regarding the latter's friends. Nevertheless, parents of a teenager are still responsible for doing whatever they reasonably can to keep their child from being harmed or from harming others.

In dealing with your teenage child's popularity-based concerns, you'll probably have little choice but to be exceptionally tactful and watchful. Assuming that your child is devoted to a particular group of friends, you must try as best you can to learn more about that group—its other members, its activities, and its norms—without offending your child or inspiring deception. Assuming your child clearly suffers from *not* being a popular member of a group, you must try to find out why your child isn't popular without causing her or him undue embarrassment. In either case, you must use the knowledge you gain with great care so that you can step in to help your child whenever it's appropriate, without inadvertently making matters worse.

Here are guidelines to assist you in these complicated endeavors:

■ *Set reasonable rules and policies regarding your child's social life.*

Your child should know the parameters within which she or he is free—and trusted—to operate. Meet with your child for the specific purpose of setting these parameters and do so again whenever circumstances warrant reinforcement or renegotiation.

Among the rules and policies to consider are the following:

> ■ Establish the times when you expect your child to be home (e.g., for meals, to do homework or chores, or to go to bed).

> ■ Establish how many evenings—and what evenings—during the week it's permissible for your child to socialize with friends.

> ■ Agree upon a standard procedure that each of you will follow to let the other one know what you are doing and—if possible— how you can be reached (e.g., by always leaving a note when you can't tell the other one verbally or by making sure to telephone if you're away from home for a longer period of time than you anticipated).

> ■ Let your child know that you expect arrangements to be made for you to meet her or his friends at an early stage of the relationship (e.g., by inviting the friend home to dinner).

> ■ State clearly anything that your child is not allowed to do with peers (e.g., go to a place where alcohol is being served or leave the city limits without permission).

■ *Keep track of your child's day-to-day activities.*

Monitor where your child goes, with whom (if anyone), and what she or he does by questioning her or him directly. Note any patterns of behavior that emerge in your child's social life over time, such as a long period of being alone, socializing with the same person, or spending hours just roaming around the mall with friends. When you put these patterns together with other factors in your child's life, they may prove to be significant.

Try to avoid being dictatorial or judgmental in monitoring your child's purportedly "free" time but don't abandon your need to know.

Teenagers are so self-absorbed by nature and so inclined to forget—
or avoid —keeping their parents informed, that it's dangerously easy
to lose touch with what's happening in their lives.

■ As often as practical, observe how your child plays and socializes.

The more you watch how your child interacts with others when she
or he isn't especially conscious of being observed, the better idea you
will have of her or his overall emotional maturity and security in
social situations as well as particular social habits, inclinations, resources, talents, and problems.

Avoid outright spying on your child by, for example, eavesdropping
on conversations, reading her or his mail, or following her or him
clandestinely. If you do spy on your child, you risk making both of
you suspicious about each other and destroying any trust between
you. Should specific circumstances seem to warrant such intrusions
into your child's privacy, consider seeking advice from a mental-health
professional before taking any action you may regret.

■ Take your child's concerns about popularity seriously.

Whether or not you're able to agree with your child in matters having
to do with popularity, or lack thereof, always take a sympathetic
interest when she or he talks to you about such matters. More than
anything else, it's crucial for you to understand what's important to
your child and for your child to feel that you do understand.

Above all, guard against dismissing or ridiculing your child's friendships or lack of them. A teenager is especially susceptible to feeling
disregarded, embarrassed, or humiliated and may not respond well to
even the most innocuous and well intended teasing. Try to treat your
child—and any friends she or he may make—at least as seriously as
you expect her or him to treat you and your friends.

■ Offer advice in a casual, nonjudgmental manner.

Being a tactful, supportive, and good listener in conversations about
popularity with your child does *not* mean that you can't give her or
him advice. Teenagers often use such conversations to "think out
loud," and they actually want feedback from their parent.

For example, if your child expresses dissatisfaction with a certain
group of friends, she or he may be indirectly seeking a push from you
to leave that group. If you sincerely feel that such an action is warranted, then by all means let your child know—just as you would one
of your own, same-age confidants in a similar situation.

Don't insist that your child follow your advice or imply that she or
he would be foolish not to do so. But do go ahead and share your

experience and opinions whenever this course of action seems appropriate.

■ *Be alert for signs of possible trouble.*

If you observe any of the following negative patterns, bring it to your child's attention as a pretext for having a calm but serious discussion about the nature of her or his social life:

> ■ chronic violation of "house rules," especially with one particular friend or group of friends;

> ■ a dramatic change in your child's attitude, behavior, physical state, or emotional state that is adversely affecting her or his school life or family life (e.g., pronounced and frequent fatigue, impatience, use of foul language, distractedness, or rebelliousness);

> ■ repeated episodes of otherwise inexplicable anger, withdrawal, or depression;

> ■ repeated incidents when your child has suffered serious physical or emotional hurt, especially from one particular child or group;

> ■ repeated incidents when your child—or your child's group—has inflicted serious physical or emotional hurt upon another child, especially one particular child;

> ■ a dramatic and inexplicable change in your child's apparent financial status (i.e., unusual wealth, poverty, or need for substantial amounts of money);

> ■ frequent and escalating incidence of lying and/or stealing;

> ■ radical, adverse change in your child's ethical and moral standards as evidenced by her or his statements or conduct;

> ■ perseverance in not letting you meet her or his friends even after several direct requests from you.

■ *Consistently work to bolster your child's self-esteem and self-reliance.*

The more teenagers value themselves and their independence, the less susceptible they are to the pressures and problems associated with popularity or the lack thereof. Express your love and admiration to your child frequently. Guide her or him toward activities and interests that will nourish her or his pride, self-confidence, and appreciation of solitude.

■ *Consider seeking professional help for especially problematic situations.*

In order to be popular, or to cope with not being popular, a teenager can get into all sorts of serious trouble. Beyond simply failing in school, alienating the family, and becoming deeply depressed, there are the myriad dangers of substance abuse, compulsive sex, suicidal thrill seeking, or such crimes as stealing, assaulting, raping, destroying property, or disturbing the peace.

If your child seems caught in a pattern of negative behavior and nothing you do seems to help, don't hesitate to consult with a psychiatrist, psychologist, or qualified mental-health professional. This individual can offer both you and your child vital, even lifesaving support.

Interpersonal Versus Intrapersonal Intelligence

In psychological and psychiatric terms, "*inter*personal intelligence" refers to a child's knowledge and skills involving social relationships. By contrast, "*intra*personal" intelligence refers to a child's knowledge and skills involving her or his own, inner self—independent of the outside world.

A teenager with a high degree of interpersonal intelligence is one who makes friends easily, can lead others effectively, and can cooperate, compromise, and resolve conflicts within a group context. Interpersonal intelligence tends to be acquired by extensive socialization in a variety of contexts, such as assuming an active role in a large family, engaging in different types of play and competition with diverse friends, and performing tasks in concert with other individuals and work teams.

A teenager with a high degree of intrapersonal intelligence is one who is adept at cultivating self-knowledge as well as knowledge for the sake of personal development, is capable of enjoying solitude for extended periods of time, and can identify her or his personal needs, motivations, and feelings apart from those of others.

Every child has some degree of both types of intelligence, but most children become more intelligent in one of these two ways than in the other. Typically, a child who is extroverted by nature will wind up having a better-developed interpersonal intelligence; one who is introverted by nature will wind up having a better-developed intrapersonal intelligence.

As a result, extroverted children often suffer psychological problems because of a deficiency in intrapersonal intelligence (i.e., a lack of knowing their "inner selves"). Introverted children generally have the opposite problem: They suffer psychological problems because of a deficiency in interpersonal intelligence (i.e., a lack of knowing how to interact effectively with others).

When such imbalances are first detected by parents or educators, they are often treated inappropriately. Simply pressuring an apparent bookworm into joining a soccer team to become more interpersonally intelligent could easily backfire. The bookworm may experience so much unpleasantness and even trauma playing soccer that she or he will retreat even further into books. The same kind of thing might happen if a soccer lover is forced to read the complete works of Shakespeare in order to become more intrapersonally intelligent. The soccer lover's dislike of reading may instead be reinforced.

Much can be done to correct a troubled child's imbalance in interpersonal versus intrapersonal intelligence, but it must be done carefully, with full respect for the child's personal capabilities and vulnerabilities. Fortunately, most psychologists and psychiatrists are well qualified to assist individual children (along with their parents, teachers, and caretakers) in identifying the particular training methods and experiences that will most help them develop the type of intelligence they lack.

Cosmetic Surgery: Yes or No?

As cosmetic surgery becomes increasingly easier, quicker, more comfortable, and less expensive, more and more teenage girls and boys are seeking it to solve what they consider life-disfiguring problems with their appearance. Among the more common flaws that teenagers hope to correct are bumpy noses, receding chins, or large, floppy ears, but the list also includes everything from tiny moles to sunken cheekbones to large breasts.

For the dissatisfied teenager, the issue pretty much boils

down to this: "I would be so much more attractive and therefore popular if I only had [desired version of feature] instead of [feature in its present state]." Cosmetic surgery seems a simple and clear-cut matter. For the dissatisfied teenager's parent, however, the issue of whether to undertake surgery is far more problematic.

In the first place, the parent is almost always unable to see the offending feature in quite the same light as the teenager. To the typical parent in such a situation, the feature in question just doesn't appear significantly unattractive. In many cases, the parent actually possesses the identical feature, in which case its rejection by the teenager can be almost insulting.

In the second place, the parent knows from her or his greater experience in life that altering the way one looks—however dramatically—is not guaranteed to help one gain, retain, or increase one's personal popularity. Nor is it certain to provide the same sense of private, inner satisfaction that one might have anticipated.

In the event that your child expresses an interest in having cosmetic surgery, keep the following tips in mind:

■ *Acknowledge your child's concern.*

Although cosmetic surgery may strike you as an absurd or impractical course of action, your child takes it quite seriously. And behind that seriousness lurk complex emotions—including embarrassment, self-hatred, pride, and ambition—that deserve your sympathy and attention.

Listen thoughtfully and respectfully to what your child has to say about the matter. Indicate that you understand her or his frustration. Ask questions that will help both of you put the issue into a fuller, more realistic perspective: for example, "What has happened to make you feel that [the feature] is unattractive?" and "How long have you felt this way?"

■ *Reassure your child of your love and high regard.*

Tell your child that you care deeply for her or him regardless of how she or he looks. In addition, tell your child that the feature she or he personally finds so bothersome does not seem unattractive to you and may, in fact, not seem unattractive to others. In many cases, this type of reassurance, especially from several different sources, succeeds in putting off any further consideration of cosmetic surgery.

■ *Seek evidence to support or refute the argument for cosmetic surgery.*

First and foremost, talk with and observe your child to determine how deeply she or he is troubled by the offending feature. Is it causing serious and lasting emotional problems, or is it, instead, a source of *occasional* worry and frustration? Assuming the former is true, the case for surgery is stronger. Does the feature itself genuinely seem to be the focus of your child's displeasure, or is it instead merely a convenient symbol for some other, more complicated issue? Again, assuming the former is true, the case for surgery is stronger.

Next, discuss with your child what, specifically, she or he anticipates will happen *after* the surgery: How and why will life be different from the way it is now? If your child's expectations seem illogical or inflated, then the case for surgery is weaker.

Finally, give careful thought to how your child has behaved in the past regarding matters of personal appearance. Has your child repeatedly changed her or his mind about preferred hairstyles, clothing, and other forms of personal adornment? Has your child frequently gone through brief periods of dissatisfaction or disappointment with the way she or he looks, targeting different features at different times? If the answer to either of these questions is yes, then you have grounds for not wanting to go ahead with the surgery.

■ *Proceed slowly and cautiously.*

Assuming both you and your child come to agree that cosmetic surgery is a viable possibility, wait at least a couple of years, if possible, before having it done. You and your child both need to bear in mind that cosmetic surgery will create an irrevocable difference in your child's appearance. Therefore, it's reasonable to test your child's resolve to have cosmetic surgery by postponing any action for an extended period of time. If your child reiterates a desire for the surgery several times during this waiting period, then you can be more assured that she or he is committed to it and will accept the results.

In some situations, waiting may be a necessity. Very rarely is it advisable to undergo cosmetic surgery before the feature being altered has reached its full growth. Ears, for example, are usually fully developed by the time a child reaches adolescence; but the nose may continue to evolve until age fifteen; the chin, until age twenty.

3.

Depression

Adolescence is a period when simple, moment-to-moment childhood fears are gradually replaced by more complex and lingering adult-style concerns. Like younger children, thirteen- to nineteen-year-olds continue to worry about matters of the present. In the case of adolescents, these matters include sexuality and self-image as well as social life and school performance. But unlike younger children, thirteen- to nineteen-year-olds also spend a great deal of time worrying about the future.

Some future-related concerns that bother teenagers are basically realistic in nature, such as whether and how they can get a good job, pay for college, or start a close family of their own. Other future-related concerns, however, are very idealistic in nature, such as whether and how they can find meaning in their life, purpose in their work, or peace in a world that is so politically, economically, and culturally unstable.

A teenager's vague status as a transitional being—not quite kid, not quite adult—can make any one of these worries all the more difficult to bear. Segregated from the rest of society, teenagers must continually wrestle with shifting feelings of isolation, disconnection, powerlessness, and absurdity.

Generally, adolescents are no longer raised as attentively and affectionately as they were when they were younger, which causes many of them, consciously or subconsciously, to mourn their lost childhoods or to think of themselves as neglected. At the same time, they feel pressured by their parents and society not just to grow up but to excel as individuals.

It's little wonder that an individual teenager's specific concerns, magnified by the general insecurity of adolescence, so often lead to depression. Medically, depression is an extended (two weeks or longer) episode of emotional and physical lethargy, characterized by ongoing feelings of personal worthlessness and despair. In human terms, it can mean living in purgatory, or hell itself, without any sense that things might ever change for the better.

Depression can manifest itself in many different ways, some of which may seem only dimly related, or unrelated altogether, to what people commonly associate with the word "depression." Thus, an individual case of depression may be difficult to detect.

For example, a depressed teenager may experience recurring psychosomatic symptoms, like headaches, indigestion, sleeplessness, fatigue, or rashes. For a time at least, these physical symptoms may mask the real underlying problem: emotional depression. Or a depressed teenager may resort to symptomatic behaviors, such as withdrawing from family or friends, abusing drugs, or engaging in promiscuous sex—activities that might easily and erroneously be written off as "typical acts of teenage rebelliousness."

Teenage girls suffer much higher rates of depression than teenage boys. Scientists suspect that biological factors are partly responsible (possibly relating to hormonal changes); but a great deal of the difference has to do with the culture in which we live. Females—in particular teenage females—are compelled to worry much more about personal appearance and "good" behavior than males. Moreover, their overall life expectations (the roles society casts for them and therefore the roles they envision for themselves) are far more limited. To make matters even worse, they are much more culturally conditioned than males to internalize their hostility, as opposed to discharging it on someone, or something, else.

Some scientists believe that as a result of these gender-related differences in *experiencing* depression, there are also gender-related differences in *responding* to depression. Depressed teenage boys may be more inclined to adopt "rejecting" behaviors, such as breaking off friendships, ceasing to care about schoolwork, or cursing the world, while depressed teenage girls may be more apt to adopt "self-punishing" behaviors, such as binging on food, starving themselves, or lamenting their faults and failures.

Other indicators of depression, for both teenage boys and teenage girls, include any combination of several of the following signs, extending over a period of three weeks or longer:

■ a radical and otherwise inexplicable personality change of any type;

■ consistently sleeping more or less than usual;

■ repeated attempts to run away;

■ frequent and lengthy bouts of anger or violent behavior;

■ chronic boredom;

■ ongoing inability to concentrate, pay attention, or think clearly;

■ loss of interest in activities formerly enjoyed;

■ persistent lack of tolerance for compliments or rewards;

■ continual and pronounced pessimism about the future;

■ repeated and uncharacteristic episodes of crying or tearfulness;

■ increasing tendency toward lying, thoughtlessness, carelessness, or sloppiness.

Parents of depressed teenagers are frequently advised by well-meaning friends or family members to ignore their child's depression; but, in fact, this is bad advice. Although few interpersonal activities are more challenging than communicating with a teenager who is stuck in a negative rut, her or his parents should make every reasonable effort to do so. It is precisely because teenagers are so capable of becoming stuck in a negative rut that they need all the help they can get. Parents of teenagers must never forget that teenage depression in its most extreme form can be literally a matter of life and death.

Whenever your teenage child seems depressed, try following these guidelines:

■ Be especially loving and supportive.

Remember that teenagers often feel that their parents don't love them as warmly or as much as when they were younger and "cuter." During a period of depression, this feeling can be painfully acute—whether or not there is a basis for it in reality.

Try returning in spirit to the time when your depressed child was much younger. Demonstrate your love and support in some of the same ways that used to please her or him then, modified slightly to suit her or his present age. For example, increase the amount of times that you touch your child affectionately, make praising reference to her or his good qualities, or simply "goof around." The goal is not necessarily to "baby" your child but to ensure that you don't inadvertently give your child any reason to doubt that you care.

■ Take the initiative in talking with your child.

Don't wait anxiously for your depressed child to come to you. Show your concern about the symptoms you've noticed and indicate your desire to talk about whatever might be bothering her or him.

It is certainly appropriate to give your depressed child *some* time and space to be alone and quiet. However, it doesn't make sense to leave your child entirely on her or his own, expecting her or him to take the lead in communicating with you or even to meet you halfway. A depressed person—teenage or not—can easily be incapable of making such gestures. It's up to you, as the more emotionally stable person, to coax your child into opening up.

■ *Help your child think constructively instead of destructively.*
A depressed person is inclined to see only the darkest aspects of a situation. The best way to help such a person conquer depression is to assist her or him in seeing brighter possibilities.

Suppose, for example, that your depressed child insists on maintaining a discouragingly single-minded and extremist point of view, making statements like "There's nothing I can do about it," "I always wind up making a mess of things," or "There's only one thing that can happen." In a tactful but persistent manner, point out that there are indeed positive alternatives that she or he is overlooking.

In other words, get your child to *start* thinking about various ways to get out of the rut of depression and to *stop* thinking merely about the rut itself. Don't expect an instant, positive response to your efforts. Your child may even fight against you temporarily. But the overall effect will be to restimulate her or his healthy imagination.

■ *Guide your child toward activities that are creative or self-affirming.*
Try to interest your depressed child in some form of artistic self-expression. Often depressed people can cure themselves by discharging their emotional strife into paintings, poems, sculptures, compositions, songs, dances, or crafts.

Another way for a person to dispel her or his depression is to become involved in helping others. Search for possible volunteer groups, community service activities, or social service programs that might be appropriate for your child and encourage her or him (perhaps by joining in yourself) to take part in one or more of them.

Finally, identify your depressed child's personal talents (e.g., in athletics or science) and social strengths (e.g., in teaching or teamwork) and then steer her or him toward activities in which these talents and strengths can be exercised. You'll be helping your child rebuild self-esteem and in the process recover her or his good spirits.

■ *Teach your child how to relax.*
Many depressed individuals simply don't know how to comfort themselves or put themselves in a better, more congenial frame of mind. Let your child know what you yourself do to relax by yourself, especially if it's something simple and easy to appreciate, like walking in a nearby park, shooting baskets, sketching outdoor scenes, or taking a long, hot bath.

You might also try researching several of the more popular and effective formal relaxation techniques: for example, deep breathing, visualization, meditation, or yoga. Gather information at your local library, health club, or stress-reduction center. Then either share what you learn directly with your child or arrange for your child (and perhaps yourself as well) to be instructed by a qualified teacher.

■ *Provide diversionary entertainments.*

As much as is practical, set up fun things for your child, you and your child together, and the whole family to do. For example, arrange a video night, a picnic, a boat trip, a visit to an amusement park, or a night out at a roller rink. The more novel the entertainment, the more likely it is to jolt your child out of her or his depression.

In trying to show your depressed child a good time, guard against making her or him too self-conscious about your intentions or expecting her or him to respond at the time in a positive or even noticeable manner. The good effects of the experience may be slow to reveal themselves. On the other hand, your child may continue to be— or appear—just as depressed as ever.

The most important point of providing diversionary entertainments is not to let your child wallow in uninterrupted gloom; rather, to give fun every possible chance. If at first you don't succeed, keep on trying.

■ *Do whatever you reasonably can to reduce stress at home.*

In many cases, one of the main factors contributing to a teenager's depression is stress at home. Common stressors of this type include marital discord, separation, or divorce; fighting between siblings; overcrowding; a serious illness, misfortune, or death suffered by a family member; economic insecurity; a recent or impending move; or simple disorganization: a lack of comforting order and dependable routines.

Even in cases of teenage depression when stress at home is *not* one of the main initiating factors, it definitely deepens the depression and makes it last longer. No matter how unrelated the stress at home may originally be to the teenager's depression, she or he will ultimately come to feel personally responsible for that stress. From the distorted and egocentric point of view of a typical depressed teenager, she or he is a psychic stress generator or stress magnet that can't help but cause trouble for everyone else.

For some depressed teenagers, this "irrational" sense of responsibility leads to overwhelming guilt and shame, which, in turn, renders them exceedingly passive. For others, it leads to resentment and rebellion. Unable to tolerate feeling personally guilty or ashamed, they actively project blame onto everyone around them. In either scenario, the sad consequence can be not only a self-destructing individual life but also a ruined family life.

To help your depressed teenager and your family avoid such crises, make every effort to keep family life running smoothly; for example:

■ Maintain a structure of regular mealtimes, playtimes, and work times that everyone can rely on.

■ Avoid any dramatic household disruptions, such as putting up guests for a week or conducting major renovations.

■ See to it that everyone respects each other's rights, including some degree of privacy.

■ Build opportunities into each day for rewarding person-to-person contact not only with your depressed teenager but also with other members of your family, who, during such a crisis, are also in need of special love and understanding.

■ *Consider seeking professional help.*

A teenager's depression is never something to take lightly. While it lasts, it can wreak havoc on her or his personal, family, social, and school life. And at its most extreme, it can result in seriously abusive behavior and even suicide.

If repeated attempts to rouse your teenage child from depression have had no success after several weeks and if you are worried that the depression may, in fact, be getting worse, think about getting professional help. Psychological treatment can be very effective in helping teenagers overcome their depression. And there is also the medical angle. Many cases of depression—especially severe depression—have biochemical causes that can be greatly alleviated with medication. By taking quick, responsible action to investigate the psychological and medical aspects of your child's depression, you may be sparing yourself, your child, and your family months and even years of turmoil and grief.

At PCGC:
The Onset of Adulthood

Adolescence is an awkward time from start to finish, but the years between ages seventeen and twenty-one—when an individual isn't so much a "teenager" as a "young person"—can be particularly difficult. For some individuals, the sheer accumulation of new responsibilities, demands, freedoms, and constraints that are associated with this final period of transition to adulthood can be unbearable.

Caught in a downward spiral of self-doubt, self-defeat, and

self-destructiveness, these particularly traumatized individuals may exhibit several signs of severe depression:

■ extreme moodiness;

■ recurring thoughts of death and/or suicide;

■ frequent displays of temper;

■ long periods of withdrawal;

■ intense substance abuse;

■ sexual promiscuity and/or abuse;

■ eating disorders;

■ chronic health or hygiene problems.

In such cases, professional intervention may well be required if the downward spiral is ever to be reversed. And the sooner the intervention occurs, the better.

Increasingly, hospitals and clinics are providing therapeutic programs to deal with the special needs of troubled adolescents and their families. The goal of such programs is to identify the problem *quickly* and initiate *rapid* change. They help the young person alter self-defeating behaviors, reestablish productive relationships within the family, and develop the emotional resources and coping skills needed to succeed as an adult. At the same time, other members of the young person's family are frequently assisted in resolving their interpersonal conflicts and in building stronger relationships with one another so that the family as a whole can provide a supportive context for the young person's renewed growth as an emotionally healthy human being.

PCGC offers a program of this type called the Transitions Program. The success of the Transitions Program has been guided by the philosophy that each patient presents a unique combination of strengths and weaknesses, difficulties and capabilities, needs and opportunities. The program's focus is to help each patient make the most of this combination, that is, to capitalize on her or his strengths and capabilities, to effect positive change in her or his difficulties and weaknesses, and to fulfill her or his needs and opportunities.

A patient in the Transitions Program always benefits from talking privately with an understanding professional. However, our experience supports the fact that the entire family working together can provide additional and unparalleled assistance to the young person in her or his efforts toward achieving independence and assuming a valued new role in the family as an adult. For this reason, the family as a whole usually participates in the intervention.

The first step in the Transitions Program is a general assessment of the young person's life situation and emotional well-being. It's made to help us understand the young person in the context of her or his family, school, peers, and community. A detailed treatment plan is then developed, which is typically implemented on an outpatient basis, and may include any—or all—of the following components:

■ specialized psychological, psychiatric, and/or neurological evaluations;

■ individual therapy;

■ family therapy;

■ psychopharmacological therapy (i.e., therapy involving medications);

■ psychoeducational counseling for the patient and family.

These outpatient services are offered through the Professional Services Group, Inc., the private practice affiliate of PCGC. Locations include PCGC's main facility in University City, Philadelphia, and satellite locations throughout suburban Philadelphia and southern New Jersey.

In the more serious diagnostic or treatment conditions, inpatient hospitalization may be indicated. Given such a case, a multidisciplinary team, in consultation with the family and referring therapist(s), develops a specific treatment plan to stabilize the crisis at hand and to meet the immediate, most pressing needs of the patient and her or his family. The plan includes specific short-term goals and tasks to help the young person and her or his family disrupt self-defeating patterns and achieve rapid and positive change. Thereafter, for as long a period of time as necessary, the plan is repeatedly reviewed with the patient and her or his family so that it can be revised as appropriate.

If your child, or a child you know, seems to be suffering serious emotional problems in making the transition from adolescence to adulthood, this type of program—or therapeutic approach—may be very helpful. Contact local mental-health authorities for information and guidance.

Preventing Teenage Suicide

Suicide is the most drastic manifestation of depression; among American teenagers, it is the third leading cause of death. In a 1991 Gallup poll, 6 percent of the teenagers interviewed admitted to having attempted suicide at least once in their lives, and 15 percent said they had "come very close to trying."

These percentages may not seem large in themselves, but they are appalling when one considers the age of the victims and how desperate they must have been to try to end their lives so prematurely.

To the tormented adolescent psyche, still so vulnerable to stress, self-doubt, pessimism, grief, and hopelessness, suicide can appear to be a very compelling means of escaping pain. Indeed, it can sometimes seem to be the ideal, perhaps the only, solution to the problem at hand: for example, what to do after a love affair has ended, how to end the messy conflicts surrounding the divorce of one's parents, what to do with an unwanted body or mind, or how to deal with the threat of possible annihilation in a nuclear war or ecological disaster. In situations like these, a teenager can feel especially powerless, lacking either the ability to change, or the coping skills to deal with what's happening. To teenagers who feel this way, the act of suicide can appear to be the only powerful act they're capable of performing.

Depressed teenagers are also highly susceptible to contemplating or committing suicide after learning that a peer has done so. Thus, the suicide of one teenager is sometimes quickly followed by the suicides of other teenagers in her or his community.

Known scientifically as the "cluster effect," this phenomenon of one teenage suicide prompting others offers yet one more example of an adolescent's tendency to identify so strongly with her or his peers and to react so emotionally to what they say and do. Having been swept away by the drama of another teenager's suicide, a depressed adolescent may be all the more likely to view it as a possible and even glamorous alternative to her or his present, miserable existence.

The danger signals of suicidal feelings are similar to those of depression, with the possible addition of any one or more of the following behaviors:

■ complaining about being "rotten inside" or "dying" (e.g., "I feel like I'm going to die");

■ expressing verbal hints, such as "You won't have to worry about me much longer" or "I can't put up with feeling this way anymore";

■ putting her or his affairs in order, for example, by giving away possessions, ending relationships, cleaning her or his room especially well;

■ becoming suddenly and inexplicably composed or cheerful after a long period of depression;

■ making secret arrangements for some sort of atypical outing or private ceremony.

The most effective step that concerned parents can take to prevent their depressed teenager from committing suicide is to be extravigilant. People who are thinking about suicide almost always give clues, intentionally or unintentionally; and this type of clue giving is especially prevalent among teenagers. Whenever such a clue appears, parents should take it very seriously and intervene as quickly as possible.

Here are some guidelines for intervening effectively to prevent your teenager from contemplating, attempting, or committing suicide:

■ *Ask your child if she or he is depressed or thinking of suicide.*

It may be awkward to bring up these subjects or talk about them once they are out in the open, but there's nothing to lose and everything to gain. Your child may be too inhibited in general or too immersed in her or his specific problems to confide in you without some prompting.

Don't hesitate to confront your child with these matters out of a fear that you will be putting negative or dangerous ideas into her or his head. Suicidal ideation (the formal term for "seriously thinking along suicidal lines") is not provoked in this way. Instead, you will be letting your child appreciate how much you care, rescuing her or him from any self-imposed spell of secrecy, and making it easier for him or her to be frank with you.

■ *Work with your child to find constructive solutions to her or his suicide-related problems.*

With tact and compassion, suggest ways that your child might go about addressing her or his suicide-related problems both with and without your help. Encourage your child to talk about possible problem solutions with specific individuals whom you trust—people who will be discreet, patient, supportive, and upbeat and who don't necessarily need to know that your child has been, or may be, contemplating suicide.

■ *Talk with your child about local teenage suicides that come to your attention.*

The more that the two of you discuss such suicides up front, the less chance that your child will fantasize about them, take them too much to heart, or imitate them in a "cluster effect" reaction. Together with your child, talk realistically and in detail about what circumstances and feelings may have led up to that particular suicide, what more constructive actions the victim might have taken, and what effects the suicide may be having on the victim's friends and family members as well as on strangers hearing about it.

■ *Set and enforce rules and routines that will give your child's daily life a healthy structure.*

Arrange your family's day-to-day home life so that it is more predictable, less stressful, and less conducive to providing your child with incentives or opportunities to engage in suicidal thoughts or activities. Taking care to elicit and honor any wishes your child may have regarding confidentiality, involve all family members in planning these arrangements.

Avoid making changes that are too extreme or abrupt or that appear too obviously related to your child's confessed inclination toward suicide. Otherwise, you might make your child feel punished or confined. But *do* make changes that will encourage your child, yourself, and others of your family to act more responsibly and considerately toward each other.

Among the policies to consider instituting or reinforcing are the following:

■ making sure that family members keep each other informed about their daily schedules;

■ setting up regular and peaceful times when family members are expected to be together (e.g., at supper) as well as regular and peaceful times that you and your depressed child can be together;

■ not leaving your depressed child (or any other child in the family) alone for extended periods of time without adult supervision;

■ establishing a strict curfew at night for all children and a limited number of nights per week when they can be away from home;

■ not permitting your children to tease, provoke attack, or otherwise bother each other and not allowing any such incident to pass by unmentioned.

■ *Get professional help.*

Severe depression and suicidal ideation are serious mental disorders. They are also treatable. If you have any reason to believe that your child is suffering from these disorders, then arrange to have her or him evaluated by a psychiatrist, psychologist, or mental-health professional.

A psychological evaluation will not obligate your child to enter a treatment program, nor will it have an adverse impact on your child's emotional well-being. On the contrary, it can help both of you face your child's emotional problems more directly and intelligently, and it provides both of you with an invaluable contact and resource in the event of a future crisis.

CASE:

The Double Deal

Ed remembered the event vividly as "the worst night in my life." It had happened three months ago, shortly after his fifteenth birthday. His parents had gone out in his father's car for dinner at a friend's house. On a very uncharacteristic impulse, he had decided to take a short, forbidden, and illegal drive in his mother's car, not only just for the fun of it but also to get some practice driving so that he wouldn't look so amateurish when the "formal" lessons with his father began.

As luck would have it, Ed drove right past his parents, who were returning home unexpectedly. Stepping on the gas to get away before they could see him, he jumped the curb and drove onto someone's lawn. As soon as he got back onto the street, his father pulled in behind him.

Understandably torn by anger, fear, disappointment, and disbelief, Ed's father yelled at him for risking his life, stealing the car, and digging up the lawn. Then, shaking his head over his otherwise mild-mannered, law-abiding son's bad luck at being caught, his father exclaimed, "You're such a loser!"

Thereafter, both Ed and his father appeared to have put the incident behind them. But Ed gradually spent less and less time with the family and more and more time alone in his room listening to music with his headphones on. Since he wasn't causing any noticeable problems, his parents just decided to let him be. He was eating much less, but then he had needed to lose weight, anyway. A month after the car-stealing incident, his report card showed a significant drop in his grades, so his parents applied more pressure on him to do his homework and hoped for the best.

Finally, three weeks later, something happened that Ed's parents couldn't excuse or ignore: They caught him smoking marijuana in his bedroom. An immediate search of his bedroom revealed several ounces of marijuana and a half-empty bottle of scotch. Concerned that their otherwise quiet, solitary, and well-behaved child might get into serious trouble by using drugs, they sought family counseling.

The counselor supported Ed's parents' drug-prohibition policy: Drugs and drug use were *not* to be permitted in the house; and any evidence or reasonable suspicion that drugs *were* in the house or that drug use *was* taking place would warrant a full search. But more important, the counselor enabled Ed and his parents to see that the problem was not the drugs per se but an underlying depression.

Ed had been devastated by hearing his father call him "a loser" on the night he had stolen his mother's car. That one remark had brought to the surface all the feelings of foolishness, incompetence, worthlessness, and hopelessness that he had been suppressing since puberty, when the awkward process of going through adolescence had begun. During the weeks that had followed his father's remark, he had not been able to rid his mind of those feelings. All he could do was occasionally drown them out with music and drugs.

Working with the counselor, Ed came to understand that he needed to confront his parents about things they did that upset him rather than simply brooding about them. As it turned out, Ed's father had completely forgotten the offending remark and had certainly not meant it as seriously as his son had taken it. Ed's father also said that he had felt for some time like sitting down with his son and asking him why he had been so withdrawn lately—something the counselor agreed would have been a good thing to do—but that he had been too embarrassed or afraid to do so.

Moved by the knowledge that his father, too, suffered from

embarrassment and fear, Ed was more willing to admit his own role in letting himself become so depressed. He grew to appreciate that his father couldn't turn him into a loser just by saying he was. Only Ed himself could do that. And with his newfound appreciation came a resolve never to let that happen.

After the counseling, two deals were made. Ed and his parents struck a bargain with each other that whenever a conflict arose, everyone involved would discuss it as soon as they were calm in order to eliminate misunderstandings and resolve hurt feelings. And Ed struck a bargain with himself that he would not blame someone else for getting him down as long as it was in his power to pick himself back up.

At PCGC: Seasonal Affective Disorder

Seasonal affective disorder, or SAD, is a form of depression that appears to be related to seasonal changes in natural light, as registered on the retina and processed in the brain. Other factors that may trigger SAD are wintertime temperature and humidity changes. SAD may also be experienced in summer instead of winter, a condition called reverse SAD. This latter condition, far less prevalent than SAD itself, may be caused by a latent summer-hibernation drive in the victim's brain, like the one that is activated in many animals during hot and dry seasons. In either case—SAD or reverse SAD—the symptoms are similar: decreased alertness, increased sleepiness, and sustained lack of enthusiasm for life.

The Mood, Sleep, and Seasonality Program at PCGC studies how child and adolescent depression relates to the seasons and what long-term effects such depression may have on its sufferers. The program has established that adolescents with SAD regularly exhibit various combinations of the following symptoms during the winter months:

■ extreme tiredness and listlessness;

■ appetite changes: most often an *increase* in appetite (possibly as the result of winter-triggered carbohydrate-craving obesity syndrome [COS]);

■ recurring general complaints of "not feeling well";

■ frequent irritability, negativity, and impatience;

■ persistent and pronounced sadness;

■ difficulty in concentrating, often accompanied by a slowness in thinking and causing a downward trend in school performance;

■ sleep changes: either too much or too little;

■ withdrawal from family and peer social activities.

According to what the Mood, Sleep, and Seasonality Program has learned to date, adolescent SAD is less severe than adult SAD but more severe than cases of school-age SAD. The implication is that an untreated case of SAD worsens over time and that early intervention can make a significant difference in the victim's lifelong emotional state.

An adolescent is referred to PCGC's Mood, Sleep, and Seasonality Program by her or his parents and/or teachers. A psychiatrist then assesses the various biological, psychological, environmental, and family elements that may be contributing to the adolescent's apparently season-related depression. One such element may be heredity. Both SAD and other forms of extreme seasonal mood and energy variation tend to occur in family groups; and family members from different generations may go through persistent seasonal mood changes of differing intensities.

Ultimately, the program psychiatrist arrives at a specific diagnosis, which may point to season-related depression but not SAD itself. Then the psychiatrist outlines a treatment plan tailored to the particular needs of the adolescent and her or his family.

Among the most successful treatments for SAD is phototherapy, which involves daily exposure for approximately an hour or more (depending on the case) to banks of high-intensity light. This type of exposure has worked to counteract many of the effects of SAD in approximately 80 percent of the patients admitted to the program.

If you think your child, or a child you know, may be suffering from SAD, consult your psychiatrist, psychologist, or mental-health professional. He or she can help you arrange for diagnosis and (if necessary) treatment.

4.

Discipline

A mong all the tasks associated with raising children, disciplining a teenager typically causes the greatest amount of emotional wear and tear for parent and child alike. In fact, it is the complexity of this task and not really the nature of being a teenager in itself that gives adolescence its bad reputation of being such a disturbing and turbulent developmental period.

Once adolescence begins, parents can no longer rely so much on their superior physical, social, and intellectual status to compel obedience to their authority. Instead, their teenage children are increasingly capable of seeing through that authority and challenging it. And no longer are adolescents so attached to small pleasures, like dessert and a night's worth of television, or so terrified by small pains, like having to stay in their room for a few hours. Instead, they are increasingly more interested in waging and winning power struggles over their long-range rights and liberties.

The upshot is that parents have less and less control over their teenage child as she or he gets older and older. This process is inevitable no matter what approach to discipline parents may take. It is also, in essence, appropriate and desirable. Adolescents need to learn how to control themselves rather than depending on their parents to perform that function for them. Otherwise, they will be at a serious disadvantage when they eventually leave home and are obliged to make their own way in life.

Understandably, parents of teenagers find it very difficult to yield their hard-won child-governing powers or to stand by helplessly as they lose them. Their loss of power is even harder to accept given the dangers that individual teenagers can encounter or create for themselves during their quest for independence.

Wrestling with this dilemma, parents often subconsciously turn situations that seem to call for disciplinary measures into opportunities to discharge their personal anger, frustration, and fear. Ultimately, this strategy is as futile as it is unfair. Having lost their composure, parents wind up even more upset; and having been subject to such raw antagonism, their children wind up even more alienated and therefore uncooperative.

Meanwhile, teenagers are not nearly as strong-willed or ready for self-determination as they may *appear* to be. Nor are they always capable of seeing the lack of logic or the inconsistencies that exist in their thoughts and behaviors. Their strong degree of self-absorption frequently renders them blind to their faults and mistakes no matter how apparent they may be to a parent or how well a parent may describe them and point them out.

Many parent-child disciplinary struggles that occur during a child's teenage years are triggered by deep conflicts that are common within the adolescent psyche. While teenagers may consciously believe that they want to break away from their parents, subconsciously they still desire a certain amount of parental attention, concern, and guidance. And while they may consciously think they are old enough to be treated as adults, subconsciously they know that they are not sufficiently mature in emotional or intellectual terms to appreciate many of the values and responsibilities that adult life entails.

Taking into account this fragile balance within the adolescent ego, parents must discipline their teenage children with extreme caution. They must be careful not to alienate their children by appearing to "baby" them. At the same time, they must not only give their children a clear and palpable sense of how they are expected to behave but also help them accept and meet those behavioral standards.

To discipline your thirteen- to nineteen-year-old child with a maximum of constructive guidance and a minimum of destructive stress, try following these basic recommendations:

■*Always strive to educate rather than to dictate.*

Your primary disciplinary objective is to influence your teenage child toward becoming more self-disciplined. After all, it won't be long before she or he will be outside the pale of your day-to-day support and authority.

With this in mind, make every effort to appeal to your child's reason and common sense. Involve her or him in negotiating rules. Check to be sure that she or he understands the rationale behind requests and policies that affect her or his life-style and behavior. Avoid issuing commands in a spirit of "do it because I say so."

In other words, as your teenager grows up, treat her or him more and more like an adult and less and less like a child. Build on your successes in this endeavor and involve your child in seeking alternatives to strategies that clearly aren't working.

■*Accept as much as possible in your child's behavior, even if you can't approve.*

Because of their rapidly changing physical, emotional, and social lives and their increasing desire and need to exercise their independence, teenagers are bound to behave more erratically and generate more potential conflict than they did as younger children. This calls for a more tolerant and judicious response on the part of parents. Requiring your teenager to conform to household rules and family standards just as much as she or he used to do is only inviting an ever-increasing degree of friction and hostility at home.

Reserve disciplinary actions for situations that are truly serious, that is, situations in which your child has interfered with someone else's rights, has caused harm to someone else's person or property, or has placed someone else's welfare in jeopardy. The same goes for criticisms and complaints, which, to a thin-skinned teenager, can seem just as harsh and insulting as disciplinary action.

This approach means being careful in the first place not to set up too many rules, regulations, and guidelines governing your teenager's behavior. Otherwise, you put your teenager at risk of repeatedly doing something offensive and yourself at risk of repeatedly having to express your displeasure with your child—or else lose your credibility as a parent. Keep official rules to the bare minimum and give your child as much freedom as practical to learn from her or his own mistakes.

■*Be firm and consistent in administering discipline.*

Although it may not be apparent on the surface, your teenager depends on you to establish and uphold *some* degree of order in her or his life. Stand behind whatever disciplinary rules and policies you do set up with your teenager, such as curfews, reporting procedures, or household chores. Never ignore a violation and try not to be noticeably inconsistent in addressing it—treating the same degree of violation very lightly on one occasion and very harshly on another. Instead, try to address each violation with approximately equal seriousness.

In addition, strive to maintain control over every phase of the disciplinary process. Of course, it is appropriate and desirable to negotiate rules with your teenage child rather than simply imposing your own rules. It is also appropriate and desirable to listen to what your teenager has to say about any violations that occur rather than simply leveling accusations and judgments. However, set a reasonable limit to such open-ended discussions. Your word should be the final one.

■ *Try not to get emotionally involved or upset during disciplinary confrontations.*

In the heat of an argument, an angry or frustrated teenager is likely to say all sorts of things that are capable of hurting your feelings. Don't take such statements too much to heart; rather, recognize them for what they are: desperate and, more often than not, thoughtless attempts to throw you off balance.

Alternatively, guard against getting carried away yourself and saying things that you don't want or mean to say. If you feel yourself becoming too angry or frustrated to continue a particular confrontation wisely and compassionately, then discontinue the confrontation, setting up a specific time in the near future (preferably that same day) to discuss the matter more calmly.

At all times, remember that your objective is to get your child to *behave* well, not to force her or him to have the same *feelings* as you about a particular incident or rule. Your child may not have the privilege of acting in whatever way she or he pleases but does have a right to her or his own personal opinions and attitudes.

■ *Avoid administering specific punishments unless absolutely necessary.*

Punishments for a teenage child do not have the same effect as they do for a preschooler or school-age child. A teenager is much less likely to be intimidated or reformed by having to do a particular penance for some transgression.

Nor is punishment of a teenager as easy to devise and enforce. The most common forms of teenage punishment are grounding, the imposition of special chores, or the reduction of certain privileges (e.g., using the family car, talking on the telephone, or watching television). A teenager is not only more capable of tolerating or working around such temporary inconveniences but also more capable of defying them.

Never forget that a teenager is determined to be treated as an adult and therefore frequently responds as one. This means that a well-managed disciplinary criticism or confrontation in itself may often turn out to be a sufficiently effective form of punishment.

Whenever it seems necessary to discipline your teenage child, try limiting yourself at first to confrontation and constructive criticism. Only resort to a specific punishment if the initial tactic fails to prevent repetition of the same wrongdoing.

Experiment with asking your misbehaving teenager what punishment would be appropriate, given the situation at hand. Your teenager may be harder on her- or himself than you would or could be. Besides, your teenager will have no legitimate grounds for complaining that the punishment is unfair if she or he actually determines it.

■ *Don't embarrass or humiliate your child.*

Teenagers have a great deal of pride. They can be very easily and severely wounded by sharp, punishing references to their inadequacies, vulnerabilities, and mistakes, however warranted you may feel such references are. And once wounded in this manner, teenagers usually become even more resentful, obstinate, and prone to bad behavior.

As much as possible, spare your child's feelings. Focus on what is wrong with the *act* your child has committed rather than on what is wrong with her or him. Give your child reason to believe that she or he is capable of behaving better and express your faith that she or he *will* behave better.

■ *Set a good example.*

Your child can't be expected to abide by rules for good behavior if you don't. Furthermore, your child can't be expected to know how to manage self-discipline in general if she or he can't look to you as a model.

Exercise self-control and respect for others in your personal habits. Live up to your side of any bargain that you strike with your child— or any bargain that your child knows you have struck. Obey all rules that apply to the family in general (e.g., reporting whereabouts, showing up for meals, keeping common spaces tidy, not disturbing each other's privacy). And do your best to obey all rules that apply to society in general.

■ *Recognize when matters have worsened beyond your ability to cope and seek appropriate help.*

You should never be ashamed to admit your helplessness in dealing with a particular teenage discipline problem or with your teenager's disciplinary problems in general. The potential price of not admitting your helplessness is the emotional well-being of every member of your family as well as those individuals outside your family who are heavily influenced by your teenager's behavior.

In any of the following situations, consider contacting a psychiatrist, a psychologist, a mental-health professional, or any adult whose judgment you respect and whose experience seems applicable:

> ■ Your child persists in ignoring or violating all household rules and policies.

> ■ You are unable to maintain control of your own behavior in confrontations with your child.

■ Your child is suffering from severe depression, perhaps even having suicidal thoughts.

■ Your child is developing serious health problems, such as poor eating or sleeping habits.

■ Your child shows signs of being addicted to a drug.

■ Your child appears unable to stop tormenting or abusing another child, either inside or outside the family.

■ Your child's school performance is irreversibly deteriorating.

■ Your child is unable to break a pattern of consistent lying or stealing.

■ Your child is repeatedly absent from home or truant from school for long periods of time without explanation.

■ You are often—or persistently—afraid of your child.

■ You realize your child has a serious problem of some sort, but you can't identify it.

CASE:

A Lesson in Responsibility

Marsha was a stable and trustworthy sixteen-year-old with a streak of wildness. Her classmate Kate, on the other hand, was basically wild—too wild for Marsha ever to let her mother, Phyllis, meet her or even know that they sometimes hung out together.

One weekend afternoon while Phyllis was away, Marsha invited Kate over to her house. Phyllis returned just as Kate's car was pulling out of the driveway. An hour later, Phyllis discovered fifty dollars missing from her top bureau drawer.

Without making any direct accusations, Phyllis informed Marsha that she had placed the fifty dollars in her drawer just before she had gone out that afternoon and asked Marsha if she knew anything about its disappearance. At first, Marsha denied that she or Kate had any knowledge of what might have happened to it. But when Phyllis finally stated that she had no reasonable alternative but to believe that either Marsha or Kate had taken the money, Marsha admitted that Kate had wandered freely throughout the house and might have taken the money.

Phyllis refrained from scolding her daughter. Instead, she stated clearly and firmly that she held Marsha responsible for the theft and in the future would continue to hold her responsible for whatever might happen inside the house while she was home alone and in charge. Then Phyllis secured Marsha's agreement to repay the money personally. Finally, Phyllis established a new policy: If Marsha ever again let someone who was a stranger to Phyllis into the house while she was away, Phyllis would feel compelled to make sure that Marsha was not left home alone thereafter.

Marsha was appreciative of the fact that Phyllis didn't blame her for inviting Kate into the house in the first place—or even for associating with Kate—something Marsha no longer felt inclined to do, anyway. She was also grateful that she was still trusted at home alone. And she had no trouble accepting the new policy of no strangers in the house. After all, she might not be able to afford them!

Authoritarian-Restrictive Versus Authoritative

In all dealings with your teenage child, it is helpful to bear in mind the distinction between an *authoritarian-restrictive* parenting style and an *authoritative* parenting style. The latter style tends to be far more productive and satisfying than the former style from both the parents' perspective and that of the child.

An authoritarian-restrictive parent is one whose disciplinary efforts mainly involve negative-oriented behaviors: saying "No!" or "Wrong," setting rules and limits to curb "bad" behavior, and administering punishment. On the other hand, an authoritative parent is one whose disciplinary efforts mainly involve positive-oriented behaviors: saying "Yes!" or "Right," setting a good example, and administering praise for "good" behavior.

In essence, an authoritarian-restrictive parent inspires fear and resentment in a child; an authoritative parent, love and respect. You may not always be able to avoid making your child afraid of you or to keep your child from resenting you. But you can prevent yourself from drifting into the habit of disciplining your child in a manner that is *primarily* negative.

Concentrate on phrasing disciplinary measures in terms of what is good or right to do (and why) instead of what your child is *not* allowed to do. Scrupulously practice the behavior that you want emulated and make it a point to compliment far more often than you correct your child.

5.
Substance Abuse

The United States of America is a drug culture. The majority of its citizens rely on drugs to pursue their normal lives: coffee in the morning to wake up, a cigarette, beer, or glass of wine in the evening to relax, and/or an occasional pill to fight a cold, lose weight, escape depression, or restore bowel regularity.

It's easy for parents to overlook this fact when they consider their teenage child's possible abuse of controlled substances—alcohol being the number-one most-abused substance, followed by amphetamines ("uppers"), barbiturates ("downers"), marijuana, and cocaine. Much of a child's attraction to drugs in general is preconditioned by society at large. In discouraging a child from abusing drugs, parents must accept this reality and be careful to approach the abuse problem with compassion and practical help instead of disbelief, outrage, and condemnation.

By far the most apparent reason why adolescents first begin to experiment with drugs and then go on to become habitual drug abusers is to fit in with their peers. Not only do many adolescents use drugs simply because that's what their friends do (a basic "mirroring" behavior); they also use them in order to feel more comfortable and emotionally in tune with their friends (a more complex "adapting" behavior).

Other apparent reasons why adolescents turn to drug experimentation and abuse are as follows (in no specific order):

■ to cope with loneliness or boredom;

■ to satisfy a personal curiosity—about oneself as well as about individual drugs;

■ to defy rules or authority;

■ to challenge "common sense" (so-called risk-taking behavior);

■ to appear more adult (or not to appear to be a "baby");

■ to transcend a "self" they do not value;

■ to escape specific emotional or psychosomatic pains;

■ to punish themselves (so-called self-destructive behavior);

■ to gain self-confidence or courage.

While it's important to consider and address any of these *apparent* reasons for an individual teenager's drug experimentation and abuse, there is almost always one *underlying* reason why a child incorporates drug use into her or his personal life-style: to experience pleasure. For at least a short time, a drug can help the user feel good or at least better than she or he naturally feels at the time. Unfortunately, if the user becomes addicted to a particular drug (which is very likely, given habitual use of any of the above-mentioned drugs), she or he can't feel good about it.

Here are guidelines for preventing and coping with teenage substance abuse:

■ *Maintain an active involvement in your child's day-to-day life.*
The more you know about what your child does with her or his leisure time, who your child's friends are, and how your child feels, the better able you will be to detect whether your child is using drugs and, if so, to help her or him stop. Encourage your child to share this information with you in a comfortable and trusting manner by arranging to spend time together frequently and regularly.

Assuming your child feels estranged from you or the family as a whole, she or he is all the more susceptible to relying on drugs to feel "at home." To prevent this from happening, always keep the channels of communication open, involve your child in family events, and make sure she or he is aware of your love and interest.

■ *Set a firm and clear policy prohibiting drug use.*
Don't take it for granted that your child knows that using drugs is wrong or that she or he is forbidden to use them. Explicitly state that you do not approve of teenagers using drugs and that you'll do everything you possibly can to keep your child from using them.

At the same time—or times—that you announce this policy, explain the medical, legal, and social reasons for it as well as the consequences your child will face if she or he should violate it. Just be careful to avoid arguing that drug use is forbidden as long as your child remains "under your roof." This type of argument can backfire, encouraging your child to run away, leave home prematurely, or establish a "home base" somewhere else—steps that are likely to escalate the odds that she or he will abuse drugs.

■*Educate your child to handle situations that foster drug use.*
Try role-playing with your child what she or he should say and do if
drugs are being used or offered. Go beyond advising your child simply
to say no, although this response may occasionally work. Develop
together a number of different and more substantive ways to avoid or
refuse drug-use opportunities without losing face with her or his peers.
Among the possibilities are the following:

REJECTING DRUGS INSTEAD OF THE DRUG OFFERER

■ "I'm saving my brains for something better."

■ "I don't need the poison."

■ "I don't like what it does to me."

■ "I don't like the way it tastes."

■ "That stuff always backfires on me."

OFFERING AN EXCUSE

■ "I'm allergic."

■ "I'm in training for [sport or activity]."

■ "I don't want to mess up the rest of the day."

USING HUMOR

■ "Sorry, not my brand."

■ "I'd rather just watch you guys act stupid."

TAKING THE OFFENSIVE

■ "I can't believe you really use that stuff."

■ "You guys are too smart for that."

■ "Don't ask me that again if you want to stay friends."

OFFERING AN ALTERNATIVE

■ "Let's get some real food instead."

■ "No, I'd rather play [sport or game]."

Advise your child to walk away if these strategies don't work, either
making an excuse or not, depending on the particular situation. Also,
give your child pointers on how to initiate conversations about rejecting drugs with friends or prospective friends, not only for her or
his personal benefit but also for the friends' benefit.

■ *Educate your child about how to exercise self-control.*
Take every opportunity, whether it involves substance abuse or not, to teach your child the following skills:

- ■ how to set healthy self-development goals;

- ■ how to stick to one's principles;

- ■ how to delay gratification when appropriate;

- ■ how to self-reward and self-discipline based on one's behavior.

The more guidance your child has in such matters, the easier it will be for her or him to resist the most common temptations to use drugs.

If your child is currently wrestling with actual drug-abuse problems, assist in setting up and follow a specific self-improvement program to overcome those problems. Let your child steer this program but hold on to your role as an ongoing consultant.

■ *Motivate your child to participate in activities and assume responsibilities that will make more constructive use of her or his leisure time.*
Given that boredom and low self-esteem are major factors contributing to teenage drug abuse, encourage your child to do things that are personally interesting, challenging, and morale building: sports, physical-fitness programs, volunteer work, hobbies, part-time jobs, home-improvement projects, and/or extension classes.

If possible, guide your child toward activities and responsibilities involving other kids her or his age who are similarly inclined to use their leisure time productively. These kinds of peer experiences can help your child develop social skills and value social interactions that are not oriented around drug use.

■ *As often as practical, arrange for your child to be supervised.*
If it doesn't cause too much trouble, avoid leaving your adolescent child entirely alone when you are away from home for more than a few hours. Get another adult to be there or to look in during your absence. This policy is appropriate for teenagers under any circumstances, but it's especially advisable if you suspect or know that your child has used—or is using—drugs.

In arranging for supervision, try not to imply that you don't trust your child. You don't want your child to feel like a prisoner, and she or he is entitled to a certain amount of independence. However, you also have a responsibility to ensure that both your child and your home are safe and sound. With these objectives in mind, make sure that the supervision is benevolent and discreet.

■ *Seek all available outside help when appropriate.*

To improve your knowledge and understanding of adolescent drug abuse, gather pertinent information from every school, community, and church/synagogue-sponsored drug-prevention program in your area. This information will also help you discuss drug abuse with your child and, if necessary, deal with any abuse problems your child may develop.

Assuming your child already does have an abuse problem, you should also consider enlisting the help of a professional mental-health therapist, psychologist, or psychiatrist. Often a major cause of a drug-abuse problem is a deeply rooted emotional problem. And if your child is already addicted to drugs, she or he will have to go through a considerable amount of emotional turmoil in order to break that addiction.

■ *Punish substance abuse in an appropriate fashion.*

You shouldn't punish your child too severely for casual experimentation with drugs, especially if she or he has confessed to you about it. However, if your child has engaged in relatively heavy drug use, strong, firmly administered punishment is definitely warranted.

Make sure that your child knows in advance what kind of consequences to expect if she or he starts using drugs. This knowledge may help act as a deterrent.

Ideally, such consequences should include measures that work directly toward keeping your child away from drugs: for example, prohibiting your child from participating in certain events, friendships, or activities that can be associated with her or his drug use. It might also include general "grounding" and/or a reduction or withdrawal of privileges.

By all means avoid referring to *rehabilitative* steps, like attending drug counseling programs or spending more time doing homework, as "punishments." Instead, they should be presented to your child as helpful, rewarding, and unique opportunities to turn her or his life around.

■ *Set a good example.*

It's difficult to convince a teenager not to indulge in controlled substances if the teenager sees her or his parents doing so. Restrict any such indulgence on your part as much as possible, try not to indulge in the presence of your child, and avoid referring to your own drug taking, or another adult's, in favorable terms (e.g., "I need a drink to relax" or "He's much nicer when he's had a few drinks").

In addition, explain to your child the developmental, social, and legal reasons why you and other adults *can* indulge to a certain extent in controlled substances while she or he and other teenagers *cannot*. Make sure that your child understands and accepts these distinctions.

Your child should also know that you have personal rules regulating your drug use: strict limits regarding kinds of drugs, amounts, rate of intake, occasions when you'll allow yourself to take drugs, and what you will and won't do while under the influence of drugs (such as not driving). State these rules specifically so that your child can use them later as possible models governing her or his drug consumption in adulthood.

Signs of Possible Substance Abuse

■ any dramatic change for the worse in behavior, appearance, school performance, friends, or sleeping/eating patterns

■ frequent incidents of memory lapse, sluggishness, or incoherent speech (e.g., unfinished sentences, irrational statements)

■ non-illness-related pupil dilation, bloodshot eyes, runny nose, cough, vomiting

■ repeated incidents of clumsiness or loss of coordination

■ major swings in mood (e.g., from depressed to elated) or energy level (e.g., from lethargic to hyperactive)

■ frequent inappropriate responses to outside events (e.g., unprovoked anger, insensitive laughter, unwarranted fear)

■ repeated incidents of lying, stealing, or criminal behavior

■ frequent failure to appear as promised, be on time, or meet responsibilities

■ increasing secretiveness, preoccupation, withdrawal, and avoidance

■ general loss of motivation and former interests

■ escalated use of breath and air fresheners (or such odor maskers as heavy perfumes and incense)

■ possession of drug-related paraphernalia (e.g., flasks, cigarette papers, rollers, plastic Baggies, pipes, scales, pill bottles, coke spoons, razor blades, needles, atomizer bottles, butane minitorches)

■ possession of items referring to drug use (e.g., books, magazines, recordings, printed T-shirts, posters, videocassettes, artwork)

■ frequent reference to drugs in word choices, jokes, and conversations

■ chronic and otherwise inexplicable lack or abundance of money

The Dangers of Substance Abuse

ALCOHOL

■ has a much greater impact on teenagers than adults due to smaller body size of teenagers;

■ is a natural depressant that ultimately results in listlessness, apathy, and despair;

■ impairs coordination and slows reflexes;

■ increases one's vulnerability to physical and mental coercion;

■ causes indigestion, nausea, headache, and such "hangover" symptoms as hypersensitivity and shakiness;

■ reduces inhibitions so that emotional impressions and displays are out of one's control;

■ can cause unpredictable memory "blackouts";

■ over time, weakens the immune system, ruins the complexion, damages the liver and brain, and induces psychoses.

BARBITURATES ("DOWNERS")

■ can trigger unpredictable stupor, loss of consciousness, and even death;

■ are highly addictive, necessitating increasing amounts for equal effect;

■ can result in sleepiness, confusion, despair, uncontrollable crying "jags," and loss of coordination;

■ increase, over time, general irritability and impatience;

■ can render one exceptionally vulnerable to physical and mental coercion;

■ can cause headache and "hangover" symptoms.

AMPHETAMINES ("UPPERS")

■ increase restlessness and irritability;

■ can induce feelings of anger and paranoia;

■ result in loss of coordination and muscle control;

■ produce, over time, insomnia, skin disorders, damage to the digestive system, and/or convulsions;

■ are highly addictive, necessitating increasing amounts for equal effect;

■ can trigger hallucinations;

■ render one incapable of completing thoughts or concentrating on tasks;

■ can have emotionally and physically exhausting "crash" aftereffects.

MARIJUANA

■ diminishes short-term memory, with permanent damage over time;

■ results in dramatic loss of initiative and, ultimately, energy;

■ can occasionally induce paranoia and hallucinations;

■ causes severe misjudgments regarding time and space;

■ can disrupt, over time, menstrual cycle and reduce sperm count;

■ damages the lungs (as much as one pack of cigarettes per joint);

■ is attended by long-lasting aftereffects, including difficulty in concentrating and problems in coordinating thoughts and movements.

COCAINE

■ causes general irritability and anxiety;

■ can trigger unpredictable psychosis, heart failure, respiratory collapse, and death;

■ dramatically impairs physical reflexes and judgment;

■ results, over time, in depression and loss of initiative;

■ is highly addictive, necessitating increasing amounts for equal effect.

Resources

American Council for Drug Education
5820 Hubbard Drive
Rockville, MD 20852
(301) 984-5700

National Federation of Parents for Drug-Free Youth
1820 Farnwell Avenue, Suite 16
Silver Spring, MD 20902
(800) 544-5437

Parent Resource Institute on Drug Education
100 Edgewood Avenue, Suite 1216
Atlanta, GA 30303
(800) 241-9746

Alcoholics Anonymous
Box 459, Madison Square Garden
New York, NY 10163
(check local telephone directory for local chapter)

Al-Anon and Alateen
(for relatives and friends of alcohol abusers)
P.O. Box 182, Madison Square Garden
New York, NY 10159
(check local telephone directory for local chapter)

Alcohol and Drug Helpline
(800) 252-6465

Cocaine Hotline
(800) COCAINE (262-2463)

6.

Running Away

Hanging over the teenage years for every child, especially the car-driving years after age sixteen, is the question "What will life be like when I leave home?" One in seven children between the ages of thirteen and sixteen and one in five children between the ages of sixteen and eighteen actually run away from home to find out.

For some of these children, running away from home is primarily a sincere, if misguided, effort to achieve independence. For others, it's primarily a gesture of defiance aimed at parents who are viewed as uncaring, overly strict, or otherwise intolerable. For both groups, it's a sign of emotional instability.

Instead of arranging to leave home in a mature and responsible fashion or attempting to resolve their problems while staying at home, runaways are simply trying to escape pain. In doing so, they are taking a rash flight away from the known but apparently unacceptable into the unknown and definitely unpredictable.

Since the outside world is so dangerous, teenagers who are upset emotionally and cut off from home can easily get into trouble. Trying to survive on their own, they might wind up sick, broke, hungry, and without shelter; they might be robbed, beaten, sexually abused, or seduced into a life of drugs or crime; or they might even resort to victimizing others, in which case they invite anger and retaliation.

Just as dangerous and unpredictable, however, is the *internal* world of the teenage runaway: that is, the child's *emotional* state once she or he has abandoned the relative security of the home. A teenage runaway can quickly be overwhelmed by feelings of fear, guilt, remorse, shame, foolishness, worthlessness, self-hatred, and depression.

These negative feelings can penetrate deeply and last for a long time, darkly coloring the runaway's sense of self and the world at large. This happens even in cases when the running-away experience is fairly brief and uneventful, followed by a return to home life as usual. Assuming the running-away experience is especially negative or the reentry into home life is poorly managed, then the chance that the runaway will suffer seriously from such negative feelings is quite high.

Most teenagers who run away ultimately come back home on their own, usually within one to three days and usually in a contrite frame of mind. Most of them will try running away again, usually several times in the course of their teenage years.

Indeed, while *any* history of repeated attempts to run away needs to be taken very seriously, most are not causes for unusual alarm unless they include more than one runaway attempt during a given three-month period, coupled with little or no initiative on the part of the returning runaway to try to make her or his home life succeed. In these latter cases, psychiatric intervention is almost always warranted, given the strong indication that the runaway child and her or his family are unable to work out matters for themselves, even on a short-term basis.

Here are some guidelines to help you work out matters successfully with your runaway, or would-be runaway, teenage child:

■ *Watch for signs that your child may be considering running away.*

Teenagers don't often announce beforehand their intentions to run away. Instead, their parents have to be on the lookout for clues. This is especially true in the following situations:

> ■ The teenager wants to run away because she or he feels neglected by her or his parents. Feeling this way, the teenager plans secretly in order to fulfill the self-torturing fantasy: "My parents won't even notice I've gone." She or he assumes that once they *do* notice, they will be all the more guilt stricken.

> ■ The teenager wants to go it alone but simply can't face hurting her or his parents in person. In this kind of situation, the teenager actually believes she or he is acting out of love and is left with no other reasonable choice but to depart in this manner.

> ■ The teenager wants to run away out of a feeling of guilt, shame, or embarrassment. Typically, such teenagers believe that they have irretrievably failed their parents' expectations or that they are a burden to their parents or would become so if they stayed.

With these possible situations in mind, be extra alert for running-away clues during particularly stressful times for your child (e.g., a romantic crisis), for you and your child (e.g., an ongoing argument), or for your family as a whole (e.g., a divorce, a household move, or an economic crisis). Be especially loving and supportive toward your child during such times so that she or he will be less likely to contemplate running away.

Here are the most common "unspoken" running-away clues:

■ a recent marked and steady increase in the time your child spends away from home, especially if such absences tend to be unexplained;

■ a sustained and otherwise inexplicable effort on your child's part to accumulate money and/or resources;

■ an increase in the amount of "secret" phone conversations, correspondence, and meetings;

■ an unusual and otherwise inexplicable "cleaning up" of possessions and affairs (perhaps including giving things away);

■ an unusual and otherwise inexplicable effort to clear away a block of time in the near future or to avoid—or cancel— plans for the near future.

If any of these clues, or others, give you reason to suspect that your child may be considering running away, try talking with her or him honestly and comfortably about your concerns and about what is going on in her or his life. Remember that there may in fact be no connection between the two.

You don't necessarily have to confront your child directly with your suspicions that she or he may be planning to run away. But you should make every effort to dispel some of the mysteries that are cropping up between you and your child and to improve your person-to-person relationship.

■ *Avoid directly or indirectly daring your child to leave home.* Try as much as possible not to use phrases like "As long as you're living under this roof . . ." or "Not in my house, you aren't" or "Once you get out on your own, you're free to do what you want." Such statements encourage your child to imagine a better world outside the home. In certain particularly stressful situations, she or he may even follow such implicit suggestions to run away simply in order to make you regret what you've said and, by extension, your style as a parent in general.

Never allow yourself to get so carried away with anger or exasperation that you say something like "I can't wait until you get out on your own" or "Go ahead, leave home, see if I care." Don't say such things even in a spirit of mocking humor. They can resonate in your insecure teenage child's psyche much more profoundly than you can imagine.

■ *Respond calmly but firmly to any direct threat to run away that your child makes.*

If your teenage child does express an inclination or an intention to run away, take it very seriously. It may well be that your child doesn't actually mean what she or he says. In many cases, an expression of this nature is no more than a masked cry for more attention, affection, or respect. Nevertheless, you can't afford to assume that your child won't carry out her or his threat, if only to save face.

Whenever your child makes such a threat, tell her or him immediately, and in no uncertain terms, that you love her or him and that you don't want her or him to run away. Then try to use the occasion to talk more honestly and openly about the things that are bothering her or him. Perhaps these conversations will help both of you work out some mutually acceptable changes at home that will preclude any future thoughts on your child's part about running away. In any event, the most important thing for you to do during these conversations is to *listen* to your child so that she or he feels heard. Many times, this kind of attention is all that's required to remedy matters.

■ *Don't cooperate in your child's running away.*

Assuming your child is determined to leave home, don't make it easy for her or him to do so. Rather than passively allowing your child to go away, restate your disapproval of this strategy and do what you reasonably can to stop her or him from acting upon it.

You might try to engage your child in exploring alternatives to running away, depending on the situation at hand and on the resources that are available. Maybe your child could spend a brief period away from home with a relative or a friend whom both of you trust and respect. Maybe you could both seek professional counseling to improve your relationship. Maybe your child would be satisfied to spend some time away from home in the near future, either with you (e.g., on a special outing or vacation) or by her- or himself (e.g., at a camp or job site).

You might also want to let your would-be runaway child know what the consequences will be if she or he should actually run away. Be sure she or he realizes, for example, the goods, resources, and services that will be forsaken; the problems likely to be encountered in trying to live away from home; and, if relevant, the stricter rules that will have to be imposed (especially regarding time allowed away from home and reporting procedures) upon her or his return.

This latter kind of conversation has to be handled carefully. You don't want it to degenerate into an angry tirade, you don't want to make exaggerated statements that will inspire disbelief and contempt on your child's part, and above all, you don't want to imply to your child that there's no turning back once she or he has left. On the other hand, you *do* want your child to have a realistic picture of what to expect. Children caught up in the drama of running away are apt to have a very distorted sense of things.

Express yourself calmly, with due consideration for your child's seriousness and self-esteem. First, ask for your child's patience in hearing you out. Then state your case. Finally, request that your child take some time to think about what you have said before doing anything that she or he might regret and that you most definitely can't condone. This thinking period, which honors—and appeals to—your child's sense of reason, will provide your child with an opportunity to decide *not* to run away without losing face.

■ *If your child does run away, make every reasonable effort to locate her or him as soon as possible and to encourage her or him to return.*

Too many dangerous possibilities await the teenage runaway for her or his parents to assume a wait-and-see role, hoping that their child will come to her or his senses sooner rather than later. Remember that most runaway teenagers want—in fact, need—their parents to pay more attention to them, which would certainly include looking for them if they should run away and then trying to get them to come back home.

Immediately upon suspecting or discovering that your child has run away, try contacting anyone and everyone who may know her or his whereabouts. Personally investigate places where she or he may have gone. And notify the police right away. They may not be authorized to conduct an official search until a certain period of time has gone by (usually twenty-four hours), but they can provide you with possible leads and strategies for your own search efforts based on their experience with numerous different types of situations involving teenage runaways.

■ *Throughout the time your child is involved in running away, distinguish between the pain you are feeling or causing yourself and that which your child is feeling or causing.*

When their teenage child runs away, most parents are understandably consumed with worry, which leaves them vulnerable to all sorts of other negative and energy-draining emotions. By far the most common feeling is that they have lost control of their child. Parents of runaways need to work hard to disabuse themselves of the feeling that they *should* be able to control their child.

A teenage child has a mind of her or his own and is capable of acting on her or his own. While it may be appropriate for parents to regret specific things that they did or did not do in the course of raising their child, it is not appropriate for parents to blame themselves for *not* controlling their teenage child. Nor should they blame their child for wanting to be independent.

If your child has run away, stay focused on those emotions that are not self-punishing or punitive toward your child. Although you may not be able to help feeling rejected, try to bear in mind that runaway teenagers are almost always motivated, consciously or subconsciously, by a desire to get their parents to care more for them or to care for them in a different, more agreeable manner. In other words, they are not motivated by a desire to be rid of their parents' care. In effect, they're running away to try to make *you* feel the pain of separation and miscommunication that *they* feel.

Given this aspect of most teenage runaway situations, your most appropriate and constructive emotional response—that is, the emotional frame of mind you should try hardest to maintain—is compassion and love for your child and acceptance and forgiveness of yourself. Recognizing these truths will help you cope more easily with your child's running away and ultimately restore the relationship with your child.

■ *Welcome your child back with love, compassion, and concern.* When your child returns home, either voluntarily or under your guidance, your first and foremost act should be to express your love for her or him and your joy that she or he is back. Many ex–runaway children can't help but display excitement about being back home; but whether or not they do, they're bound to be very emotionally confused at that time, feeling awkward and embarrassed at best and devastated and ashamed at worst. Your warm reception will do wonders to restore your child's sense of self-worth and to set both of you on the path to a better relationship.

You may feel compelled to introduce new policies aimed at closer supervision of your child, especially if you cited them before she or he ran away as possible consequences of a running-away attempt. However, avoid punishing your child for the attempt to run away. It can't do any good, and it can do a considerable amount of harm, instantly and automatically reviving the worst images she or he may have of your authoritarianism and lack of understanding.

■ *After your runaway child returns, be prepared to make changes in your home life and in your relationship with your child.*

As soon as your child has had sufficient time to settle down and feel somewhat natural at home—say, after two or three days—you and your child should arrange to spend some private, uninterrupted time together discussing how the home-life situation might be improved so that your child won't feel driven to run away and you won't feel obligated to behave like her or his jailer.

First, set up a specific time for this meeting with your child and let her or him know the purpose of it: to work out a more satisfying home life. That way, both of you can prepare for the meeting in advance. Then, having thought before the meeting of various possibilities concerning the future, establish in your own mind what you might reasonably expect your child to do, what you yourself might be willing to do, and where you feel you might have to draw certain lines. Finally, use the meeting itself to come to mutually acceptable terms with your child on how things will be in the future so that after the meeting both of you can get on with your lives—separately as well as together.

7.

Overeating

The leading nutritional problem among American children is obesity. A quarter of the population between ages thirteen and twenty suffers from it, with male and female sufferers in roughly equal proportions. According to the U.S. Public Health Service, a teenager is technically considered obese if she or he is 20 percent over her or his ideal weight; and by far the most common reason why a teenager becomes and remains obese is overeating.

Although overeating may be the main *physical* cause of obesity, there are almost always significant *emotional* causes. An obese child typically overeats to compensate for being undernourished emotionally. Perhaps she or he feels neglected, incompetent, or inferior in some way. Maybe she or he is experiencing trouble dealing with day-to-day stress in her or his home life, school life, or social life. Possibly she or he is bothered—consciously or subconsciously—by a specific psychological conflict, such as a phobia about becoming ill or a suppressed desire to inflict harm on someone.

Whatever the case, overeaters in general tend to have low self-esteem, which, in turn, leads to poor self-control and difficulty in making decisions. Unfortunately, low self-esteem is not only the most common emotional *cause* but also the most common emotional *effect* of overeating. Thus, teenage overeaters find themselves caught in a vicious circle: They don't care about themselves, which gives them an excuse to indulge in eating behavior that is not good for them, which makes them disgusted with themselves, which leads them not to care about themselves, and so on.

The long-range consequences of overeating can be devastating. Emotionally, an overeater may fall victim to chronic depression or anxiety. Physically, she or he may develop heart disease, high blood pressure, a high cholesterol level, difficulty in breathing, or a blood-sugar irregularity. Any one of these conditions, emotional or physical, can reduce life expectancy.

Unfortunately, the most obvious solution to overeating, dieting, is not necessarily the best solution. In many instances, the stresses and strains of trying to maintain a diet only aggravate the overeater's problems with self-esteem, self-control, and self-satisfaction. Every time an overeater fails to stick to her or his diet, she or he can become even more hopeless and self-punishing about the obesity, which increases the chances of discontinuing dieting altogether and resuming overeating on a regular basis.

Such diet-related problems are common to people of any age, but they are compounded in the teenager living at home. Even if the dieter's parents try to stay as far removed from their child's efforts as possible, they are still close enough to witness all the inevitable struggles, frustrations, and setbacks associated with them.

Most of the time, the teenage dieter's parents are *not* far removed from their child's diet. Instead, they feel personally obliged, or are directly recruited, to become active partners in their child's diet, helping their child plan it, motivating her or him to stick with it, and organizing meals to accommodate it.

In either case, but especially in the latter, the parent-child relationship can easily and quickly become soured by mutual resentment, disappointment, and exasperation. The same thing can happen when an obese teenager initiates, or is coerced into following, a strict exercise program to lose weight. Anytime the teenager fails to meet the demands of such a program, she or he may also feel like a failure in the eyes of her or his parents, regardless of how sensitive or detached those parents try to be.

Avoiding such problems does not mean abandoning all efforts aimed at influencing your obese child to eat more responsibly and exercise more extensively. It's simply a matter of degree. The gradual introduction of a mild, informal trend toward eating healthier foods in more modest portions at less frequent intervals stands a much better chance of creating a positive and lasting change in your child's eating habits than the sudden imposition of a drastic and detailed diet. A gradual, mild, and informal approach also works better to get your child more productively involved in exercise.

If your child is obese or a chronic overeater, consider taking the following steps:

■ *Check for every possible physical cause of your child's obesity.* Before doing anything else, you and your child should consult a physician. Find out if there is any constitutional factor contributing to your child's obesity or overeating: for example, sluggish thyroid activity, a blood-sugar problem, anemia, or a food allergy. Although these conditions are relatively rare among obese teenagers, it's best to test for them as soon as possible.

Also, ask the physician for dietary and exercise recommendations.

While you may not want detailed plans (for reasons already stated), you can definitely profit from expert general advice.

■ *Inform your child about good eating and exercise habits without nagging.*

Guard against assuming the role of a coach. Instead, assume the less active and therefore less abrasive role of an adviser. In other words, be prepared to help your child as much as she or he wants without taking it upon yourself to force your child to help her- or himself.

To be a good adviser, first become informed about common-sense foods, eating habits, and exercise routines that are healthy and practical for teenagers in general and have a good chance of appealing to your child in particular. Then use this information not only to educate your overweight child whenever an opportunity presents itself but also to guide your "normal" planning of family meals and recreation.

Be careful not to initiate talk about healthy eating or healthy exercise too often or to lecture at length when you talk. Share your knowledge with your child at appropriate times in your ongoing dialogue—that is, when you and your child are already talking about such matters, when your child actually asks you about them, or when it's obvious that your child is doing something inappropriate due to a lack of information about diet or nutrition.

To test whether you may be overdoing your role as an adviser, keep track of each time you talk with your child about food, exercise, or being overweight both when the discussion occurred and what specifically you said. If these occasions tend to occur more than once or twice a week or if, as a whole, they represent a sizable percentage of the total number of times that the two of you have a serious conversation, then you are probably pressuring your child too much. Saying the same things about your child's weight problem over and over again clearly does not help the situation.

In addition, avoid at all times making statements that will cause your child to feel unduly guilty or embarrassed about being overweight, such as, "You'd be so much prettier if you'd only lose ten pounds!" or "How can you just stuff yourself like that?" or "Don't be such a pig." Instead, emphasize the overall health value that every human being derives from maintaining an appropriate weight and always express confidence in your child's ability to achieve this goal for him- or herself.

■ *Establish and enforce sensible policies regarding family meals and mealtimes.*

Among the policies to consider adopting in your household are the following:

■ Have rules about regular mealtimes and snack times. Stick to the rules so that your child does not wind up eating or snacking whenever it's personally convenient or desirable.

■ Set appropriate limits on the total amount of food you make available at mealtimes. Then let each person fill her or his own plate. This makes your child personally responsible for monitoring her or his food intake, and it prevents you from inadvertently giving your child more food than she or he wants or needs.

■ Be sensible in your food shopping and menu planning. Cut out exceedingly rich foods but don't eliminate all sauces or desserts. Introduce more fruits and vegetables into your family's diet gradually rather than abruptly. Minor adjustments are much easier to accept and much more likely to last than major ones.

■ Shop, plan menus, and cook according to a regular schedule. The more control you build in to food purchasing and preparation, the less chance there is for "trouble" foods or meals to wind up on your table. Make all members of the family aware of these routines so that they will all develop more respect for food purchasing and preparation.

■ *Make sure that all meals take place in a relaxed and pleasant environment.*

Encouraging your child to look forward to eating experiences rather than to eating in itself will change her or his entire attitude toward food. The more aesthetically and socially appealing mealtimes are, the less inclined your child will be either to derive pleasure simply from shoveling food into her or his mouth or to eat food thoughtlessly, without appreciating what—or how much—is being consumed.

As much as possible, transform each mealtime into a special occasion on which to enjoy not only the food but also pleasant physical surroundings and easygoing, nonbusiness-oriented conversation. The serving area should be attractive and compelling, and so should the food presentation itself. Also, eliminate distractions; for example, don't eat in front of the television set and don't answer the telephone during meals.

■ *Involve your child in choosing and preparing healthy foods.*

Your child already thinks about food a great deal, so why not capitalize on this interest? She or he will be much more motivated to eat judiciously upon assuming an active role in putting healthy food on the table.

Take your child grocery shopping with you and look together for nourishing as well as taste-tempting foods that are low in fat and calories. Plan, tend, and harvest a garden together, whether it's an indoor herb garden in front of a sunny window or a full-fledged vegetable garden in the backyard. Finally, work together to turn the foods you have purchased and grown into sensible as well as delicious meals.

■ Don't use food as a punishment or reward.

Resist the temptation to celebrate your obese child's achievements and good fortune with snacks, favorite dishes, or fancy desserts. Conversely, don't forbid or withhold such food items to indicate your displeasure with your child. Otherwise, you'll be inadvertently training your child to associate eating with happiness and not eating with unhappiness.

In addition, try to avoid directly linking food with love, for example, by saying, "I baked this cake especially for you" or "I know how much you like macaroni and cheese." Moreover, do not use food as a pacifier, for example, by serving popcorn or potato chips to your child in the evening as a means of soothing restlessness. As much as possible, you should be influencing your obese child to regard eating as a pleasant life-supporting activity rather than as a form of recreation, relaxation, or emotional self-management.

■ Seek opportunities to praise your child and acknowledge her or his strong points.

A significantly overweight child is one who is not happy with her- or himself. If you can raise this child's self-esteem, you'll also be increasing her or his interest in making positive and lasting changes in eating and exercise habits.

Be alert for occasions when you can express sincere admiration for your child's behavior and accomplishments. Encourage your child to engage in activities that are likely to bolster her or his pride, self-confidence, and sense of accomplishment.

■ Examine your child's home life, school life, and social life for stress factors.

Regularly talk with your child about what's going on in her or his world and keep your ears open for any signs of experiencing an emotionally distressing problem. Alleviating this problem may release your child from an inner compulsion to overeat.

Also, do whatever you reasonably can to create and maintain a happy and stress-free environment at home, especially during times when your child regularly eats (snack times as well as mealtimes). Make sure that your child gets frequent, regular, and dependable personal attention of a nonjudgmental nature and that others in the family treat her or him with respect.

■ *Consider arranging for a professional evaluation of your child's emotional well-being.*

If you suspect that there are specific emotional issues troubling your child—especially if she or he manifests emotional disturbance in ways other than overeating—don't hesitate to consult a psychiatrist, psychologist, or other mental-health professional. Begin by asking for a general evaluation. Then, if the evaluation warrants it, you can arrange for this person to treat your child.

In any event, bear in mind that it is much easier to conquer an overeating problem during the teenage years than during the adult years, and the odds of an overeating teenager turning into an overeating adult are very high. If your obese teenager is having no success conquering her or his overeating problems after several years despite her or his best efforts coupled with your best efforts, then it may be advisable to seek professional help whether or not you suspect an underlying emotional problem.

At PCGC:
Helping Obese Teenagers

One of the most daunting tasks any individual can face is achieving and maintaining an ideal weight; but for adolescents, who are going through uniquely dramatic physical and life-style changes, this task can be especially difficult. The challenge for psychotherapists is to devise treatment modes that affect multiple, complex aspects of an obese teenager's life, not just a diet-and-exercise regimen, in order to encourage weight loss and stabilization.

One of the pioneering responses to this challenge has been PCGC's Adolescent Weight Management Study. It focuses on the adolescent subgroup that most commonly needs help in weight management: girls between ages fourteen and sixteen who have to lose forty or more pounds in order to reach their ideal weight. Although the study itself features a program of *professional* intervention in specific cases of obesity, its primary aim is to assist *families* in managing such cases. The guiding philosophy of the study is that the family is often at the root of a teenager's obesity problem.

To date, the study has confirmed the following specific ways in which the family most commonly contributes to an obese teenager's overeating:

■ by insisting—or implying—that everybody's plate must be cleaned—a typical phenomenon in households governed by parents who were raised under restrictive economic circumstances;

■ by equating food with love, that is, by functioning as if dispensing huge amounts of food were the same as doling out similar amounts of love and, conversely, as if eating large servings of food were the same as receiving a great deal of love;

■ by using food for the express purpose of pacifying emotional pain—a psychosomatic "nursing" approach that sometimes works but never more than temporarily;

■ by depending too much on food—or occasions when food is served—to unite family members, an especially prevalent tactic within families that are experiencing interpersonal conflicts.

The experiences encountered in the PCGC Adolescent Weight Management Study also suggest that heredity and environment are equally responsible for causing obesity in teenage children. Most overweight children do come from overweight families. And in some of these cases biological factors are being passed along from parent to child that make the body store more fat than usual, as if to protect the individual against famine. But just as frequently, biological factors are *not* contributing to a family's tendency toward obesity. Instead, family members as a rule—often from generation to generation—are inclined to fall victim to *situational* factors that promote obesity: a high-fat, high-calorie diet and/or the type of bad eating habits and attitudes mentioned above.

Among the recommendations for at-home weight management that have emerged from the study so far are the following:

■ Address obesity problems seriously as soon as they appear in a child's life. It's much easier to tackle and reverse obesity at an earlier age than at a later one.

■ Remember that there's a strong link between depression and obesity; that is, either condition can easily lead to, and sustain, the other condition. With this in mind, parents of an obese child should be on the alert for possible overeating problems if their child appears depressed and for possible depression problems if their child is obese or appears to be overeating.

■ In order for a child to lose weight, it's absolutely critical that she or he believes in her or his ability to do so. Therefore, parents of obese children should always express confidence in their child's efforts to lose weight and maintain weight loss. They should also assist their child in following sensible weight-losing strategies that offer the greatest chance for step-by-step success.

8.

Psychotherapy

I t's a common misconception that all teenagers are by nature a little bit crazy. Adolescence in general is assumed to be a time of great psychological turmoil, as opposed to the "happy" years of childhood and the "stable" years of adulthood. Thus, while some teenagers are considered more crazy than others, each one is regarded somewhat suspiciously, as if she or he were a risky experiment in living that might backfire at any moment, given the right—or, rather, wrong— circumstances.

Obviously, teenagers face psychological crises and pressures that are unique to their particular age group. Among the major ones are dealing with puberty and a newly emergent sexuality, planning and preparing for life after high school, breaking away from the world of the family, and assuming an increasingly independent personal and social identity. However, the early years of childhood, from birth to age six; the middle years of childhood, from age six to age thirteen; and the adult years, beginning around age twenty-one, each have their unique psychological crises and pressures as well.

The bottom line is that no one age group is basically "crazier" than another. To tag adolescence with the reputation of being an excep- tionally trouble-ridden period of life is not only unjust; it is potentially harmful. Such a common value judgment predisposes many adoles- cents to be even more insecure about themselves than is warranted. It also encourages many parents to read psychological problems into their teenage child's behavior that in fact do *not* exist and—even more damaging—to dismiss psychological problems that *do* exist on the grounds that their child is no more disturbed than any other teenager is likely to be.

In determining whether or not to seek psychotherapeutic help for a teenage child, the challenge for parents is to distinguish between the *appearance* of emotional instability on the one hand and the *reality* of it on the other. This particular challenge is indeed more troublesome during a child's teenage years than it is during any other time in childhood.

If adolescence in general *appears* to be the most psychologically turbulent period of a child's life, it's largely a matter of the parents' built-in perspective. As a rule, parents tend to worry much more about the emotional welfare of their child during adolescence than they do during the years immediately preceding her or his adolescence.

There's no doubt that the potential consequences of an emotional disturbance during a child's adolescent years are much scarier for a parent to contemplate. Aside from the fact that adolescents are bigger, stronger, and more sexually developed than younger children and therefore more physically capable of inflicting violence upon themselves and others, adolescents are not nearly as responsive to parental control.

This loss of control is extremely difficult for any parent to handle with equanimity, even in the best of cases. Unfortunately, many parents unwittingly project their own emotional disturbance over their loss of control directly onto their teenage child, thereby making her or him appear to be the emotionally upset party instead of themselves.

In addition, parents can't help but feel that a psychological problem during a child's adolescent years poses a much more serious threat to her or his future success as an adult than one that occurs during the younger years. In other words, a preadolescent child is tacitly afforded more license to have emotional difficulties—whether they occur or not—than an adolescent child.

Admittedly, this is a shortsighted point of view. Unresolved psychological problems dating from early childhood are likely to have a far more entrenched and devastating effect on an adult's life than similar ones dating only from adolescence. However, it's understandable that parents are more and more inclined to worry about their child's future as that future looms closer and closer.

For example, parents are usually much more concerned about the negative effects that an emotional disturbance might have on their child's *high school* grades than they are about the negative effects that it might have on their child's *elementary school* performance. And parents are more apt to worry about society's opinion of their child's stealing, lying, or otherwise acting out psychological problems when she or he is a teenager than they are to worry about society's opinion of similarly motivated behaviors when she or he is only age seven, or nine, or eleven.

To make matters even more complicated, parents' memories of their own adolescence are generally more vivid, more extensive, and more emotionally charged than those of earlier childhood years. As a result, they have a greater ability to recall, imagine, and fear the emotional traumas that an adolescent might experience than those a younger child might face.

Here are some other "appearance-versus-reality" factors that can make it difficult for parents of an adolescent child to recognize if and when their child is experiencing serious psychological problems:

■ Adolescents spend a large percentage of time, day by day and week by week, away from their parents. Much of this separation is deliberately engineered: Adolescents crave the freedom to behave as they choose, without parental supervision. Thus, parents may not have sufficient exposure to their teenage child to detect that she or he is suffering emotional problems or, conversely, to appreciate that she or he is emotionally well adjusted and "normal" within her or his age range.

■ Adolescents are adept at "masking" their true state of mind. Instead of acting happy when they're happy, or sad when they're sad, they may display a neutral, "all purpose" demeanor that they maintain as often as possible—the classic "sullen" expression associated with adolescents. Or they may intentionally try to look annoyed when they're pleased, or content when they're troubled. These masking behaviors represent yet another extension of the typical teenager's intense desire for privacy. And they make it difficult for parents to determine how their teenage child truly feels.

■ Adolescents are often adamant about *not* letting their parents know that they're experiencing *any* problems, much less emotional problems. In some cases, the motivation is a desire not to appear incompetent or "babyish." In other cases, the motivation is more commendable, if equally self-centered: The teenager simply doesn't want to burden her or his parents with something that she or he personally finds so hard to bear.

■ Parents of adolescents are frequently unaware, or loath of admit, that they themselves are contributing to their child's emotional problems: for example, by being inappropriately overbearing, lenient, competitive, or distant. Thus, they literally don't see their child's emotional disturbances for what they really are. Instead, they perceive these problems more simplistically as "quirks" in their child's personality and behavior, "phases" in their child's progress through adolescence, or "attitudes" that their child is willfully and temporarily assuming for her or his own purposes.

Because so many factors can make it difficult for the parents of teenagers to determine whether or not their child is suffering from a serious emotional problem, they should be especially alert for the following most common indicators that a psychiatric evaluation might be useful:

■ a significant change for the worse in school performance;

■ evidence of prolonged substance abuse;

■ a consistent inability to cope with day-to-day activities and problems;

■ a dramatic change in sleeping or eating habits;

■ repeated complaints about physical ailments;

■ a persistent pattern of violating the rights of others;

■ a continual opposition to authority;

■ repeated incidents of illegal, illicit, or antisocial behavior (e.g., stealing, lying, truancy, vandalism);

■ a strong, irrational fear of becoming obese;

■ a persistent depression, characterized by negative mood, poor appetite, general passivity, and/or withdrawal;

■ a threat to commit suicide or a persistent, morbid interest in death or suicide;

■ repeated attempts to run away within a three-month period.

If you have any reason to believe that your teenage child's emotional health should be evaluated by a professional, don't hesitate to take action. The sooner you arrange for this evaluation, the better the chances are that you can catch any problems before they become even more serious. The evaluation itself may or may not reveal the need for actual psychotherapy.

As a rule, psychotherapeutic interventions involving adolescent children are relatively brief and pragmatic. Individual sessions typically last from forty-five minutes to two hours. In some cases, one or two sessions may be sufficient. For example, a concerned parent and child may just need professional reassurance that the child's psychological development is progressing normally or professional advice on strategies and activities that will foster more satisfying parent-child relations. In other cases, effective intervention may require weekly or biweekly sessions for several months or even hospitalization for anywhere from a few weeks to a year or more (although a year or more of hospitalization is very rare).

Specific goals for the psychotherapy of adolescent children generally include helping parents and child alike to interpret the latter's emotional state more accurately, increasing the quality and quantity of a child's—and a family's—social supports, and assisting all family members in coping with extrafamilial stressors in a more productive manner.

Case-by-case diagnostic techniques and treatments involving teenage children vary considerably according to the specific situation and the actual age of the child. Generally, parental interviews are always a major part of the process. Parents are asked about their perceptions of their child, their relationship with their child, and their relationships with other family members, including their own parents.

Here are some issues to consider in finding the right doctor or therapist and the right type of therapy for you, your child, and your family:

1. Before you begin your search, establish what you consider is the problem that you want addressed and the goal that you want achieved.

First, write down your answers to the following five questions, bearing in mind that some of your answers may overlap:

a. What specific signs have I observed indicating that my child may be experiencing emotional turmoil? (As much as possible, give dates, times of day, settings, and circumstantial surroundings.)

b. How would I define this emotional turmoil? (In other words, if you had to make a diagnosis, what would it be?)

c. What might be the cause(s) of this turmoil? (Include any speculations you may have as well as any more conclusive opinions—being careful to distinguish between these two categories.)

d. In what different ways has this emotional turmoil been bothersome or detrimental to my child, to me, and to other members of the family? (Be as specific as possible, as you were directed to be in answering question a.)

e. How have I tried to better this situation? (Indicate which methods have been at least partially successful and which have failed altogether.)

Once you have answered all five questions to the best of your ability, write down a fairly succinct (one- or two-sentence) description of what you think the *problem* is. Next, write a similarly succinct description of the *goal* that you want to achieve related to this problem: that is, what you would like to see happen *as a result* of psychotherapeutic intervention.

These statements, as well as the question-and-answer background material, will be enormously helpful to you in interviewing possible doctors or therapists. They will also be enormously helpful to the doctor or therapist you choose in her or his efforts to diagnose and treat your child successfully.

2. Familiarize yourself with the major types of therapy that are available.

The sheer variety of therapy labels is bewildering to the outsider: psychoanalytic (Freudian, Jungian, Adlerian, or otherwise), cognitive, behavioral, existential, Gestalt, transactional, reality-oriented, rational-emotive, and so on. However, for the purpose of interviewing potential doctors or therapists to work with a teenage child, all you need is a very basic awareness of three broad categories of psychotherapy: psychodynamic therapy, behavioral therapy, and family-oriented therapy.

Let's consider each category individually:

■ *Psychodynamic therapy* is geared toward getting the child to identify, understand, and self-manage her or his emotional problems. It depends heavily on effective verbal communication between the doctor or therapist and the child. It also tends to be relatively long-term compared to the other categories of psychotherapy, often involving multiple sessions per week for up to a year or two.

■ *Behavioral therapy* is geared toward getting the child to change the way she or he behaves. Instead of focusing squarely on the causes of a particular problem, it concentrates on the symptoms. For example, it might help children learn to control their anger without necessarily getting them to appreciate why they get angry, to be less afraid of nightmares regardless of whether they know about their possible source, or to interact more cooperatively with other people even if their feelings about them remain unresolved. It typically takes at least a few months of weekly or biweekly sessions before satisfactory results can be expected.

■ *Family-oriented therapy*, sometimes known as "systems therapy," is the type of therapy practiced at Philadelphia Child Guidance Center (PCGC) and the type that PCGC recommends most highly for children of any age. Drawing upon both psychodynamic therapy and behavioral therapy, family-oriented therapy is geared toward generating positive awareness and change in all aspects of the child's world: her or his own mind and behavior as well as the minds and behaviors of those people who directly influence her or his life. The focus of the therapy is on interactions among family members and how these interactions influence each family member. In comparison to the other therapies, it is much more adaptable to the situation at hand. Satisfactory results may be achieved in just one or two sessions or may take up to a year or two to achieve.

Use these very basic distinctions as starting points for discussing with other people (such as knowledgeable advisers and potential doctors or therapists) the particular type or types of psychotherapy that may be appropriate for your unique situation. Investigate the literature about child psychotherapy that's available at local libraries and bookstores. The more informed you are about child psychotherapy— whatever form it may take—the more benefit you'll derive from the type you finally choose, whatever it may be.

3. Familiarize yourself with the major types of doctors and therapists that are available.

The three most common practitioners of child-oriented psychotherapy are psychiatrists, psychologists, and social workers. Regardless of the specific title (e.g., "child psychiatrist"), not all of these practitioners have special training or experience in treating children in particular, as opposed to people in general. This is an important issue that you will want to investigate with individual practitioners that you interview.

Also, keep in mind that one type of practitioner, all else being equal, is not necessarily more or less desirable than another type. Your final determination should be based on how appropriate the individual practitioner is, given the following factors: your child's problem, the goals you've established relating to that problem, the type of therapy you're interested in pursuing, your financial resources, and most important of all, the overall personalities of you and your child.

These warnings having been given, here are brief descriptions of each major type of practitioner:

■*Psychiatrists* are medical doctors (M.D.s), which means that they have had four years of medical school, one year of internship, and at least two years of residency training in psychiatry. In addition, virtually all child psychiatrists have had two-year fellowships in child psychiatry and are board certified.

One major advantage of a psychiatrist over other types of practitioners is that she or he can diagnose and prescribe treatment for physical problems that may be causing or aggravating a child's emotional problems. A possible disadvantage, depending on your particular situation, is that most psychiatrists are inclined to practice only psychodynamic forms of therapy.

■*Psychologists* have usually earned a doctorate (Ph.D.) in psychology, typically the result of five years of graduate training, including several supervised clinical programs and a year of formal internship. Most states also require postdoctoral experience before licensing. Some states, however, require only a master's degree (M.A.) to become a psychologist.

Although psychologists themselves cannot offer physical diagnosis and prescription, they almost always have close professional relationships with M.D.s whom they can recommend for such services. They are also likely to be more eclectic in their therapeutic style, although there is still a trend among psychologists to favor behavioral therapy.

■ *Social workers* have earned a master's degree in social work (M.S.W.), a process that involves two years of classes and fieldwork. In addition, some states require two or more years of postgraduate experience before licensing.

While social workers may not have had the extensive academic and clinical training that psychiatrists and psychologists have had, they are, as a rule, much more familiar with—and knowledgeable about—the home, community, and school environments of their clients. This background inclines them to practice family-oriented or systems-oriented therapy more than other types of therapy.

Another major issue to consider in choosing a particular type of doctor or therapist is whether the therapy will take place in a *private office* or in a *clinic*. Other factors aside, therapy performed in a clinic tends to be more multidimensional—a by-product of the fact that clinics are so often staffed with different types of doctors and therapists who not only practice different types of therapy but also conduct different kinds of research projects.

4. Make a rough estimate of how much you can afford to spend on your child's therapy.

It may be impossible to put a price on a child's emotional well-being. However, it's quite possible to determine how much you can afford to spend for psychotherapy without making life much more difficult for yourself and your family—a situation that could only exacerbate your child's emotional problems.

You may have insurance that will cover some or all of the expenses directly incurred as a result of your child's therapy; but in the best of situations there are bound to be some hidden costs. Factor into your budget such possibilities as lost income for days off work, transportation and parking for therapy sessions, and baby-sitting care for other children while you are at the sessions.

In estimating how much you can afford for the therapy itself, take into account that private therapy is almost certain to be more expensive than therapy in a clinic. Also, clinics may offer lower fees if you accept therapy from a supervised student therapist or agree to participate in a research project (which typically means being observed, taped, and/or interviewed).

5. Seek several recommendations from a variety of qualified sources.

Ask relatives and friends who have benefited from the services of child psychiatrists, psychologists, or social workers for their opinions but also seek leads from more experienced and disinterested parties, such as your pediatrician, family physician, school counselor, and/or clergyperson. For the names of certified practitioners in your area, contact the local and national mental-health and professional organizations (see Appendix for a list of suggestions).

6. Interview different doctors and therapists thoroughly about their credentials, areas of expertise, and therapeutic techniques.

Among the specific questions you should ask are the following:

■ What is your educational and training background (see issue 3)?

■ Are you board certified? By whom?

■ With what professional organizations are you affiliated (see Appendix for a list)?

■ How long have you practiced in your current capacity?

■ What is your general or preferred style of therapy (see issue 2)?

■ What are your areas of special expertise?

■ How much work have you done with children who are the same age as my child?

■ How much work have you done with the type of problem(s) my child is having (see issue 1)?

■ Would you feel committed to achieving the goal I have in mind (see issue 1)?

■ What kinds of services can I expect from you toward meeting this goal?

■ What kinds of commitment and cooperation would you expect from me and my family in the course of my child's therapy?

■ How, and at what rate, will you keep me informed of the progress my child is making in therapy?

■ How much time do you estimate the therapy might take?

■ How much will it cost, will my insurance or medical assistance help pay the cost, and are there ways to reduce the cost (see issue 4)?

7. Make sure that you choose a doctor or therapist who respects you and with whom you are comfortable.

Some doctors or therapists may unintentionally cause you to feel guilty or incompetent, in which case you should look for someone else. The doctor or therapist you select should be a person who inspires you to feel good about yourself: *re*moralized, instead of *de*moralized.

Your answer to each of the following questions should be yes both during your initial interview with a doctor or therapist and for the time period that the therapy itself takes place.

■ Does the doctor or therapist take into account *your* theories, opinions, and concerns as well as her or his own?

■ Does the interaction you have with the doctor or therapist seem like a dialogue rather than a monologue on the doctor's or therapist's part?

■ Does the doctor or therapist seem genuinely interested in you and your situation (evidenced by paying close attention to you, maintaining fairly consistent eye contact with you, and regularly soliciting your comments and reactions)?

■ Does the doctor or therapist seem genuinely interested in your child and her or his problems?

■ Does the doctor or therapist take it upon her- or himself to make sure that you understand what she or he is doing and saying?

■ Does the doctor or therapist answer all your questions promptly, thoughtfully, and to the best of her or his ability?

■ Do you leave the doctor's or therapist's company feeling clear about the direction that your child's case will be taking?

■ Do you leave the doctor's or therapist's company feeling generally stronger rather than weaker?

Special Diagnoses: Adolescents

DEPRESSION

It used to be thought that so-called clinical depression was an adult psychiatric disorder. Over the past twenty years, it has increasingly been diagnosed among adolescents as well. Clinical depression for either an adult or an adolescent refers to a syndrome of multiple and severe depressive symptoms lasting for over three months (see pages 334–35 in this book for a list of adolescent depressive symptoms).

Psychotic features, such as hallucinations, obsessive thoughts, compulsive actions, or phobias, are often present in cases of clinical depression involving an adolescent, especially in extreme cases. But it is not *required* that such features be present to warrant a formal diagnosis. The same is true of suicidal thoughts or impulses toward self-destruction.

Typically, an episode of clinical depression in an adolescent is triggered by situational factors, for example, a poor adjustment to a new school, a major failure in peer relationships, a crisis in the family, or a severe dissatisfaction with one's performance or behavior. However, the serious nature of such a depression also suggests preexisting psychological and/or biochemical factors, which, if left untreated, are very likely to cause recurring and perhaps progressively worsening attacks of depression throughout the victim's life.

Successful psychotherapeutic treatment of a clinically depressed adolescent generally involves several months or more of individual and/or group sessions and sometimes one or more short periods of hospitalization (especially if the victim is suicidal). It may also involve antidepressant medication.

ANOREXIA NERVOSA

The most common psychiatric eating disorder afflicting teenagers, especially girls, is anorexia nervosa, or simply speaking, self-imposed starvation. Although the expressed purpose of a teenager's refusal to eat may be to lose weight or remain trim, the real motivation is a desperate need to experience a sense of mastery over life.

Typically, the anorexic teenager is a perfectionist who suffers from low self-esteem. This diminished self-esteem leads to an irrational self-image: The teenager persists in seeing her- or himself as too fat and too susceptible to self-indulgence regardless of how thin and self-denying she or he becomes.

Teenage girls are more subject to becoming victims of anorexia nervosa than teenage boys because of cultural factors. Not only do prevailing standards of beauty put far more pressure to be thin on women than on men, but also women are provided with fewer opportunities to feel that they have mastery over their lives.

In a relentless effort to avoid gaining weight (which, in itself, is a masked form of self-punishment), the anorexic teenager may actually starve her- or himself to the point where physical deterioration is irreversible, resulting in certain death if there is no medical intervention (and, in some cases, if medical intervention does not occur at a sufficiently early stage in the process). For this reason, it is vital to seek professional help for your child immediately if you have any reason to suspect anorexia.

BULIMIA

Bulimia is characterized by compulsively binging on huge quantities of high-calorie food and then purging oneself by self-induced vomiting or by using laxatives. The motivational pattern among teenage bulimics is similar to the pattern among teenage anorexics. Indeed, bulimic binges are often preceded or followed by periods of severe dieting.

Bulimia is much more widespread among female than male teenagers due to the same cultural differences that incline more women than men to become anorexic. Like anorexics, bulimics tend to be highly secretive about what they are going through. For example, a bulimic may hoard food or only binge during the middle of the night, while everyone else is asleep, or try to hide signs of throwing up by running water while spending long periods of time in the bathroom.

Among the possible negative effects of bulimia on the victim's physical health are severe dehydration, hormonal imbalance, and/or the depletion of important minerals. Fortunately, professional intervention at an early point stands an excellent chance of curing the victim of the compulsion toward bulimia.

Adolescence: Selected Terms and Concepts

acting out indirectly expressing emotional conflicts—or "forbidden feelings"—through negative behavior. Such behavior is typically overdramatic and designed to attract attention. It may or may not be overtly self-punishing or injurious to others.

For example, a child who feels rejected by a parent may "act out" that feeling by refusing to speak to that parent, constantly trying to distract the parent, talking back, or picking fights with a sibling who appears to be getting more attention.

affective disorder also known as *emotional disorder* or *mood disorder,* a specifically defined psychological illness relating to the emotions (e.g., *bipolar disorder*). Generally, such a disorder is apparent in the problematic manner in which a child physically displays her or his emotions (hence, the root "affect"). The disorder may also have a physical cause.

behavior modeling a therapeutic technique by means of which the child is taught or encouraged to replace negative behaviors with more positive ones. The teaching or encouraging process involves modifying the way that each parent or caretaker interacts with the child so that the child learns by example or direct experience (e.g., a reward system) to behave more constructively.

bipolar disorder also known as *manic-depressive disorder,* a psychological illness characterized by extreme mood swings back and forth between depression and elation. Each mood phase lasts for an indeterminant amount of time, varying from individual to individual and from episode to episode. The disorder has a biological basis and can often be controlled by medication.

cognitive disorder a specifically defined mental problem relating to a child's perception, thought, learning, and/or memory processes. Such an illness generally has a biological cause and psychological effects.

A child may have suffered a particular cognitive disorder

from a very early age, or it may have developed over time. In either case, it is frequently not detected and diagnosed until adolescence, when a child's cognitive development is assumed to have reached maturity.

compliance   the tendency to respond effectively—both in emotional and behavioral terms—to scheduling arrangements, rules, and discipline.

conflict resolution   a therapeutic technique in which a child is assisted in alleviating or managing chronic interpersonal conflict. Often group therapy is involved, bringing together the child with the other person or persons involved in the conflict. The therapy may also, or alternatively, feature one-on-one teaching, whereby the child learns general strategies for handling interpersonal conflicts more effectively.

defense mechanism   according to Sigmund Freud's terminology, a means unconsciously and automatically employed by the psyche to avoid emotional pain, such as *denial*, *projection*, or *repression*.

delinquency   also known as *juvenile delinquency,* a legal term applied to the antisocial, immoral, or transgressive behavior of minors (who, in most states, are children under eighteen years old). Manifested by an adult, the same behavior would most likely be construed as criminal and therefore legally liable.

In psychological terms, such behavior in a child is often motivated by emotional problems relating to adjustment, identity, or conduct. However, the behavior may also be partly or entirely motivated by social, economic, cultural, or "life-style" forces (e.g., peer pressure, discrimination, poverty, substance abuse).

denial   a conscious or unconscious refusal to acknowledge or accept unpleasant thoughts or situations. An automatic, self-protective measure, denial is particularly apparent among adolescents because of their heightened self-awareness and expanded social horizons.

depression   more technically known as *unipolar disorder*, a term that refers to a distinct psychological illness characterized by chronic apathy, hopelessness, and fatigue—physical as well as emotional.

dysfunctional   as opposed to *functional*, a term used to describe a personality or family unit that does not operate effectively or satisfactorily to meet day-to-day life challenges. In some cases, there is apparent effectiveness or satisfaction, but achieving it causes underlying psychological damage. In other cases, the personality or family unit is clearly having problems that pose a threat to its survival.

This term is sociological in origin and is rapidly losing currency in the field of psychology. Many therapists consider it too negative and abstract to be useful diagnostically.

emotional disorder   (see *affective disorder*)

functional   (see *dysfunctional*)

juvenile delinquency   (see *delinquency*)

maladaptation   also known as *maladjustment*, this term refers to a child's inability to respond in a calm, effective, or successful manner either to a single life change or to the demands of life in general.

maladjustment   (see *maladaptation*)

manic-depressive disorder   (see *bipolar disorder*)

medical intervention   in most cases, the use of medication (e.g., tranquilizing drugs) to alleviate the cause or symptoms of a psychological problem.

mood disorder   (see *affective disorder*)

neurosis   as opposed to the more serious condition *psychosis*, a psychological problem that still allows the victim to maintain reasonably good contact with reality and perform intellectually in a reasonably acceptable manner.

This term does not refer to a specific illness. Therefore, it is technically not accurate to say that a child is suffering from a *neurosis*. Because of this fact, the term is rapidly being replaced by the expression "neurotic process" (e.g., "If treatment is not applied, this child's emotional problem could trigger a neurotic process").

obsessive-compulsive disorder   a psychological problem characterized by intense, highly disruptive preoccupation with performing a certain ritualized activity. This activity may or may not be related to "normal life" tasks. For example, one person suffering from obsessive-compulsive disorder may be fanatically neat in her or his personal grooming (a "normal life" task); another person suffering from the disorder may be driven to scrub her or his bedroom walls every week (not a "normal life" task).

Such a disorder generally does not manifest itself in an individual's life prior to adolescence. However, early signs that such a disorder may be developing can occur during a child's middle years, in behaviors that are indeed obsessive but far less disruptive to the child and those around her or him (e.g., frequent and ritualized hand washing).

overcorrection a negative effect of the parent-child relationship in which the discipline or punishment imposed on a child's conduct—or the child's "reforming" response to discipline or punishment—exceeds appropriate limits.

pathology (see *psychopathology*)

personality disorder a psychological problem relating to acquired and entrenched character traits or patterns of personal behavior that are injurious to the child or to others. Generally, the child does not realize such traits or behaviors are problematic, but those who are in contact with the child easily and quickly do.

projection an unconscious, self-protecting measure in which a child denies her or his own negative, forbidden, or unpleasant feelings and instead attributes them to someone else. In most cases, the person upon whom the child projects such feelings is the trigger for them. For example, a child who is angry at Mother may unconsciously reclaim her or his innocence by believing instead that Mother is angry with her or him.

psychoanalysis as opposed to the broader term *psychotherapy*, a mode of diagnosing and treating a child's psychological problems through one-on-one patient-therapist dialogue. There are many different schools of psychoanalysis, each based on a particular philosophy regarding how the psyche functions.

psychopathology the study of mental illnesses. The term *pathology* refers to a disease or disorder, as opposed to a less severe problem.

psychosis as opposed to the less serious condition *neurosis*, a psychological problem that often or continuously prevents the victim from maintaining reasonably good contact with reality or from performing intellectually and socially in a reasonably acceptable manner.

A particular psychotic disorder may be psychological in origin, biological in origin, or both. Among the distinctive indicators that an emotional problem is psychotic rather than neurotic are the presence of delusions (irrational beliefs) or hallucinations (distorted perceptions).

psychotherapy   a professional method of treating emotional problems and *affective disorders*. Psychotherapy can take a number of different forms, such as *psychoanalysis*, or varying therapies designed to provide appropriate *behavior modeling*.

repression   a means of emotional self-protection in which traumatic or unpleasant thoughts or memories are automatically relegated to the unconscious mind and forgotten by the conscious mind.

resilience   a child's ability to adapt effectively to change or recover effectively from a crisis. The more resilient a child's emotional nature is, the psychologically healthier she or he is.

resistance   in the context of psychotherapy, a child's conscious or unconscious refusal to cooperate with the therapist or the therapy.

suicidal ideation   a child's thoughts or verbal expressions having to do with suicide. Some verbal expressions may be direct (e.g., the statement "I feel like killing myself"); others may be indirect (e.g., "Life just doesn't seem worth living"). For safety's sake, expressions of either type should always be regarded as possible indicators of serious suicidal intention. (For more information, see the "Depression" section, especially "Preventing Teenage Suicide.")

unipolar disorder   (see *depression*)

withdrawal   a child's willful separation, emotionally and/or physically, from an event or person that is somehow distressing. Long-term withdrawal, or an ever-widening pattern of withdrawal, can be a sign of an underlying psychological problem.

Appendix

Organizations to Contact

I f you believe your child is having serious problems dealing with her or his emotions or behavior, it's a good idea to get a professional evaluation of your child's emotional health and, possibly, professional help for your child. These services should be provided by a well-qualified child psychiatrist, child psychologist, or social worker whom both you and your child like and trust.

To find the professional that's right for your situation, first consult friends and relatives who have had experience with such services, your pediatrician, and your child's school counselor. Also try local organizations, such as medical societies, psychiatric societies, and city, county, and state mental-health associations.

If you are unable to get satisfactory references or locate an acceptable professional using these sources, or if you'd like more background information on the subject and practice of psychotherapy for children, try contacting any of the following organizations for assistance:

American Academy of Child and Adolescent Psychiatry
3615 Wisconsin Avenue, NW
Washington, DC 20016
(800) 222-7636

■ professional society for degreed physicians who have completed an additional five years of residency in child and adolescent psychiatry

■ forty-three regional groups in the United States, equipped to provide information (including consumer guidance on insurance benefits covering child and adolescent psychiatry) and referrals

American Academy of Community Psychiatrists
P.O. Box 5372
Arlington, VA 22205
(703) 237-0823

■ professional society for psychiatrists and psychiatry residents practicing in community mental-health centers or similar programs that provide care regardless of their client's ability to pay

■ seven regional groups in the United States that are equipped to inform the public about a community psychiatrist's training and role and about how to obtain services

American Association of Psychiatric Services for Children
1200-C Scottsville Road, Suite 225
Rochester, NY 14624
(716) 235-6910

■ accrediting service and information clearinghouse for clinics and other institutions offering psychiatric services for children

■ equipped to provide information and referrals

National Association of Social Workers
7981 Eastern Avenue
Silver Spring, MD 20910
(800) 638-8799

■ professional society for people who hold a minimum of a baccalaureate degree in social work (B.S.W.)

■ fifty-five state, district, and protectorate groups that are equipped to inform the public about the services provided by social workers and how to obtain them

American Association for Marriage and Family Therapy
1717 K Street, NW #407
Washington, DC 20006
(202) 429-1825

■ professional society for marriage and family therapists

■ maintains thirty-nine training centers throughout United States that are equipped to provide information and referrals

Psychology Society
100 Beekman Street
New York, NY 10038
(212) 285-1872

■ professional society for psychologists who have a doctorate and are certified/licensed in the state where they practice

■ equipped to provide information and referrals

*National Association for the Advancement of Psychoanalysis
and the American Boards for Accreditation and Certification*
80 Eighth Avenue, Suite 1210
New York, NY 10011
(212) 741-0515

■ professional society for psychoanalysts that sets standards for training, accredits institutions, certifies individual practitioners, and evaluates institutions and practitioners

■ equipped to offer information and referrals (publishes an annual directory, *National Registry of Psychoanalysts*, with geographic index: $15)

Council for the National Register of Health Service Providers in Psychology
1730 Rhode Island Avenue, NW, Suite 1200
Washington, DC 20036
(202) 833-2377

■ registry for psychologists who are licensed or certified by a state board of examiners of psychology and who have met additional council criteria as health service providers in psychology

■ equipped to provide referrals

National Council of Community Mental Health Centers
12300 Twinbrook Parkway
Rockville, MD 20852

■ membership organization of community mental-health centers

■ not equipped to provide referrals by telephone but publishes a bi-annual *National Registry*, which lists centers by geographic area

Federation of Families for Children's Mental Health
1021 Prince Street
Alexandria, VA 22314
(703) 684-7710

■ organization for parents looking for support and advocacy groups

■ equipped to provide contacts

Index

Index